A Primer for Unit Root Testing

Other books by Kerry Patterson

Patterson, K. D. *An Introduction to Applied Econometrics: A Time Series Approach*

Mills. T. C., and K. D. Patterson. (eds) *Palgrave Handbook of Econometrics, Volume 1, Econometric Theory*

Mills. T. C., and K. D. Patterson. (eds) *Palgrave Handbook of Econometrics, Volume 2, Applied Econometrics*

PalgraveTexts in Econometrics

General Editor: Kerry Patterson

Titles include:

Simon P. Burke and John Hunter
MODELLING NON-STATIONARY TIME SERIES

Michael P. Clements
EVALUATING ECONOMETRIC FORECASTS OF ECONOMIC AND FINANCIAL VARIABLES

Lesley Godfrey
BOOTSTRAP TESTS FOR REGRESSION MODELS

Terence C. Mills
MODELLING TRENDS AND CYCLES IN ECONOMIC TIME SERIES

Kerry Patterson
A PRIMER FOR UNIT ROOT TESTING

Palgrave Texts in Econometrics

Series Standing Order ISBN 978–1–4039–0172–9 (hardback)
978–1–4039–0173–6 (paperback) (outside North America only)

You can receive future titles in this series as they are published by placing a standing order. Please contact your bookseller or, in case of difficulty, write to us at the address below with your name and address, the title of the series and the ISBN quoted above.

Customer Services Department, Macmillan Distribution Ltd, Houndmills, Basingstoke, Hampshire RG21 6XS, England

---

A Primer for Unit Root Testing

Kerry Patterson

palgrave
macmillan

First published 2010 by
PALGRAVE MACMILLAN

Palgrave Macmillan in the UK is an imprint of Macmillan Publishers Limited, registered in England, company number 785998, of Houndmills, Basingstoke, Hampshire RG21 6XS.

Palgrave Macmillan in the US is a division of St Martin's Press LLC, 175 Fifth Avenue, New York, NY 10010.

Palgrave Macmillan is the global academic imprint of the above companies and has companies and representatives throughout the world.

ISBN: 978–1–403–90204–7 hardback
ISBN: 978–1–403–90205–4 paperback

This book is printed on paper suitable for recycling and made from fully managed and sustained forest sources. Logging, pulping and manufacturing processes are expected to conform to the environmental regulations of the country of origin.

A catalogue record for this book is available from the British Library.

A catalog record for this book is available from the Library of Congress.

10 9 8 7 6 5 4 3 2 1
19 18 17 16 15 14 13 12 11 10

Printed and bound in Great Britain by
CPI Antony Rowe, Chippenham and Eastbourne

To Kaylem, Abdullah, Isaac, Ana and Hejr

Contents

Detailed Contents

Tables

Figures

Symbols and Abbreviations

$\rightarrow_{as}$	almost sure convergence
$\Rightarrow_{D}$	convergence in distribution (weak convergence)
$\rightarrow_{P}$	convergence in probability
$\rightarrow_{r}$	convergence in r-th mean
$\mapsto$	mapping
$\rightarrow$	tends to, for example ε tends to zero, $\varepsilon \rightarrow 0$
$\subset$	a proper subset of
$\subseteq$	a subset of
$\times$	Cartesian product (or multiplication, depending on context)
$\equiv$	definitional equality
$\Rightarrow$	implies
$\cap$	intersection of sets
$\sim$	is distributed as
$\wedge$	minimum
$\neq$	not equals
$\varnothing$	the null set
$\approx$	approximately equals
$\Re$	the set of real numbers; the real line ($-\infty$ to ∞)
$\Re^{+}$	the positive half of the real line
$\cup$	union of sets
$\in$	an element of
♦	ends each example
$\|a\|$	the absolute value (modulus) of a
$\Pi_{j=1}^{n} x_j$	the product of x_j, $j = 1, \ldots, n$
$\Sigma_{j=1}^{n} x_j$	the sum of x_j, $j = 1, \ldots, n$
a.s	almost surely
B^{-1}	inverse of B if B is matrix
$f^{-1}(x)$	pre-image, where f(x) is a function
$\Phi(z)$	the cumulative distribution function of the standard normal distribution
ε_t	white noise unless explicitly excepted
B(t)	standard Brownian motion, that is with unit variance
iid	independent and identically distributed
niid	independent and identically normally distributed

m.d.s	martingale difference sequence
N	the set of integers
N^+	the set of non-negative integers
$N(0, 1)$	the standard normal distribution, with zero mean and unit variance
plim	probability limit
W(t)	non-standard Brownian motion

Preface

The purpose of this book is to provide an introduction to the concepts and terminology that are particularly appropriate to random walks, Brownian motion and unit root testing. However, these concepts are also inextricably bound into probability, stochastic process and time series and so I hope that there will be some broader gains to the reader in those areas. The prerequisites for the material in this book are two-fold. First, some knowledge of basic regression topics, such as least squares estimation, 't' statistics and hypothesis testing. This could be provided by such excellent introductory texts as Gujarati (2006), Dougherty (2007), Ramanathan (2002) and Stock and Watson (2007). Second, some knowledge of probability at an elementary level would also be useful, such as provided by Hodges and Lehman (2004) and Suhov and Kelbert (2005).

Since Nelson and Plosser's (1982) seminal article, which examined a number of macroeconomic time series for nonstationarity by way of a unit root, the literature on unit root test statistics and applications thereof has grown like no other in econometrics; but, in contrast, there is little by way of introductory material in one source to facilitate the next step of understanding the meaning of the functional central limit theorem or the continuous mapping theorem applied to functionals of Brownian motion. The steps to understand such concepts are daunting for a student who has only undertaken introductory courses in econometrics and/or probability.

At one level, the application of a unit root test requires little knowledge other than how to apply a test statistic, the prototypical case being the 't' test for the significance of an individual regression coefficient. At an introductory level, students become aware of the testing framework comprising a null hypothesis, an alternative hypothesis, a test statistic, a critical value for a chosen significance level and a rejection region. The rest is a matter of simple mechanical routine of comparing a sample value of the test statistic with a critical value.

Unit root tests can, of course, be approached in the same way. However, a deeper understanding, for example of the probability background and distribution of the test statistic under the null hypothesis, requires a set of concepts that is not usually available at an introductory level, indeed possibly even at an intermediate level. However, there are some

excellent references at an advanced level, for example Billingsley's classic (1995) on probability and measure, Hamilton's (1994) text on time series analysis and Davidson's (1994) monograph on stochastic limit theory. But such references are beyond the step needed from introductory texts that are widely used in second year courses in introductory econometrics. For example, a student may well have a basic understanding of probability theory, for example being aware of such important distributions as the binomial and the normal, but the concepts of measure theory and probability space, which are essential to an understanding of more advanced work, are generally unfamiliar and anyway seem rather too analytical.

This book hopes to bridge that gap by bringing a number of key concepts, such as the functional central limit theorem and the continuous mapping theorem, into a framework that leads to their use in the context of unit root tests. A complementary motivation for the book is to provide an introduction to the random walk model and martingales, which are of interest in economics because of their relationship with efficient markets.

There are worked examples throughout the book. These are integrated into the text, where the completion of an example is marked by the symbol ♦, and at the end of each chapter.

The central topics covered in the book are as follows. Probability and measure in Chapter 1; this chapter starts the task of converting and developing the language of probability into the form used in more advanced books. Chapter 2 provides an introduction to time series models, particularly the ARMA and ARIMA models, which are widely used in econometrics. Of course there exist extensive volumes on this topic, so the aim here is to introduce the key concepts for later use. An underlying and connecting theme in random walks, Brownian motion and unit root tests, is the extent of dependence in a stochastic process, and Chapter 3 introduces some essential concepts, again with a view to later developments. Chapter 4 is concerned with the idea that one stochastic process converges to another is a key component in the development of unit root tests. This concept of convergence extends that of the simpler case in which the n-th term in a sequence of random variables converges in some well-defined sense either to a random variable or a constant. Chapter 5 starts with the basic ideas underlying random walks, which motivate their use as prototypical stochastic processes in economics. Random walks also turn out to be at the heart of Brownian motion, which is introduced in Chapter 6. The differentiation and integration of stochastic processes involving Brownian motion is considered in

Chapter 7. Strictly, Brownian motion is nowhere differentiable, but the reader may have seen expressions that look like differentials or derivatives being applied to Brownian motion: what, therefore, is meant by dB(t) where B(t) is Brownian motion? Finally, Chapter 8 'dips' into some unit root tests and gives examples of parametric and nonparametric tests. Despite the extent of research on the topic of unit root testing, even some 30 years after the seminal contributions by Dickey and Fuller (see, for example, Fuller, 1976, and Dickey and Fuller, 1981), and hundreds of articles on theory and applications, there are still unresolved issues or areas where practical difficulties may arise; Chapter 8 concludes with a brief summary of some of these areas.

The graphs in this book were prepared with MATLAB, which was also used together with TSP (www.tspintl.com) and RATS (www.estima.com), for the numerical examples. Martinez and Martinez (2002) provides an invaluable guide to statistics, with many MATLAB examples; and guides to MATLAB itself include Hanselman and Littlefield (2004), Moler (2004) and Hahn and Valentine (2007).

My sincere thanks go to Lorna Eames, my secretary at the University of Reading, who has always responded very positively to my many requests for assistance in preparing the manuscript for this book.

A website has been set up to support this book. It gives access to more examples, both numerical and theoretical, a number of the programs that have been used to draw the graphs, estimate the illustrative models and the data that has been used. Additionally, if you have comments on any aspects of the book please contact me at my email address given below.

Website and email details

Book website: http://www.palgrave.com/products/title/aspx?PID=266278

Authors: email address: k.d.patterson@reading.ac.uk

Palgrave Macmillan Online: http://www.palgrave.com/economics/econometrics.asp

Palgrave Macmillan email address: orders@palgrave.com

1
An Introduction to Probability and Random Variables

Introduction

This chapter is a summary of some key concepts related to probability theory and random variables, with a view to the developments in subsequent chapters. Essential concepts include the formalisation of the intuitive concept of probability, the related concepts of the sample space, the probability space and random variable, and the development of these to cases such as uncountable sample spaces, which are critical to stochastic processes. The reader is likely to have some familiarity with the basic concepts in this chapter, perhaps in the context of countably discrete random variables and distributions, such as the binomial distribution and for continuous random variables that are normally distributed.

This chapter is organised as follows. The idea of a random variable, in contrast to a deterministic variable, underlies this chapter and Section 1.1 opens with this concept. The triple of the probability space, that is the sample space, a field and a probability measure, is developed in Section 1.2 applied to a random variable, with various subsections dealing with concepts such as countable and uncountable sample spaces, Borel sets and derived probability measures. A random vector, that is a collection of random variables, is considered in Section 1.3, and is critical to the definition of a stochastic process, which is introduced in Section 1.4. Section 1.5 considers summary measures, such as the expectation and variance, which are associated with random variables and these are extended to functions of random variables in Section 1.6. The idea of constructing a random variable by conditioning an existing random variable on an event in the sample space of another random variable is critical to the concepts of dependence and independence and is considered in Section 1.7; some useful properties of conditional

expectations are summarised in Section 1.8. The final substantive section, 1.9, considers the property of stationarity, which is critical to subsequent analysis.

1.1 Random variables

Even without a formal definition, most will recognise the outcomes of random 'experiments' that characterise our daily lives. Describing some of these will help to indicate the essence of a random experiment and related consequences that we model as random variables. In order to reach a destination for a particular time, we may catch a bus or drive. The bus will usually have a stated arrival time at the bus stop, but its actual arrival time will vary, and so a number of outcomes are possible; equally its arrival at the destination will have a stated time, but a variety of possible outcomes will actually transpire. Driving to the destination will involve a series of possible outcomes depending, for example, on the traffic and weather conditions. A fruitful line of examples to illustrate probability concepts relate to gambling in some form, for example betting on the outcome of the toss of a coin, the throw of a dice or the spin of a roulette wheel.

So what are the key characteristics of an 'experiment' that generates a random variable? An essential characteristic is that the experiment has a number of possible outcomes, in contrast to the certain outcome of a deterministic experiment. We may also link (or map) the outcomes from the random experiment by way of a function to a variable. For example, a tossed coin can land heads or tails and then be mapped to the outcomes +1 and –1, or 1 and 0. A measure of the chance of each outcome should also be assigned and it is this measure that is referred to as the probability of the outcome; for example, by an admittedly circular argument, a probability of ½ to each outcome. However, one could argue that repeating the experiment and recording the proportion of heads should in the limit determine the probability of heads. Whilst this relative frequency (frequentist) approach is widely adopted it is not the only view of what probability is and how it should be interpreted; see Porter (1988) for an account of the development of probability in the nineteenth century and for an account of subjective probability see Jeffrey (2004) and Wright and Ayton (1994). Whatever view is taken on the quantification of uncertainty, the measures so defined must satisfy properties P1–P3 detailed below in Section 1.2.3.i.

Notation: the basic random variables of this chapter are denoted either as x or y, although other random variables based on these, such as the

sum, may also be defined. The distinction between the use of x and y is as follows: in the former case there is no presumption that time is necessarily an important aspect of the random variable, although it may occur in a particular interpretation or example; on the other hand, the use of y implies that time is an essential dimension of the random variable.

1.2 The probability space: Sample space, field, probability measure (Ω, F, P)

The probability space comprises three elements: a sample space, Ω; a collection of subsets or events, referred to as a field or algebra, *F*, to which a probability measure can (in principle) be assigned; and the probability measure, *P*, that assigns probabilities to events in *F*. Some preliminary notation is first established in Section 1.2.1.

1.2.1 Preliminary notation

Sample space: Ω, or Ω_j if the sample space is part of a sequence indexed by j.

An event: an event is a subset of Ω. Typically this will be denoted by an upper case letter such as A or B, or A_j.

The sure event: the sure or certain event is Ω, since it defines the sample space.

The null set: the null set, or empty set, corresponding to the impossible event is $\Omega^c = \varnothing$, where Ω^c indicates the complement or negation of a set. For example, in the case of two consecutive tosses of a coin, let A denote the event that at least one head occurs, then A = {*HH, HT, TH*}; the complement (or negation) of the event A is denoted A^c, in this case A^c = {*TT*}.

Union of sets: the symbol denoting the union of events is ∪, read as 'or'; for example A or B, written A ∪ B. Let A be the event that only one head occurs in two tosses of the coin then A = {*HT, TH*} and let B be the event that only two tails occurs, B = {*TT*} then A ∪ B = {*HT, TH, TT*} is the event that only one head or two tails occurs.

Intersection of sets: the symbol to denote the intersection of events is ∩, read as 'and'; for example A and B, written A ∩ B. Let A be the event that at least one head occurs in two tosses of the coin, then A = {*HH, HT, TH*} and let B be the event that only one tail occurs, B = {*HT, TH*}, then A ∩ B = {*HT, TH*} is the event that one head and one tail occurs.

Disjoint events: disjoint events have no events in common and, therefore, their intersection is the null set; in the case of sets A and B,

$A \cap B = \emptyset$. For example, let A be the event that two heads occur in two tosses of the coin, then A = {*HH*} and let B be the event that two tails occur, B = {*TT*}, then $A \cap B = \emptyset$; the intersection of these sets is the empty set.

The power set: the power set is the set of all possible subsets, it is denoted 2^{Ω}, and may be finite or infinite. It should not be interpreted literally as raising 2 to the power Ω; the notation is symbolic.

1.2.2 The sample space Ω

The sample space, denoted Ω is the set of all possible outcomes, or realisations, of a random 'experiment'. A typical element or sample point in Ω is denoted ω, thus $\omega \in \Omega$; a subscript will be added to ω where this serves to indicate the multiplicity of outcomes in Ω. To consider the sample space further, braces {.} will be used for a set where the order is not essential, whereas the parentheses (.) indicate that the elements are ordered.

A sequence of sample spaces is indicated by Ω_j, where j is increasing; for example, consider two consecutive tosses of a coin, then the sample space is Ω_2 = {(*HH*), (*HT*), (*TT*), (*TH*)}, which comprises $2^2 = 4$ elements, denoted, respectively, ω_1, ω_2, ω_3 and ω_4, where each ω_i is an ordered sequence (ξ_1, ξ_2) and ξ_i is either *H* or *T*. The subscripting on ξ_i could be more explicit to capture the multiplicity of possible outcomes for ξ_i; for example, let $\xi_{i,1} = H$ and $\xi_{i,2} = T$, then $\omega_1 = (\xi_{1,1}, \xi_{2,1})$, $\omega_2 = (\xi_{1,1}, \xi_{2,2})$, $\omega_3 = (\xi_{1,2}, \xi_{2,2})$ and $\omega_4 = (\xi_{1,2}, \xi_{2,1})$. If the random experiment was the roll of a dice, then there would be $6^2 = 36$ elements in Ω_2, each (still) comprising an ordered pair of outcomes, for example (1, 1), (1, 2) (1, 3) and so on.

Continuing with the coin-tossing experiment, the sample space for three consecutive tosses of a coin is Ω_3 = {(*HHH*), (*HHT*), (*HTH*), (*HTT*), (*TTT*), (*TTH*), (*THT*), (*THH*)}, which comprises $8 = 2^3$ elements, $\{\omega_i\}_{i=1}^{8}$, where each ω_i is an ordered sequence (ξ_1, ξ_2, ξ_3) and ξ_i is either $\xi_{i,1} = H$ or $\xi_{i,2} = T$. In general, for n tosses of the coin, there are 2^n elements, $\{\omega_i\}_{i=1}^{n}$, in the sample space, Ω_n, each comprising an ordered sequence of length n, $(\xi_i, \ldots, \xi_n)$, where ξ_i is either *H* or *T*; (more explicitly $\xi_{i,j}$, j = 1, 2). The simplest case is n = 1, so that $\Omega_1 = \{\omega_1, \omega_2\}$ where $\omega_1 = \xi_{1,1} = H$ and $\omega_2 = \xi_{1,2} = T$; that is two elements with a sequence of length 1. It is also sometimes of interest to consider the case where $n \to \infty$, in which case the sample space is denoted $\Omega_\infty = \{\omega_1, \ldots, \omega_i, \ldots\}$, where ω_i is an ordered sequence $(\xi_1, \ldots, \xi_j, \ldots)$.

In the example of the previous paragraph, Ω_1 is the sample space of the (basic) random experiment of tossing a coin; however, it is often

more useful to map this into a random variable, typically denoted x, or x_1, where the subscript indicates the first of a possible multiplicity of random variables. To indicate the dependence of x on the sample space, this is sometimes written more explicitly as $x_1(\omega)$. For example, suppose we bet on the outcome of the coin-tossing experiment, winning one unit if the coin lands heads and losing one unit if the coin lands tails; then the sample space $\Omega_1 = (H, T)$ is mapped to $\Omega_{x,1} = (+1, -1)$. The new sample space now comprises sequences with the elements 1 and –1, rather than (*H*, *T*); for example, in two consecutive tosses of the coin, the sample space of $x_2(\omega)$ is $\Omega_{x,2} = \{(1, 1), (1, -1), (-1, 1), (-1, -1)\}$.

These examples illustrate that a random variable is a mapping from the sample space Ω to some function of the sample space; the identity mapping is included to allow for Ω being unchanged. Indeed, the term random variable is a misnomer, with random function being a more accurate description; nevertheless this usage is firmly established. Usually, the new space, that of the random variable, is $\Re$ and that of an n-vector of random variables is $\Re^n$. Consider the coin-tossing experiment, then for each toss separately $x_i(\omega)$: $\Omega_1 \mapsto \Re$. For example, in the case of n = 2, two possibilities may be of interest to define random variables based on the underlying sample space. First, construct a new random variable as the sum of the win/lose amounts, say $S_2(\omega) = x_1(\omega) + x_2(\omega)$, with sample space $\Omega_{S_2} = \{-2, 0, +2\}$; this is a mapping of Ω_2 into $\Re$, that is $S_2(\omega) : \Omega_2 \mapsto \Re$ and by simple extension for n consecutive tosses, $S_n(\omega) : \Omega_n \mapsto \Re$. The second possibility is to recognise the sequential nature of the coin tosses and define two random variables, one for each toss of the coin, $x(\omega) = (x_1(\omega), x_2(\omega))$, with a sample space that is the Cartesian product (defined in the glossary) of Ω_1 with itself and, hence, contained in $\Re^2$. In general, n coin tosses is a mapping into $\Re^n$.

The next step, having identified the sample space of the basic experiment, is to be able to associate probabilities with the elements, collections of elements, or functions of these as in the case of random variables, in the sample space. Whilst this can be done quite intuitively in some simple cases, the kinds of problems that can be solved in this way are rather limited. For example, let a coin be fair, and the experiment is to toss the coin once; we wish to assign a probability, or measure, that accords with our intuition that it should be a non-negative number between 0 and 1. In this set up, we assign the measure ½ to each of the two elements in Ω_1, and call these the probabilities of tossing a head and a tail, respectively. The probabilities sum to one.

By extension of the example, let there be n = 3 (independent) tosses of the coin; then to each element in Ω_3 we assign the measure of $^1/_8$;

again the probabilities sum to one. Now let $n \to \infty$ and apply the same logic: the probability of a particular $\omega \in \Omega_n$ tends to zero, being $½^n$; since each element of Ω_n has a probability of zero, then by extension the sum of any subset of such probabilities is also zero, since a sum of zeros is zero!

This suggests that we will need to consider rather carefully experiments where the sample space has an infinite number of outcomes. That we can make progress by adopting a different approach is evident from the elementary problem of determining the probability of a random number, generated by a draw from the normal distribution, falling between *a* and *b*, where $a < b$. On the basis of the argument that the probability of a particular element is zero, this probability is zero; however, a solution is obtained by finding the distribution function for the random variable x and taking the difference between this function evaluated at *b* and *a*, respectively.

This last point alerts us to the important distinction between discrete and continuous random variables, which will be elaborated below. The nature of a random variable (and of the random experiment underlying it) is that, a priori, a number of outcomes or realisations are possible. If the number of distinct values of these outcomes is countable, then the random variable is discrete. The simplest case is when there is a finite number of outcomes, such as in a single throw of a dice; this is a number that is finite and, therefore, clearly countable. However, the number of outcomes may be countably infinite or denumerable, by which is meant that they stand in a one-to-one relationship with the (infinite) set of integers. If the number of possible outcomes of a random variable is not denumerable, then the random variable is said to be continuous.

1.2.3 Field (algebra, event space), F: Introduction

At an abstract level a field is a collection of subsets, here combinations from the sample space Ω. The generic notation for a field, also known as an algebra, is *F*. What we have in mind is that these subsets will be the ones to which we seek to assign a probability (measure). At an introductory level, in the case of a random experiment with a finite number of outcomes, this concept is implicit rather than explicit; the emphasis is usually on listing all the possible elementary events and then assigning probabilities, P(.), to them and then combining the elementary events into other subsets of interest. For example, consider rolling a 6-sided dice then the elementary events are the six integers, 1–6, $\omega_j = j$, $j = 1, \ldots, 6$, with $P(x = \omega_j) = 1/6$. The sample space is $\Omega = \{\omega_1, \ldots, \omega_6\}$. We could, therefore,

define the collection of subsets of interest as $(\emptyset, \Omega)$, where the null set is included for completeness since it is the complement of Ω, $\Omega^c = \emptyset$. This is the simplest 'field', since it is a collection of subsets of Ω, that could be defined, say $F_0 = (\emptyset, \Omega)$.

Rather than the individual outcomes, we may instead be interested in whether the outcome was odd; this is the (combined) event or subset C_{odd} that can be obtained either as the union $C_{odd} = \{\omega_1 \cup \omega_3 \cup \omega_5\}$ or as the complement of the union C_{even}, $C^c_{even} = \{\omega_2 \cup \omega_4 \cup \omega_6\}^c$. Either way, the component subsets are mutually exclusive, that is $\{\omega_1 \cap \omega_3\} = \{\omega_1 \cap \omega_5\} = \{\omega_3 \cap \omega_5\} = 0$, so that $P(C_{odd}) = P(\omega_1) + P(\omega_3) + P(\omega_5)$. Thus, we could extend the subsets of interest to the field $F_1 = (\emptyset, C_{odd}, C_{even}, \Omega)$ and assign probabilities by combining the probabilities from the elementary events. By extension, we might be interested in many other possible events, for example the event that the number is less than 2, so that, say, $A_1 = 1$, or greater than or equal to 4, say $A_2 = \{4 \cup 5 \cup 6\}$, and so on. To be on the 'safe' side, perhaps we could include all possible events in the field; this is known as the power set, but this set, even with this relatively small example, is quite large, here it comprises 2^6 events, and, practically, we might need a field less extensive than this, but more complete than F_0, to be the one of interest. More generally, as the maximum dimension of the power set increases, we seek a set of 'interesting' events, an event space, to which we will, potentially, assign probabilities.

1.2.3.i *Ω is a countable finite sample space*

If Ω is a countably finite sample space then F is defined as follows. Let Ω be an arbitrary nonempty set, then the class or collection of subsets of Ω, denoted F, is a field or algebra if:

F1. $\Omega \in F$, that is Ω is contained in F;
F2. $A \in F$ implies $A^c \in F$, that is both A and its complement belong to F;
F3. if $A \in F$ and $B \in F$, then $A \cup B \in F$, that is the union of A and B is in F; equivalently, by an application of De Morgan's law, $A \cap B \in F$.

Note that $F_1 = (\emptyset, C_{odd}, C_{even}, \Omega)$, as in the previous subsection, is a field; condition **F1** is satisfied; condition **F2** is satisfied as $C_{even} = C^c_{odd}$, and, condition **F3** is satisfied as, if $A = C_{odd}$ and $B = C_{even}$, then $A \cup B \in F$.

A probability measure, generically denoted P, is a function defined on the event space of F. Let F be a field of Ω, then a probability measure is a function that assigns a number, $P(A)$, to every event (set) $A \in F$,

such that:

P1. $0 \leq P(A) \leq 1$ for A, the number assigned to A is bounded between 0 and 1;
P2. $P(\Omega) = 1$, $P(\emptyset) = 0$, so that the sure event and the null event are included;
P3. if $A_1 \in F$ and $A_2 \in F$ are disjoint subsets in *F*, then $P(A_1 \cup A_2) = P(A_1) + P(A_2)$.

The probability space (or probability measure space) is the triple that brings together the space Ω, a field *F*, and the probability measure associated with that field, usually written as the triple (Ω, *F*, *P*).

Provided the conditions **P1**, **P2** and **P3** are met, the resulting function *P* is a probability measure. Usually, considerations such as the limiting relative frequency of events will motivate the probabilities assigned. For example, in the dice-rolling experiment, setting $P(\omega_j) = \frac{1}{6}$ might be justified by an appeal to a 'fair' dice in the sense that each outcome is judged equally likely; however, the assignment ($\frac{1}{4}$, $\frac{1}{12}$, $\frac{1}{6}$, $\frac{1}{6}$, $\frac{1}{6}$, $\frac{1}{6}$), is also a probability measure as it satisfies properties **P1–P3**.

1.2.3.ii Ω is a countably infinite sample space; σ–field or σ–algebra

The problem with the field and probability measure defined upon is that, so far, it is confined to a finite, and so countable, sample space. This is captured in condition **F3** and the associated condition **P3**. However, we will need to consider sample spaces that comprise an infinite number of outcomes. The case to consider first is where the number of outcomes is countably infinite (or denumerable), in that the outcomes can be mapped into a one-to-one correspondence with the integers. Thus, Ω comprising the set of all positive integers, Ω = (1, 2, ... ,) is countably infinite; outcomes of the form $\omega_i = \alpha + hi$, so that h is the step size, are countably infinite. Condition **F3** limits the subsets in the field to a finite union of events, which means that many subsets of interest, including Ω itself, cannot be generated. What is required is an extension of conditions **F3** and **P3**, to allow infinite unions of events. When this is done the field *F* is known as a σ–field or σ–algebra (of Ω). The condition and its extension to the probability measure are as follows.

The field *F* is said to be a σ–field or σ–algebra (of Ω) if, in place of condition **F3** we have the following.

F4. Whenever the sequence of sets $\{A_i\}_{i=1}^{\infty} \in F$, then the union of the component sets, written $\cup_{i=1}^{\infty} A_i$, also belongs to *F*; equivalently, by De Morgan's law, $\cap_{i=1}^{\infty} A_i$, also belongs to *F*.

There is an equivalent extension of **P3** as follows. Let *F* be a σ–field of Ω, then a probability measure is a function that assigns a number, P(A), to every event (set) $A \in F$, such that, with conditions **P1** and **P2**, as before:

P4. if $\{A_i\}_{i=1}^{\infty} \in F$ is a sequence of disjoint sets in *F*, and $\cup_i^{\infty} A_i \in F$, then $P(\cup_{i=1}^{\infty} A_i) = \Sigma_{i=1}^{\infty} P(A_i)$.

See, for example, Billingsley (1995, chapter 1).

If *F* is a σ–field *F* of Ω, then the associated probability space is the triple that brings together the space Ω, a σ–field *F* and the probability measure *P*, written as the triple (Ω, σ(*F*), *P*).

1.2.3.iii Ω is an uncountably infinite sample space

The final case to consider is when Ω is an infinite sample space that is not countable, which is the most relevant specification for stochastic processes (see Section 1.4). A set that is not countable is said to be uncountable; in an intuitive sense it is just too big to be countable – it is nondenumerable. Although we are occasionally interested in the underlying sample space, here the emphasis will be on a random function (or random variable) that maps the original sample space into $\Re^n$, starting with the simplest case where n = 1. (The general case is considered in Section 1.3.)

To return to the problem at hand, the question is how to define a field, that is a collection of subsets representing 'interesting' events, and an associated probability measure in such a case. It should be clear that we cannot make progress by (only) trying to assign probabilities to the singletons, which are sets but comprise just single numbers in ℜ or single elementary events; rather, we focus on intervals defined on the real line, ℜ. For example, instead of asking if a probability measure can be assigned to the occurrence of $x(\omega) = a$, where a is a real number, we seek to assign a probability to the occurrence of $x(\omega) \in B$, where B is a set comprising elements in the interval [a, b], (a, b], [a, b) or (a, b), where $a < b$. This makes sense from a practical viewpoint; for example, the ingestion of drugs over the (infinitely divisible) time interval (0, b] or a tolerance requirement in a manufacturing process that has to fall

with a certain probability within prescribed tolerances; and from an econometric viewpoint, if we are interested in the probability of a test statistic falling in the interval $(-\infty, b]$ or in the combined interval $(-\infty, b] \cup [c, \infty)$.

This approach suggests that the sets that we would like to assign probabilities to, that is define a probability measure over, be quite general and certainly include open and closed intervals, half-open intervals and, for completeness, ought to be able to deal with the case of singletons. On the other hand, we don't need to be so general that every possible subset is included. The field, or collection of subsets, that meets our requirements is the Borel field of $\Re$.

1.2.3.iii.a Borel sets; Borel σ–field of $\Re$

Consider the case where the sample space is $\Re$. This can occur because the original sample space Ω is just $\Re$ or $\Omega \neq \Re$ but, as noted, interest centres on a random variable that provides the mapping: $\Omega \mapsto \Re$. We will distinguish the two cases in due course, but for now we concentrate on ways of generating the Borel σ–field, *B*, of $\Re$. There are a number of equivalent ways of doing this, equivalent because one can be generated from the other by a countable number of the set operations of union, intersection and complementation. Thus, variously, the reader will find the Borel σ–field of $\Re$ defined as the collection (on $\Re$) of all open intervals, the collection of all closed sets, the collection of all half-open intervals of the form $(-\infty, b]$, $-\infty < b \in \Re$, and so on. For example, if the Borel σ–field is defined as the collection of all open intervals which are of the form,

$$I^{(1)} = \{(a, b), -\infty < a < b < \infty\} \tag{1.1}$$

where a and b are scalars, then closed sets, which are the complements of open sets, are included in the field, so we might equally have started from closed sets. If we start from closed intervals, we can get all the open intervals from the relation $(a, b) = \cup_{n=1}^{\infty} [a + 1/n, b - 1/n]$. Note that despite the upper limit of ∞, the unions are countable because of their one-to-one correspondence with the integers. Singletons can be generated as $b = (-\infty, b] \cap (-\infty, b)^c$; visually on $\Re$, this intersection just isolates b. For example, suppose interest centres on the interval $[0, b)$, so that outcomes cannot be negative, then this is included as $[0, b) = \cap_{n=1}^{\infty} (-1/n, b)$. What this means is that Borel sets, and the associated Borel σ–field of $\Re$, are quite general enough to consider the subsequent problem of associating a probability measure with the σ–field so defined.

1.2.3.iii.b Derived probability measure and Borel measurable function
If the Borel sets relate to the underlying random experiment, then the probability space follows as: $(\Re, B, P)$. Generally, it is more likely to be the case, as in the focus of this section, that a random variable x based on the original sample is of interest; two cases being where x maps Ω to $\Re$, that is x: $\Omega \mapsto \Re$ and x maps $\Re^n$ to $\Re$, that is x : $\Re^n \mapsto \Re$. In these cases, the probability measure that we seek is a derived probability measure and the triple of a sample space, a σ–field on the Borel sets and a measure, is a derived probability space $(\Re, B, P_x)$, where P_x is the probability measure on B and is distinguished by an x subscript. The question then is whether there are any complications or qualifications that arise when this is the case? The answer is yes and relates to being able to undertake the reverse mapping from $\Re$ to Ω.

The notation assumes that x: $\Omega \mapsto \Re$, and the random variable is assumed to be defined on the Borel σ–field of $\Re$. The measurable spaces are $(\Omega, \sigma\text{–}F)$ and $(\Re, B)$, with corresponding probability space $(\Omega, \sigma\text{–}F, P)$ and derived probability space $(\Re, B, P_X)$, respectively. The requirement is that of measurability defined as follows. The function x: $\Omega \mapsto \Re$, is said to be measurable, relative to $\sigma\text{–}F$ and B, if $x^{(-1)}(B) \subset \sigma\text{–}F$. (The operator indicated by the superscript (–1), to distinguish it from the inverse operator, is the pre-image) That is the pre-image of X is in the σ–field of the original random experiment. Intuitively, we must be able to map the event(s) of interest in x back to the field of the original sample space. (A brief outline of the meaning of image and pre-image is provided in the glossary.)

1.2.4 The distribution function and the density function, cdf and pdf

The task now is to assign probability measures to sets of interest where the sets are Borel sets; that is we seek P(A) where A is an event (set) in B. This is approached by first defining the distribution function associated with a probability measure on $(\Re, B)$. The distribution function also referred to as the cumulative distribution function, abbreviated to cdf, uniquely characterises the probability measure.

1.2.4.i The distribution function

The distribution function for the measurable space $(\Re, B)$ is the function such that:

$$F(a) = P(x(\omega) \leq a) \tag{1.2}$$

An equivalent way of writing this for a random variable x is F(X) = P(x(ω) ≤ X). The properties of a distribution function are:

D1. F(a) is bounded, F(–∞) = 0 and F(∞) = 1;
D2. it is non-decreasing, F(b) – F(a) ≥ 0 for a < b;
D3. it is continuous on the right.

For example, consider a continuous random variable that can take any value on the real line, R, and A = [a, b] where –∞ < a ≤ b < ∞, then what is the probability measure associated with A? This is the probability that x is an element of A, given by:

$$\begin{aligned} P(x(\omega) \in A) &= F(b) - F(a) \\ &= P(x(\omega) \leq b) - P(x(\omega) \leq a) \geq 0 \end{aligned} \qquad (1.3)$$

An identifying feature of a discrete random variable is that it gives rise to a distribution function that is a step function; this is because there are gaps between adjacent outcomes, which are one-dimensional in $\Re$, so the distribution function stays constant between outcomes and then jumps up at the next possible outcome.

1.2.4.ii The density function

In the case of continuous random variables, we can usually associate a density function f(X), sometimes referred to as the (probability) density function, pdf, with each distribution function F(X). If a density function exists for F(X) then it must have the following properties:

f1. it is non-negative, f(X) ≥ 0 for all X;
f2. it is integrable in the Reimann sense (see Chapter 7, Section 7.1.1);
f3. it integrates to unity over the range of x, $\int_c^d f(X)dX = 1$, typically c = –∞ and d = ∞.

If a density function exists for F(x) then:

$$F(x \leq a) = \int_{-\infty}^{a} f(X)dX \qquad (1.4)$$

in which case P(x ∈ A), where A = [a, b], is given by:

$$P(x \in A) = \int_{a}^{b} f(X)dX \qquad (1.5)$$

The definition of A could replace the closed interval by open intervals at either or both ends because the probability of a singleton is zero.

Example 1.1: Uniform distribution

Consider a random variable that can take any value in an interval with range $[a, b] \subset \Re$, and a uniform distribution over that range; that is, the probability of x being in any equally sized interval is the same. The density function, f(X), assigns the same (positive) value to all elements in the interval or equal sub-intervals. To make sense as a density function, the integral of all such points must be unity. The density and distribution functions for the uniform distribution are:

$$f(X) = \frac{1}{a_2 - a_1} \qquad \text{if } a_1 \le X \le a_2 \tag{1.6a}$$

$$f(X) = 0 \qquad \text{if } X < a_1 \text{ or } X > a_2 \tag{1.6b}$$

$$\begin{aligned} F(X \le a_2) &= \int_{a_1}^{a_2} f(X)dX \\ &= \int_{a_1}^{a_2} \left(\frac{1}{a_2 - a_1} \right) dX \\ &= \frac{1}{a_2 - a_1} a_2 - \frac{1}{a_2 - a_1} a_1 \\ &= 1 \end{aligned} \tag{1.7}$$

Now consider the Borel set $A = [c, d]$ where $a_1 < c$, $d < a_2$, what is $P(x \in A)$? In this case the density function exists, so that:

$$\begin{aligned} P(x \in A) &= F(x \le d) - F(x \le c) \\ &= \int_{-\infty}^{d} f(X)dX - \int_{-\infty}^{c} f(X)dX \\ &= \int_{c}^{d} f(X)dX \\ &= \int_{c}^{d} \left(\frac{1}{a_2 - a_1} \right) dX \\ &= \frac{d - c}{a_2 - a_1} \end{aligned} \tag{1.8}$$

The distribution function is non-decreasing and, therefore, $P(x \in A)$ is non-negative. This is also an example of Lebesgue measure, which is a measure defined on the Borel sets of $\Re$ and corresponds to the intuitive notion of the length of the interval [c, d]. ♦

Example 1.2: Normal distribution

A particularly important pdf is that associated with the normal density, which gives rise to the familiar symmetric, bell-shaped density function:

$$f(X) = \frac{1}{\sqrt{2\pi}} \exp\left\{-\frac{1}{2}\sigma^2 (X-\mu)^2\right\} \tag{1.9}$$

where μ is the expected value of x and σ^2 is the variance, defined below (Section 1.5). The cdf associated with the normal pdf is, therefore:

$$F(x < b) = \frac{1}{\sqrt{2\pi}} \int_{-\infty}^{b} \exp\left\{-\frac{1}{2}\sigma^2 (X-\mu)^2\right\} dX \tag{1.10}$$

The pdf and cdf are shown in Figures 1.1a and 1.1b, respectively. The normal distribution is of such importance that it has its own notational

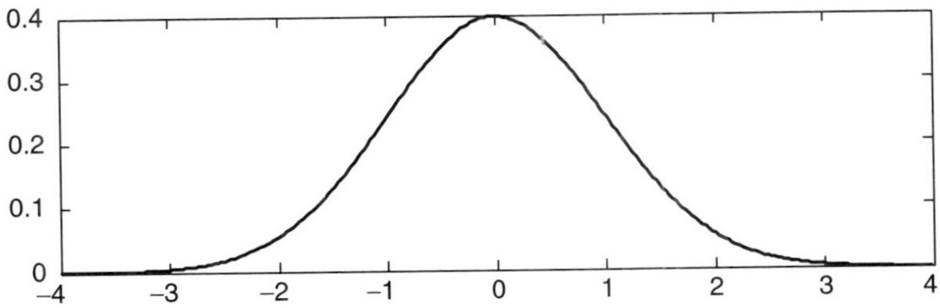

Figure 1.1a pdf of the standard normal distribution

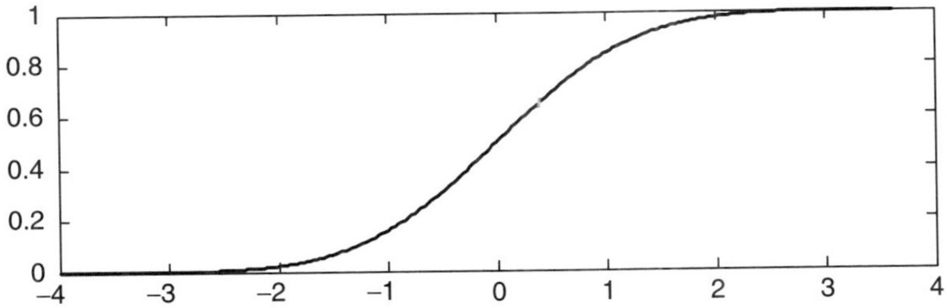

Figure 1.1b cdf of the standard normal distribution

representation with $\Phi(z)$ often used to denote the normal distribution function. Some probability calculations are well known for the normal density; for example, let $A = (-1.96, 1.96)$, then $P(x \in A) = \Phi(1.96) - \Phi(-1.96) = 0.95$, that is 95% of the distribution lies between ±1.96. ♦

1.3 Random vector case

We are typically interested in the outcomes of several random variables together rather than a single random variable. For example, interest may focus on whether the prices of two financial assets are related, suggesting we consider two random variables x_1 and x_2, and the relationship between them. More generally, define an n-dimensional random vector as the collection of n random variables:

$$x = (x_1, x_2, \ldots, x_n)' \tag{1.11}$$

where each of the x_j is a real-valued random variable. For simplicity assume that each random variable is defined on the measurable space $(\Re, B)$. (This will often reflect the practical situation, but it is not essential.) By letting the index j take the index of time, x becomes a vector of a random variable at different points in time; such a case is distinguished throughout this book by reserving the notation y_j or y_t where time is of the essence.

By extension, we seek a probability space for the vector of random variables. The sets of interest will be those in the Borel σ–field of $\Re^n$. For example, when n = 2, this is the σ–field of the two-dimensional Borel sets, that is rectangles in $\Re^2$, of the form:

$$I^{(2)} = \{(\mathbf{a}, \mathbf{b}), -\infty < a_1 < a_2 < \infty, -\infty < b_1 < b_2 < \infty\} \tag{1.12}$$

where $\mathbf{a} = (a_1, a_2)$ and $\mathbf{b} = (b_1, b_2)$. A particular subset is a Borel set if it can be obtained by repeated, countable operations of union, intersection and complementation.

The distribution function extends to the joint distribution function of the n random variables, so that:

$$F(X_1, \cdots, X_n) = P(x_1 \le X_1, \ldots, x_n \le X_n) \tag{1.13}$$

The properties of a distribution function carry across to the vector case, so that $F(X_1, \ldots, X_n) \ge 0$, $F(-\infty, \ldots, -\infty) = 0$, $F(\infty, \ldots, \infty) = 1$.

If the density function, $f(X_1, \ldots, X_n)$, exists then the distribution function can be written as:

$$F(X_1, \cdots, X_n) = \int_{-\infty}^{X_1} \ldots \int_{-\infty}^{X_n} f(X_1, \ldots, X_n) dX_1, \ldots, dX_n \tag{1.14}$$

Assuming that ∞ is the upper limit of each one-dimensional random variable, then:

$$\begin{aligned} F(\infty, \ldots, \infty) &= \int_{-\infty}^{\infty} \ldots \int_{-\infty}^{\infty} f(X_1, \ldots, X_n) dX_1, \ldots, dX_n \\ &= 1 \end{aligned} \tag{1.15}$$

Example 1.3: Extension of the uniform distribution to two variables

In this case we consider two independent random variables x_1 and x_2, with a uniform joint distribution, implying that each has a uniform marginal distribution. The sample space is a rectangle $\subset \Re^2$, the two-dimensional extension of an interval for a single uniformly distributed random variable. Thus, x_1 and x_2 can take any value at random in the rectangle formed by $I_1^{(1)} = [a_1, a_2]$ on the horizontal axis and $I_2^{(1)} = [b_1, b_2]$ on the vertical axis, $a_1 < a_2$ and $b_1 < b_2$. A natural extension of the probability measure of example 1.1, which is another example of Lebesgue measure, is to assign the area to any particular sub-rectangle, so that the joint pdf is:

$$f(X_1, X_2) = \frac{1}{(a_2 - a_1)(b_2 - b_1)} \tag{1.16}$$

The joint distribution function integrates to unity over the range of the complete sample space and is bounded by 0 and 1;

$$F(X_1 \in I_1^{(1)}, X_2 \in I_2^{(1)}) = \int_{a_1}^{a_2} \int_{b_1}^{b_2} f(X_1, X_2) dX_2 dX_1 = 1 \tag{1.17a}$$

$$0 \le F(X_1 \le a_2, X_2 \le b_2) = \frac{(X_1 - a_1)(X_2 - b_1)}{(a_2 - a_1)(b_2 - b_1)} \le 1 \tag{1.17b}$$

For example, if $X_1 = \frac{1}{2}(a_2 - a_1)$ and $X_2 = \frac{1}{4}(b_2 - b_1)$ then $F(X_1, X_2) = \frac{1}{8}$.

In fact, as the reader may already have noted, the assumption of independence (defined in Section 1.7 below) implies that $f(X_1, X_2) = f(X_1)f(X_2)$, $f(X_1 \mid X_2) = f(X_1)$ and $F(X_1 \in A \mid X_2 \in B) = F(X_1 \in A)$. ♦

1.4 Stochastic process

From the viewpoint of time series analysis, typically we are not interested in the outcome of a random variable at a single point in time, but in a sample path or realisation of a sequence of random variables over an interval of time. To conceptualise how such sample paths arise, we introduce the idea of a stochastic process, which involves a sample space Ω and time. Superficially, a stochastic process does not look any different from the random vector case of the previous section and, indeed, technically, it isn't! The difference is in the aspects that we choose to emphasise.

One difference, purely notational, is that a stochastic process is usually indexed by t, say $t = 1, \ldots, T$, to emphasise time, whereas the general random vector case uses $j = 1, \ldots, n$. Following the notational convention in this chapter the components of the stochastic process will be denoted $y_t(\omega)$ for a discrete-time process and $y(t, \omega)$ for a continuous-time process; the reference to $\omega \in \Omega$ is often suppressed. In the discrete-time case, $t \in T$, where, typically T comprises the integers $N = (0, \pm1, \pm2, \ldots)$ or the non-negative integers $N^+ = (0, 1, 2, \ldots)$. In the continuous-time case, T is an interval, for example $T = \Re$, or the positive half line $T = \Re^+$ or an interval on R, for example $T = [0, 1]$.

A stochastic process is a collection of random variables, denoted Y, on a probability space (see, for example, Billingsley, 1995), indexed by time $t \in T$ and elements, ω, in a sample space Ω. A discrete-time stochastic process with $T \subseteq N^+$ may be summarised as:

$$Y = (y_t(\omega) : t \in T \subseteq N^+, \omega \in \Omega) \tag{1.18}$$

For given $t \in T$, $y_t(\omega)$ is a function of $\omega \in \Omega$ and is, therefore, a random variable. A realisation is a single number – the point on the sample path relating to, say, $t = s$; by varying the element of Ω, whilst keeping $t = s$, we get a distribution of outcomes at that point.

For given $\omega \in \Omega$, $y_t(\omega)$ is a function of time, $t \in T$. In this case an 'outcome' is a complete sample path, that is a function of $t \in T$, rather than a single number. A description of the sample path would require a functional relationship rather than a single number. By varying ω we

now get a different sample path; that is (potentially) different realisations for all $t \in T$.

We will often think of the index set T as comprising an infinite number of elements, even in the case of discrete-time processes, where N is (countably) infinite; in the case of a continuous-time stochastic process even if T is an finite interval of time, such as [0, 1], the interval is infinitely divisible. In either case, the collection of random variables in Y is infinite.

Often the reference to $\omega \in \Omega$ is suppressed and a single random variable in the stochastic process is written y_t, but the underlying dependence on the sample space should be recognised and means that different $\omega \in \Omega$ give rise to potentially different sample paths (this will be illustrated in Chapter 5 for random walks and in Chapter 6 for the important case of Brownian motion).

A continuous-time stochastic process may be summarised as:

$$Y = (y(t, \omega) : t \in T \subseteq \Re, \omega \in \Omega) \tag{1.19}$$

The continuous-time stochastic process represented at a discrete or countably infinite number of points is then written as: $y(t_1)$, $y(t_2)$,..., $y(t_n)$, where reference to ω has been suppressed.

We can now return to the question of what is special about a stochastic process, other than that it is a sequence of random variables. To highlight the difference it is useful to consider a question that is typically considered for a sequence of random variables, in the general notation $(x_1, \ldots, x_n)$; then it may be of interest to know whether x_n converges in a well-defined sense to a random variable or a constant as $n \to \infty$, a problem considered at length in Chapter 4. For example, suppose that x_n is distributed as Student's t with n degrees of freedom; then as $n \to \infty$, $x_n \to x$, where x is normally distributed. Such an example occurs when the distribution of a test statistic has a degrees of freedom effect. In this case we interpret the sample space of interest as being that for each x_n, rather than the sequence as a whole. In the case of a stochastic process, the sample space is the space of a sequence of length n (or T in the case of a random variable with an inherent time dimension).

If we regard n tosses of a coin as taking place sequentially in time, then we have already encountered the sample space of a stochastic process in Section 1.2.2. If the n tosses of the coin are consecutive, then the sample space, of dimension 2^n, is denoted Ω_n, where the generic element of Ω_n, ω_i, refers to an n-dimensional *ordered* sequence. In the usual case that the coin tosses are independent, then the sample space

Ω_n is the product space, $\Omega_n = \Omega_1 \times \Omega_1 \times \ldots \times \Omega_1 = \Omega_1^n$ (where the $\times$ symbol indicates the Cartesian product, see glossary).

We now understand by fixing ω that we fix a whole path, not just a single element at time j (or t); thus as ω is varied, the whole sample path is varied, at least potentially. This is why the appropriate space for a stochastic process is a function space: each sample path is a function not a single outcome. The distribution of interest is not the distribution of a single element, say y_t, but the distribution of the complete sample paths, which is the distribution of the functions on time. Thus, in terms of convergence, it is of limited interest to focus on the t-th or any particular element of the stochastic process. Replication of the process through simulation generates a distribution of sample paths associated with different realisations over the *complete* sample path and convergence is a now a question of the convergence of one process to another process; for example, the convergence of the random walk process, used in Chapter 5, to another process, in this case Brownian motion, considered in Chapter 6.

Of interest in assessing convergence of a stochastic process are the finite-dimensional distributions, fidis; in the continuous-time case, these are the joint distributions of the n-dimensional vector $y(t_1)$, $y(t_2)$, ..., $y(t_n)$, where t_1, t_2, ..., t_n is a finite-dimensional sequence. Although it is not generally sufficient to establish convergence, at an intuitive level one can think of the distribution of the stochastic process Y as being the collection of the fidis for all possible choices of sequences of time, t_1, t_2, ..., t_n. This becomes relevant when providing a meaning to the idea that one stochastic process converges to another; we return to this question in Chapter 4, Section 4.4.

1.5 Expectation, variance, covariance and correlation

We shall be interested not only in the distribution and density of a random variable, but also some other characteristics that summarise features likely to be of use. The first of these is the expectation of a random variable, which accords with the common usage of the average or mean of a random variable; the second is the variance, which is one measure of the dispersion in the distribution of outcomes of a random variable; the third necessarily involves more than one random variable and relates to the covariance between random variables; and, finally, the correlation coefficient which is a scaled version of the covariance. A particular important case of the covariance and correlation between random variables occurs when in the case of two random variables, say, one random variable is a lag of the other. This case is of such importance that whilst the basic

concepts are introduced here, they are developed further in Chapter 2, Section 2.3.1, in the explicit context of time series analysis.

1.5.1 Expectation and variance of a random variable

1.5.1.i Discrete random variables

By definition, a discrete random variable, x, has a range R(x), with a countable number of elements. The probability density function associated with a discrete random variable is usually referred to as the probability mass function, pmf, because it assigns 'mass', rather than density, at a countable number of discrete points. An example is the Poisson distribution function, which assigns mass at points in the set of non-negative integers, see Section 3.5.3.

In the case of a discrete random variable, the expected value of x is the sum of the possible outcomes each weighted by the probability of occurrence of the outcome, that is:

$$E(x) = \sum_{i=1}^{n} X_i P(x = X_i) \tag{1.20}$$

Recall the notational convention that x denotes the random variable, or more precisely random function, and X denotes an outcome; thus $x = X_i$ means that the outcome of x is X_i and $P(x = X_i)$ is the assignment of probability (mass) to that outcome; the latter may more simply be referred to as $P(x = X_i)$ or P(X) when the context is clear.

In a shorthand that is convenient, E(x) can be expressed as:

$$E(x) = \sum_{X \in R(x)} XP(X) \tag{1.21}$$

The summation is indicated over all X in the range of x, R(x). A common notational convention is to use μ to indicate the expectation of a random variable, with a subscript if more than one variable is involved, for example μ_x is the expected value of x.

The existence of an expected value requires that the absolute convergence condition is satisfied: $\Sigma_{X \in R(x)}|X|P(X) < \infty$. This condition is met for a finite sample space and finite R(x), but it is not necessarily satisfied when R(x) is countably infinite.

The variance of x, var(x), abbreviated to σ_x^2, is a measure of the dispersion of x about its expected value:

$$\sigma_x^2 = E[x - E(x)]^2 \tag{1.22}$$

In the case of a discrete random variable, the variance is:

$$\sigma_x^2 = \sum_{i=1}^{n} [X_i - E(x)]^2 P(x = X_i) \tag{1.23}$$

The variance is the sum of the deviations of each possible outcome from the expected value, weighted by the probability of the outcome. The square root of the variance is the standard deviation, σ_x (conventionally referred to as the standard error in a regression context).

1.5.1.ii Continuous random variables

In the case of a continuous random variable case, the range of x, R(x), is uncountably infinite. The pdf, f(X), is then defined in terms of the integral, where $P(x \in A) = \int_{X \in A} f(X)dX$. Correspondingly, the expectation and variance of x are:

$$E(x) = \int_{-\infty}^{\infty} XdF(X) \tag{1.24a}$$

$$= \int_{-\infty}^{\infty} Xf(X)\,dX \qquad \text{when f(X) exists} \tag{1.24b}$$

$$\sigma_x^2 = \int_{-\infty}^{\infty} [X - E(x)]^2 dF(X) \tag{1.25a}$$

$$= \int_{-\infty}^{\infty} [X - E(x)]^2 f(X)dX \qquad \text{when f(X) exists} \tag{1.25b}$$

In each case, the second line assumes that the probability density function exists. Also, in each case, the integral in the first line is the Lebesgue-Stieltjes integral, whereas in the second line it is a (ordinary) Reimann integral; for more on this distinction see Rao (1973, especially Appendix 2A) and Chapter 7, Sections 7.1.1 and 7.1.2. The absolute convergence condition for the existence of the expected value is $\int_{-\infty}^{\infty} |X|\, f(X)\, dX < \infty$. In some practical cases, the limits of integration may be those of a finite interval [a, b], where $-\infty < a < b < \infty$.

1.5.2 Covariance and correlation between variables

One measure of association between two random variables x and z is the covariance, denoted cov(x, z) and abbreviated to σ_{xz}:

$$\sigma_{xz} = E[x - E(x)][z - E(z)] \tag{1.26}$$

with some simple manipulation σ_{xz} may be expressed as:

$$\sigma_{xz} = E(xz) - E(x)E(z) \tag{1.27}$$

The units of measurement of the covariance are the units of x times the units of z, hence σ_{xz} is not invariant to a change in the units of measurement and its magnitude should not, therefore, be taken to indicate the strength of association between two variables. The correlation coefficient, ρ_{xz}, standardises the covariance by scaling by the respective standard deviations, hence producing a unit free measure, with the property that $0 \leq |\rho_{xz}| \leq 1$:

$$\rho_{xz} = \frac{\sigma_{xz}}{\sigma_x \sigma_z} \tag{1.28}$$

1.5.2.i *Discrete random variables*

For case of the discrete random variables, σ_{xz} is:

$$\begin{aligned} \sigma_{xz} &= E[x - E(x)][z - E(z)] \\ &= \sum\nolimits_{i=1}^{n} \sum\nolimits_{j=1}^{m} [X_i - E(x)][Z_j - E(z)] P(x = X_i) \cap P(z = Z_j) \end{aligned} \tag{1.29}$$

where $P(x = X_i) \cap P(z = Z_i)$ is the probability of the joint event $x = X_i$ and $z = Z_j$; this is an example of a joint pmf for which the notation may be shortened to P(X, Z).

1.5.2.ii *Continuous random variables*

When x and z are each continuous random variables, then the covariance between x and z is:

$$\sigma_{xz} = \int_{-\infty}^{\infty} \int_{-\infty}^{\infty} [X - E(x)][Z - E(z)] f(X, Z) dX dZ \tag{1.30}$$

where f(X, Z) is the joint pdf of x and z.

Example 1.4: Bernoulli trials

We have already implicitly set up an example of Bernoulli trials in the coin-tossing random experiment of Section 1.2.2. In a Bernoulli trial, the random variable has only two outcomes, typically referred

to as 'success' and 'failure', with probabilities p and q, where q = 1 – p; additionally, the trials are repeated and independent, for example tossing a coin three times, with p = P(*H*) and q = P(*T*). The sample space is Ω_3 = {(*HHH*), (*HHT*), (*HTH*), (*HTT*), (*TTT*), (*TTH*), (*THT*), (*THH*)}, to which we assign the following probabilities (measures): $P_3 = (p^3, p^2q, p^2q, pq^2, q^3, pq^2, p^2q)$; if the coin is fair then P(*H*) = P(*T*) = ½ and each of these probabilities is $(^1/_2)^3 = {}^1/_8$.

It is convenient to define a random variable that assigns +1 to *H* and 0 to *T*, giving rise to sequences comprising 1s and 0s. (In a variation, used below in example 1.6 and extensively in Chapter 5, that reflects gambling and a binomial random walk, the assignment is +1 and –1.) For a single trial and this assignment of x_1, say, then $E(x_1) = 1p + 0q = p$, and variance $\sigma^2_{x_1} = (1-p)^2 p + (0-p)^2 q = (1-p)^2 p + p^2 q = p(1-p)$ using q = 1 – p. When the coin is tossed twice in sequence, we can construct a new random variable (which is clearly measurable) that counts the number of heads in the sequence and so maps Ω_2 into *N* (the set of non-negative integers) say, $S_2 = x_1 + x_2$, with sample space $\Omega_{S,2} = \{0, 1, 2\}$ and probabilities $\{q^2, 2pq, p^2\}$; if p = q = ½, then these probabilities are {¼, ½, ¼}. The expected number of heads is $E(S_2) = 2pq + 2p^2 = 2p$, and the variance of S_2 is $\sigma^2_{S_2} = (1-2p)2pq + (2-2p)\,p^2 = 2p(1-p)$.

This direct way of computing the mean and variance of Bernoulli trials is cumbersome. It is easier to define the indicator variable I_i, which takes the value 1 if the coin lands head on the i-th throw and 0 otherwise, these events have probabilities p and q, respectively, and are independent; hence, $E(S_n) = E(\Sigma^n_{i=1} I_i) = \Sigma^n_{i=1} E(I_i) = np$ and $\sigma^2_{S_2} = var(\Sigma^n_{i=1} I_i) = \Sigma^n_{i=1} var(I_i) = npq = np(1-p)$. ♦

1.6 Functions of random variables

Quite often functions of random variables will be important in the subsequent analysis. This section summarises some rules that apply to the expectation of a function of a random variable. Although similar considerations apply to obtaining the distribution and density of a function, it is frequently the case that the expectation is sufficient for the purpose. There is one case in Chapter 8 (the half-normal) where the distribution of a nonlinear function is needed, but that case can be dealt with intuitively.

1.6.1 Linear functions

The simplest case is that a new random variable is defined as a linear function of component random variable or variables. For example,

consider two random variables x_1 and x_2, their sum being defined as $S_2 = x_1 + x_2$, then what is the expectation and variance of S_2? The expectation is simple enough as expectation is a linear operator, so that $E(S_2) = E(x_1) + E(x_2)$. The variance of S_2 will depend not just on the variances of x_1 and x_2, but also on their covariance; it is simple to show, as we do below, that the variance of S_2, say $\sigma^2_{S_2}$, is $\sigma^2_{S_2} = \sigma^2_{x_1} + {}^2\sigma_{x_2} + 2\sigma_{x_1x_2}$, where $\sigma_{x_1x_2}$ is the covariance between x_1 and x_2. The reader may note that an extension of this rule was used implicitly in example 1.4.

Some rules for the expectation and variance of simple linear functions of random variables follow. Let $w = cx + b$, where x is a random variable with variance σ^2_x, and b and c are constants, then:

L1. $E(w) = cE(x) + b$
L2. $\sigma^2_w = c^2\sigma^2_x$

Let $\{x_i\}^n_{i=1}$ be a sequence of random variables and define a related sequence by $\{S_i\}^n_{i=1} = \Sigma^n_{i=1} x_i$, then, by the linearity of the expectation operator, we have:

L3. $E(S_n) = \sum^n_{i=1} E(x_i)$

If $E(x_i) = \mu$ for all i, then $E(S_n) = n\mu$ and $E(n^{-1}S_n) = \mu$.

The variance of S_n is given by:

L4. $\text{var}(S_n) = \sum^n_{j=1} \text{var}(x_j) + 2\sum^{n-1}_{k=1}\sum^n_{j=k+1} \text{cov}(x_j x_{j-k})$

For example, if n = 3 then $\text{var}(S_n)$ is given by:

$$\text{var}(S_n) = \sum^3_{j=1} \text{var}(x_j) + 2[\text{cov}(x_2x_1) + \text{cov}(x_3x_2) + \text{cov}(x_3x_1)] \tag{1.31}$$

If $\text{var}(x_j) = \sigma^2_x$, a finite constant, then:

$$\text{var}(S_n) = n\sigma^2_x + 2\sum^{n-1}_{k=1}\sum^n_{j=k+1} \text{cov}(x_j x_{j-k}) \tag{1.32}$$

The general result of (1.32) can be obtained by direct, but tedious, multiplication as in (1.31); however, a more economical way to obtain the result is to first let $x' = (x_1, x_2, ..., x_n)$, see (1.11), and then:

$$\text{var}(S_n) = E\{[x - E(x)]'\Lambda[x - E(x)]\} \tag{1.33}$$

where $\Lambda = ii'$ and $i = (1, ..., 1)'$, so that Λ is an n x n matrix comprised entirely of 1s; for a variation on this theme, see **Q2.5** of Chapter 2. If $E(x) = 0$, this reduces to:

$$\text{var}(S_n) = E(x'\Lambda x) \tag{1.34}$$

Example 1.5: Variance of the sum of two random variables

Consider $S_2 = x_1 + x_2$, then the variance of S_2 is:

$$\begin{aligned}\text{var}(S_2) &= E\{(x_1 + x_2) - E(x_1 + x_2)\}^2 \\ &= E\{[x_1 - E(x_1)] + [x_2 - E(x_2)]\}^2 \\ &= E[x_1 - E(x_1)]^2 + E[x_2 - E(x_2)]^2 + 2E[x_1 - E(x_1)][x_2 - E(x_2)] \\ &= \text{var}(x_1) + \text{var}(x_2) + 2\,\text{cov}(x_1 x_2)\end{aligned} \tag{1.35}$$

In abbreviated notation, this is: $\sigma^2_{S_2} = \sigma^2_{x_1} + \sigma^2_{x_2} + 2\sigma_{x_1x_2}$. Applying (1.33), we obtain the following:

$$\text{var}(S_2) = E\left\{(x_1 - E(x_1) \quad x_2 - E(x_2))\begin{bmatrix}1 & 1\\ 1 & 1\end{bmatrix}\begin{pmatrix}x_1 - E(x_1)\\ x_2 - E(x_2)\end{pmatrix}\right\}$$

with the result as before. ♦

1.6.2 Nonlinear functions

Given a random variable x, a simple nonlinear function that has already proved to be of interest is the variance. We start with this case and then generalise the argument. To simplify suppose that x has a zero expectation, then $E(x^2)$ is the variance of x; in effect we first define $z = x^2$ and then evaluate E(z). In the case that x is a discrete random variable then the following should be familiar from introductory courses (see also Equation (1.23)):

$$E(z) = E(x^2) = \sum_{i=1}^{n} X_i^2 P(x = X_i) \tag{1.36}$$

(Note that here the upper limit n refers to the finite number of outcomes of the random variable x.) What is perhaps not apparent here is why the probability in (1.36) refers to x rather than z. It turns out that this is an application of a theorem that greatly simplifies the evaluation of the expectation for nonlinear functions; for a formal statement of the theorem and proof see, for example, Ross (2003).

Turning to the more general case, let z = g(x) be a Borel measurable (non-linear) function of the random variable x, then, from general principles:

$$E(z) = \sum_{i=1}^{n} Z_i P(z = Z_i) \tag{1.37}$$

This implies that to obtain E(z), we appear to need the pmf of z, that is, in effect the distribution of z. However, this is not in fact the case and we may proceed by replacing $P(z = Z_i)$ by $P(x = X_i)$ and noting that $Z_i = g(X_i)$, so that:

$$E(z) = \sum_{i=1}^{n} g(X_i) P(x = X_i) \tag{1.38}$$

Consider $z = x^2$ where $x = (X_1 = -1, X_2 = 0, X_3 = 1)$ with probabilities $(\frac{1}{6}, \frac{1}{3}, \frac{1}{2})$, then $z = (Z_1 = 0, Z_2 = 1)$ with probabilities $(\frac{1}{3}, \frac{2}{3})$, so that working with z directly $E(z) = 0 \times \frac{1}{3} + 1 \times \frac{2}{3} = \frac{2}{3}$; in terms of x, $E(z) = (-1)^2 \times \frac{1}{6} + 0 \times \frac{1}{3} + (1)^2 \times \frac{1}{2} = \frac{2}{3}$. The answers are, of course, the same. In this case it is simple enough to obtain the pmf of z from the pmf of x, however, this is not always the case and it is in any case unnecessary. This property also holds for continuous random variables, so that:

$$\begin{aligned} E(z) &= \int_{-\infty}^{\infty} Z dG(Z) \\ &= \int_{-\infty}^{\infty} g(X) dF(X) \end{aligned} \tag{1.39}$$

where G(Z) is the distribution function of z and, as usual, F(X) is the distribution function of x, see Rao (1973, p. 93) and Billingsley (1995, p. 274).

In general $E[g(y)] \neq g(E[y])$; in words the expectation of the function is not the function of the expectation; the exception is when g(.) is a linear function, see **L1** and **L3**. In some cases we can say something about E[g(x)] from knowledge of g(x). If g(x) is a convex function then from Jensen's inequality, see, for example, Rao (1973), then $E[g(x)] \geq g[E(x)]$. A convex function requires that the second derivative of g(x) with respect to x is positive; for example, for positive x, the slope of g(x) increases with x. An example will illustrate the application of this inequality. Consider x to be the random variable with outcomes equal to the number of spots on the face of a rolled dice and $z = g(x) = x^2$; then x is positive and the second derivative is 2x, which is positive for x positive, hence the function g(x) is convex. The expected value of z is $E[g(x)] = E(x^2) = 91/6$, whereas $E(x)^2 = (7/2)^2 = 49/4 < 91/6$.

1.7 Conditioning, independence and dependence

This section reviews some concepts related to dependence between random variables, including conditional probability and conditional expectation. There is no presumption here that the random variables have an index of time that is important to their definition. For example, in a manufacturing process, the two random variables x_1 and x_2 may measure two dimensions of an engineered product. Section 1.9 considers dependence over time as an essential part of the characteristics of the random variables in a sequence.

The simplest case to start with is that random variables are independent. The idea of stochastic independence of random variables captures the intuitive notion that the outcome of the random variable x_1 does not affect the outcome of the random variable x_2, for all possible outcomes of x_1 and x_2. It is thus rather more than just that two events are independent, but that any pairwise comparison of events that could occur for each of the random variables, leads to independence. An example presented below in Table 1.1 illustrates what is meant for a simple case.

1.7.1 Discrete random variables

It is helpful to consider first the case of two random variables, x_1 and x_2, each of which is discrete. A standard definition of independent random variables is that they satisfy:

$$P(x_2 \mid x_1) = P(x_2) \tag{1.40}$$

where | indicates that the probability of x_2 is being considered conditional on x_1. This notation is shorthand for much more. More explicitly we are concerned with a conditioning event (set) in the range of x_1, say $X_1 \in A$ and an event (set) in the range of x_2, say $X_2 \in B$. Sometimes, in the case of discrete random variables, the sets A and B will comprise single values of x_1 and x_2 in their respective outcome spaces, but this is not necessary; for example, in a sequence of two throws of a dice, the conditioning event could be that the outcome on the first throw is an odd number, so that A = (1, 3, 5) and the second event is that the outcome on the second throw is an even number, so that B = (2, 4, 6). The definition of independence (1.40) then implicitly assumes that the condition of the definition holds whatever the choices of A

and B. For this reason, some authors emphasise this point by referring to the global independence of events for random variables. It is against this background that simple statements such as (1.40) should be interpreted.

Provided that $P(x_1) > 0$, then the conditional probability mass function is given by:

$$P(x_2 \mid x_1) = \frac{P(x_2 \cap x_1)}{P(x_1)} \tag{1.41}$$

where $P(x_2 \cap x_1)$ is shorthand for the probability that the joint event x_2 and x_1 occurs. Under independence $P(x_2 \mid x_1) = P(x_2) \Rightarrow P(x_2 \cap x_1) = P(x_2) P(x_1)$. Indeed, the definition of independence of two random variables is sometimes given directly as:

$$P(x_2 \cap x_1) - P(x_2)P(x_1) = 0 \tag{1.42}$$

This is the definition we will use below in defining α-mixing (see Chapter 3, Section 3.1.2). The subtle difference is that whilst (1.41) implies (1.42), the former requires $P(x_1) > 0$ otherwise (1.41) is not defined, whereas (1.42) does not require this condition.

The conditional expectation of x_2 given x_1 follows using the conditional probabilities, but note that there is one expectation for each outcome value of x_1. For example, $E(x_2 \mid x_1 = X_{1,i})$ is given by:

$$E(x_2 | x_1 = X_{1,i}) = \sum\nolimits_{j=1}^{m} (x_2 = X_{2,j} | x_1 = X_{1,i}) \frac{P(x_2 = X_{2,j} \cap x_1 = X_{1,i})}{P(x_1 = X_{1,i})} \tag{1.43}$$

If independence holds for $x_1 = X_{1,i}$ and $x_2 = X_{2,j}$, $j = 1, \ldots, m$ (remember the index i is fixed in 1.43) then the joint probability in the numerator of (1.43) factors as:

$$P(x_2 = X_{2,j} \cap x_1 = X_{1,i}) = P(x_2 = X_{2,j})P(x_1 = X_{1,i}) \tag{1.44}$$

for $j = 1, \ldots, m$. Substituting the right-handside of (1.44) into (1.43), shows that in terms of expectations (provided they exist), then independence implies:

$$E(x_2 | x_1 = X_{1,i}) = E(x_2) \tag{1.45}$$

If conditional expectations are being taken conditional on each of the values taken by the conditioning variable, then the notation can be simplified to $E(x_2 \mid x_1)$, so that independence implies that $E(x_2 \mid x_1) = E(x_2)$.

The conditional expectation is a random variable unlike the ordinary expectation; the values it takes depend on the conditioning event. The conditional expectation can be 'unconditioned' by obtained by taking the expectation of the conditional expectations; for example,

$$\sum_{i=1}^{n} E(x_2 \mid x_1 = X_{1,i})P(x_1 = X_{1,i}) \tag{1.46}$$

this will be equal to $E(x_2)$. The equality follows because the conditional expectation is evaluated over all possible values of the conditioning event; see **Q1.4** for the technical details and Section 1.7.2 for a development of this concept. Of course the equality follows trivially for independent random variables, but remember this is just a special case of the general result: $E[E(x_2 \mid x_1)] = E(x_2)$.

Other moments, such as the variance, can be conditioned on events in the space of the random variables. In a simple extension of the procedure adopted for the conditional expected value, the conditional variance is

$$\sigma^2_{x_2|x_{1,i}} = E\{(x_2 | x_1 = X_{1,i}) - E(x_2 \mid x_1 = X_{1,i})\}^2 \tag{1.47}$$

It is also of note that whilst the independence of x_1 and x_2 implies that their covariance is zero, the reverse implication does not hold unless x_1 and x_2 are normally distributed. This property becomes particularly important in a time series context when x_2 is a lag of x_1, in which case the covariance and correlation between these two variables are referred to as the autocovariance and autocorrelation; for example, if x_k is the k-th lag of x_1, then the covariance of x_1 and x_k is known as the k-th order autocovariance and scaling by the square root of the variance of x_1 times the variance of x_k results in the k-th order autocorrelation coefficient, see Chapter 2, Section 2.3.

Example 1.6: The coin-tossing experiment with n = 2

Consider the coin-tossing experiment with n = 2, with random variables $\{x_j\}_{j=1}^{2}$, where the outcome on the j-th toss is mapped into (+1, –1). Then there are four sets of outcomes: $\Omega_{x,2} = \{(1, 1), (1, -1), (-1, -1), (-1, 1)\}$. Under independence the joint event table has the following entries.

Table 1.1 Joint event table: Independent events

	$X_{1,1} = 1$	$X_{1,2} = -1$	$P(x_2)$
$X_{2,1} = 1$	$P(1, 1) = 0.25$	$P(1, -1) = 0.25$	$P(x_2 = X_{2,1}) = 0.5$
$X_{2,2} = -1$	$P(1, -1) = 0.25$	$P(-1, -1) = 0.25$	$P(x_2 = X_{2,2}) = 0.5$
$P(x_1)$	$P(x_1 = X_{1,1}) = 0.5$	$P(x_1 = X_{1,2}) = 0.5$	1

The event $(X_{1,1} = 1) \cap (X_{2,1} = 1)$ is a joint event, with probability under independence of $P(x_1 = 1) \times P(x_2 = 1) = 0.5 \times 0.5 = 0.25$. The probabilities in the final row and final column are just the probabilities of the events comprising x_1 and x_2, respectively; these are referred to as the marginal probabilities, and their whole as the marginal distribution(s), to distinguish them from the conditional probabilities and conditional distributions in the body of the table. Note that summing the joint probabilities across a row (or column) gives the marginal probability.

The conditional expectations are obtained taking one column, or one row, at a time; for example, consider the expectations taken over the first and second columns of the table, respectively:

$$
\begin{aligned}
E(x_2 | x_1 = X_{1,1} = 1) &= \sum\nolimits_{i=1}^{2} (x_2 = X_{2,i} \mid x_1 = 1) \frac{P(x_2 = X_{2,i} \cap x_1 = 1)}{P(x_1 = 1)} \\
&= (1) \times \frac{0.25}{0.5} + (-1) \times \frac{0.25}{0.5} \\
&= 0
\end{aligned}
$$

$$
\begin{aligned}
E(x_2 \mid x_1 = X_{1,2} = -1) &= \sum\nolimits_{i=1}^{2} (x_2 = X_{2,i} \mid x_1 = -1) \frac{P(x_2 = X_{2,i} \cap x_1 = -1)}{P(x_1 = -1)} \\
&= (1) \times \frac{0.25}{0.5} + (-1) \times \frac{0.25}{0.5} \\
&= 0
\end{aligned}
$$

An implication of independence is that $E(x_2 \mid x_1) = E(x_2)$, which can be verified in this case as follows:

$$
\begin{aligned}
E(x_2) &= E(x_2 \mid x_1 = 1)p(x_1 = 1) + E(x_2 \quad x_1 = -1)p(x_1 = -1) \\
&= (0) \times 0.5 + (0) \times 0.5 \\
&= 0
\end{aligned}
$$

Similarly it is easy to show that in this case $E(x_1 \mid x_2) = E(x_1)$. ♦

The order of the random variables in the conditioning affects none of the general principles. In example 1.6, the conditioning could have been taken as x_1 on an event in the sample space of x_2, thus the conditional probability would be written as $P(x_1 \mid x_2)$, with conditional expectation $E(x_1 \mid x_2)$. However, in the case of stochastic processes, there is a natural ordering to the random variables: x_2 comes after x_1 in the time series sequence, hence it is more natural to condition x_2 on x_1. This has relevance to a more formal approach to conditional expectations in which the σ–fields (or conditioning information sets) form an increasing nested sequence over time, see Section 1.8.

Example 1.7: A partial sum process

The example of Table 1.1 could be reinterpreted as simultaneously tossing two coins, and so time is not of the essence, therefore another process will serve to show the essential element of time-ordering and the sequential nature of the kind of processes that are of interest in random walks and unit root tests. In a partial sum process, the order of the sequence, which is usually related to an index of time, is important. Consider a discrete-time stochastic process $Y = (y_t : 0 \le t \le T)$, then the corresponding partial sum process, psp, of Y is $S = (S_t : 0 \le t \le T)$, where $S_t = \Sigma_{j=1}^{t} y_j$, so that $\{S_t\}_{t=1}^{T} = \{y_1, y_1 + y_2, \ldots, \Sigma_{j=1}^{T} y_j\}$. The coin-tossing experiment is an example of a psp provided that tosses of the coin are inherently consecutive and the random variable is that which keeps a running tally (sum) of the number of heads (or tails). Time is usually an essential aspect of a partial sum process and so the input random variable is referred to generically as y_t, although when the input is white noise we set $y_t = \varepsilon_t$; where ε_t is white noise (WN), defined by the properties: $E(\varepsilon_t) = 0$; $var(\varepsilon_t) = \sigma^2$ and $cov(\varepsilon_t\, \varepsilon_s) = 0$, for $t \neq s$, see Chapter 2, Section 2.2.1.

The variance of S_t depends essentially on its ordered place in the sequence. Consider the variance of S_2 : $var(S_2) = var(y_1 + y_2) = var(y_1) + var(y_2) + 2cov(y_1, y_2)$; if y_1 and y_2 are independent or there is no (serial) correlation, which is the weaker assumption, then $cov(y_1, y_2) = 0$, and, hence, $var(S_2) = 2\sigma_y^2$. In general, $var(S_t) = t\sigma_y^2$, so that the variance of the terms in the partial sum process are not constant and increase linearly with time. This example is considered further in example 1.9. ♦

1.7.2 Continuous random variables

The aim in this section is to generalise the concepts of independence, dependence and conditional expectation to the case of continuous random variables. The development is not completely analogous to the

discrete case because if the conditioning event is a single value it is assigned a zero probability and so an expression analogous to (1.41) would not be defined. To outline the approach, but to avoid this difficulty in the first instance, we consider the conditioning event to have a non-zero probability.

Independence in terms of distribution functions is the condition that the joint distribution function factors into the product of the (marginal) distribution functions:

$$F(X_2, X_1) - F(X_1)F(X_2) = 0 \tag{1.48}$$

In terms of density functions, the condition of independence is that the joint pdf factors into the product of the individual or marginal pdfs:

$$f(X_1, X_2) - f(X_1)f(X_2) = 0 \tag{1.49}$$

These conditions are not problematical as assuming that the density functions exist then all component functions are well defined.

In seeking a conditional expectation, we could approach the task by first defining a conditional distribution function, by analogy with the discrete case, as the ratio of the joint distribution function to the (conditioning) marginal distribution function, or in terms of density functions as the ratio of the joint density function to the (conditioning) marginal density function. As the density functions exist for the distributions considered in this book, we will approach the conditional expectation from that viewpoint.

1.7.2.i Conditioning on an event $A \neq a$

In this section, the exposition is in terms of x_2 conditional on x_1. The problem to be considered is to obtain the probability of $X_2 \in B \subseteq \Re$ given that $X_1 \in A \subseteq \Re$, the latter being the conditioning event, which is not a single element. This conditional probability is:

$$P(X_2 \in B \mid X_1 \in A) = \frac{\int_{X_1 \in A}\int_{X_2 \in B} f(X_1 \in A, X_2 \in B)dX_1 dX_2}{\int_{X_1 \in A} f(X_1 \in A_1)dX_1} \tag{1.50a}$$

This notation is explicit but cumbersome and is sometimes shortened to:

$$P(X_2 \in B \mid X_1 \in A) = \frac{\int_{X_1 \in A}\int_{X_2 \in B} f(X_1, X_2)dX_1dX_2}{\int_{X_1 \in A} f(X_1)dX_1} \tag{1.50b}$$

The conditional pdf is given by:

$$f(X_2 \in B \mid X_1 \in A) = \frac{f(X_1 \in A, X_2 \in B)}{f(X_1 \in A)} \tag{1.51}$$

where A and B are Borel sets. Where the context is clear, the notation is simplified by omitting explicit reference to the sets, for example $f(X_2 \mid X_1) = f(X_1, X_2)/f(X_1)$ in place of (1.51).

The expression (1.51) is well defined provided that the denominator is positive, which we can ensure by setting A to be a nondegenerate interval, $A = [A_2 - A_1] > 0$. This rules out singletons, that is single points on the X_1 axis; these are Borel sets, but lead to the problem that zero probability is assigned to such events for a continuous random variable. Graphically, the set $B = [B_2 - B_1] \geq 0$ defines an interval on the X_2 axis and the set A defines an interval on the X_1 axis; their intersection is a rectangle.

A definition of the conditional expectation then follows as:

$$E(x_2 \mid X_1 \in A) = \int_{X_2 \in R(x_2)} X_1 f(X_2 \mid X_1 \in A)dX_2 \tag{1.52}$$

If x_1 and x_2 are independent for all choices of sets in the event spaces of x_1 and x_2 then:

$$E(x_2 \mid x_1 = X_1) = E(x_2) \tag{1.53}$$

Example 1.8: The uniform joint distribution

To illustrate some of the key points so far, consider again the example of two (independent) random variables x_1 and x_2, with a uniform joint distribution, see example 1.3.

In this case the conditional probability function is:

$$P(X_2 \in B \mid X_1 \in A) = \int_{X_1 \in A} \int_{X_2 \in B} \frac{\dfrac{(A_2 - A_1)(B_2 - B_1)}{(a_2 - a_1)(b_2 - b_1)}}{\dfrac{(A_2 - A_1)}{(a_2 - a_1)}} dX_1 dX_2 \tag{1.54a}$$

$$= \frac{(B_2 - B_1)}{(b_2 - b_1)} \leq 1 \tag{1.54b}$$

If we let $B_1 = b_1$, with $B_2 \geq B_1$, then this defines a function that has the properties required of a conditional distribution function, so that we may write:

$$F(X_2 \in B \mid X_1 \in A) = P(X_2 \in B \mid X_1 \in A) \tag{1.55}$$

Note that if $B_2 - B_1 = 0$ then $F(X_2 \in B \mid X_1 \in A) = 0$ and if $B_1 = b_1$ and $B_2 = b_2$ then $F(X_2 \in B \mid X_1 \in A) = 1$, as required in a probability measure. Independence is easily confirmed in this case: $f(X_1, X_2) = f(X_1)f(X_2)$, $f(X_1 \mid X_2) = f(X_1)$, $F(X_1, X_2) = F(X_1)F(X_2)$ and $F(X_2 \in B \mid X_1 \in A) = F(X_2 \in B)$.

A conditional expectation may also be defined as:

$$E(x_2 \mid X_1 \in A) = \int_{b_1}^{b_2} X_2 f(X_2 \mid X_1 \in A) dX_2 \tag{1.56}$$

In this illustration x_1 and x_2 are independent, so the conditional expectation reduces to:

$$\begin{aligned} E(x_2 \mid X_1 \in A) &= \int_{b_1}^{b_2} X_2 f(X_2) dX_2 \\ &= E(x_2) \end{aligned} \tag{1.57}$$

for all B. ♦

1.7.2.ii Conditioning on a singleton

Although these definitions, for example (1.50) and (1.51), seem straightforward extensions of the discrete random variable case, they raise a problem. From the start, the situation in which $\int_{X_1 \in A} f(X_1)dX_1 = 0$ was ruled out, so that the set A could not be a single point in the range of X_1 or a set with measure zero.

To see the problem, note that in the case of a discrete random variable, a conditional probability mass function is obtained by taking a

value for, say, X_1, as given; this fixes a row of the joint event table. Each cell entry in that row is then normalised by the sum of such entries, which necessarily results in each new probability being non-zero with a sum that is unity. The extension by analogy to a continuous random variable breaks down because the normalising factor is zero.

There are two ways forward. One is to redefine the conditional probability as a limit and the second is to go directly to the concept of a conditional expectation without first defining a conditional distribution or conditional density function. The solution outlined here is of the former kind and follows Mittelhammer (1996); for an earlier reference see Feller (1966). The second approach is adopted in more advanced treatments, where the emphasis is on a measure-theoretic approach; the interested reader may like to consult Davidson (1994, chapter 10) and Billingsley (1995, chapter 6).

The idea taken here is to construct an interval set that shrinks to a single point in the limit; thus, let $A = a \pm \varepsilon$, where $\varepsilon \geq 0$, which collapses to a in the limit as $\varepsilon \to 0^+$. The conditional probability is now defined in terms of this limit as:

$$P(X_2 \in B \mid X_1 = A) = \lim_{\varepsilon \to 0} P(X_2 \in B \mid X_1 \in a \pm \varepsilon) \tag{1.58a}$$

$$= \lim_{\varepsilon \to 0^+} \left[\frac{\int_{X_2 \in B} \int_{X_1 = a-\varepsilon}^{a+\varepsilon} f(X_1, X_2) dX_1 dX_2}{\int_{X_1 = 1-\varepsilon}^{1+\varepsilon} f(X_1) dX_1} \right] \tag{1.58b}$$

$$= \int_{X_2 \in B} \frac{f(X_2, X_1 = a)}{f(X_1 = a)} dX_2 \tag{1.58c}$$

$$= \int_{X_2 \in B} \frac{f(X_2, a)}{f(a)} dX_2 \tag{1.58d}$$

The last line is just a matter of a shorthand notation. More substantively, the penultimate line follows from the mean value theorem for integrals and the continuity of $f(X_1)$ and $f(X_1, X_2)$ in X_1 for $X_1 \in A$, see Mittelhammer (1996) for details. The difference between (1.50) and (1.58) is that, in the limit, there is no need for the integral over $X_1 \in A$, because the set A collapses to a single point. The end result is simple enough and does have the same form as the discrete case. Thus, as (1.58) holds for all A, the conditional pdf, when conditioning on a singleton, is:

$$f(X_2 \mid X_1 = a) = \frac{f(X_2, X_1 = a)}{f(X_1 = a)} \tag{1.59}$$

where $f(X_1 = a) > 0$. This means that we can go straight to the conditional expectation using this density:

$$E(x_2 \mid X_1 = a) = \int_{X_2 \in R(x_2)} X_1 f(X_2 \mid X_1 = a) dX_2$$

Moreover we may now take the expectation of the conditional expectation by integrating out all possible values of a:

$$\begin{aligned} &E[E(x_2 \mid X_1 = a)] \\ &\quad = \int_{X_1 \in R(x_1)} \left(\int_{X_2 \in R(x_2)} X_2 f(X_2 \mid X_1 = a) dX_2 \right) f(X_1) dX_1 \\ &\quad = E(x_2) \end{aligned} \tag{1.60}$$

The proof of the second line is left to a question, see **Q1.4.** The result states that taking the expected value conditional on the event $X_1 = a$, and then weighting the resulting conditional expectations over all possible values of X_1 undoes the conditioning.

1.7.3 Independence in the case of multivariate normality

Multivariate normality is often important, for example in the properties of stochastic processes, so that a notation that allows the generalisation of the bivariate case will be worthwhile. Consider the random vector $x = (x_1, ..., x_n)'$ with expected value $\mu = (\mu_1, ..., \mu_n)'$. The covariance matrix of x is the n x n matrix Σ, where:

$$\Sigma = \begin{bmatrix} \sigma_1^2 & \sigma_{2,1} & \cdots & \sigma_{n,1} \\ \sigma_{2,1} & \sigma_2^2 & \cdots & \sigma_{2,n-1} \\ \vdots & \vdots & \vdots & \vdots \\ \sigma_{n,1} & \sigma_{2,n-1} & \cdots & \sigma_n^2 \end{bmatrix} \tag{1.61}$$

Σ is assumed to be non-singular (no linear dependencies among the n random variables) and σ_{ij} is the covariance between variables i and j. The joint pdf is

$$f(X) = (2\pi)^{-n/2} \mid \Sigma \mid^{-1/2} \exp\left\{ -\frac{1}{2}(X - \mu)'\Sigma^{-1}(X - \mu) \right\} \tag{1.62}$$

where $\mid \Sigma \mid$ is the determinant of Σ.

A case of particular interest is when normal random variables are independent, in that case Σ will be scalar diagonal and the joint pdf simplifies to:

$$f(X) = (2\pi)^{-n/2}(\Pi_{i=1}^{n}\sigma_i)^{-1}\exp\left\{-\frac{1}{2}\sum_{i=1}^{n}\left(\frac{X_i - \mu_i}{\sigma_i}\right)^2\right\} \tag{1.63}$$

where $\Pi_{i=1}^{n}$ is the product symbol. Also of interest in deriving maximum likelihood based estimators is the log of the joint pdf. In the case of independent x_i, the log of (1.63) is:

$$\ln\{f(X)\} = -(n/2)\ln(2\pi) - \sum_{i=1}^{n}\ln\sigma_i - \frac{1}{2}\sum_{i=1}^{n}\left(\frac{X_i - \mu_i}{\sigma_i}\right)^2 \tag{1.64}$$

1.8 Some useful results on conditional expectations: Law of iterated expectations and 'taking out what is known'

This subsection outlines two results that are particular useful in analysing partial sum processes. The first is the law of iterated expectations (sometimes called the 'tower' property of expectations). The emphasis here is on the time series context. Consider the stochastic process (y_t, $0 \leq t \leq T$) generating $Y = (y_0, y_1, \ldots, y_T)$ and the following two conditional expectations: $E(y_t \mid F_0^{t-1})$ and $E(y_t \mid F_0^{t-2})$, where $F_0^{t-s} = (y_{t-s}, \ldots, y_0)$ is regarded initially as an information set; then $F_0^{t-2} \subseteq F_0^{t-1}$, thus F_0^{t-1} does not contain less information than F_0^{t-2}, in this example the difference is the observation y_{t-1}. Now consider the iterated expectation given by:

$$E[E(y_t | F_0^{t-1}) | F_0^{t-2}] = E(y_t | F_0^{t-2}) \tag{1.65}$$

In effect the second (or outer) conditioning removes what information there is in F_0^{t-1} that is not in F_0^{t-2}, so that it has no effect. The iterating can be continued. For example:

$$E\{E[E(y_t | F_0^{t-1}) | F_0^{t-2}] | F_0^{t-3}\} = E(y_t | F_0^{t-3}) \tag{1.66}$$

This result holds because of the nested sequence of conditioning information. A more formal way of stating this result is in terms of σ–fields

rather than the concept of information sets. Thus, to reinterpret, let F_0^{t-s} be the σ–field $\sigma(y_{t-s}, \ldots, y_0)$, then $F_0^{t-2} \subseteq F_0^{t-1}$, so that F_0^{t-2} is a subfield of F^{t-1}, then the law of iterated expectations states that:

$$E[E(y_t \mid F_0^{t-1}) \mid F_0^{t-2}] = E(y_t \mid F_0^{t-2}] \tag{1.67}$$

For a proof along general lines see, for example, Mikosch (1998).

For the second property, start by considering the product of two random variables, x and z. Then, in general, E(xz) ≠ E(x)E(z), equality holding for independent random variables; however, if x is a constant then E(xz) = xE(z). There is an important case in the context of conditional expectations where, in the product of random variables one random variable can, in effect, be treated like a constant.

The general result is stated as follows, see for example Jacod and Protter (2004, Theorem 23.7), Mikosch (1998, Rule 5) and Davidson (1994, Theorem 10.10). Let x and z be random variables on the probability space (Ω, F, P), where x is measurable with respect to G, a σ–subfield such that $G \subseteq F$, and assuming that x, z and xz are integrable, then:

$$E(xz \mid G) = xE(z \mid G) \tag{1.68}$$

The intuition for the result is based on $G \subseteq F$: x is known from the information in G and adds nothing to the information in F on z, it can, therefore, be treated as known and taken outside the expectation.

In a time series context, consider $G = \sigma(y_{t-1}, \ldots, y_0)$ and $F = \sigma(y_t, \ldots, y_0)$, then:

$$E(y_{t-1}y_t \mid G) = y_{t-1}E(y_t \mid G) \tag{1.69}$$

Because y_{t-1} is measurable with respect to G and $G \subset F$, it can be treated as known in the conditional expectation.

1.9 Stationarity and some of its implications

At an intuitive level, stationarity captures the idea that certain properties of a (data generating) process are unchanging. If the process does not change at all over time, it does not matter which sample portion of observations we use to estimate the parameters of the process; we may as well, therefore, use all available observations. On the other hand, this may be too strict a requirement for some purposes. There may be a break

in the mean of the process, whilst the variance of the process remains the same. In that case, assuming that the mean is unchanging, which is a form of nonstationarity, is clearly wrong and will lead us into error; but rather than use only that part of the sample where the mean is constant, we may be able to model the mean change and use all of the sample.

The leading case of nonstationarity, at least in econometric terms, is that induced by a unit root in the AR polynomial of an ARMA model for y_t, considered more extensively in Chapter 2. This implies that the variance of y_t is not constant over time and that the k-th order autocovariance of y_t depends on t. This is, however, just one example of how nonstationarity can be induced.

Note that stationarity refers to a property of the process generating the outcomes – or data – that we observe; thus we should refer to a stationary or nonstationary process, not to stationary or nonstationary data. Notwithstanding this correct usage, it is often the case that sample data is referred to as stationary or nonstationary. This is particularly so in the case of data generated from a stochastic process and presented in the form of a time series, when one finds a sample, for example data on GDP for 1950–2000, being referred to as nonstationary. This usage is widespread and does no particular harm provided that the correct meaning is understood.

1.9.1 What is stationarity?

Consider the coin-tossing experiment, where a single coin is tossed sequentially T times: what is the joint pmf for the resulting sequence $Y = \{y_1, y_2, ..., y_T\}$, where y_t is the mapping $\{H, T\} \mapsto \{+1, -1\}$? By independence, we can multiply together the pmfs for each $P(y_t)$ and as, by assumption, each of these is identical, the joint pmf is:

$$P(y_1, y_2, \ldots, y_T) = \prod_{t=1}^{T} P(y_t) \tag{1.70}$$

These assumptions mean that we can answer a number of elementary questions about sequence patterns. For example, what is the probability of the sequence (–1, +1, –1, –1, +1)? As $P(-1) = P(+1) = \frac{1}{2}$, the answer is $(\frac{1}{2})^5$; indeed as the outcomes have equal probabilities, all outcome sequences for a given T are equally likely, and as there are 2^5 possible sequences, each equally likely, then the probability of each must be $2^{-5} = (\frac{1}{2})^5$.

Suppose we wanted to assess the assumption that the two outcomes for each t were, indeed, equally likely. Now the order in the sequence is not vital, so that one line of enquiry would be to count the number of –1 (or +1) outcomes in the sequence and divide by the number in the

sequence. This uses the 'outcome' average to estimate the probability $P(y_t = -1)$, say $\hat{P} = \#I(-1)/T$, which is the number of observed occurrences of –1 divided by T, where I(–1) = 1 if the outcome is –1 and 0 otherwise, and # indicates the counting operator. This is a sensible estimator given that the probability structure over the sequence is unchanging (see Chapter 3, Section 3.3 on ergodicity).

However, suppose that the coin-tossing 'machine' develops a fault and $P(y_t = -1)$ becomes more likely from a point halfway through the sequence; then the time average is misleading due to the change in the underlying structure. In this case, it is necessarily the case that the mean and the variance of the process have changed; that is key elements of the underlying probability structure are not constant or 'stationary'. This illustration uses the independence property explicit in the random experiment of coin tossing, but it is not a part of the definition of stationarity. The next two subsections show what is required depending on the particular concept of stationarity.

1.9.2 A strictly stationary process

Let $\tau \neq s$ and T be arbitrary, if Y is a strictly stationary, discrete-time process for a discrete random variable, y_t, then:

$$P(y_{\tau+1}, y_{\tau+2}, \ldots, y_{\tau+T}) = P(y_{s+1}, y_{s+2}, \ldots, y_{s+T}) \tag{1.71}$$

That is, the joint pmf for the sequence of length T starting at time $\tau + 1$ is the same for any shift in the time index from τ to s and for any choice of T. This means that it does not matter which T-length portion of the sequence we observe. Since a special case of this result in the discrete case is for T = 1, that is $P(y_\tau) = P(y_s)$, the marginal pmfs must also be the same for $\tau \neq s$ implying that $E(y_\tau) = E(y_s)$. These results imply that other moments, including joint moments, such as the covariances, are invariant to arbitrary time shifts.

If the random variables are continuous and defined in continuous time, a strictly stationary random process must satisfy the following:

$$F(y(\tau+t_1), y(\tau+t_2), \ldots, y(\tau+t_T)) = F(y(s+t_1), y(s+t_2), \ldots, y(s+t_T)) \tag{1.72}$$

where $t_1 < t_2 \ldots < t_T$, $\tau \neq s$ and F(.) is the joint distribution function. If the probability density functions exist, then an analogous condition holds, replacing F(.) by f(.):

$$f(y(\tau+t_1), y(\tau+t_2), \ldots, y(\tau+t_T)) = f(y(s-t_1), y(s+t_2), \ldots, y(s+t_T)) \tag{1.73}$$

An iid stochastic process, as in the example opening this section, is strictly stationary.

1.9.3 Weak or second order stationarity (covariance stationarity)

A less demanding form of stationarity is weak or second order stationarity, which requires that the following three conditions are satisfied for arbitrary τ and s, $\tau \neq s$:

SS1. $E(y_\tau) = E(y_s) = \mu$
SS2. $var(y_\tau) = var(y_s) = \sigma^2$
SS3. $cov(y_\tau, y_{\tau+k}) = cov(y_s, y_{s+k})$

The moments in **SS1–SS3** are assumed to exist. The first condition states that the mean is constant, the second that the variance is constant and the third that the k-th order autocovariance is invariant to an arbitrary shift in the time origin. The extension to continuous time is straightforward, replacing y_τ by $y(\tau)$ and so on. From these three conditions, it is evident that a stochastic process could fail to be weakly stationary, because at least one of the following holds over time:

i. its mean is changing;
ii. its variance is changing;
iii. the k-th order autocovariances depend on time for some k.

A stochastic process that is not stationary is said to be nonstationary. A nonstationary process could be: nonstationary in the mean; nonstationary in the variance; and/or nonstationary in the autocovariances. Usually it is apparent from the context whether the stationarity being referred to is strict or weak. When the word stationary is used without qualification, it is taken to refer to weak stationarity, shortened to WS, but, perhaps, most frequently referred to as covariance stationarity. (Weak or covariance stationarity is also referred to as wide-sense stationary, leading to the initials WSS.)

Ross (2003) gives examples of processes that are weakly stationary but not strictly stationary; however, note that, exceptionally, a process could be strictly stationary, but not weakly stationarity by virtue of the non-existence of its moments. For example, a random process where the components have unchanging marginal and joint Cauchy distributions will be strictly stationary, but not weakly stationary because the moments do not exist.

Example 1.9: The partial sum process continued (from Example 1.7)

An example of a process that is stationary in the mean, but nonstationary in the variance, is the partial sum process (introduced earlier in example 1.7) with iid inputs, as in the case of Bernoulli or white noise inputs. If the process starts at j = 1, then $S_t = \sum_{j=1}^{t} y_j$, with $E(y_j) = 0$, and $E(S_t) = \sum_{j=1}^{t} E(y_j) = 0$. The variance of S_t is given by:

$$\begin{aligned} var(S_t) &= var\left(\sum_{j=1}^{t} y_j\right) \\ &= E\left(\sum_{j=1}^{t} y_j\right)^2 && \text{using } E(y_j) = 0 \text{ for all j} \\ &= t\sigma_y^2 + 2\sum_{i=1}^{t}\sum_{j>i}^{t} cov(y_i, y_j) && \text{using } var(y_j) = \sigma_y^2 \text{ for all i} \\ &= t\sigma_y^2 && (1.74) \end{aligned}$$

where the last line uses $cov(y_i, y_j) = 0$. In passing note that this result only requires that the sequence $\{y_t\}$ is white noise rather than iid (hence we could have written $\{y_t\} = \{\varepsilon_t\}$).

From (1.74) note that the variance is not constant and the partial sum process is, therefore, nonstationary in the variance. The process also becomes nonstationary in the mean if $E(y_j) = \mu \neq 0$ as when $E(S_t) = t\mu$, as well as $var(S_t) = t\sigma_y^2$. Finally, $\{S_j\}_{j=1}^{t}$ is also nonstationary in the autocovariances, even if $cov(y_i, y_j) = 0$ for $i \neq j$. To illustrate consider the following two first-order autocovariances, $cov(S_1, S_2)$ and $cov(S_2, S_3)$, then:

$$\begin{aligned} cov(S_1, S_2) &= cov(y_1, y_1 + y_2) \\ &= \sigma_y^2 + cov(y_1, y_2) \\ cov(S_2, S_3) &= cov(y_1 + y_2, y_1 + y_2 + y_3) \\ &= 2\sigma_y^2 + 2cov(y_1, y_2) + cov(y_1, y_3) + cov(y_2, y_3) \end{aligned}$$

These differ, although both refer to a first order autocovariance; hence, the process is nonstationary as the translation in time does affect the joint probability mass function.

1.10 Concluding remarks

This chapter has introduced a number of concepts and some language and terminology that are vital to later chapters. One cannot make sense of random walks and Brownian motion without a background knowledge of probability or of, for example, memory and persistence in a stochastic process without the concept of dependence. The partial sum

process is critical to not only random walks and Brownian motion but also to the development of the distribution theory of unit root tests.

There are a number of excellent texts on probability and stochastic processes that can serve as a follow up to this chapter. On probability, these include Larson (1974), Fristedt and Gray (1997), Jacod and Protter (2004), Koralov and Sinai (2007), Ross (2003) and Tuckwell (1995); a classic, but advanced, reference on the measure theory approach to probability is Billingsley (1995) and Feller's (1966, 1968) two volumes on probability theory are classic and timeless texts. On stochastic processes see, for example, Brzeźniak and Zastawniak (1999), Mikosch (1998) and Stirzaker (2005). Classic texts on stochastic processes include Doob (1953) and Cox and Miller (1965); and Karlin and Taylor's (1975a, 1975b) two volumes on stochastic processes provide an excellent graded introduction and development of a great deal of relevant material.

Questions

Q1.1 Suggest some possible examples of random variables from everyday life and state whether the random variable so defined is discrete or continuous.

A1.1 The time you wake in the morning (continuous); the number of arrivals at the supermarket checkout in given interval of time (discrete);

Q1.2 Consider a random experiment where a fair coin is tossed ten times and the number of times that the coin lands heads is noted. A student argues that since the coin is fair, the probability of 5 heads out of 10 is ½. Is he correct?

A1.2 First note that this is a Bernoulli trial with n = 10 and probability of success $P(H) = p = ½$ and $q = 1 - p = ½$, and let k denote the number of heads. There are various ways that k = 5 can occur, for example, the coin lands heads on the first 5 throws and then tails on the next 5; it lands tails on the first throw and then lands heads on the next 5 followed by 4 tails. Each of these outcomes taken individually has a probability of occurrence of $p^k q^{(n-k)}$; with n = 10, k = 5 and p = ½, this probability is $\frac{1}{2}^5 \frac{1}{2}^{(10-5)} = \frac{1}{2}^{10}$. However, we also need to consider how many ways 5 heads can occur in 10 tosses. To do this we need the number of ways that we can choose k from n without regard to order, this is the combinatorial factor ${}_nC_k = n!/[(n-k)!k!]$, where $n! = n(n-1)\ldots 1$, read as n factorial. The required probability is then ${}_nC_k p^k q^{(n-k)} = {}_nC_k p^n$; for n = 10, k = 5 and p = ½, ${}_{10}C_5 p^5 q^5 = 252 \times (\frac{1}{2})^5 = 0.2461$; the student is wrong! (This example is due to Bean, 2009.)

Q1.3 Let C = (A, B) where $A, B \subset \Omega$: generate the σ–field of C, denoted σ(C).

A1.3 The first condition for a σ–field requires that ∅, Ω be in σ(C); then include all unions and unions of complements, $A \cup B$, $A^c \cup B$, $A \cup B^c$ and $A^c \cup B^c$; therefore, $\sigma(C) = (\varnothing, A \cup B, A^c \cup B, A \cup B^c, A^c \cup B^c, \Omega)$.

Q1.4 Show that in both the discrete and continuous cases $E[E(x_1 \mid X_2)] = E(x_1)$.

A1.4 Consider the discrete case first as it will provide a clue for the continuous case. We want to evaluate the expectation of the conditional expectation:

$$
\begin{aligned}
E[E(x_1 \mid x_2 = X_{2,i})] &= \sum\nolimits_{i=1}^{n} E(x_1 \mid x_2 = X_{2,i}) p(x_2 = X_{2,i}) \\
&= \sum\nolimits_{i=1}^{n}\left(\sum\nolimits_{j=1}^{m} X_{1,j} \frac{p(x_1 = X_{1,j} \cap x_2 = X_{2,i})}{p(x_2 = X_{2,i})}\right) p(x_2 = X_{2,i}) \\
&= \left(\sum\nolimits_{j=1}^{m} X_{1,j} \sum\nolimits_{i=1}^{n} p(x_1 = X_{1,j} \cap x_2 = X_{2,i})\right) \\
&= \left(\sum\nolimits_{j=1}^{m} X_{1,j} p(x_1 = X_{1,j})\right) \\
&= E(x_1)
\end{aligned}
$$

The second line follows by substitution for the conditional expectation and the conditional probability; the third line follows by cancellation of $p(x_2 = X_{2,i})$; the summations are interchanged in the fourth line, then the sum over all joint probabilities (that is one row or column of the joint event table) results in the marginal probability.

In the case of a continuous random variable, the starting expression is:

$$
\begin{aligned}
E[E(x_1 \mid X_2 = b)] &= \int_{X_2 \in R(x_2)} \left(\int_{X_1 \in R(x_1)} X_1 f(X_1 \mid X_2 = b) dX_1\right) f(X_2) dX_2 \\
&= \int_{X_2 \in R(x_2)} \left(\int_{X_1 \in R(x_1)} X_1 \frac{f(X_1, X_2 = b)}{f(X_2 = b)} dX_1\right) f(X_2) dX_2 \\
&= \int_{X_1 \in R(x_1)} X_1 \left(\int_{X_2 \in R(x_2)} \frac{f(X_1, X_2 = b)}{f(X_2 = b)} f(X_2) dX_2\right) dX_1 \\
&= \int_{X_1 \in R(x_1)} X_1 \left(\int_{X_2 \in R(x_2)} f(X_1, X_2 = b) dX_2\right) dX_1 \\
&= \int_{X_1 \in R(x_1)} X_1 f(X_1) dX_1 \\
&= E(x_1)
\end{aligned}
$$

The line operations are analogous to the discrete case; of note is the integrating out of the conditioning event such that $\int_{X_2 \in R(x_2)} f(X_1, X_2 = b)\, dX_2 = f(X_1)$.

2
Time Series Concepts

Introduction

This chapter brings together a number of concepts that are essential in characterising and analysing time series models. The reader is likely to be familiar with series of observations that are ordered by time and arranged into a sequence; for example quarterly observations on GDP from 1950q1 to 2009q4 (T = 240 observations). In practice we observe one set of observations, but conceptualise these as outcomes from a process that is inherently capable of replication. In order to do this, each sample point of the 240 is viewed as an outcome, or 'draw', from a random variable; there are, therefore, in the conceptual scheme, 240 random variables, arranged in a sequence, $Y = (y_1, y_2, ..., y_{240})$, each with a sample space corresponding to the multiplicity of possible outcomes for each random variable, and a sample space for the entire sequence. In Chapter 1, this sequence was referred to as a stochastic process, where an outcome of such a process is a path function or sample path, not a single point.

This chapter proceeds as follows. The lag operator is introduced in Section 2.1; its many uses include obtaining the autocovariance generating function, measuring persistence, obtaining impulse response functions, finding the roots of dynamic models and calculating mean lags. The ARMA model, which is central to many unit root tests, is outlined in Section 2.2. As a key preliminary in this chapter is characterising the degree of dependence, autocovariances, autocorrelations and variances are introduced in Section 2.3; this section also includes an introduction to the long-run variance. Section 2.4 is concerned with some simple, but widely used, tests for dependence. One use of the lag operator, that is in defining the autocovariance generating function, ACGF, is dealt

with in Section 2.5. Estimation of the long-run variance is considered in 2.6; and Section 2.7 includes some empirical examples. Throughout this chapter, time is of the essence and, therefore, the adopted notation is of the form for a discrete-time random variable.

2.1 The lag operator L and some of its uses

The lag operator is an essential tool of time series econometric analysis. We outline some basic principles in this subsection; a more extensive discussion can be found in Dhrymes (1981).

2.1.1 Definition of lag operator L

The lag operator, sometimes referred to as the backshift operator, is defined by:

$$L^j y_t \equiv y_{t-j} \tag{2.1}$$

A negative exponent results in a lead, so that:

$$L^{-j} y_t \equiv y_{t-(-j)} = y_{t+j} \tag{2.2}$$

Lag operators may be multiplied together as follows:

$$L^j L^i y_t \equiv y_{t-(j+i)} \tag{2.3}$$

Setting j = 0 in $L^j y_t$ leaves the series unchanged, thus $L^0 y_t \equiv y_t$, and $L^0 \equiv 1$ can be regarded as the identity operator. If the lag operator is applied to a constant, the constant is unchanged; that is, $L^j \mu \equiv \mu$, where μ is a constant.

In the backshift notation, often preferred in the statistics literature, the notation for the lag operator is B, thus $B^j y_t \equiv y_{t-j}$. The lag operator is more than just a convenience of notation; it opens the way to write functions of the lags and leads of a time series variable that enable some quite complex analysis.

2.1.2 The lag polynomial

A polynomial in L can be defined using the lag operator notation, thus $\phi(L) = 1 - \Sigma_{j=1}^{p} \phi_j L^j$; for example, the second order lag polynomial is $\phi(L) = 1 - \phi_1 L - \phi_2 L^2$. Note that this is a special form of the polynomial

$\phi(L) = \phi_0 - \phi_1 L - \phi_2 L^2$, with $\phi_0 = 1$. The lag polynomial can be applied to the random variable y_t at time t, as well as to the sequence of random variables $\{y_t\}_{t=1}^{t=T}$ to obtain a new sequence. In the case of the second order polynomial $\phi(L)y_t \equiv (1 - \phi_1 L - \phi_2 L^2)y_t \equiv y_t - \phi_1 y_{t-1} - \phi_2 y_{t-2}$ and this operation defines a new random variable, which is a linear combination of y_t, y_{t-1}, and y_{t-2}; when applied to $\{y_t\}_{t=1}^{T}$ a new sequence of random variables is defined.

2.1.3 Roots of the lag polynomial

Writing the lag structure using the lag operator enables some simple algebraic operations, but we have to be careful not to use the lag operator L both as an operator and a variable, which would contradict its definition (2.1). Instead, the variable z takes the place of the operator L and the analysis is pursued in terms of $\phi(z)$. For example, the first order polynomial is written as $\phi(z) = 1 - \phi_1 z$. To obtain the root of this polynomial involves solving for the value of z such that $\phi(z) = 0$; the solution is $z = 1/\phi_1$, which gives rise to the terminology that $\phi(z)$ has the root $1/\phi_1$, which is a unit root if $\phi_1 = 1$.

At this point, it is useful to clarify a distinction in approach that arises in connection with the roots of polynomials. Note that nothing fundamental changes in seeking the solutions (zeros) of $\phi(z) = 0$ on dividing the lag polynomial through by the coefficient on z^p; it implies that z^p has a coefficient of unity, but the solutions are unchanged. The benefit is a neater way of representing the roots. In the case of a quadratic lag polynomial, the form of the factorisation is $(z - \lambda_1)(z - \lambda_2) = 0$, and λ_1 and λ_2 are the two roots of this quadratic. This approach and factorisation separates the use of variable z from the roots λ_i and is a preferable notation. This procedure generalises in a straightforward manner: let $\phi(z) = 1 - \sum_{j=1}^{p} \phi_j z^j$, then the polynomial factors as $\prod_{i=1}^{p} (z - \lambda_i) = 0$, where λ_i, $i = 1, \ldots, p$ are the p roots of $\phi(z)$. Notice that if one or more of the roots is unity, then $\phi(1) = 0$, where $\phi(1)$ is shorthand for $\phi(z)$ evaluated at $z = 1$, so that $\phi(1) = 1 - \sum_{j=1}^{p} \phi_j$.

The inverse of the lag polynomial, if it exists, is defined such that $\phi(L)^{-1}\phi(L) = 1$, and the lag polynomial is said to be invertible. Consider the first order polynomial $\phi(L) = 1 - \phi_1 L$ and note that provided $|\phi_1| < 1$ the inverse of this polynomial can be defined; in this case $(1 - \phi_1 L)^{-1}(1 - \phi_1 L) = 1$, where $(1 - \phi_1 L)^{-1} = 1 - \sum_{j=1}^{\infty} \phi_1^j L^j$ and convergence of the infinite sum is assured by the condition $|\phi_1| < 1$. More generally the condition that ensures invertibility is that the roots of the lag polynomial have moduli greater than unity, $|\lambda_i| > 1$, said to be 'outside the unit circle'.

Example 2.1: Roots of a second order lag polynomial

Obtain the roots of the lag polynomial $y_t - 1.25y_{t-1} + 0.25y_{t-2}$ and check for invertibility. The roots are the solutions to $1 - 1.25z + 0.25z^2 = 0$. Divide the lag polynomial through by 0.25 to obtain $\phi(z) = 4 - 5z + z^2 = 0$, which factors as $(z - 1)(z - 4) = 0$. This is an example of $(z - \lambda_1)(z - \lambda_2) = 0$, so that the roots are $\lambda_1 = 1$ and $\lambda_2 = 4$. The lag polynomial is not invertible because one root, λ_1, is on the unit circle. Note that isolating the unit root and rewriting the lag polynomial in terms of the remaining root, results in an invertible polynomial, specifically: $y_t - 1.25y_{t-1} + 0.25y_{t-2} = (1 - L)y_t - (1 - L)0.25Ly_t$ and, as usual, define $\Delta y_t \equiv (1 - L)y_t$, so that this can be written as $\Delta y_t - 0.25L\Delta y_t$, then the polynomial $(1 - 0.25L)$ is invertible, indeed we know that, by construction, it has one root = 4.

2.2 The ARMA model

The autoregressive, moving average model is a special but important case of a linear process relating y_t to stochastic inputs. It features widely in tests for a unit root, which in effect focus on the AR component of the model. This section outlines some important features of this class of model; and subsequent sections use some simple ARMA models for illustration. References to follow up this important area of time series analysis are given at the end of the chapter.

2.2.1 The ARMA(p, q) model using lag operator notation

The lag operator notation allows an economic way of writing the familiar ARMA(p, q) model, where p and q refer to the lag lengths on the AR and MA components of the model, respectively. The ARMA(p, q) model is:

$$y_t = \sum_{i=1}^{p} \phi_i y_{t-i} + \varepsilon_t + \sum_{j=1}^{q} \theta_j \varepsilon_{t-j} \tag{2.4}$$

The AR part of the specification refers to the lags on y_t and the MA part to the lags on ε_t; these are p and q, respectively. For simplicity the specification in (2.4) implicitly assumes $E(y_t) = 0$, if this is not the case, say $E(y_t) = \mu_t$, then y_t is replaced by $y_t - \mu_t$, in which case (2.4) becomes:

$$\tilde{y}_t = \sum_{i=1}^{p} \phi_i \tilde{y}_{t-i} + \varepsilon_t + \sum_{j=1}^{q} \theta_j \varepsilon_{t-j} \tag{2.5}$$

where $\tilde{y}_t \equiv y_t - \mu_t$. The two most familiar cases are $\mu_t = \mu$ and $\mu_t = \beta_0 + \beta_1 t$. The usual procedure in these cases is to replace μ_t by a consistent

estimator; in the former case, μ is usually estimated by the sample mean and in the latter case β_0 and β_1 are estimated by a LS regression of y_t on a constant and t (with ^ over indicating an estimator) and $\hat{\tilde{y}}_t = y_t - \hat{\mu}_t$, where $\hat{\mu}_t = \hat{\beta}_0 + \hat{\beta}_1 t$, is referred to as the detrended data. In the case of a trend other methods are available see, for example, Canjels and Watson (1997) and Vogelsang (1998).

It is usual to add a specification of ε_t to complete the ARMA model, and we digress briefly to cover this point. The intention of the specification is to ensure that the ε_t, $t = 1, \ldots, T$, are not serially dependent. However, there are various 'strengths' of the assumptions that can be made. To understand these we start with the assumption that ε_t is white noise (WN), defined as: $E(\varepsilon_t) = 0$; $var(\varepsilon_t) = \sigma^2$, a constant for all t; and $cov(\varepsilon_t \varepsilon_s) = 0$, for $t \neq s$, that is the (auto)covariance between ε_t and ε_s is zero. A slightly stronger version of white noise (strong or independent white noise) is to specify that the sequence, $\{\varepsilon_t\}_{t=1}^{T}$ comprises ε_t that are independently and identically distributed (iid) for all t, written as $\varepsilon_t \sim iid(0, \sigma^2)$. Normality of ε_t is not an essential part of either of these specifications; if it assumed then we write $\varepsilon_t \sim niid(0, \sigma^2)$, so that the ε_t are independent not just uncorrelated. Another possibility requires us to look ahead to a martingale difference sequence (MDS), see Chapter 3, Section 3.5.1. For present purposes, we note that an MDS allows some heteroscedasticity, and we may alternatively specify that $\{\varepsilon_t\}$ is a stationary MDS with finite variance. Our default assumption is that $\varepsilon_t \sim WN(0, \sigma^2)$, with the notational convention that ε_t and σ^2 are generally reserved for this specification. Hayashi (2000) shows that in terms of increasing strength of assumptions, the relationships are: white noise $\subset$ MDS $\subset$ strong white noise.

Returning to the main issue, in terms of lag polynomials, the ARMA(p, q) model is written as one of the following:

$$\phi(L)y_t = \theta(L)\varepsilon_t \tag{2.6a}$$

$$\phi(L)\tilde{y}_t = \theta(L)\varepsilon_t \tag{2.6b}$$

where $\phi(L) = 1 - \sum_{i=1}^{p} \phi_i L^i, \theta(L) = 1 + \sum_{j=1}^{q} \theta_j L^j$ and $\varepsilon_t \sim WN(0, \sigma^2)$.

Example 2.2: ARMA(1, 1) model

The specification of this model is:

$$(1 - \phi_1 L)y_t = (1 + \theta_1 L)\varepsilon_t$$

The polynomial $(1 - \phi_1 L)$ has an inverse provided that $|\phi_1| < 1$, so that the model is invertible. Multiplying through by the inverse polynomial results in:

$$\begin{aligned} y_t &= (1 - \phi_1 L)^{-1}(1 + \theta_1 L)\varepsilon_t \\ &= \left(1 + \sum\nolimits_{j=1}^{\infty} \phi_1^j L\right)(1 + \theta_1 L)\varepsilon_t \\ &= \left(1 + (\phi_1 + \theta_1)L + \phi_1(\phi_1 + \theta_1)L^2 + \phi_1^2(\phi_1 + \theta_1)L^3 \ldots\right)\varepsilon_t \\ &= \sum\nolimits_{j=0}^{\infty} \omega_j L^j \varepsilon_t \end{aligned}$$

where $\omega_0 = 1$ and $\omega_j = \phi_1^{j-1}(\phi_1 + \theta_1)$ for $j \geq 1$. This is the MA(∞) representation of the original ARMA(1, 1) model. ♦

The polynomials $\phi(L)$ and $\theta(L)$ in Equation (2.6) are assumed to have no roots in common. To give a counter-example suppose it was the case in the ARMA(1, 1) model $(1 - \phi_1 L)y_t = (1 + \theta_1 L)\varepsilon_t$, that $\phi_1 = -\theta_1$, then the polynomials would cancel to leave $y_t = \varepsilon_t$. In practice, such exact cancellation is rare, but near-cancellation does occur especially as p and q are increased.

At this point, it is worth pointing out a departure from the notation of Equation (2.4) in the case of the AR(1) model. It is conventional in the area of unit root tests to adopt the notation that ρ rather than ϕ_1 is the coefficient on y_{t-1}, so that the commonplace (and equivalent) notation is $y_t = \rho y_{t-1} + \varepsilon_t$. This simple model, or a slight generalisation of it, is an often used vehicle for unit root tests. In fact, this notational convention has a substantive base in terms of the formulation of a model for unit root testing, see Chapter 8.

2.2.2 Causality and invertibility in ARMA models

An ARMA(p, q) model is described as being causal if there exists an absolutely summable sequence of constants $\{\omega_j\}_0^{\infty}$, such that:

$$\begin{aligned} y_t &= \sum\nolimits_{j=0}^{\infty} \omega_j L^j \varepsilon_t \\ &= \omega(L)\varepsilon_t \end{aligned} \tag{2.7}$$

The condition of absolute summability is $\sum_{j=0}^{\infty} |\omega_j| < \infty$. The lag polynomial $\omega(L)$ is the casual linear filter governing the response of $\{y_t\}$ to $\{\varepsilon_t\}$. The representation in (2.7) is the MA form of the original model, which will be MA(∞) if $\phi(L)$ is not redundant. The MA polynomial is

$\omega(L) = \Sigma_{j=0}^{\infty} \omega_j L^j = \phi(L)^{-1}\theta(L)$, with $\omega_0 = 1$; for this representation to exist the roots of $\phi(L)$ must lie outside the unit circle.

The MA form (2.7) provides the basis of a number of tools of interpretation of the original model. A measure of persistence based on (2.7) is considered in Section 2.2.3, and Section 2.6 considers the related concept of the long-run variance.

Note that (2.7) defines a linear filter since y_t is expressed as an additive function of current and past values of ε_t. Provided that $\phi(L)$ is invertible, the ARMA model of (2.4) necessarily implies a linear filter of the form in (2.7); however, one could start an analysis by assuming that y_t was generated by a linear filter, without necessarily specifying that the filter was generated by an ARMA model; for an application of this idea in the context of unit root tests, see Phillips and Solo (1992).

Although the condition of causality requires the invertibility of $\phi(L)$, the term invertibility is more usually taken to refer to the MA polynomial in the ARMA model. That is suppose $\theta(L)^{-1}$ exists, then the ARMA(p, q) model has the invertible representation:

$$\pi(L)y_t = \varepsilon_t \tag{2.8a}$$

where $\pi(L) = \Sigma_{j=0}^{\infty} \pi_j L^j = \theta(L)^{-1}\phi(L)$ and $\pi_0 = 1$. Thus (2.8a) may be written explicitly in infinite AR form as:

$$\begin{aligned} y_t &= [1-\pi(L)]y_t + \varepsilon_t \\ &= -\sum\nolimits_{j=1}^{\infty} \pi_j L^j y_t + \varepsilon_t \end{aligned} \tag{2.8b}$$

Analogous to the condition on $\phi(L)$, the representation in (2.8) requires that the roots of $\theta(L)$ lie outside the unit circle and that the sequence of coefficients in $\pi(L)$ is absolutely summable, that is $\Sigma_{j=0}^{\infty} |\pi_j| < \infty$. Consider the MA(1) case. Then $y_t = (1 + \theta_1 L)\varepsilon_t$ and invertibility requires that the following representation exists:

$$\pi(L)y_t = \varepsilon_t$$

where $\pi(L) = (1 + \theta_1 L)^{-1}$; provided that $|\theta_1| < 1$, then the inverse exists and is given by:

$$(1 + \theta_1 L)^{-1} = 1 + \sum\nolimits_{j=0}^{\infty} \theta_1^j (-1)^j L^j$$

This example illustrates the general condition that the modulus of the root(s) of the MA polynomial must lie outside the unit circle for the ARMA model to be invertible.

It is usual to impose an invertibility condition on the MA polynomial to ensure identifiability of the MA coefficients. This is because different sets of MA coefficients give rise to the same autocorrelation structure. The problem can be illustrated most simply with the MA(1) model. The first order autocorrelation coefficient ρ_1 (defined in Section 2.3.1, below), for this case is exactly the same if θ_1^{-1} replaces θ_1, that is:

$$y_t = (1+\theta_1 L)\varepsilon_t \Rightarrow \rho_1 = \frac{\theta_1}{(1+\theta_1^2)}$$

$$y_t = (1+\theta_1^{-1} L)\zeta_t \Rightarrow \rho_1 = \frac{1/\theta_1}{(1+(1/\theta_1)^2)} = \frac{1}{\theta_1(\theta_1^2+1)/\theta_1^2} = \frac{\theta_1}{(1+\theta_1^2)}$$

However, whilst ρ_1 is unchanged, the root of $(1 + \theta_1 L)$ is $-1/\theta_1$, whereas the root of $(1 + \theta_1^{-1} L)$ is $-\theta_1$ and, if $|\theta_1| < 1$ then only the first of these polynomials is invertible. Given that ρ_1 can be mapped back into different sets of MA coefficients then imposing invertibility ensures that one particular set is chosen (or identified).

2.2.3 A measure of persistence

The idea here is to determine the effect on y_t of a unit increase in ε_t which, when calculated as the total effect, is one measure of the persistence embodied in the model. The moving average representation of (2.7) is the most efficient way to obtain the required quantities.

For illustrative purposes, initially assume that $\omega(L)$ is the second order polynomial given by:

$$y_t = \varepsilon_t + \omega_1\varepsilon_{t-1} + \omega_2\varepsilon_{t-2}$$

The (finite) order of $\omega(L)$ will be denoted S, so in this case S = 2. Now consider a one unit one-off shock at time t; this can be represented as $\varepsilon^*_{t+s} = \varepsilon_{t+s} + 1$ for s = 0, and $\varepsilon^*_{t+s} = \varepsilon_{t+s}$ for $s \geq 1$. This shock will trace through time as follows:

$$\begin{aligned}
y^+_t &= \varepsilon_t + 1 + \omega_1\varepsilon_{t-1} &&= y_t + 1 \\
y^+_{t+1} &= \varepsilon_{t+1} + \omega_1(\varepsilon_t + 1) + \omega_2\varepsilon_{t-1} &&= y_{t+1} + \omega_1 \\
y^+_{t+2} &= \varepsilon_{t+2} + \omega_1\varepsilon_{t+1} + \omega_2(\varepsilon_t + 1) &&= y_{t+2} + \omega_2 \\
y^+_{t+s} & &&= y_{t+s} \quad \text{for } s \geq 2
\end{aligned}$$

From this pattern, we can infer that $y^{+}_{t+s} - y_{t+s} = \omega_s$ for $s \le S$ and $y^{+}_{t+s} - y_{t+s} = 0$ for $s > S$. Evidently, the lag coefficients in the moving average representation capture the differences due to the unit shock.

If the shock is sustained, that is $\varepsilon^{*}_{t+s} = \varepsilon_{t+s} + 1$ for $s \ge 0$, then following through the pattern over time, we can establish that $y^{+}_{t+s} - y_{t+s} = \sum_{j=0}^{s} \omega_j$ for $s < S$, and $y^{+}_{t+s} - y_{t+s} = \sum_{j=0}^{S} \omega_j$ for $s \ge S$. So, in this case, it is the partial sum of the lag coefficients that capture the sustained one unit shock if $s < S$ and the sum of the lag coefficients if $s \ge S$. The sum $\sum_{j=0}^{S} \omega_j$ is a measure of persistence, in that it shows how much y^{+}_{t+S} differs from y_{t+S}.

Increasing S, for example letting $S \to \infty$, does not change any aspect of principle outlined here. Thus, the limiting (or long-run) effect of a sustained one unit shock, where $\omega(L)$ is a lag polynomial of infinite order is:

$$\Lambda(\infty) = \lim_{S\to\infty} \sum_{j=0}^{S} \omega_j \tag{2.9}$$

To put this another way $\lim_{S\to\infty} (y^{+}_{t+S}) = y_{t+S} + \Lambda(\infty)$, so that in the limit y^{+}_{t+S} and y_{t+S} differ by $\Lambda(\infty)$. It is for this reason that $\Lambda(\infty)$ can be interpreted as a measure of persistence; for example, suppose that $\Lambda(\infty) = 0$, then the sustained unit shock has no effect in the long run. To illustrate the other extreme, consider the AR(1) model given by $y_t = \rho y_{t-1} + \varepsilon_t$; provided that $|\rho| < 1$, then this has the infinite MA representation $y_t = (1 - \rho L)^{-1} \varepsilon_t$. That is:

$$\begin{aligned} y_t &= (1 - \rho L)^{-1} \varepsilon_t \\ &= (1 + \rho L + \rho^2 L^2 + \ldots)\varepsilon_t \\ &= (\omega_0 + \omega_1 L + \omega_2 L^2 + \ldots)\varepsilon_t \end{aligned}$$

where $\omega_0 = 1$ and $\omega_j = \rho^j$ for $j \ge 1$. From the definition of persistence, we obtain $\Lambda(S) = 1 + \sum_{j=1}^{S} \omega_j = 1 + \sum_{j=1}^{S} \rho^j$ and hence: $\Lambda(\infty) = 1 + \sum_{j=1}^{\infty} \rho^j = (1 - \rho)^{-1}$

Note that as $\rho \to 1$, then $\Lambda(\infty) \to \infty$. Thus as the unit root is approached, persistence, as measured by $\Lambda(\infty)$, increases without limit. This result generalises: all that is required is that the AR polynomial includes at least one unit root.

Finally, $\Lambda(\infty)$ can be obtained very simply on noting that it is the (limiting) sum of the moving average coefficients, but rather than working out the sum, which could be tedious, it can be obtained by setting $z = 1$

in the MA lag polynomial w(z). That is:

$$\begin{aligned}\Lambda(\infty) &= \omega(z|\, z = 1) \\ &= \left(\sum_{j=0}^{\infty} \omega_j z^j \mid z = 1\right) \\ &= \sum_{j=0}^{\infty} \omega_j\end{aligned} \tag{2.10}$$

The shorthand notation for $\omega(z \mid z = 1)$ is $\omega(1)$, see also Section 2.1. Moreover if $\omega(1)$ is a rational polynomial, as in the invertible ARMA model, then $\Lambda(\infty)$ is obtained by setting L = 1 in each component polynomial, thus:

$$\Lambda(\infty) = \omega(1) = \frac{\theta(1)}{\phi(1)} \tag{2.11}$$

Example 2.3: ARMA(1, 1) model (continued)

In the case of the ARMA(1, 1) model of example 2.1, the persistence measure $\Lambda(\infty)$ is:

$$\Lambda(\infty) = \omega(1) = \frac{(1 + \theta_1)}{(1 - \phi_1)}$$

For example, if $\theta_1 = -0.3$ and $\phi_1 = 0.9$, then $\Lambda(\infty) = 7$. This calculation is clearly much more efficient than computing the infinite sum using ω_j as determined in example 2.2. ♦

2.2.4 The ARIMA model

The case of a unit root in the AR component of an ARMA model is sufficiently important to separate it from the general case. By way of motivation, consider the ARMA(2, 0) model, with the lag polynomial of example 2.1, that is:

$$(1 - 1.25L + 0.25L^2)y_t = \varepsilon_t$$

so that $\phi(L) = (1 - 1.25L + 0.25L^2)$. The roots of $\phi(L)$ were obtained as $\lambda_1 = 1$ and $\lambda_2 = 4$, so $\phi(L)$ is not invertible. However, the AR polynomial is invertible if the variable is redefined to include the unit root, that is $\phi(L)y_t = \phi^{(p-1)}(L)\Delta y_t$, where $\phi^{(p-1)}$ is of one lower order than $\phi(L)$. In

example 2, we saw that $\phi^{(p-1)} = (1 - 0.25L)$, which is invertible. In this case, there is d = 1 unit root, which can be extracted to leave an invertible polynomial.

This idea generalises, so that if there are d ≥ 1 unit roots, then:

$$\phi(L)y_t = \theta(L)\varepsilon_t \Rightarrow \phi^{(p-d)}(L)\Delta^d y_t = \theta(L)\varepsilon_t \qquad (2.12)$$

where $\phi^{(p-d)}$ is an invertible polynomial and $\Delta^d \equiv (1 - L)^d$ is the d-th differencing operator, which necessarily has d unit roots. The resulting model is described as an autoregressive integrated moving average model, ARIMA(p – d, d, q), which corresponds to the underlying ARMA(p, q) with d unit roots in the AR polynomial. Sometimes the ARIMA model is written as ARIMA(p, d, q), in which case the underlying ARMA model is ARMA(p + d, q).

When y_t is generated by an ARIMA(p – d, d, q) process, it also integrated of order d, written $y_t \sim I(d)$, in that modelling in terms of the d-th difference of y_t results in a casual (AR invertible) and stationary model. The most familiar case is d = 1, that is $y_t \sim I(1)$, so that the unit root is accommodated by modelling Δy_t rather than y_t. The concept of an integrated process is intimately related to the concept of stationarity, which was considered in Chapter 1, Section 1.9 and is considered further in Chapter 3, Section 3.2.

2.3 Autocovariances and autocorrelations

This section introduces a number of basic building blocks with which to analyse time series. A key aspect in characterising a time series is the extent of its dependence on itself, usually referred to as serial dependence, and for linear time series, the basic concept is the autocovariance, considered in the next section.

2.3.1 k-th order autocovariances and autocorrelations

The k-th order autocovariance is a measure of the (linear) dependence between y_t and its k-th lag, y_{t-k} (equivalently, the k-th lead, if the process generating the data is covariance stationary, see Chapter 1, Section 1.9 and Chapter 3, Section 3.2). It is defined as:

$$\gamma_k = E\{y_t - E(y_t)\}\{(y_{t-k} - E(y_{t-k})\} \qquad k = \pm 1, 2, 3, \ldots \qquad (2.13)$$

For k = 0, γ_0 is the variance, given by:

$$\gamma_0 = E\{y_t - E(y_t)\}^2 \tag{2.14}$$

Notice that if $E(y_t) = 0$ for all t, then $\gamma_0 = E(y_t^2)$ and $\gamma_k = E(y_t y_{t-k})$.

The k-th order autocorrelation coefficient ρ_k is γ_k scaled by the variance, γ_0, so that:

$$\rho_k = \frac{\gamma_k}{\gamma_0} \tag{2.15}$$

The scaling ensures that $0 \leq |\rho_k| \leq 1$. A word on notation at this point: ρ_k is the conventional notation for the autocorrelation coefficient, which we have followed here – it will *always* have a subscript; ρ, without a subscript, is the notation reserved for the coefficient on y_{t-1} in the AR(1) model. Considered as a function of k, γ_k and ρ_k give rise to the autocovariance and autocorrelation functions; the latter portrayed graphically, with k on the horizontal axis and ρ_k on the vertical axis, is referred to as the correlogram.

The existence of γ_k and ρ_k requires that $E(y_{t-k})$ exists. There are some distributions for which this is not the case; for example, these expectations do not exist for the Cauchy distribution, a feature that arises intuitively because the 'fat' tails of the Cauchy imply that there is 'too' much probability mass being applied to outlying realisations and, as a result, the weighted integral in $E(y_t)$ does not converge to a finite constant.

The autocovariance function of pure MA processes, which are just linear combinations of white noise (and hence uncorrelated) inputs, are particularly easy to obtain. These are as follows, where $y_t = \theta(L)\varepsilon_t$, with $\theta(L) = 1 + \Sigma_{j=1}^{q}\theta_j L^j$, $\varepsilon_t \sim WN(0, \sigma^2)$ and finite q, then we have:

$$\gamma_0 = \sigma^2 \sum_{j=0}^{q} \theta_j^2 \tag{2.16a}$$

$$\gamma_k = \sigma^2 \sum_{j=0}^{q-|k|} \theta_j \theta_{j+|k|} \qquad \text{for } k = 1, \ldots, q \tag{2.16b}$$

where $\theta_0 = 1$. It then follows that the autocorrelations are given by:

$$\gamma_k = \sum_{j=0}^{q-|k|} \theta_j \theta_{j+|k|} \Big/ \sum_{j=0}^{q} \theta_j^2 \tag{2.17}$$

For example:

$$q = 1, \quad \gamma_0 = (1+\theta_1^2)\sigma^2, \gamma_1 = \theta_1\sigma^2, \rho_1 = \theta_1/(1+\theta_1^2), \gamma_k = \rho_k = 0 \text{ for } k \geq 2;$$

$$q = 2, \quad \gamma_0 = (1+\theta_1^2+\theta_2^2)\sigma^2, \gamma_1 = (\theta_1+\theta_2\theta_1)\sigma^2, \gamma_2 = \theta_2\sigma^2;$$

$$\rho_1 = (\theta_1+\theta_2\theta_1)/(1+\theta_1^2+\theta_2^2), \rho_2 = \theta_2/(1+\theta_1^2+\theta_2^2), \gamma_k = \rho_k = 0 \text{ for } k \geq 3.$$

In the case of MA processes that result from the inversion of a casual ARMA model, then the MA coefficients are denoted ω_j, which is the j-th coefficient of $\omega(L)$. The autocovariances and autocorrelations are then given by:

$$\gamma_0 = \sigma^2 \sum_{j=0}^{\infty} \omega_j^2 \tag{2.18a}$$

$$\gamma_k = \sigma^2 \sum_{j=0}^{\infty} \omega_j \, \omega_{j+|k|} \qquad \text{for } k \geq 1 \tag{2.18b}$$

$$\rho_k = \sigma^2 \sum_{j=0}^{\infty} \omega_j \, \omega_{j+|k|} \Big/ \sum_{j=0}^{\infty} \omega_j^2 \quad \text{for } k \geq 1 \tag{2.18c}$$

An example is given below, see example 2.4. An alternative method of obtaining the autocovariance and autocorrelation functions is by way of the autocovariance generating function, see Section 2.5.

2.3.2 The long-run variance

It is also useful at this stage to introduce the concept of the long-run variance, which is the limiting value as $T \to \infty$ of $\text{var}(\sqrt{T}\bar{y})$, denoted $\sigma^2_{lr,y}$. Consider the following:

$$\begin{aligned} s^2_{lr,y} &= \lim_{T\to\infty} \text{var}\left(\sqrt{T}\bar{y}\right) \\ &= \lim_{T\to\infty} \text{var}\left(T^{-1/2}\sum_{t=1}^{T} y_t\right) \\ &= \lim_{T\to\infty} T^{-1}\,\text{var}(S_T) \end{aligned} \tag{2.19}$$

Notice the third line introduces the sum $S_T = \Sigma_{t=0}^{T} y_t$. If y_t has a zero mean, then $\text{var}(S_T) = E(S_T^2)$, and Equation (2.19) becomes,

$$\sigma^2_{lr,y} = \lim_{T\to\infty} T^{-1}E(S_T^2) \tag{2.20}$$

The form in (2.20) is the one that is often used for unit root tests, with S_T constructed from the sum of residuals (rather than y_t), which have zero mean by construction (otherwise the mean is subtracted from the original observations).

Multiplying out the terms in (2.19), $\sigma^2_{lr,y}$ can be expressed in terms of the autocovariances as follows:

$$\begin{aligned}\sigma^2_{lr,y} &= \sum\nolimits_{k=-\infty}^{\infty} \gamma_k \\ &= \gamma_0 + 2\sum\nolimits_{k=1}^{\infty} \gamma_k\end{aligned} \tag{2.21}$$

see Hayashi (2000, Proposition 6.8). Implicit in (2.21) are the assumptions that the (unconditional) variance of y_t is constant and that the autocovariances are invariant to a translation in the time index, so that $\gamma_k = \gamma_{-k}$; these, together with the assumption that the expectation of y_t is a constant, are the conditions of weak or covariance stationarity, see Chapter 1, Section 1.9. Example 2.4 shows how to obtain $\sigma^2_{lr,y}$ for an AR(1) model; however, in practice for ARMA or other linear models, it is usually easiest to use a result on the autocovariance generating function, ACGF, to obtain the long-run variance, see Equations (2.44) and (2.45).

The justification for describing $\sigma^2_{lr,y}$ as the 'long-run' variance requires some knowledge of a central limit theorem (CLT) for processes that generate serially dependent errors, which is deferred until Chapter 4, Section 4.2.3.

2.3.3 Example 2.4: AR(1) model (extended example)

Consider the simple AR(1) model:

$$y_t = \rho y_{t-1} + \varepsilon_t \tag{2.22}$$

where $\{\varepsilon_t\}$ is an WN(0, σ^2) sequence. First note that σ^2 is the variance of y_t conditional on y_{t-1}; that is $\text{var}(y_t \mid y_{t-1}) = \text{var}(\varepsilon_t) = \sigma^2$. Next repeated back substitution, assuming an infinite past, gives:

$$\begin{aligned}y_t &= \rho^2 y_{t-2} + \rho\varepsilon_{t-1} + \varepsilon_t \\ &= \rho^3 y_{t-3} + \rho^2\varepsilon_{t-2} + \rho\varepsilon_{t-1} + \varepsilon_t \\ &\vdots \\ &= \sum\nolimits_{i=0}^{\infty} \rho^i \varepsilon_{t-i}\end{aligned} \tag{2.23}$$

The last line assumes an infinite past and $|\rho| < 1$, so that $\lim_{i \to \infty}(\rho^i y_{t-i}) = 0$ for $|\rho| < 1$. The (unconditional) variance of y_t, $\sigma_y^2 = \gamma_0$, is obtained on exploiting the white noise nature of the sequence of ε_t, so that:

$$\begin{aligned}\gamma_0 &= Var(\sum_{i=0}^{\infty} \rho^i \varepsilon_{t-i}) \\ &= \sum_{i=0}^{\infty} \rho^{2i} Var(\varepsilon_{t-i}) \\ &= \frac{1}{(1-\rho^2)}\sigma^2 \end{aligned} \tag{2.24}$$

The last line uses three properties: ε_t has zero autocovariance with ε_s for $t \neq s$ by the assumption of white noise or the stronger assumption of iid; the variance of ε_t is a constant, σ^2, for all t; and $|\rho| < 1$, and, hence, $\lim_{K\to\infty} \sum_{i=0}^{K} \rho^{2i} = (1-\rho^2)^{-1}$.

To obtain ρ_k, multiply y_t by y_{t-k} and take expectations:

$$E(y_t y_{t-k}) = \rho E(y_{t-1} y_{t-k}) + E(\varepsilon_t y_{t-k}) \tag{2.25}$$

(For simplicity, $k > 0$ is assumed.) The last expectation is zero because y_{t-k} is a function of $(\varepsilon_{t-k}, \varepsilon_{t-k-1}, \ldots)$ but is uncorrelated with $(\varepsilon_{t-k+1}, \varepsilon_{t-k+2}, \ldots \varepsilon_t)$; intuitively y_{t-k} occurs before ε_t and the independence part of the assumption for ε_t means that it unrelated to predetermined events. Thus,

$$\gamma_k = \rho\gamma_{k-1} \tag{2.26}$$

As γ_0 is known, the sequence of γ_k, $k > 0$, is obtained from:

$$\gamma_k = \frac{\rho^k}{(1-\rho^2)}\sigma^2 \tag{2.27}$$

Further, the autocorrelations are then given by:

$$\begin{aligned}\rho_k &= \frac{\rho^k(1-\rho^2)^{-1}\sigma^2}{(1-\rho^2)^{-1}\sigma^2} \\ &= \rho^k \end{aligned} \tag{2.28}$$

If $k < 0$, then $|k|$ replaces k in the exponent of (2.28).

It is evident that a characteristic of the autocovariance and autocorrelation functions of the AR(1) process is that they decline geometrically. Also, as this example shows, γ_k and ρ_k are even functions, so that $\gamma_k = \gamma_{(-k)}$ and $\rho_k = \rho_{(-k)}$, which is a component of the definition of (weak) stationarity. Furthermore, the sequences of autocovariances and autocorrelations are clearly summable. The respective limits are:

$$\sum_{k=0}^{\infty} \gamma_k = \frac{\sigma^2}{(1-\rho^2)} \sum_{k=0}^{\infty} \rho^k = \frac{\sigma^2}{(1-\rho^2)} \frac{1}{(1-\rho)} \tag{2.29}$$

$$\sum_{k=0}^{\infty} \rho_k = \sum_{k=0}^{\infty} \rho^k = \frac{1}{(1-\rho)} \tag{2.30}$$

Notice that as $\rho \to 1$ these limits $\to +\infty$, indicating the lack of convergence to a finite limit as the positive unit root is approached; that is, in the limit, these sequences cease to be summable. A commonly used definition of a 'short-memory' process is one such that $\lim_{K\to\infty} \sum_{k=0}^{K} |\gamma_k| < \infty$. This is satisfied for the AR(1) process provided that $|\rho| < 1$.

Using (2.24) and (2.27), the long-run variance is obtained as follows:

$$\begin{aligned}
\sigma_{lr,y}^2 &= \sum_{k=-\infty}^{\infty} \gamma_k = \gamma_0 + 2\sum_{k=1}^{\infty} \gamma_k \\
&= \frac{1}{(1-\rho^2)} \sigma^2 \left[1 + 2\left(\frac{1}{(1-\rho)} - 1 \right) \right] \\
&= \frac{1}{(1-\rho^2)} \sigma^2 \left[1 + 2\left(\frac{\rho}{(1-\rho)} \right) \right] \\
&= \frac{1}{(1-\rho)(1+\rho)} \sigma^2 \left[\frac{(1+\rho)}{(1-\rho)} \right] \\
&= \frac{1}{(1-\rho)^2} \sigma^2
\end{aligned} \tag{2.31}$$

It is natural to extend the examples to consider higher order MA and AR models; and an easy way to do this is using the ACGF, see Section 2.5.

To complete this extended example, we confirm the autocovariance function can be obtained as $\gamma_k = \sigma^2 \sum_{j=0}^{\infty} \omega_j \omega_{j+|k|}$. Only k = 0, 1 are dealt

with explicitly as the principle soon becomes clear:

$$\begin{aligned}\gamma_0 &= \sigma^2 \sum_{j=0}^{\infty} \omega_j^2 \\ &= \sigma^2 (1 + \rho^2 + \rho^4 + \ldots +) \\ &= \frac{\sigma^2}{(1+\rho^2)} \qquad \text{confirms (2.24)}\end{aligned}$$

$$\begin{aligned}\gamma_1 &= \sigma^2 \sum_{j=0}^{\infty} \omega_j \omega_{j+1} \\ &= \sigma^2 (\rho + \rho\rho^2 + \rho^2\rho^3 + \ldots + \rho^j\rho^{j+1} + \ldots) \\ &= \sigma^2 \rho (1 + \rho^2 + \rho^4 + \ldots + \rho^{2j} + \ldots) \\ &= \rho\gamma_0\end{aligned}$$

The latter confirms Equation (2.26) for k = 1. ♦

2.3.4 Sample autocovariance and autocorrelation functions

So far the discussion has referred to the population concepts of the autocovariance and autocorrelation. In practice, these are replaced by their sampling counterparts. Given a sample of $t = 1, \ldots, T$ observations, possible estimators of γ_k and ρ_k are:

$$\hat{\gamma}_k = T^{-1} \sum_{t=k+1}^{T} (y_t - \bar{y})(y_{t-k} - \bar{y}) \tag{2.32}$$

$$\begin{aligned}\hat{\rho}_k &= \hat{\gamma}_k / \hat{\gamma}_0 \\ &= \frac{\sum_{t=k+1}^{T} (y_t - \bar{y})(y_{t-k} - \bar{y})}{\sum_{t=1}^{T} (y_t - \bar{y})^2}\end{aligned} \tag{2.33}$$

where $\bar{y} = T^{-1} \sum_{t=1}^{T} y_t$. Some variations on the estimator of γ_k include dividing by the number of observations in the summation, that is $T - k$; however, using T ensures that the autocovariance matrix, with the (i, j)-th element equal to $\hat{\gamma}_k$ where $k = |i - j|$, is non-negative definite, see Brockwell and Davis (2006). Also, rather than using $\bar{y}$, the estimator of $E(y_{t-k}) = \mu$ is adjusted for the lag (or lead) length, giving $\bar{y} = (T - k)^{-1} \sum_{t=k+1}^{T} y_t$. These variations affect the small sample properties, but have no effect asymptotically.

2.4 Testing for (linear) dependence

There are several tests for (linear) dependence based on the autocovariances or autocorrelations. In Section 2.4.1 we describe two of the most

widely used, which are the Box-Pierce (BP) statistic and the Ljung-Box (LB) modification of that statistic. Additionally, in Section 2.4.2, two widely used information criteria for selecting the orders of an ARMA model are introduced.

2.4.1 The Box-Pierce and Ljung-Box statistics

These tests were derived on the basis that $y_t \sim \text{niid}(0, \sigma^2)$; the zero mean can be ensured by first centring or detrending the data. The null hypothesis for these tests is $H_0 : \rho_k = 0, k = 1, \ldots, p$, whereas the alternative hypothesis is that at least one of ρ_k is non-zero.

The basic BP statistic is:

$$Q_p = T\sum\nolimits_{k=1}^{p} \hat{\rho}_k^2 \tag{2.34}$$

Under the null hypothesis, this test statistic is asymptotically distributed as $\chi^2(p)$ with p degrees of freedom: $Q_p \Rightarrow_D \chi^2(p)$, see Box and Pierce (1970); thus, large values of Q_p relative to the $(1 - \alpha)\%$ quantile of $\chi^2(p)$, lead to rejection at the $\alpha\%$ significance level. The notation $\Rightarrow_D$ means convergence in distribution, sometimes referred to as weak convergence; it is considered in detail in Chapter 4, Section 4.2.1.

Ljung and Box (1978) noted that the BP test statistic was derived as an approximation to the following test statistic:

$$\breve{Q}_p = T(T+2)\sum\nolimits_{k=1}^{p} \frac{\hat{\rho}_k^2}{(T-k)} \tag{2.35}$$

where $\breve{Q}_p \Rightarrow_D \chi^2(p)$. LB (ibid) showed that $\breve{Q}_p$ has better small sample properties compared to Q_p; for example, using critical values from $\chi^2(p)$ for $\breve{Q}_p$, resulted in an empirical size that was closer to the nominal size. They also showed, by means of some Monte-Carlo experiments, that $\breve{Q}_p$ was robust to departures from normality of y_t. (See also Anderson and Walker (1964) who had previously shown that the asymptotic normality of the $\hat{\rho}_k$ did not require normality of y_t). One of the most frequent uses of the BP and LB tests is as a 'portmanteau' test of model adequacy; that is where an ARMA(p, q) model had been estimated and the model's residuals are examined for remaining autocorrelation, the presence of which suggests that the estimated model is not yet adequate. The tests are, however, also applied as tests of (in)dependence to the levels of series, see, for example, Escanciano and Lobato (2009).

In the case of a single autocorrelation coefficient, the null hypothesis is $H_0 : \rho_k = 0$, and it can be shown that $\hat{\rho}_k \Rightarrow_D N(0, 1/T)$; that is $\hat{\rho}_k$ is asymptotically distributed as normal, with zero mean and variance 1/T, so that the asymptotic standard error of $\hat{\rho}_k$ is $1/\sqrt{T}$. A two-sided confidence interval at the level $(1-\alpha)\%$ is then formed as $\hat{\rho}_k \pm z_{\alpha/2}(1/\sqrt{T})$, where $z_{\alpha/2}$ is the $(\alpha/2)\%$ critical value from the standard normal distribution; for example, the 95% confidence interval with T = 100, is $\hat{\rho}_k \pm 1.96(1/10) = \hat{\rho}_k \pm 0.196$. The correlogram is often drawn with the 95% confidence interval overlaid. However, it is important to bear in mind the underlying hypothesis tests implied by this multiple testing approach. This procedure implies $H_{0,k} : \rho_k = 0$, for $k = 1, \ldots, m$, so that there are m multiple tests. The upper limit to the type 1 error, when each test is applied at the $\alpha\%$ significance level, is $\alpha_m = 1 - (1 - \alpha)^m$, this being the upper limit achieved by independent tests; for example, if $\alpha = 0.05$ and m = 10, then α_m is just over 40%, which may not be what was intended. The overall type 1 error can be controlled by solving for α given a particular value of α_m as follows: $\alpha = 1 - (1 - \alpha_m)^{1/m}$. For example, if $\alpha_m = 0.05$ and m = 10, then each test should be carried out at $\alpha = 1 - (0.05 - 1)^{1/10} = 0.0051$, that is at a significance level just above ½%, rather than 5%; alternatively, one could entertain a higher cumulative type 1 error; for example, $\alpha_m = 0.10$ implies $\alpha = 0.0105$, that is approximately a 1% significance level for each of the m tests.

2.4.2 Information criteria (IC)

The question of determining the order of a model often arises in practice. In the context of ARMA models, this is known as the *identification* of the model and there is an extensive literature on this subject, see, for example, Brockwell and Davis (2006, chapter 9). In this section we note two variations of a frequently used selection method based on information criteria, IC; the criteria used are Akaike IC (AIC, Akaike 1974), and the Bayesian IC (BIC), also referred to as the SIC after Schwarz (1978). These are examples of selection criteria that penalise the addition of terms that improve the fit of the model. In general terms, the idea is to choose the lag or model order, generically indexed by k, to minimise a function of the form:

$$IC(k) = T \ln \tilde{\sigma}^2(k) + k\{f(T)\} \tag{2.36}$$

where $\tilde{\sigma}^2(k) = T^{-1}\sum_{t=1}^{T} \tilde{\varepsilon}_t^2(k)$; $\tilde{\sigma}^2(k)$ is the maximum likelihood estimator of the regression variance and $\tilde{\varepsilon}_t(k)$ is the t-th residual which depends

upon the sample size and the parameter, k, which is the total number of coefficients in the model, for example p + q + 1 in an ARMA (p, q) model with an intercept. (Also, notice there is no degrees of freedom adjustment made in $\tilde{\sigma}^2(k)$). Minimising the first term alone is the same as the familiar criterion of minimising the (ML) residual standard error as a function of k; however, as $\tilde{\sigma}^2(k)$ cannot increase with k, this does not result in a practical answer to the question of determining k. The role of the second term is to impose a penalty on increasing k. Different choices of the penalty function give different information criteria (IC). Two common choices are as follows:

$$AIC(k) = T\ln\tilde{\sigma}^2(k) + 2k \qquad (2.37a)$$
$$BIC(k) = T\ln\tilde{\sigma}^2(k) + k\ln T \qquad (2.37b)$$

The idea is to set an upper limit to k, say k* and, correspondingly, set a common sample period, then calculate the information criterion over the range k = 1,..., k*, selecting that value of k, say $\tilde{k}(IC)$, that results in a minimum to the chosen information criterion. (AIC and BIC are sometimes presented in a form that divides (2.37a) and (2.37b) by T, but this does not affect the resulting choice of k.) One can establish from a comparison of (2.37a) and (2.37b) that $\tilde{k}(SIC) \leq \tilde{k}(AIC)$ for T > 8, see Lütkepohl (1993, Proposition 4.3). Some variations on AIC and BIC include using T*, the effective (actual) sample size, rather than T in (2.37a) and (2.37b); for example, in an AR(k*) model with a constant, the sample period is k* + 1,..., T, resulting in T* = T – k*.

Both AIC and BIC are in frequent use. AIC is not consistent for an AR(p) model in that there is a positive probability that is it overparameterises asymptotically, whereas BIC is consistent, see Lütkepohl (1993, Corollaries 4.2.1 and 4.2.2) and Hayashi (2000): however, the former is often preferred for its finite sample properties – see Jones (1975), Shibata (1976) and Koreisha and Pukkila (1995). Also, in practice, the use of an information criterion may be joined by another criterion, such as no evidence of serial correlation in the residuals of the resulting model.

2.5 The autocovariance generating function, ACGF

Consider the causal, invertible ARMA(p, q) model as defined in (2.6), that is:

$$\phi(L)y_t = \theta(L)\varepsilon_t \qquad (2.38)$$

The autocovariance generating function, ACGF, is given by:

$$\text{ACGF}(z) = \frac{\theta(z)\theta(z^{-1})}{\phi(z)\phi(z^{-1})}\sigma^2 \tag{2.39}$$

The notation $\phi(z^{-1})$ does not refer to the inverse polynomial but to the polynomial evaluated with the argument z^{-1} rather than z. The k-th order autocovariance is read off the ACGF as the coefficient on the k-th power of z. Some examples will illustrate the use of the ACGF (throughout $\gamma_k = \gamma_{-k} = \gamma_{|k|}$).

Example 2.5: MA(1) model

This is a simple example to show how the general principle works. The ACGF for this model is (noting that $\phi(z)$ is redundant in this example):

$$\begin{aligned}\text{ACGF}(z) &= (1+\theta_1 z)(1+\theta_1 z^{-1})\sigma^2 \\ &= \left((1+\theta_1^2 + \theta_1(z+z^{-1})\right)\sigma^2\end{aligned}$$

Hence, 'picking' off the appropriate powers of z, that is 0 for γ_0, +1 for γ_1 and k for γ_k, gives:

$$\gamma_0 = (1+\theta_1^2)\sigma^2, \gamma_1 = \theta_1\sigma^2 \text{ and } \gamma_k = 0 \text{ for } k \geq 2.$$

Note the symmetry of the terms in z and z^{-1}, so that we could have written the powers as ±1 for γ_1 and ±k for γ_k. The autocorrelations are then obtained as:

$$\rho_1 = \frac{\theta_1}{(1+\theta_1^2)}, \rho_k = 0 \text{ for } k \geq 2. \blacklozenge$$

Example 2.6: MA(2) model

The ACGF is given by (note that $\phi(z)$ is again redundant):

$$\begin{aligned}\text{ACGF}(z) &= (1+\theta_1 z+\theta_2 z^2)(1+\theta_1 z^{-1}+\theta_2 z^{-2})\sigma^2 \\ &= \left((1+\theta_1^2+\theta_2^2)+\theta_1(1+\theta_2)(z+z^{-1})+\theta_2(z^2+z^{-2})\right)\sigma^2\end{aligned}$$

Thus, $\gamma_0 = (1 + \theta_1^2 + \theta_2^2)\sigma^2$, $\gamma_1 = \theta_1(1 + \theta_2)\sigma^2$, $\gamma_2 = \theta_2\sigma^2$ and $\gamma_k = 0$ for $k \geq 3$; and the autocorrelations are, therefore, as follows.

$$\rho_1 = \frac{\theta_1(1+\theta_2)}{(1+\theta_1^2+\theta_2^2)}, \quad \rho_2 = \frac{\theta_2}{(1+\theta_1^2+\theta_2^2)}, \quad \rho_k = 0 \text{ for } k \geq 3.$$

Example 2.7: AR(1) model

This example revisits example 2.4, but applies the approach of the ACGF. In this case we adopt the notational convention that the simple AR(1) model is written as $(1 + \rho L)y_t = \varepsilon_t$, so that ρ replaces ϕ_1. Applying (2.39) we obtain:

$$\begin{aligned}
\text{ACGF}(z) &= \frac{1}{(1-\rho z)(1-\rho z^{-1})}\sigma^2 \\
&= (1 + \rho z + \rho^2 z^2 + \ldots)(1 + \rho z^{-1} + \rho^2 z^{-2} + \ldots)\sigma^2 \\
&= (1 + \rho^2 + (\rho^2)^2 + \ldots)\left((1 + \rho(z + z^{-1}) + \rho^2(z + z^{-2}) + \ldots\right)\sigma^2
\end{aligned}$$

First note the notational equivalence $\rho \equiv \phi_1$. The second line follows by expanding $(1 - \rho z)^{-1}$ and $(1 - \rho z^{-1})^{-1}$, respectively, and the third line follows by simplifying and collecting like powers (the derivation of this line is left as a question). Hence, $\gamma_0 = (1 - \rho^2)^{-1}\sigma^2$ and $\gamma_k = \rho^k(1 - \rho^2)^{-1}\sigma^2$; which is as before, but using the general AR coefficient notation, where $\phi_1 \equiv \rho$. ♦

2.6 Estimating the long-run variance

This section follows on from Section 2.3, which considered estimating the variance and autocovariances of the process generating y_t (the data generation process, DGP) given a sample of observations. In this section, we consider how to estimate the long-run variance $\sigma^2_{lr,y}$ defined in Section 2.3.2. Two methods predominate. The first makes no assumption about the parametric form of the DGP and bases the estimator on the sample variance and autocovariances; the second, assumes either that the DGP is an ARMA(p, q) model or can be reasonably approximated by such a model.

2.6.1 A semi-parametric method

Recall from (2.21) that $\sigma^2_{lr,y} = \gamma_0 + 2\sum_{k=1}^{\infty}\gamma_k$; and a consistent estimator of $\sigma^2_{lr,y}$ is, in principle, obtained by replacing γ_k, $k = 0, 1, \ldots, \infty$, by

consistent estimators as defined in (2.32). The practical problem here is that the upper summation limit cannot extend to infinity; therefore, an estimator is defined by truncating the upper limit to a finite number m < T – 1, such that:

$$\hat{\sigma}^2_{lr,y}(m) = \hat{\gamma}_0 + 2\sum\nolimits_{k=1}^{m} \hat{\gamma}_k \qquad (2.40)$$
$$= T^{-1}\sum\nolimits_{t=1}^{T} \hat{\tilde{y}}_t^2 + 2T^{-1}\sum\nolimits_{k=1}^{m}\sum\nolimits_{t=k+1}^{T} \hat{\tilde{y}}_t \hat{\tilde{y}}_{t-k}$$

where $\hat{\tilde{y}}_t = y_t - \hat{\mu}_t$. The argument for the use of $\hat{\sigma}^2_{lr,y}(m)$ is that the omitted autocovariances must be 'small' in some well-defined sense. Phillips (1987, theorem 4.2) shows that, given certain regularity conditions, if $m \to \infty$ as $T \to \infty$ such that $m \sim o(T^{1/4})$, then $\hat{\sigma}^2_{lr,y}(m)$ is a consistent estimator for $\sigma^2_{lr,y}$, see also Phillips and Ouliaris (1990) for details. (The notation $m \sim o(T^{1/4})$ is, as yet, unfamiliar, but is explained in Chapter 4, Section 4.3.1. It relates to the rate at which m increases as a function of T; it is read as m must increase with T, but at an order which is smaller than $o(T^{1/4})$, so that the ratio $m/T^{1/4}$ tends to zero.)

The estimator $\hat{\sigma}^2_{lr,y}(m)$ may be negative if there are large negative sample autocovariances; to avoid this problem a kernel estimator can be used, which defines a weighting function for the sample autocovariances. The kernel function $\psi(k)$ defines the weights $\psi_{m,k}$ and the revised estimator $\hat{\sigma}^2_{lr,y}(m, \psi)$ is given by:

$$\hat{\sigma}^2_{lr,y}(m, \psi) = \hat{\gamma}_0 + 2\sum\nolimits_{k=1}^{m} \psi_{m,k} \sum\nolimits_{t=k+1}^{T} \hat{\gamma}_k \qquad (2.41)$$
$$= T^{-1}\sum\nolimits_{t=1}^{T} \hat{\tilde{y}}_t^2 + 2T^{-1}\sum\nolimits_{k=1}^{m} \psi_{m,k} \sum\nolimits_{t=k+1}^{T} \hat{\tilde{y}}_t \hat{\tilde{y}}_{t-k}$$

The Newey-West/Bartlett kernel is often used in this context and is given by:

$$\psi_{m,k} = 1 - k/(m+1) \qquad k = 1, \ldots, m. \qquad (2.42)$$

The notation $\hat{\sigma}^2_{lr,y}(m, \psi)$ is rather cumbersome, so where no confusion arises, this will be shortened to $\hat{\sigma}^2_{lr,y}$.

The guidance on choosing m does not offer an immediate solution to choosing m in a single sample: the condition that $m = o(T^{1/4})$ ensures that $(m/T) \to 0$ as $T \to \infty$, but does not otherwise say what m should be for a fixed T. In practice a simple truncation rule is often used, such as $m = \{K(T/100)^{1/4}]$, where [.] is the integer part and K is a constant, with

typical choices being 4 and 12. If the truncation rule is correct, then increasing m should not make a noticeable difference to the estimate of $\sigma^2_{lr,y}$, and some informal guidance can be provided by inspecting the autocorrelation function.

2.6.2 An estimator of the long-run variance based on an ARMA(p, q) model

Recall that in the case that y_t is generated by an causal ARMA(p, q) model, then it has the MA form given by:

$$y_t = \omega(L)\varepsilon_t \tag{2.43}$$

where $\omega(L) = \phi(L)^{-1}\theta(L)$. The corresponding ACGF is:

$$\begin{aligned} ACGF(z) &= \omega(z)\omega(z^{-1})\sigma^2 \\ &= \frac{\theta(z)\theta(z^{-1})}{\phi(z)\phi(z^{-1})}\sigma^2 \end{aligned} \tag{2.44}$$

The ACGF offers an economical way of obtaining the long-run variance. To obtain $\sigma^2_{lr,y}$ set z = 1 in the ACGF, so that:

$$\begin{aligned} \sigma^2_{lr,y} &= \omega(1)^2\sigma^2 \\ &= \frac{\theta(1)^2}{\phi(1)^2}\sigma^2 \end{aligned} \tag{2.45}$$

The first line follows on noting that $z = z^{-1} = 1$ when evaluated at $z = 1$.

The practical problem is to determine the orders p and q and estimate the associated AR and MA parameters. One often used method for the first part of the problem is to select the orders by an information criterion, such as AIC or BIC (see also the modified AIC, MAIC, suggested by Ng and Perron, 2001). As to estimation, standard econometric software packages, such as Eviews, RATS and TSP, offer estimation routines based on the method of moments, conditional least squares and exact maximum likelihood; when available, the latter is usually to be preferred. Let ~ over a coefficient denote a consistent estimator, then the model-based estimator of $\sigma^2_{lr,y}$ is given by:

$$\begin{aligned} \tilde{\sigma}^2_{lr,y} &= \omega(1)^2\tilde{\sigma}^2 \\ &= \frac{\tilde{\theta}(1)^2}{\tilde{\phi}(1)^2}\tilde{\sigma}^2 \end{aligned} \tag{2.46}$$

$$\tilde{\sigma}^2 = T^{-1} \sum\nolimits_{t=p+1}^{T} \tilde{\varepsilon}_t^2 \tag{2.47}$$

The quantity $\tilde{\sigma}^2$ is an estimator of σ^2 based on the residuals $\tilde{\varepsilon}_t^2$; just how these are obtained depends on the estimation method, but by rearranging the ARMA(p, q) model, $\tilde{\varepsilon}_t$ can be expressed as:

$$\tilde{\varepsilon}_t = y_t - \tilde{\phi}_1 y_{t-1} - \ldots - \tilde{\phi}_p y_{t-p} - \tilde{\theta}_1 \varepsilon_{t-1} - \ldots \tilde{\theta}_q \varepsilon_{t-q} \tag{2.48}$$

where t = p + 1, . . . , T. Estimation methods differ in how the pre-sample values are dealt with; for example, pre-sample values of ε_t may be set to zero or they may backcast given initial estimates of the ARMA coefficients. However, once the estimates are determined, the corresponding sequence of $\tilde{\varepsilon}_t$ is available. For details of different estimation methods see, for example, Brockwell and Davis (2006, chapter 8) and Fuller (1996, chapter 8).

A variation on this method arises if ω(L) is assumed to have an AR form, with no MA component. This could arise if it is genuinely the case that q = 0, so there is no MA component, or q ≥ 1, but the MA component is approximated by increasing the AR order to, say, p*, compared to that determined by p alone, such that p* ≥ p. The resulting estimator is:

$$y_t = \sum\nolimits_{j=1}^{p^*} \phi_j L^j y_t + \varepsilon_{p^*,t} \tag{2.49}$$

where $p^* \geq p$ and $\varepsilon_{p^*,t}$ differs from ε_t if an MA component is being approximated by an AR component. The estimated coefficients from (2.49) are denoted $\hat{\phi}_j$, with residuals $\hat{\varepsilon}_{p^*,t}$. The resulting estimator of $\sigma^2_{lr,y}$ is:

$$\hat{\sigma}^2_{lr,y} = \hat{\phi}(1)^{-2} \hat{\sigma}^2 \tag{2.50}$$

$$\hat{\sigma}^2 = (T - p^*)^{-1} \sum\nolimits_{t=p^*+1}^{T} \hat{\varepsilon}^2_{p^*,t} \tag{2. 51}$$

In the case that the MA component is approximated by lengthening the AR lag, there is no finite order of p* that is 'correct' and the question is to determine an appropriate truncation point. A sufficient condition governing the expansion of p* for the consistency of the resulting estimator of $\sigma^2_{lr,y}$, is $p^*/T^{1/3} \to 0$ as $T \to \infty$, and there exist constants, ζ and s, such that $\zeta k^* > T^{1/s}$. A problem analogous to that for the choice

of m in the semi-parametric method applies here: the rule does not uniquely determine p* for a given T. In practice, an analogous rule, but of the form $p^* = [K(T/100)^{1/3}]$ is used, but the sensitivity of the results to increasing p* should be considered as a matter of course, particularly as when $\tilde{\phi}(1)$ is close to zero, which will happen when there is a near-unit root, the nonlinear form of (2.50), makes the resulting estimator very sensitive to small changes in $\tilde{\phi}(1)$. Further references on this topic include Berk (1974), Said and Dickey (1984), Pierre and Ng (1996), Ng and Perron (2001) and Sul et al. (2005).

2.7 Illustrations

This section comprises two examples to illustrate some of the concepts introduced in this chapter.

Example 2.8: Simulation of some ARMA models

In this example, two models are simulated, and the simulated data are graphed, together with the sample autocorrelation function and the cumulative sum of the sample autocorrelations. The two models are:

$$\text{AR}(1): (1-\rho L)y_t = \varepsilon_t \qquad \rho = 0.9 \qquad \text{Figure 2.1}$$
$$\text{MA}(1): y_t = (1+\theta_1 L)\varepsilon_t \qquad \theta_1 = -0.5 \qquad \text{Figure 2.2}$$

Throughout $\varepsilon_t \sim \text{niid}(0, 1)$ and T = 500 observations are generated in each case. The autocorrelations and variances for each model are:

$$\text{AR(1)}: \rho_k = \rho^k; \sum\nolimits_{k=0}^{\infty} \rho^k = (1-\rho)^{-1} = 10;$$
$$\sigma_y^2 = (1-\rho^2)^{-1}\sigma^2 = 5.26; \sigma_{lr,y}^2 = (1-\rho)^{-2}\sigma^2 = 100.$$

$$\text{MA}(1): \rho_0 = 1, \rho_1 = \theta_1/(1+\theta_1^2) = -0.497, \rho_k = 0 \text{ for } k \geq 2; \sum\nolimits_{k=0}^{1} \rho_k = 0.503;$$
$$\sigma_y^2 = (1+\theta_1^2)\sigma^2 = 1.25; \sigma_{lr,y}^2 = (1+\theta_1^2)\sigma^2 + 2\theta_1\sigma^2 = (1+\theta_1)^2\sigma^2 = 0.25.$$

There are three sub-figures for each model. The realisations from the AR(1) model are shown in Figure 2.1a, from which it is evident that there is positive dependency in the series. The sample autocorrelations are shown in Figure 2.1b and their sum in Figure 2.1c, each together with their theoretical counterparts. The geometric decline in $\hat{\rho}_k$ matches

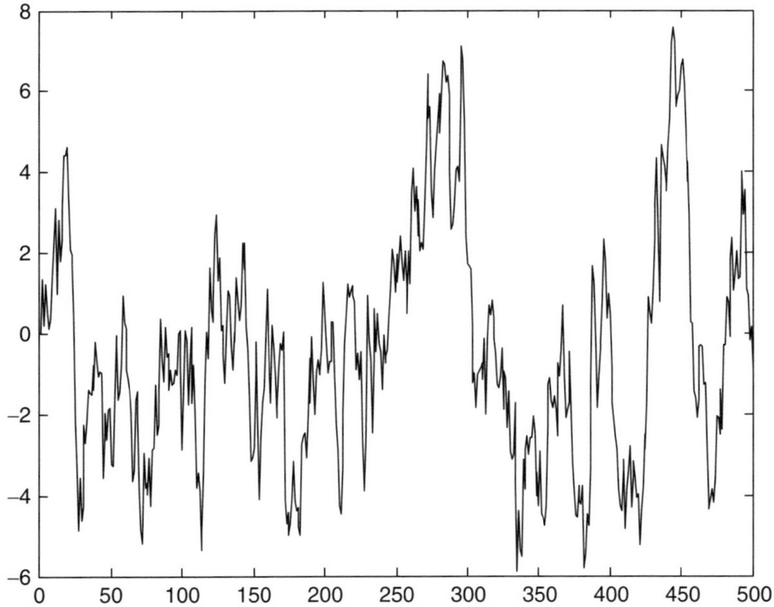

Figure 2.1a Simulated observations: AR(1)

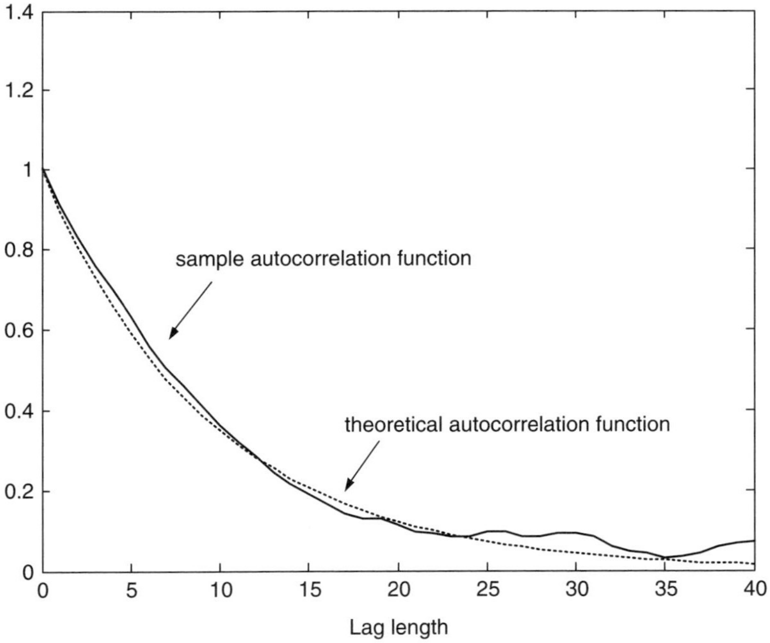

Figure 2.1b Sample autocorrelation function: AR(1)

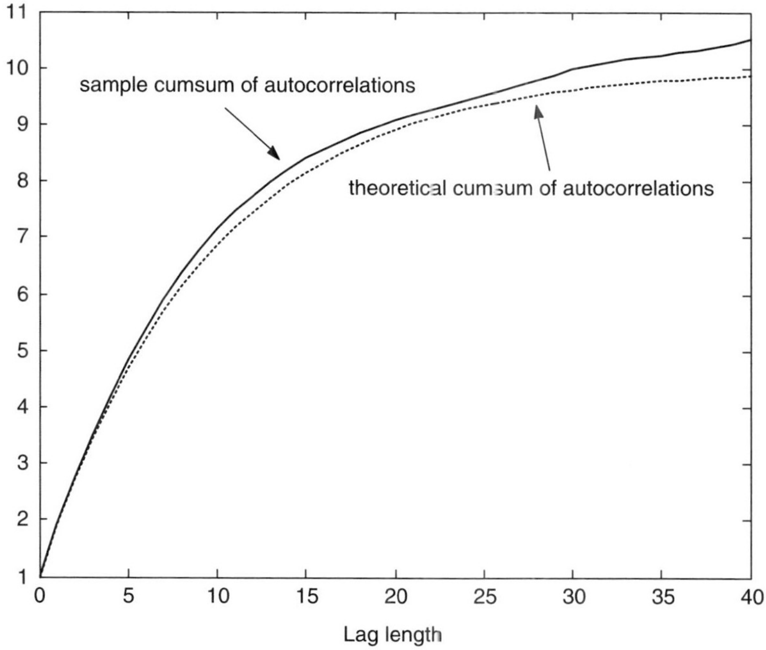

Figure 2.1c Cumulative sum of autocovariances: AR(1)

the expected theoretical pattern, and $\sum_{k=0}^{\infty}\hat{\rho}^{k}$ approaches the theoretical, and finite, limit = 10 in this case, indicating short memory in the process.

There is negative first order autocorrelation in the MA(1) model, so there are a relatively large number of changes of sign in adjacent realisations, see Figure 2.2a. The sample autocorrelations mimic the expected theoretical pattern with $\hat{\rho}_k$, $k \geq 2$, close to zero, see Figure 2.2.b; and the sum of the sample autocorrelations is close to its theoretical value of just over 0.5, see Figure 2.2c. ♦

Example 2.9: An ARMA model for US wheat data

In this example, the data is annual for US wheat production, 1864–2008. The observations, in natural logarithms, are graphed in Figure 2.3a, from which it is clear that there is a positive trend. The data is, therefore, detrended by a regression of the log of wheat production on a constant and a linear time trend; the detrended data is referred to as $\hat{y}_t$

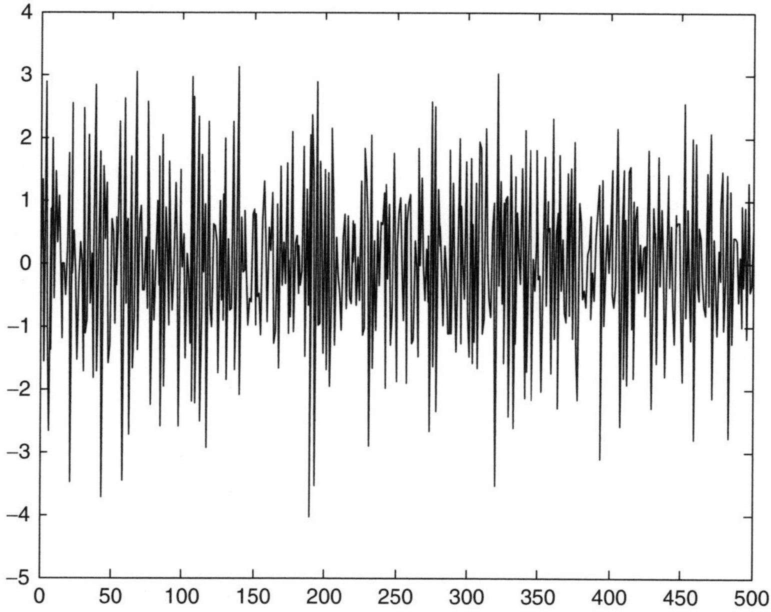

Figure 2.2a Simulated observations: MA(1)

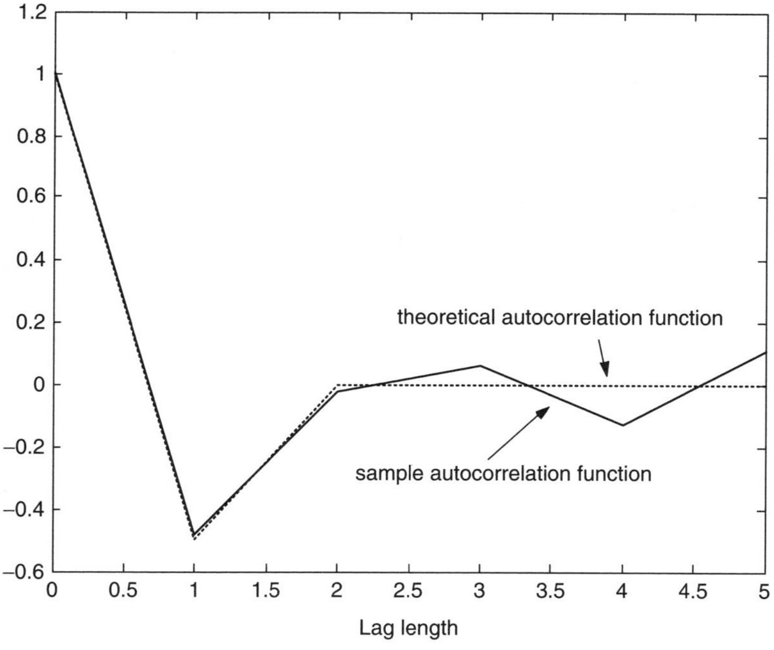

Figure 2.2b Autocorrelation functions: MA(1)

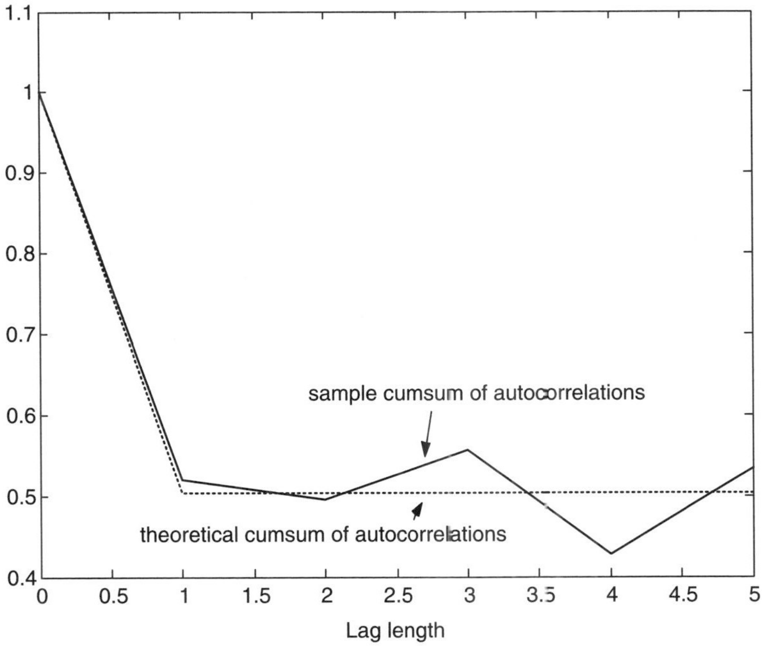

Figure 2.2c Cumulative sum of autocovariances: MA(1)

and is shown in Figure 2.3b. Clearly there is some positive dependency in the series. The sample autocorrelations, $\hat{\rho}_k$, of $\hat{y}_t$ are graphed in Figure 2.4a and the cumulative sum of the $\hat{\rho}_k$ are shown in Figure 2.4b. Figure 2.4a confirms the positive dependency, with $\hat{\rho}_k > 0$ until lag 11 and thereafter $\hat{\rho}_k$ takes small negative values. The values of the Box-Pierce and Ljung-Box test statistics for p = 10, were $Q_{10} = 176.4$ and $\breve{Q}_{10} = 184.1$, respectively, and both are clearly significant with p-values of zero (the 99% quantile for χ^2 is 23.2). The short-memory nature of the process is suggested by the finite sum of the autocorrelations in Figure 2.4b, and confirmed by the estimation results assuming a parametric model, reported next.

An ARMA(p, q) model was fitted to the data, with the upper limits of p and q set at 3. AIC suggested p = 1, q = 1 and BIC suggested p = 1, q = 0; on examination of the estimated coefficients in the ARMA(1, 1) model, the AR coefficient had a p-value of zero and the MA coefficient had a p-value of 0.9%, which suggested keeping both components. (Estimation used the BJFOR option in RATS). The estimated model was

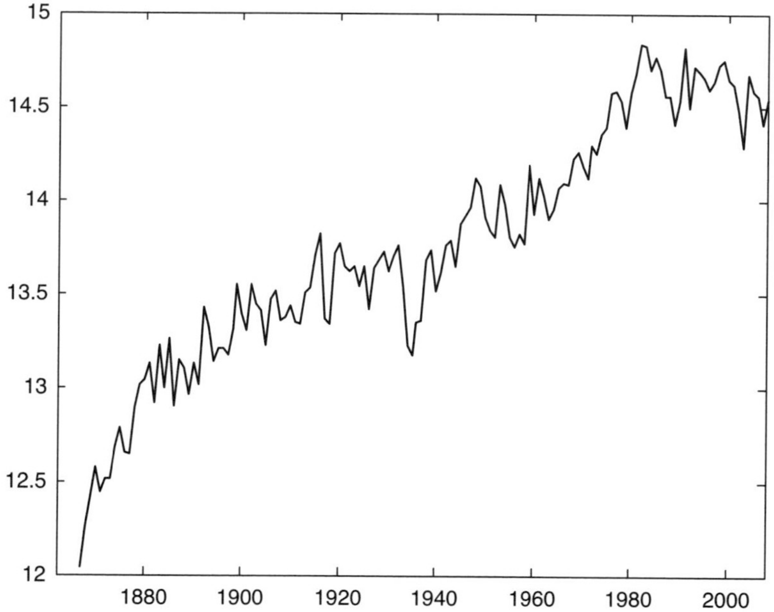

Figure 2.3a US wheat production (log)

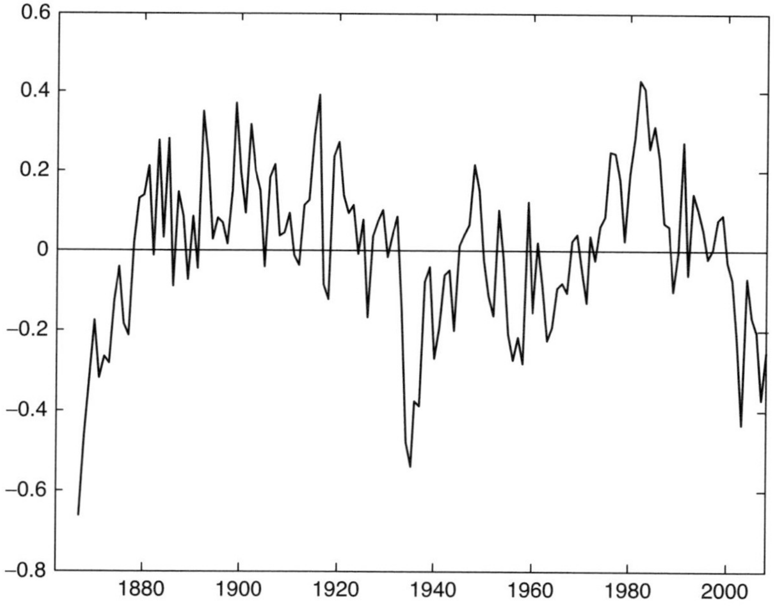

Figure 2.3b US wheat production (log, detrended)

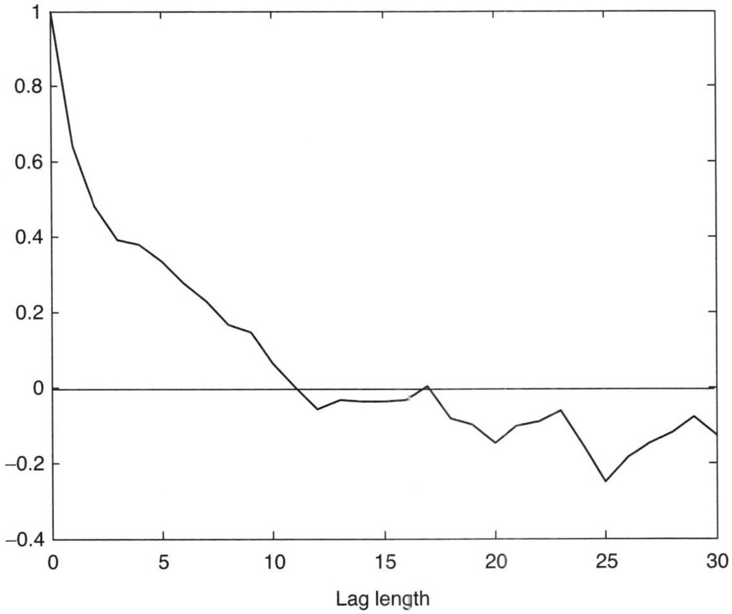

Figure 2.4a Sample autocorrelation function: US wheat

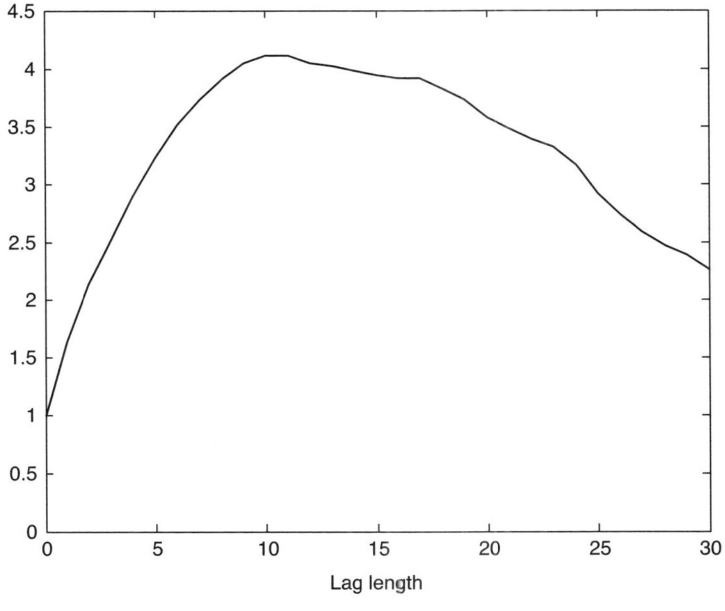

Figure 2.4b Cumulative sum of autocorrelations: US wheat

$(1 - 0.814L)\tilde{y}_t = (1 - 0.324L)\,\hat{\varepsilon}_t$, which confirms both the short-memory and the predominantly positive nature of the dependency. The estimated parameters of interest were:

$$\tilde{\sigma}^2 = 0.1438^2 \qquad \text{conditional variance}$$

$$\hat{\Lambda}(\infty) = \hat{\omega}(1) = \frac{\tilde{\theta}(1)}{\tilde{\phi}(1)} = \frac{(1-0.324)}{(1-0.814)} = 3.65 \qquad \text{persistence}$$

$$\begin{aligned}\tilde{\sigma}^2_{lr,y} &= \frac{\hat{\theta}(1)^2}{\hat{\phi}(1)^2}\tilde{\sigma}^2 = \frac{(1-0.324)^2}{(1-0.814)^2}\tilde{\sigma}^2 \qquad \text{long-run variance}\\ &= 13.24\tilde{\sigma}^2\\ &= 0.274\end{aligned}$$

If $q = 0$, then p, now in effect p*, is allowed to vary in order to approximate any MA component by extending the AR order; the AIC selects p* = 2, whilst the BIC selection is unchanged, that is p = p* = 1. The estimated ARMA(2, 0) model is: $(1 - 0.542L - 0.147L^2)\tilde{y}_t = \tilde{\varepsilon}_t$, with other estimated quantities: $\tilde{\sigma} = 0.144$, $\hat{\Lambda}(\infty) = 3.22$ and $\tilde{\sigma}^2_{lr,y} = (1 - 0.542 - 0.147)^{-2}\tilde{\sigma}^2 = 10.37\tilde{\sigma}^2 = 0.216$.

Semi-parametric estimation of the long-run variance was described in Section 2.6.1; the method uses either an unweighted estimator as in $\hat{\sigma}^2_{lr,y}(m)$ of (2.40) or imposes a set of kernel weights; here we use the Newey-West weights of (2.42) combined with the estimator of (2.41), denoted $\hat{\sigma}^2_{lr,y}(m, \psi)$. The results are presented graphically in Figure 2.5, where the estimated long-run variance is a function of the truncation parameter m, referred to as the lag length. The unweighted estimator shows a more marked peak compared to the estimator using the Newey-West weights. The often-used 'rule' to select m, that is $m = [12(143/100)^{1/4}] = [13.12] = 13$, results in the unweighted estimate $\hat{\sigma}^2_{lr,y}(13) = 0.281$ and the Newey-West estimate $\hat{\sigma}^2_{lr,y}(13, \psi) = 0.216$; in this case, the former is very close to the estimate of $\tilde{\sigma}^2_{lr,y}$ from the preferred ARMA(1,1) model. ♦

2.8 Concluding remarks

There are many excellent books on time series analysis. Classic texts include Box and Jenkins (1970) and Anderson (1971), both of which are a must for serious time series analysis. The texts by Brockwell and Davis

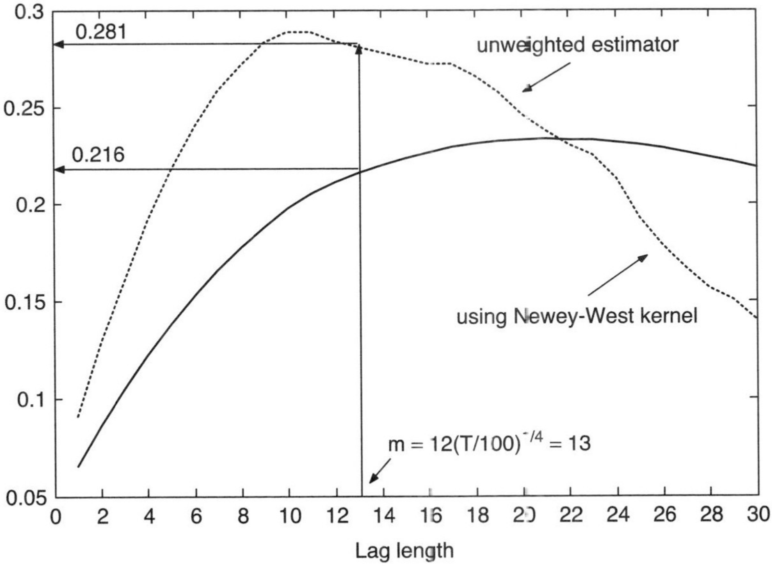

Figure 2.5 Alternative semi-parametric estimates of σ^2_{lr}

(2002) and Chatfield (2004) are appropriate to follow this chapter. In turn they could be followed by Priestley (1981), Fuller (1996), Brockwell and Davis (2006); two books with a slightly more econometric orientation are Hamilton (1994) and Harvey (1993). The problems associated with estimating the long-run variance are considered by Sul et al. (2005) and Müller (2007).

Questions

Q2.1 Obtain and interpret the roots of the following lag polynomial $(1 - 0.75L + 0.25L^2)$.

A2.1 In terms of analysis, work with $\phi(z) = (1 - 0.75z + 0.25z^2)$, and the roots are then obtained by solving $\phi(z) = 0$; however, as noted in Section 2.1.3, it is neater mathematically to divide through by the coefficient on z^2, so that the resulting polynomial and zeros are obtained from $4 - 3z + z^2 = 0$, which factors as $(z - \lambda_1)(z - \lambda_2) = 0$, with roots λ_1 and λ_2. This can be solved using the standard high school formula for the roots of a quadratic equation; however, it is easier to use a program in,

for example MATLAB, as used here, to obtain the roots. The MATLAB instructions are:

```
p = [1 -3 4]
r = roots(p)
absr = abs(r)
```

Note that the polynomial coefficients are typed in declining order of the powers in the polynomial; thus the coefficient on z^2 is read in first, and the constant is last. (Note that the same results are obtained provided that the ratio of the coefficients is maintained, so that p = [1/4 −3/4 1], gives the same results, see **Q2.3** below.) The output is:

```
p = [1 -3 4]
r = 1.5000 + 1.3229i
    1.5000 - 1.3229i
absr =
        2
        2
```

In the notation of this chapter, the roots are: $\lambda_1, \lambda_2 = 1.5 \pm 1.323i$, which is a pair of conjugate complex numbers, with the same modulus given by $|\lambda_1|, |\lambda_2| = \sqrt{(1.5^2 + 1.323^2)} = 2$. The modulus of the roots is greater than 1 and the roots are said to be 'outside the unit circle', so that the AR(2) model constructed from this lag polynomial is invertible.

To check that λ_1 and λ_2 are indeed the roots, the polynomial $(z - \lambda_1)(z - \lambda_2)$ is reconstructed using the numerical values of λ_1 and λ_2. The MATLAB instructions and output are as follows:

```
pp = poly(r)
pp = 1 -3 4
```

Q2.2 Confirm the result used in example 2.7, that:

$$\begin{aligned} \text{ACGF}(z) &= \frac{1}{(1-\rho z)(1-\rho z^{-1})}\sigma^2 \\ &= (1+\rho^2+(\rho^2)^2+\ldots)\big((1+\rho(z+z^{-1})+\rho^2(z+z^{-2})+\ldots\big)\sigma^2 \end{aligned}$$

A2.2 The first part of the answer uses the result for convergent series that:

$$\frac{1}{(1-\rho z)} = \sum_{j=0}^{\infty} \rho^j z^j$$

Also replace z by z^{-1} to obtain an analogous result for $(1 - \rho z^{-1})^{-1}$. Now write out some illustrative terms:

$$\begin{aligned}
&\left((1+\rho z+\rho^2 z^2+\rho^3 z^3+\ldots\right)\left(1+\rho z^{-1}+\rho^2 z^{-2}+\rho^3 z^{-3}+\ldots\right) \\
&\qquad 1+\ \rho z\ +\ \rho^2 z^2\ +\rho^3 z\ \ +\ldots \\
&= \qquad \rho z^{-1}+\ \rho^2\ \ +\rho^3 z\ \ +\ldots \\
&\qquad\qquad\quad \rho^2 z^{-2}\ +\rho^3 z^{-1}+\ldots
\end{aligned}$$

The trick is to pick off the coefficients on powers of z. For example, the coefficients on $z^0 \equiv 1$, z, z^2 and the general term, z^k, are, respectively:

$$\begin{aligned}
&(1+\rho^2+\rho^4+\rho^6+\ldots) &&= (1-\rho^2)^{-1} \\
&\rho(1+\rho^2+\rho^4+\rho^6+\ldots) &&= \rho(1-\rho^2)^{-1} \\
&\rho^2(1+\rho^2+\rho^4+\rho^6+\ldots) &&= \rho^2(1-\rho^2)^{-1} \\
&\qquad\vdots &&\qquad\vdots \\
&\rho^k(1+\rho^2+\rho^4+\rho^6+\ldots) &&= \rho^k(1-\rho^2)^{-1}
\end{aligned}$$

Multiplying the general term by σ^2 gives the k-th order autocovariance.

Q2.3 Compare the AR and MA roots of the following ARM(p, q) models, based on an example from Chapter 3, which uses the log ratio of the gold to the silver price. The first model is the ARMA(2, 1) given by:

$$(1 + 0.940L + 0.130L^2)\ \tilde{y}_t = (1 + 0.788L)\tilde{\varepsilon}_t,\ \tilde{\sigma} = 0.0137$$

The second model is the following ARMA(1, 0) model (estimated on the same data set):

$$(1 + 0.152L)\ \tilde{y}_t = \tilde{\varepsilon}_t,\ \tilde{\sigma} = 0.0137.$$

Why is the estimate of σ from the two models indistinguishable?

A2.3. In the first case, the roots of the AR(2) polynomial $(1 + 0.940z + 0.130z^2)$ can be obtained from MATLAB as follows:

```
p = [0.13 0.94 1]
r = roots(p)
  = –1.2962, –5.9346
```

The reciprocals of the roots are obtained as:

```
rr = 1./r
   = –0.7715, –0.1685
```

Hence, the polynomial can be factored as:

$$(1 + 0.940z + 0.130z^2) = (1 + 0.7715z)\,(1 + 0.1685z)$$

If you were tempted to obtain the measure of long-run persistence using this polynomial, the following would result:

$$\begin{aligned}\hat{\Lambda}(\infty) &= \frac{(1+0.788)}{(1+0.7715)(1+0.1685)}\\ &= 0.864\end{aligned}$$

However, note that the reciprocal of the first root, that is 0.7715, is very close to the MA(1) coefficient of 0.788, so that there is a near cancellation of roots in the AR and MA polynomials, that is:

$$\frac{(1+0.788L)}{(1+0.7715L)(1+0.1685L)} \approx \frac{1}{(1+0.1685L)}$$

Thus, moving to the ARMA(1, 0) model, the root of the AR(1) polynomial is

```
p = [0.152 1]
r = roots(p)
  = –6.5789
```

As expected, this single root is close to one of the roots of the AR(2) polynomial, confirming the suspicion of a common factor. Finally, note that the persistence measure based on the AR(1, 0) model is calculated as:

$$\begin{aligned}\hat{\Lambda}(\infty) &= \frac{1}{(1+0.152)}\\ &= 0.868\end{aligned}$$

Which differs only slightly from the over-parameterised ARMA(2, 1) model. In effect, the ARMA(2, 1) model has nothing to add over the ARMA(1, 0) model, hence their estimated standard errors and associated statistics differ only marginally.

The estimator of the long-run variance for the preferred model is then given as follows:

$$\begin{aligned}\tilde{\sigma}^2_{lr,y} &= 0.868 \times (0.0137)^2 \\ &= 0.000141 \\ \tilde{\sigma}_{lr,y} &= 0.0119\end{aligned}$$

Q2.4.i Let $y_t = \rho y_{t-1} + u_t$ and $u = (u_1, \ldots, u_T)'$. Show that the long-run variance $\sigma^2_{lr,u}$ of u_t is the limiting sum of all of the elements in the covariance matrix of u; hence, derive $\sigma^2_{lr,u} = \sum_{j=-\infty}^{\infty} \gamma_j$. Note that this set-up is the most familiar form in which the long-run variance is required; for example, it is important in the functional central limit theorem of Chapter 6; and a unit root test will generally not be valid unless an adjustment is made for $\sigma^2_{lr,u} \neq \sigma^2$, see Chapter 8.

Q2.4.ii Show that $S^2_{T,u}$ may be equivalently expressed as:

$$\begin{aligned}S^2_{T,u} &= \left(\sum\nolimits_{t=1}^{T} u_t\right)^2 \\ &= \sum\nolimits_{t=1}^{T} u_t^2 + 2\sum\nolimits_{k=1}^{T-1}\sum\nolimits_{t=k+1}^{T} u_t u_{t-k}\end{aligned}$$

Note that this is an often used form for $S^2_{T,u}$, as shown in Section 2.6.1 on estimating the long-run variance by semi-parametric methods; in that section, the notational set-up was for $\tilde{y}_t$ rather than u_t.

A2.4.i Consider the partial sum process constructed from u_t, $S_t = \sum_{j=1}^{t} u_j$ and the long-run variance $\sigma^2_{lr,u}$ of u_t. Then we have, by definition:

$$\sigma^2_{lr,u} \equiv \lim_{T\to\infty} T^{-1}E(S_T^2)$$

Next write $S_T = i'u$, where $i' = (1, \ldots, 1)$ and $u = (u_1, \ldots, u_T)'$ and, therefore:

$$\begin{aligned}E(S_T^2) &= E(i'u)(i'u) \\ &= E[i'u(u'i)] \text{ because } i'u \text{ is a scalar and, therefore, } i'u = u'i \\ &= i'E(uu')i\end{aligned}$$

$$= (1, \ldots, 1)E\begin{bmatrix} u_1^2 & u_1u_2 & \ldots & u_1u_T \\ u_2u_1 & u_2^2 & \ldots & u_2u_T \\ \vdots & \vdots & \vdots & \vdots \\ u_Tu_1 & u_Tu_2 & \ldots & u_T^2 \end{bmatrix}\begin{pmatrix} 1 \\ 1 \\ \vdots \\ 1 \end{pmatrix} \quad \text{(A2.1)}$$

Thus, note that $E(S_T^2)$ sums all the elements in the covariance matrix of u, of which there are (count the elements on the diagonals) T of the form $E(u_t^2)$, $2(T - 1)$ of the form $E(u_tu_{t-1})$, $2(T - 2)$ of the form $E(u_tu_{t-2})$ and so on until $2E(u_1u_T)$. If the $\{u_t^2\}$ sequence is covariance stationary, then $E(u_t^2) = \sigma_u^2$ (or γ_0 in the terminology of Equation 2.14) and $E(u_tu_{t-k}) = \gamma_k$ and we conclude that:

$$\begin{aligned} E(S_T^2) &= T\sigma_u^2 + 2(T-1)\gamma_1 + 2(T-2)\gamma_2 + \ldots + 2\gamma_{T-1} \\ &= T\sigma_u^2 + 2\sum\nolimits_{j=1}^{T-1}(T - j)\gamma_j \\ T^{-1}E(S_T^2) &= \sigma_u^2 + 2T^{-1}\sum\nolimits_{j=1}^{T-1}(T - j)\gamma_j \\ &= \sigma_u^2 + 2\sum\nolimits_{j=1}^{T-1}\left(1 - \frac{j}{T}\right)\gamma_j \end{aligned}$$

Taking the limit as $T \to \infty$, we obtain:

$$\sigma_{lr,u}^2 \equiv \lim_{T\to\infty} T^{-1}E(S_T^2) = \sigma_u^2 + 2\sum\nolimits_{j=1}^{\infty}\gamma_j$$

Note that in taking the limit it is legitimate to take j as fixed and let the ratio j/T tend to zero. Also as covariance stationarity implies $\gamma_k = \gamma_{-k}$, therefore $\sum_{j=-\infty}^{\infty}\gamma_j = \gamma_0 + 2\sum_{j=1}^{\infty}\gamma_j$ and one may write $\sigma_{lr,u}^2 = \sum_{j=-\infty}^{\infty}\gamma_j$.

A2.5.ii The purpose of this question is to show that a frequently occurring form of S_T^2 is:

$$S_T^2 = \sum\nolimits_{t=1}^{T}u_t^2 + 2\sum\nolimits_{k=1}^{T-1}\sum\nolimits_{t=k+1}^{T}u_tu_{t-k} \quad \text{(A2.2)}$$

Noting that $S_T = \Sigma_{t=1}^{T} u_t$, one can simple multiply out $(\Sigma_{t=1}^{T} u_t)^2$ to obtain (A2.2). Alternatively, refer back to (A2.1) and note that:

$$S_T^2 = (1, \dots, 1)\begin{pmatrix} u_1^2 + u_1u_2 + \dots + u_1u_T \\ u_1u_2 + u_2^2 + \dots + u_2u_T \\ \vdots \\ u_Tu_1 + u_Tu_2 + \dots + u_T^2 \end{pmatrix} \tag{A2.3}$$

$$= \sum_{t=1}^{T} u_t^2 + 2\sum_{k=1}^{T-1}\sum_{t=k+1}^{T} u_t u_{t-k}$$

as required.

3
Dependence and Related Concepts

This chapter introduces a number of concepts and models that have in common the central concern of characterising the dependence in a stochastic process. Intuitively we are interested in whether what happens at time t has been affected by what happened before that time, sometimes referred to the 'memory' of the process. In an economic context, the more usual situation is that stochastic processes have memory to some degree and our interest is in assessing the extent of that memory. This is important for the generalisation of the central limit theorem (CLT), see Chapter 4, Section 4.2.3, and the functional CLT, see Chapter 6, Section 6.6.1.

This chapter is organised as follows. The concept of temporal dependence is introduced in Section 3.1; and the generalisation of weak stationarity to asymptotic weak stationarity, which is particularly relevant for processes with an AR component, is considered in Section 3.2; ergodicity, and particularly ergodicity in the mean are considered in Section 3.3; Section 3.4 collects some results for ARMA models; Section 3.5 introduces two properties of particular interest in economics and finance, which serve to define a martingale sequence and a Markov process, respectively.

3.1 Temporal dependence

The idea of temporal dependence was introduced in Chapter 2; it is, for example, implicit in the concept of persistence and explicit in the autocovariances and long-run variance. In the case of persistence, the impact of a shock is captured by $\omega(L)$ and $\omega(1)$, the coefficients and sum of the coefficients in the MA representation of an ARMA process. One characterisation of a process without dependence is $\omega_j = 0$, $j = 1, \ldots \infty \Rightarrow \omega(1) = 1$; this is

a limiting and rather uninteresting case, but serves to contrast with other cases for which $\omega_j \neq 0$ for some $j \geq 1$ and $\omega(1) \neq 1$. An important way of assessing dependence is through the autocovariances, which is the subject of the next section.

3.1.1 Weak dependence

Reference was made in Chapter 2 to the summability of the autocovariance and autocorrelation sequences for an AR(1) DGP. If $|\rho| < 1$, then the process exhibits temporal dependence, but it is weak enough that the links between elements in the sequence $\{y_t\}$ are 'forgotten' for elements sufficiently far apart. This is indicated by the k-th autocovariance, γ_k, tending to zero sufficiently fast as $k \to \infty$, such that $\lim_{K\to\infty} \sum_{k=0}^{K} |\gamma_k| = c$, a finite constant. This is a condition referred to as absolute summability of the autocovariances; it is usually taken to define a 'short-memory' process. In the case of the AR(1) model, as $\rho \to 1$ then $\lim_{K\to\infty} \sum_{k=0}^{K} |\gamma_k| \to \infty$, and this is a particular form of 'long memory'. If the autocovariances are absolutely summable, then the sequence $\{y_t\}$ is said to be weakly dependent. Also note that absolute summability implies $\sum_{k=0}^{\infty} \gamma_k^2 < \infty$, but not vice-versa (Section 3.4 below for a summary of relevant results).

3.1.2 Strong mixing

As a preliminary to the formality of the condition of strong mixing, consider the straightforward definition of independence given in Chapter 1, Equation (1.42), as it is applied to y_t and y_t shifted by s periods, for example y_{t+s}. In that case y_t and y_{t+s} are independent and dependent, respectively, if:

$$P(y_t \cap y_{t+s}) - P(y_t)P(y_{t+s}) = 0 \tag{3.1a}$$

$$P(y_t \cap y_{t+s}) - P(y_t)P(y_{t+s}) \neq 0 \tag{3.1b}$$

In the latter situation an interesting case to consider is where the extent of the dependence is limited, so that it tends to zero as $s \to \infty$, that is for s 'sufficiently' far from t. Thus, the sequence $\{y_t\}$ may well exhibit short range dependence, but of a form that, in a well-defined sense, becomes less important over time. To this effect, dependence is limited if:

$$\begin{array}{l} |P(y_t \cap y_{t+1}) - P(y_t)P(y_{t+1})| < \alpha_1 < \infty \\ \vdots \qquad\qquad\qquad \vdots \\ |P(y_t \cap y_{t+s}) - P(y_t)P(y_{t+s})| < \alpha_s < \infty \end{array}$$

with the condition that $\alpha_s \to 0$ as $s \to \infty$. This is an example of a more general concept known as strong mixing, which is a way of characterising the extent of dependence in the sequence of y_t. It was introduced by Rosenblatt (1956) and is one of a number of mixing conditions; for a survey see Bradley (2005), who considers eight measures of dependence.

Strong mixing is put into a more formal context as follows. Consider the sequence of random variables $Y = \{y_t\}_{-\infty}^{\infty}$ and let F_t^{t+s} be the σ–*field* generated by the subset sequence $\{y_t\}_{t=1}^{t=1}$, $s \geq 0$. (The process could be started at $t = 0$, without altering the substance of this section.) F_t^{t+s} is the σ–field generated by a particular time series 'portion' of y_t over the period t to $t + s$, $s \geq 0$; for example, $\sigma(y_t)$ for $s = 0$, $\sigma(y_t, y_{t+1})$ for $s = 1$ and so on. Further, $\sigma(y_{t+s}, ..., y_\infty)$ is the σ–field generated by the random variables from y_{t+s} onward and $\sigma(y_{-\infty}, ..., y_t)$ is the σ–field generated by random variables from the start of the process to time t. As we are here dealing with essentially time-ordered sequences, the fields F_t^{t+s} are inclusive or nested, such that $F_t^{t+s} \subseteq F_t^{t+s+1} \subseteq F_t^{t+s+2}$ and so on, known as increasing sub-algebras; this feature of F_t^{t+s} is a property that is relevant for martingale sequences, see Section 3.5.1 below.

Let A denote a set in $F_{-\infty}^{t}$ and B a set in F_{t+s}^{∞}, so the sequences of comparison comprise, respectively, the σ–fields generated by the random variables in the two time series 'portions' $\{y_j\}_{j=-\infty}^{t}$ and $\{y_j\}_{j=t+s}^{\infty}$. Next define the mixing coefficients α_s by:

$$\sup_t \left(\sup_{A \in F_{-\infty}^t, B \in F_{t+s}^{\infty}} (|p(A \cap B) - p(A)p(B)|)\right) \equiv \alpha_s \tag{3.2}$$

The sequence $\{\alpha_j\}_{j=1}^{s}$ is a sequence of 'mixing' coefficients. If $\alpha_s \to 0$ as $s \to \infty$, then $\{y_t\}$ is said to be strong mixing, usually referred to as α-mixing.

The notation 'sup' applied to a set with elements that are real numbers means the supremum or least upper bound: it is the least (smallest) real number that is greater than or equal to every element (real number) in the set. For example, let the set A(ω), with elements a_i, be such that $A(\omega) = (a_i \in \Re : -\infty < c < a_i < b < \infty)$, then $\sup_i A(\omega) = b$; note that b is not actually in A(ω) as defined, so it differs from the maximum value ('max'), although if the sup is in the set, then it is the maximum element.

In the definition of strong mixing, the first 'sup' to consider is the inner one, which looks for the least upper bound across all elements of the sets A and B for fixed t; the second sup then just allows t to vary. The idea is that a sequence is strong mixing or α-mixing, if the (maximum)

dependence as indexed by α_s dies out for s, the time separation indicator, sufficiently large; thus, independence is achieved asymptotically.

Stationary MA(1) and AR(1) processes are generally α-mixing as are more general stationary ARMA(p, q) processes; the 'generally' implies that there are some exceptions. One such was highlighted by Andrews (1983), who showed that an AR(1) process, with $\rho \in (0, ½]$, and stochastic inputs ε_t, including ε_0, generated as Bernouilli random variables, is not strong mixing. What is required additionally is that the distribution of the random variable ε_0 is smooth. The formal condition is stated in Andrews (1983, especially Theorem 1), and is satisfied by a large number of distributions including the normal, exponential, uniform and Cauchy (which has no moments).

The importance of the concept of strong mixing is two-fold in the present context. First, in the context of the (standard) central limit theorem, CLT, see Chapter 4, Section 4.2.3, an interesting question is how much dependence is allowed in the sequence of stochastic inputs, such that the CLT still holds. The CLT can be regarded as providing an 'invariance' principle, in the sense it holds for a broad set of specifications of the marginal and joint distributions of the stochastic inputs. However, notwithstanding its importance elsewhere, what is more important in context is the extension of the CLT to the functional CLT, see Chapter 6, Section 6.6.1, which again provides an invariance principle, but this time one that is relevant to unit root testing.

3.2 Asymptotic weak stationarity

The concept of stationarity, in the forms of strict and weak or covariance stationarity, was introduced in Chapter 1, Section 1.9. A slight variation on weak stationarity (WS), which is particularly relevant for AR models, is asymptotic weak stationarity. The idea is that the process is nonstationary for a finite sample size, T, but becomes stationary as $T \rightarrow \infty$. An example will illustrate the point.

Example 3.1: AR(1) model

Consider the stochastic process generated by the AR(1) model:

$$y_t = \rho y_{t-1} + \varepsilon_t \tag{3.7}$$

where ε_t is a white noise input. Adopt the convention that y_0 (rather than $y_{-\infty}$) is the starting value, where y_0 is a bounded random variable

with $E(y_0) = 0$ and $var(y_0) < \infty$. By repeated (back)substitution using (3.7), the solution in terms of the initial condition and intervening shocks is:

$$y_t = \rho^t y_0 + \sum_{i=1}^{t} \rho^i \varepsilon_{t-i} \tag{3.8}$$

The variance of y_t is given by:

$$\begin{aligned} var(y_t) &= var\left(\rho^t y_0 + \sum_{i=0}^{t-1} \rho^i \varepsilon_{t-i}\right) \\ &= \rho^{2t} var(y_0) + var\left(\sum_{i=0}^{t-1} \rho^i \varepsilon_{t-i}\right) \\ &= \rho^{2t} var(y_0) + \sum_{i=0}^{t-1} \rho^{2i} var(\varepsilon_{t-i}) \\ &= \rho^{2t} var(y_0) + \sigma^2 \sum_{i=0}^{t-1} (\rho^2)^i \end{aligned} \tag{3.9}$$

Notice that neither term in the variance is constant as t varies, both having the feature that the dependence declines as t increases for given $|\rho| < 1$. The second term can be expressed as:

$$\sigma^2 \sum_{i=1}^{t} (\rho^2)^i = \frac{\sigma^2}{(1-\rho^2)} - \rho^{2t} \frac{\sigma^2}{(1-\rho^2)} \tag{3.10}$$

Hence, as $t \to \infty$, for $|\rho| < 1$, only the first term survives. This means that for an arbitrary $var(y_0) < \infty$ (for example, $var(y_0) = 0$ if y_0 is a constant), then $var(y_t)$ is not constant, but it converges to a constant.

Alternatively, note that setting $var(y_0) = \sigma^2(1 - \rho^2)^{-1}$, which is an option in a Monte-Carlo setting to generate the data, is equivalent to starting the process in the infinite past; then $\rho^{2t}\ var(y_0) = \rho^{2t}\rho^2(1 - \rho^2)^{-1}$, so that $var(y_t) = \sigma^2(1 - \rho^2)^{-1}$, which is a constant. This assumption is often preferred for $var(y_0)$ as it generates a weakly stationary process. ♦

3.3 Ensemble averaging and ergodicity

The problem we are usually faced with in practice is an inability to replicate the data generation process, DGP, to produce repeated samples. We observe one particular set of realisations, or sample outcomes, and the question is what can we infer from this one set? For example, suppose we would like to know the means of the variables y_t, $E(y_t)$, $t = 1, \ldots, T$, each of which is a (discrete) random variable with N possible

outcomes at time t, so that the outcome set is $(Y_{t,1}, \ldots, Y_{t,N})$. Collecting the T-length sequence of random variables together gives the stochastic process $Y = (y_1, \ldots, y_s, \ldots, y_T)$.

What we would like to do is replicate the DGP for Y, say R times; the data could then be arranged into a matrix of dimension $R \times T$, so that the t-th column is the vector of R replicated values for the random variable y_t and the r-th row is the vector of one realisation of the sequence of T random variables. The resulting matrix is as follows, where, for example, $Y_t^{(r)}$, is the outcome on the r-th replication of y_t:

$$\begin{bmatrix} Y_1^{(1)} & \cdots & Y_t^{(1)} & \cdots & Y_T^{(1)} \\ \vdots & \vdots & \vdots & \vdots & \vdots \\ Y_1^{(r)} & \cdots & Y_t^{(r)} & \cdots & Y_T^{(r)} \\ \vdots & \vdots & \vdots & \vdots & \vdots \\ Y_1^{(R)} & \cdots & Y_t^{(R)} & \cdots & Y_T^{(R)} \end{bmatrix} \Rightarrow \text{time averages} \begin{pmatrix} \sum_{j=1}^{T} Y_j^{(1)}/T \\ \vdots \\ \sum_{j=1}^{T} Y_j^{(r)}/T \\ \vdots \\ \sum_{j=1}^{T} Y_j^{(R)}/T \end{pmatrix}$$

$$\Downarrow \text{ensemble averages}$$

$$\left(\sum_{i=1}^{R} Y_1^{(i)}/R \quad \cdots \quad \sum_{i=1}^{R} Y_t^{(i)}/R \quad \cdots \quad \sum_{i=1}^{R} Y_T^{(i)}/R \right)$$

In order to estimate the mean of the random variable we could then take the ensemble average, $\hat{\mu}_t(R) = \sum_{r=1}^{R} Y_t^{(r)}/R$; that is the average of the t-th column. This gives an estimator of μ_t that converges to μ_t as $R \to \infty$. However, this option is not generally available (because of the lack of historical replication) and, instead, we take the temporal average, which is the average across a single row of the matrix (the observations actually drawn by 'history'). In practice we only have one such row, say the r-th row, so that $\hat{\mu}_r(T) = \sum_{j=1}^{T} Y_j^{(r)}/T$.

If $\lim_{T\to\infty} \hat{\mu}_r(T) = \mu_t = \mu$, then the random process is said to be ergodic in the mean. The condition $\mu_t = \mu$, for all t, is satisfied for a WS random process. In addition the condition $\lim_{T\to\infty} \text{var}[\hat{\mu}_r(T)] = 0$ is required, which is satisfied for an iid random process and by some less restrictive WS processes. For a development of this argument, with some time series examples, see Kay (2004), who also gives an example where a WS random process is not ergodic in the mean. Although this example has assumed, that y_t is a discrete-time random variable, with a discrete number of outcomes, that was simply to fix ideas; there is nothing essential to the argument in this specification, which carries across to a stochastic process comprising continuous time, continuous random variables.

3.4 Some results for ARMA models

In this section we gather together some useful results (without proof), connected to dependence, and relate them to ARMA processes. In part this just collects together previous results for convenience.

Let be $\{\zeta_k\}_{k=0}^{\infty}$ a sequence of constants, then the sequence is said to be absolutely summable if $\Sigma_{k=0}^{\infty} |\zeta_k| < \infty$. If $k = -\infty, \ldots, \infty$, the definition of absolute summability is altered accordingly through a change in the lower limit. The sequence is said to be square summable if $\Sigma_{k=0}^{\infty} \zeta_k^2 < \infty$.

Absolute summability implies square summability, but not vice-versa:

$$\sum_{k=0}^{\infty} |\zeta_k| < \infty \Rightarrow \sum_{k=0}^{\infty} \zeta_k^2 < \infty$$

If the sequence of autocovariances of y_t is absolutely summable, then y_t is said to be weakly dependent; that is, a process with weak dependence or, equivalently, short memory, necessarily has the property $\Sigma_{k=0}^{\infty} |\gamma_k| < \infty$.

Next suppose that $\{y_t\}$ is generated by a causal ARMA(p, q) process, with MA representation (see Chapter 2, Equation (2.7)) given by:

$$y_t = \sum_{j=0}^{\infty} \omega_j \varepsilon_{t-j}$$

Then, in terms of the MA coefficients and autocovariance coefficients, we have:

1. $\sum_{k=0}^{\infty} |\omega_k| < \infty \Rightarrow \sum_{k=0}^{\infty} \omega_k^2 < \infty$
2. $\sum_{k=0}^{\infty} |\gamma_k| < \infty \Rightarrow \sum_{k=0}^{\infty} \gamma_k^2 < \infty$
3. $\sum_{k=0}^{\infty} |\omega_k| < \infty \Rightarrow \sum_{k=0}^{\infty} \gamma_k^2 < \infty$
4. $\sum_{k=0}^{\infty} |\omega_k| < \infty \Rightarrow \sum_{k=0}^{\infty} |\gamma_k| < \infty$
5. $\sum_{k=0}^{\infty} \omega_k^2 < \infty \Rightarrow y_t$ is covariance stationary
6. $\sum_{k=0}^{\infty} |\omega_k| < \infty \Rightarrow y_t$ is ergodic for the mean and covariance (weakly) stationary by 1 and 5.

3.5 Some important processes

This section introduces two properties that are relevant to stochastic processes that have a particular role in subsequent chapters. The first is the martingale, which is central to financial econometrics, especially its role in the Itô calculus (see Chapters 6 and 7), and to unit root testing

through its role as a prototypical time series process. (Some of the necessary background has already been undertaken in Section 3.1.2.) The second property results is that of a Markov process which, although less significant in the present development, characterises an important feature of some economic time series.

3.5.1 A Martingale

Consider the stochastic process $Y = (y_t, 0 \leq t < \infty)$ and let the sequence of σ–fields $H = (H_0^t, 0 \leq t < \infty)$ represent 'history' to time t, not necessarily just the history of Y. Given the gambling context in which the concept of a martingale arose, the stochastic process is assumed to start at a particular finite point of history, rather than in the infinite past. (The time index assumes that time is discrete and $t \in \Re^+$, but the arguments carry across to $t \in \Re$ and to the continuous-time case replacing y_t by y(t) and so on.)

On the assumption that history is not lost, then $H_0^s \subseteq H_0^t$ for s < t, and *H* is a nested sequence, referred to as a filtration. Y is said to be adapted to the filtration *H* if $\sigma(y_s, ..., y_0) \subseteq H_0^s$ for all $s \leq t$. The natural filtration is the sequence of σ–fields associated with Y, that is $F = (F_0^t, 0 \leq t < \infty)$ where $F_0^t = \sigma(y_t, y_{t-1}, ...)$. Y is adapted to the natural filtration as $\sigma(y_s, ..., y_0) \subseteq F_0^s$. In an economic context, the filtrations can be thought of as information sets and usually no violence is done to the meaning to substitute the information set, say $(y_t, y_{t-1}, ..., y_0)$, for F_0^t; although theoretically, conditional expectations are more soundly based when viewed as being based on σ–fields, rather than information sets, see, for example, Davidson (1994) and Shreve (2004).

A martingale stochastic process is defined with respect to a filtration (or information set). Here we take that filtration to be *F*, although the definition allows other filtrations (for example *H*). Y is a martingale with respect to the filtration *F* if:

i. $E|y_t| < \infty$
ii. Y is adapted to *F*
iii. $E[y_t \mid F_0^s] = y_s$ for all s < t

As the σ–field F_0^s can be generated from $(y_s, y_{s-1}, ...)$ the last condition, in a form that is more familiar (in an economic sense of forming expectations), is:

$$E[y_t \mid y_s, y_{s-1}, \ldots] = y_s \quad \text{for all } s < t \tag{3.11}$$

For example, if s = t – 1, then the martingale property is:

$$E[y_t \mid y_{t-1}, y_{t-2}, \ldots] = y_{t-1} \tag{3.12}$$

For emphasis one might also date the expectation, say E_{t-1} for an expectation formed at time t – 1, thus (3.12) is $E_{t-1}[y_t \mid y_{t-1}, y_{t-2}, \ldots] = y_{t-1}$, but the general understanding is that the date of the formation of the conditional expectation matches the most recent date in the information set. For example, suppose that y_t is the price of a financial asset, then by taking the expectation one period forward (say 'tomorrow'), the expected value of tomorrow's price is the price today: $E[y_{t+1} \mid y_t, y_{t-1}, \ldots, y_0] = y_t$, where the expectation is implicitly dated at t.

Note that $E(y_t \mid y_t, y_{t-1}, \ldots) = E(y_t) = y_t$, as y_t is included in the filtration and so has happened at the time of the information set. Thus, an implication of the martingale condition is that:

$$E[(y_{t+1} - y_t) \mid y_t, y_{t-1}, \ldots] = 0 \tag{3.13}$$

An interpretation of this condition is that viewed as a game, the process generating y_t is said to be fair. No systematic gains or losses will be made if the game is replicated. If y_t is an asset price, and the conditioning set is current information, then the change in price is unpredictable in the mean.

As $\Delta y_{t+1} \equiv y_{t+1} - y_t$, then to focus on the differences (3.13) can be written in general terms as:

$$E[\Delta y_{t+1} \mid y_t, y_{t-1}, \ldots] = 0 \tag{3.14}$$

A sequence of differences with this property is referred to as a martingale difference sequence or MDS. An MDS has serially uncorrelated, but not necessarily independent, stochastic increments. Neither does a MDS require that the variance or higher order moments are constant. A leading example is where the squared levels depend upon past values of y_t, as in an ARCH or GARCH model, so that $E(y_t^2 \mid y_{t-1}, y_{t-2}, \ldots, y_0) = f(F_0^{t-1})$ and the variance is predictable from F_0^{t-1}.

Example 3.2: Partial sum process with –1/+1 inputs

Consider a random variable y_t with two outcomes taking the value –1 with probability p and the value +1 with probability 1 – p, so that $E(y_t) = -1 \times p + (+1) \times (1 - p) = (1 - 2p)$. Let $S_t = \Sigma_{j=1}^{t} y_j$ and the random process

comprise the sequence of S_t, where y_t is stochastically independent of y_s for $t \neq s$. Then $S_t = S_{t-1} + y_t$, which is an asymmetric random walk, but not a martingale unless $p = ½$, as in the coin-tossing game with a fair coin. First, observe that when $p \neq ½$, y_t is not a fair game. The sequence of unconditional expectations is: $E(S_1) = 1-2p$, $E(S_2) = 2(1-2p)$ and so on, with general term $E(S_t) = t(1 - 2p)$; for example if $p = ¼$, then the expected loss on the game at $t = 10$ is 5. Consider the conditional expectation (3.13) applied in this case:

$$\begin{aligned} E_t[(S_{t+1} - S_t) \mid y_t, y_{t-1}, \ldots, y_0] \\ &= E_t[(S_{t+1} - S_t) \mid y_t] \\ &= E_t[y_{t+1} \mid y_t] \\ &= E_t(y_{t+1}) \\ &= (1-2p) \end{aligned} \tag{3.15}$$

The second last equality follows from the assumption of stochastic independence. Note that $(1 - 2p) \neq 0$ unless $p = ½$, so that generally the game is not fair and not a martingale. However, a martingale can be constructed from y_t by making the game fair; that is, by removing the non-zero mean, and to this effect define the random process constructed from the random variables $z_t = S_t - t(1 - 2p)$. Then to assess the fairness of the game consider $E_t[\Delta z_{t+1} \mid z_t]$ where $\Delta z_{t+1} = \Delta S_{t+1} - \Delta(t + 1)(1 - 2p) = y_{t+1} - (1 - 2p)$; hence, $E[y_{t+1} - (1 - 2p) \mid z_t] = (1 - 2p) - (1 - 2p) = 0$, on substituting from (3.15), and the game is fair. ♦

Example 3.3: A psp with martingale inputs

Consider the partial sum process (psp) of example 1.9, so that $S_t = \sum_{j=1}^{t} y_j$ and $Y = (y_1, y_2, \ldots, y_t)$, but assume directly that Y is a martingale with respect to the natural filtration, then $E(S_t^2) = \sum_{j=1}^{t} E(y_j^2)$, a result that had previously been associated with y_j being iid$(0, \sigma^2)$. See question **Q3.3** for an outline of the proof. The impact of this property is that it enables a generalisation of some important theorems in statistics and econometrics to other than iid sequences; for example, the central limit theorem and the weak law of large numbers see Chapter 4, Section 4.2.7. ♦

3.5.2 Markov process

The Markov property characterises the memory of a stochastic process. Consider the stochastic process $Y = (y_t, 0 \leq t < \infty)$, then the Markov

property is:

$$P(y_{t+h} \in A \mid y_{t-s}, y_{t-2}, \ldots, y_0) = P(y_{t+h} \in A \mid y_{t-s}) \tag{3.16}$$

for all $h \geq 0$, $s \geq 0$ and $A \in \Re$. First note that time is of the essence in defining the Markov property. In the language of Markov chains, y_t is the 'state' at time t and the set A is specialised to a particular state, say $y_t = y$. The Markov property is then often stated for the case $h = 0$ and $s = 1$, so that:

$$P(y_t = y \mid y_{t-1}, y_{t-2}, \ldots, y_0) = P(y_t = y \mid y_{t-1}) \tag{3.17}$$

Thus, information prior to $t - 1$ has no influence on the probability that y_t is in state y; there is no memory concerning that part of the information set. Given this property it should not be a surprise that moving the index h forward leads to the same conclusion:

$$P(y_{t+1} = y \mid y_{t-1}, y_{t-2}, \ldots, y_0) = P(y_{t+1} = y \mid y_{t-1}) \tag{3.18}$$

Designating t as the present, then in calculating conditional probabilities about the future, $t + h$ with $h \geq 0$, the present is equivalent to the present *and* the entire history of the stochastic process to that point (the past). The Markov property is easily extended to stochastic processes in continuous time; all that is required is a time index that distinguishes the future, the present and the past, see for example Billingsley (1995, p. 435) and the example of the Poisson process below (Section 3.5.3).

Examples of stochastic processes with the Markov property are the Poisson process and Brownian motion (BM); this is a result due essentially to the independent increments involved in both processes. BM is considered at length in Chapter 7 and the Poisson process is described in the following section.

3.5.3 A Poisson process

A Poisson process is a particular example of a counting process. Typical practical examples of which are 'arrivals' of some form during a continuous interval; for example, the arrival of cars in a store car park on a particular day of the week; the arrival of passengers booking into the departure lounge between 10am and 11am; the calls received by a call centre on a working day between 8am and 5pm; and the number of coal mining disasters per year.

The random variables in a counting process are typically denoted $N(t)$, $t \geq 0$, where the sample space is the set of non-negative integers, $N = (0, 1, 2, 3, \ldots)$. The process starts at zero, so that $N(0) = 0$; thereafter $N(t_2) \geq N(t_1) \geq 0$, for $t_2 > t_1$; and the number of arrivals in the interval $(t_1, t_2]$ is $N(t_2) - N(t_1)$. The question then is what is a reasonable model for the arrivals? One possibility is the Poisson process. This specialises the counting process, adding the condition that the increments are independent; for example, let $\Delta N(t_j) = N(t_j) - N(t_{j-1})$, then $\Delta N(t_j)$ is stochastically independent of $\Delta N(t_k)$ for non-overlapping intervals.

The Poisson probabilities are given by:

$$P[N(t_j) - N(t_{j-1}) = n] = e^{-(\lambda\delta)} \frac{(\lambda\delta)^n}{n!} \tag{3.19}$$

where $\delta = t_j - t_{j-1}$. This is the probability of n arrivals in an interval of length δ. Letting $t_{j-1} = 0$, $t_j = t$ in (3.19) so that $\delta = t$, and noting that $N(0) = 0$, then:

$$P[N(t) = n] = e^{-(\lambda t)} \frac{(\lambda t)^n}{n!} \tag{3.20}$$

In the case that the interval δ is of unit length, $\delta = 1$, then the probability of n arrivals is:

$$P[N(t_j) - N(t_j - 1) = n] = e^{-(\lambda)} \frac{(\lambda)^n}{n!} \tag{3.21}$$

To check that these measures define a probability mass function, note that:

$$\begin{aligned} \sum\nolimits_{n=0}^{\infty} P[N(t_j) - N(t_{j-1}) = n] &= e^{-(\lambda\delta)} \sum\nolimits_{n=0}^{\infty} \frac{(\lambda\delta)^n}{n!} \\ &= e^{-(\lambda\delta)} e^{\lambda\delta} \\ &= 1 \end{aligned} \tag{3.22}$$

where the second line follows from the result that $\lim_{N\to\infty} \sum\nolimits_{n=0}^{N} \frac{x^n}{n!} = e^x$. The sum of probabilities is unity and each is ≥ 0 as required.

Moreover, the expected value $E[N(t_j) - N(t_{j-1})] = \lambda\delta$:

$$
\begin{aligned}
E[N(t_j) - N(t_{j-1})] &= \sum_{n=1}^{\infty} nP[N(t_j) - N(t_{j-1}) = n] \\
&= e^{-(\lambda\delta)} n \sum_{n=1}^{\infty} \frac{(\lambda\delta)^n}{n!} \\
&= e^{-(\lambda\delta)} (\lambda\delta) \sum_{n=1}^{\infty} \frac{(\lambda\delta)^{n-1}}{(n-1)!} \\
&= e^{-(\lambda\delta)} (\lambda\delta) e^{(\lambda\delta)} \\
&= \lambda\delta
\end{aligned} \tag{3.23}
$$

A special case of this result obtains on taking $\delta = t$, in which case:

$$E[N(t)] = \lambda t \tag{3.24}$$

A Poisson process can be viewed as the limit of repeated independent Bernoulli trials, in which an event, in this case an arrival, either does or does not occur, assigning the values 1 and 0, with probabilities p and 1 – p, respectively; the limit is then obtained by subdividing an interval of time of δ units into smaller and smaller non-overlapping subintervals; an arrival or non-arrival in one subinterval has no effect on occurrences in other time intervals, so that the increments are independent. The random variable, N, counting the number of arrivals in the time interval, has approximately a binomial distribution given by:

$$P[N = n] \approx {}_mC_n p^n (1 - p)^{m-n} \tag{3.25}$$

where $\approx$ means 'approximately' and ${}_mC_n$ is the number of ways of choosing n from m without regard to order, see Chapter 5, Section 5.3. The interval of time is δ units, which is divided into m subintervals of length Δt, so that $m\Delta t = \delta$. The probability of an arrival, p, in each subinterval is the product of the arrival rate λ and the length of time, Δt, so that $p = \lambda\Delta t = \lambda\delta/m$. Making these substitutions, (3.25) is:

$$P[N = n] \approx {}_mC_n \left(\frac{\lambda\delta}{m}\right)^n \left(1 - \frac{\lambda\delta}{m}\right)^{m-n} \tag{3.26}$$

Taking the limit of (3.26) as m increases, so that Δt decreases, results in:

$$\lim_{m\to\infty}\left({}_{m}C_{n}\left(\frac{\lambda\delta}{m}\right)^{n}\left(1-\frac{\lambda\delta}{m}\right)^{m-n}\right) = e^{-(\lambda\delta)}\frac{(\lambda\delta)^{n}}{n!} \tag{3.27}$$

see, for example, Larson (1974, p. 145) and Ross (2003, p. 32). The right-hand-side of (3.27) is exactly the Poisson probability P[N = n], as in (3.19).

A martingale is obtained from a Poisson process in the same manner as in example 3.3, that is by subtracting the expected value of the underlying random variable; thus, let P(t) = N(t) – λt, P(s) = N(s) – λs, s < t and F_0^s be the σ–field generated by {N(r), 0 ≤ r ≤ s}, then:

$$E[P(t)\,|\,F_0^s] = P(s) \tag{3.28}$$

for a proof, see Brzeźniak and Zastawniak (1999, p. 166).

A Poisson process also has the Markov property, and thus is an example of a Markov process, a result due to the independence of the increments, for a proof see Billingsley (1995, p. 436).

Example 3.4: Poisson process, arrivals at a supermarket checkout

Assume that the number of arrivals at a checkout in a one minute interval is a Poisson process with expected value = λ = 2 (on average two customers per minute); then in a unit interval, the Poisson probabilities are given by:

$$P[N(t_j) - N(t_j - 1) = n] = e^{-2}\frac{2^n}{n!} \tag{3.29}$$

A bar chart of these probabilities is shown in Figure 3.1a and the corresponding (cumulative) distribution function is shown in Figure 3.1b. The cumulative arrivals for the first ten minutes are shown in Figure 3.2. This figure also serves to illustrate a particular sample path, or path function, of the Poisson process, N: (N(t), 0 ≤ t ≤ 10). The path is right continuous and it jumps at the discrete points associated with the positive integers. If the particular element of the sample space that was realised for this illustration was realised exactly in a second replication, the whole sample path would be repeated, otherwise the sample paths

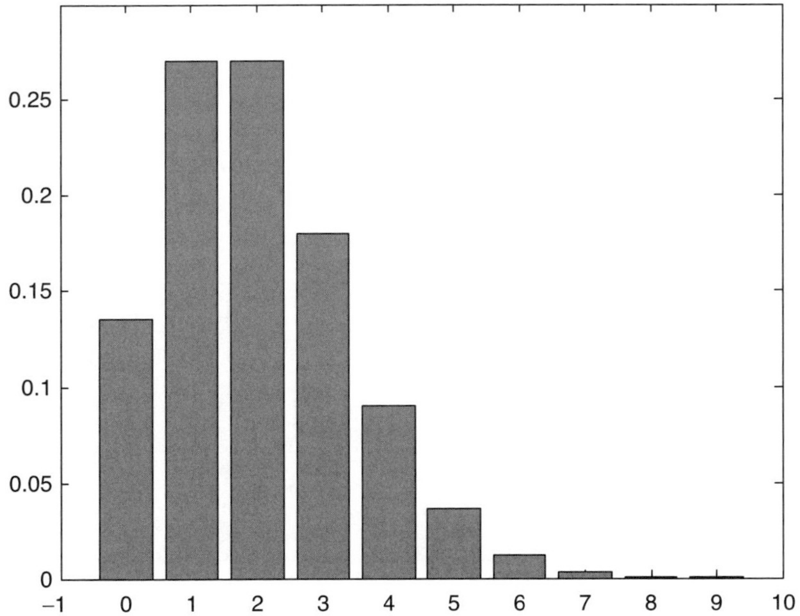

Figure 3.1a Poisson probabilities for λ = 2

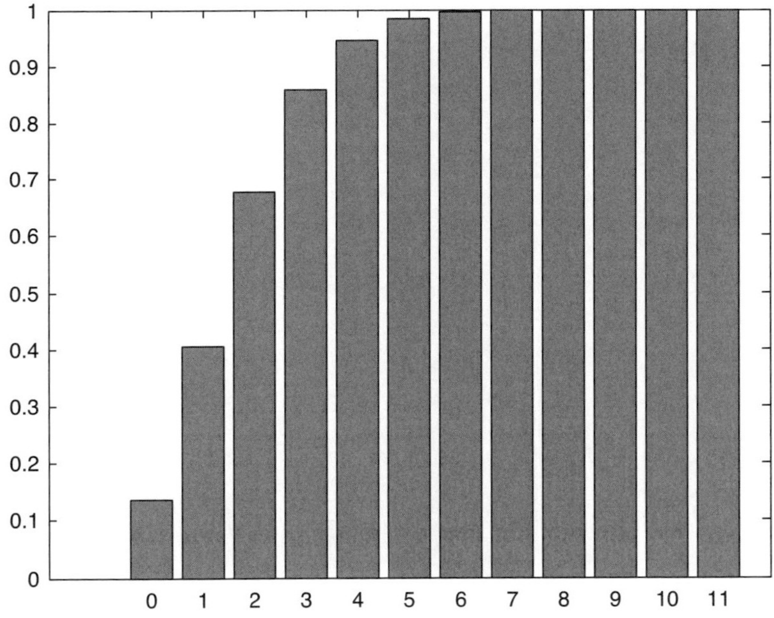

Figure 3.1b Distribution function for Poisson process, λ = 2

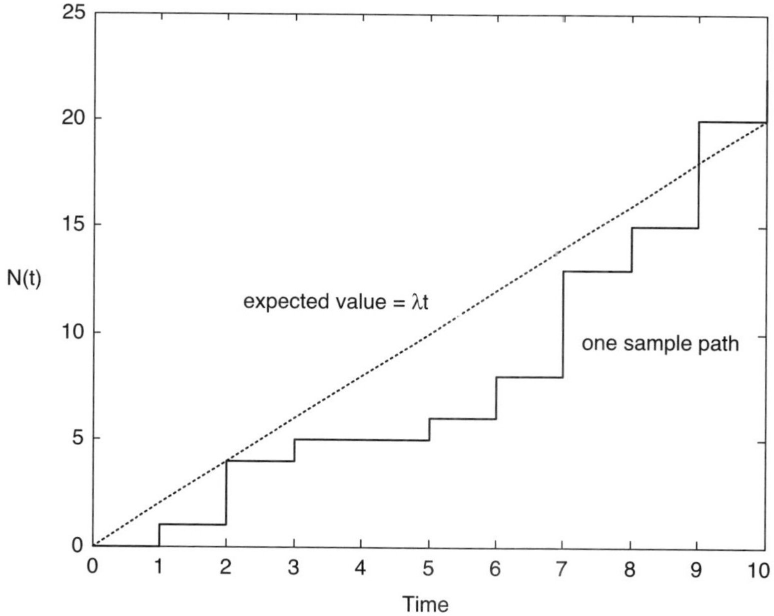

Figure 3.2 A Poisson process: The first ten minutes of arrivals

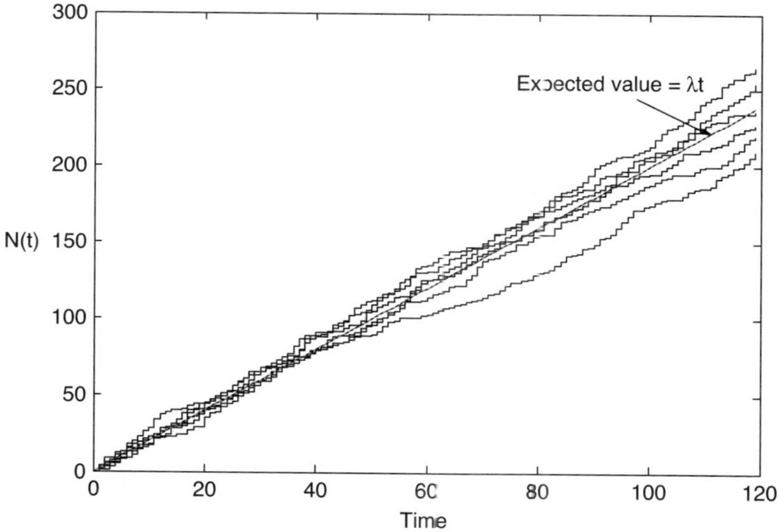

Figure 3.3 A Poisson process: Some sample paths

differ, showing that there is a distribution of sample paths. To make this point, a number of sample paths for a two hour period are shown in Figure 3.3; these are obtained by taking draws from the Poisson distribution with probabilities given by (3.19). In this example, the expected value of N(t) is $\lambda t = 2t$ and that function is overlaid on Figures 3.2 and 3.3. ♦

3.6 Concluding remarks

The concepts of the extent of dependence and strong mixing are quite technical but, intuitively, capture the idea that events separated sufficiently far in time, for example y_t and y_{t+s} for $s > 0$, become unrelated. For a survey of mixing concepts see Bradley (2005); Withers (1984) considers the relationship between linear processes and strong mixing; and for an application in the context of unit root tests, see Phillips (1987). For the connection between mixing sequences and martingale difference sequences at an advanced level, see Hall and Heyde (1980).

Martingales and Markov processes are an essential part of the ideas of probability and stochastic processes. A martingale for the variable y_t has the property that the expected value of y_t, $E(y_t)$, conditional on the history of the variable to $t - 1$, is y_{t-1}; $E(y_t)$ is thus not dependent on y_{t-s}, $s > 1$. A stochastic process with the Markov property satisfies $P(y_t = y \mid y_{t-1}, y_{t-2}, \ldots, y_0) = P(y_t = y \mid y_{t-1})$ so that it is sufficient to condition on y_{t-1} rather than the complete history of y_t. For a development of martingales see Jacod and Protter (2004, chapters 24–27), Brzeźniak and Zastawniak (1999, chapters 3 and 4) and Fristedt and Gray (1997). At a more advanced level see Hall and Heyde (1980). An econometric perspective is provided by Davidson (1994), who covers the concepts of dependence, mixing and martingales at a more advanced level; and Billingsley (1995, chapter 6, section 35) gives a similarly advanced coverage of martingales. McCabe and Tremayne (1993, chapter 11) consider dependent sequences and martingales.

Questions

Q3.1 Consider an ARMA(1, 1) model: $(1 - \phi_1 L)y_t = (1 + \theta_1 L)\varepsilon_t$, obtain $\omega(L)$ and determine the conditions for absolute summability and weak stationarity.

A3.1 Assume that the ARMA(1, 1) model is causal, thus:

$$\begin{aligned} y_t &= (1 - \phi_1 L)^{-1}(1 + \theta_1 L)\varepsilon_t \\ &= (1 + \phi_1 L + \phi_1 L^2 + \ldots)^{-1}(1 + \theta_1 L)\varepsilon_t \\ &= \sum\nolimits_{j=0}^{\infty} \omega_j L^j \varepsilon_t \end{aligned}$$

This model was considered in example 2 2, where it was shown that $\omega_j = \phi_1^{j-1} (\phi_1 + \theta_1)$ for $j \geq 1$, thus making the substitutions:

$$\begin{aligned} \sum\nolimits_{j=0}^{\infty} |\omega_j| &= 1 + \sum\nolimits_{j=1}^{\infty} |\phi_1^{j-1}(\phi_1 + \theta_1)| \\ &= 1 + \sum\nolimits_{j=1}^{\infty} |\phi_1^{j-1}||(\phi_1 + \theta_1)| && \text{using } |ab| = |a||b| \\ &= 1 + \sum\nolimits_{j=0}^{\infty} |\phi_1^{j}||(\phi_1 + \theta_1)| \\ &= 1 + |(\phi_1 + \theta_1)| \sum\nolimits_{j=0}^{\infty} |\phi_1^{j}| && \text{as } |(\phi_1 + \theta_1)| \text{ is a constant} \\ &= 1 + \frac{|(\phi_1 + \theta_1)|}{1 - |\phi_1|} && \text{if } |\phi_1| < 1 \\ &= \frac{1 - |\phi_1| + |(\phi_1 + \theta_1)|}{1 - |\phi_1|} \\ &= \frac{1 - |\phi_1| + \sqrt{(\phi_1 + \theta_1)^2}}{1 - |\phi_1|} && \text{using } |a + b| = \sqrt{(a + b)^2} \end{aligned}$$

Hence, $\Sigma_{j=0}^{\infty} | \omega_j | = c < \infty$ for $| \phi_1 | < 1$. This is the same result that obtains for the AR(1, 0) model. The presence of the MA(1) coefficient (and more generally the MA(q) coefficients), just serves to scale the magnitude of the response.

Note that if $|(\phi_1 + \theta_1)| = (\phi_1 + \theta_1) > 0$ and $\phi_1 > 0$, then:

$$\begin{aligned} \sum\nolimits_{j=0}^{\infty} |\omega_j| &= \frac{1 - \phi_1 + \phi_1 + \theta_1}{1 - \phi_1} \\ &= \frac{1 + \theta_1}{1 - \phi_1} = \omega(1) \end{aligned}$$

Further, using results 3) and 4) from Section 3.4, y_t is ergodic and weakly (or covariance) stationary; the qualification asymptotic may be necessary depending on how the initial value is determined in starting the AR(1) part of the process, see Section 3.2.

Q3.2 Consider the ARMA(1, 1) model of the previous question and obtain the condition for square summability. Obtain the unconditional variance of y_t, σ_y^2, and show that it is a finite constant if $|\phi_1| < 1$; contrast σ_y^2 with the long-run variance $\sigma_{lr,y}^2$ (see Section 2.6.2).

A3.2 In this case, we are interested in:

$$\begin{aligned}
\sum\nolimits_{j=0}^{\infty} \omega_j^2 &= 1 + \sum\nolimits_{j=1}^{\infty} [\phi_1^{j-1}(\phi_1 + \theta_1)]^2 \\
&= 1 + (\phi_1 + \theta_1)^2 \sum\nolimits_{j=1}^{\infty} \phi_1^{2(j-1)} \\
&= 1 + (\phi_1 + \theta_1)^2 \sum\nolimits_{j=0}^{\infty} \phi_1^{2j} \\
&= 1 + \frac{(\phi_1 + \theta_1)^2}{(1 - \phi_1^2)} \\
&= \frac{(1 + \phi_1^2) + (\phi_1 + \theta_1)^2}{(1 - \phi_1^2)} \\
&= \frac{(1 - \phi_1^2 + \phi_1^2 + \theta_1^2 + 2\phi_1\theta_1)}{(1 - \phi_1^2)} \\
&= \frac{(1 + \theta_1^2 + 2\phi_1\theta_1)}{(1 - \phi_1^2)}
\end{aligned}$$

The unconditional variance of y_t is therefore:

$$\begin{aligned}
\sigma_y^2 &= \sigma^2 \sum\nolimits_{j=0}^{\infty} \omega_j^2 \\
&= \sigma^2 \frac{(1 + \theta_1^2 + 2\phi_1\theta_1)}{(1 - \phi_1^2)}
\end{aligned}$$

which is a finite constant provided $|\phi_1| < 1$. As to the long-run variance recall from Chapter 2, Section 2.6.2, that:

$$\begin{aligned}
\sigma_{lr,y}^2 &= \sigma^2 \sum\nolimits_{j=0}^{\infty} \omega_j^2 \\
&= \sigma^2 \omega(1)^2 \\
&= \frac{(1 + \theta_1)^2}{(1 - \phi_1)^2} \\
&= \frac{(1 + 2\theta_1 + \theta_1{}^2)}{(1 - \phi_1)^2}
\end{aligned}$$

(Extension: note that it is not necessarily the case that $\sigma^2_{lr,y} > \sigma^2_y$; hence obtain the conditions for this inequality to hold.)

Q3.3 Let Y = $(y_1, y_2, ..., y_T)$ be a martingale with respect to the natural filtration; and assume that y_t has a finite second moment. Show that $E(S_T^2) = \sum_{t=1}^{T} E(y_t^2)$.

A3.3 Note that $S_T = \sum_{t=1}^{T} y_t$, hence:

$$\begin{aligned} E(S_T^2) &= \text{var}\left(\sum_{t=1}^{T} y_t\right) \\ &= \sum_{t=1}^{T} E(y_t^2) + 2\sum_{k=1}^{T-1}\sum_{t=k+1}^{T} E(y_t y_{t-k}) \end{aligned}$$

As to the last term, the application of three rules gives the result that $E(y_t y_s) = 0$, $s = t - k$, $k > 0$:

$$\begin{aligned} E(y_t y_s) &= E(S_t - S_{t-1})(S_s - S_{s-1}) \\ &= E\{E[(S_t - S_{t-1})(S_s - S_{s-1}) \mid F_0^{t-1}]\} \\ &= E[(S_s - S_{s-1})E[(S_t - S_{t-1}) \mid F_0^{t-1}] \\ &= E(S_t - S_{t-1})[E\{(S_t \mid F_0^{t-1}) - E(S_{t-1} \mid F_0^{t-1})\} \mid F_0^{t-1}] \\ &= 0 \end{aligned}$$

As to the detail, the second line follows by the law of iterated expectations (see Chapter 1). Let w be a random variable and F a conditioning field, then $E[E(w \mid F)] = E(w)$. To apply this result let $w = (S_s - S_{s-1})(S_t - S_{t-1})$ and $F = F_0^{t-1}$.

The third line is an application of 'taking out what is known'. The general result is $E(xz \mid F) = xE(z \mid F)$ where x and z are random variables and x is F-measurable. Set $x = (S_s - S_{s-1})$ and $z = (S_t - S_{t-1})$, then applying the general result noting that $s < t$, gives:

$$E[(S_s - S_{s-1})(S_t - S_{t-1}) \mid F_0^{t-1}] = (S_s - S_{s-1})E[(S_t - S_{t-1}) \mid F_0^{t-1}]$$

The last line follows because $E(S_t \mid F_0^{t-1}) = S_{t-1}$ from the defining condition of a martingale, and $E(S_{t-1} \mid F_0^{t-1}) = S_{t-1}$ as F_0^{t-1} includes S_{t-1}, hence $E(S_1 \mid F_0^{t-1}) - E(S_{t-1} \mid F_0^{t-1}) = S_{t-1} - S_{t-1} = 0$.

The martingale result is, therefore, $E(S_t^2) = \sum_{j=1}^{t} E(y_j^2)$. The importance of the result is that it does not require that the y_j are iid. This answer has drawn on McCabe and Tremayne (1993) and Hayashi (2000).

4
Concepts of Convergence

Introduction

The idea of convergence is an important one in econometrics. Quite often it is not possible to determine the finite sample properties of, for example, the mean or distribution, of a random variable, such as an estimator or a test statistic; but in the limit, as the sample size increases, these properties are more easily determined. There is, however, more than one concept of convergence and different concepts may be applicable in different circumstances.

The matter of convergence is more complex in the case of a sequence of random variables compared to a nonstochastic sequence, since a random variable has multiple outcomes. There are some intuitively appealing concepts of convergence; for example, perhaps we could require two random variables x_n and x to be exactly the same in the limit, so that the probability of an event $\omega \in \Omega$ in the probability space of the random variable x_n is exactly the same as for the random variable x, and this holds for all ω. This would require that x_n and x are defined on the same probability space. Overall, this is a stringent condition for convergence and some lesser form of convergence may well be sufficient for practical purposes.

Starting at the other end of the spectrum, we could ask what is the minimum form of convergence that would be helpful for a test statistic to satisfy in the event that the finite sample distribution is analytical intractable or difficult to use. In this case what it would be helpful to know is: what distribution does the distribution of x_n, the n-th random variable in a sequence or 'family' of random variables, converge to in the limit, if one exists? Even when we know the finite sample distribution, the limit distribution may be easier to use, an example being the

normal approximation to the binomial distribution, which works well even for moderate n when p and q are reasonably equal. Convergence in distribution turns out to be the weakest form of convergence that is sensible and useful. Another form of convergence that is in widespread use, which is stronger than convergence in distribution, is convergence in probability which gives rise to the much-used 'plim' notation; other concepts of convergence include almost sure convergence and convergence in mean square.

This chapter is organised as follows. Our central interest is in a sequence of random variables, for example, a test statistic indexed by the sample size, but, by way of introduction, Section 4.1 starts the chapter with a brief review of convergence concepts for a (nonstochastic) sequence of real numbers determined by a function of an index that may be increased without limit. Section 4.2 moves the concepts on to stochastic sequences and different concepts of convergence; this section includes an introduction to related results, such as the continuous mapping theorem (CMT), the central limit theorem (CLT), Slutsky's theorem and the weak and strong laws of large numbers (WLLN and SLLN, respectively). A concept related to convergence (whether, for example, in distribution or probability) is the order of convergence which, loosely speaking, is a measure of how quickly sequences converge (if they do); again this idea can be related to nonstochastic or stochastic sequences and both are outlined in Section 4.3. Finally, the convergence of a stochastic process as a whole that is viewed not as the n-th term in a sequence, but of the complete trajectory, is considered in Section 4.4.

4.1 Nonstochastic sequences

Let $\{x_j\}_{j=1}^n$ be a sequence of real numbers. Then the limit of the sequence is x if,

$$\text{for every } \varepsilon > 0, \text{ there is an integer N, such that:} \quad |x_n - x| < \varepsilon \text{ for } n > N \tag{4.1}$$

This is usually written as $\lim_{n\to\infty} x_n = x$ or $x_n \to x$; or equivalently $\lim_{n\to\infty} |x_n - x| = 0$, see, for example, Pryce (1973).

Just as we may define a sequence of real numbers $\{x_j\}_{j=1}^n$, we may define a sequence of scalar functions. Let $f_j(x)$ be a scalar function that maps $x \in S$ into the real line, $\Re$, that is $f_j(x) : S \to \Re$, then $\{f_j(x)\}_{j=1}^n$ is the associated sequence of such functions.

The sequence $\{f_j(x)\}$converges pointwise to f(x) if,

$$\text{for every } \varepsilon > 0 \text{ and every } x \in S, \text{ there is an integer N: such that } |f_n(x) - f(x)| < \varepsilon \text{ for } n > N \tag{4.2}$$

Example 4.1: Some sequences

The following examples illustrate the two concepts of convergence.

Sequences of real numbers:

Example 1: $x_j = j$ does not converge;
Example 2: $x_j = 1/j$ this is the sequence 1, $1/2$, $1/3$, which converges to $x = 0$;
Example 3: $x_j = (-1)^j$ this is the sequence –1, 1, –1,..., which does not converge;
Example 4: $x_j = (-1)^{2j}$ this is the sequence 1, 1, 1, 1,..., which does converge to 1.

Sequence of scalar functions:

Example 5: $f_j(x) = x^j$ converges to $f(x) = 0$ for $|x| < 1$, converges to $f(x) = 1$ for $x = 1$; alternates +1, –1 for $x = -1$; does not converge for $|x| > 1$. ♦

Given the sequence $\{x_j\}_{j=1}^n$, then another sequence can be obtained as the partial sum process, psp, of the original terms; that is $\{S_j\}_{j=1}^n$ where $S_j = \sum_{i=1}^j x_i$. Convergence then refers to the property in terms of S_n and convergence implies that $\lim_{n\to\infty} S_n = S$. The corresponding sequence of the partial sums does not necessarily have the same convergence property as its component elements. Consider some of the previous examples (with an S to indicate the sum).

Example 4.2: Some sequences of partial sums

Example 1S: $S_n = \sum_{j=1}^n j$ does not converge

Example 2S: $S_n = \sum_{j=1}^n (1/j)$ does not converge

Example 5S: $S_n = \sum_{j=1}^n x^j$ converges to $x/(1 - x)$ for $|x| < 1$, but does not converge for $|x| \geq 1$

Whilst it is obvious that example 2 converges, it may not be obvious that its partial sum analogue, example 2S, does not converge. The reader may recognise this as a harmonic series; the proof of its divergence has

an extensive history not pursued here. The interested reader is referred to Kifowit and Stamps (2006), who examine 20 proofs on divergence! Also note that in examples 5 and 5S, whilst $x_j = x^j$ converges for x = 1, convergence of its psp requires $|x| < 1$. ♦

4.2 Stochastic sequences

More generally, it is random rather than deterministic sequences that will be of interest, so $\{x_j\}_{j=1}^n$ is now interpreted as a sequence of random variables. A more explicit notation that emphasises this point is $\{x_j(\omega)\}_{j=1}^n$ but, generally, the simpler notation will be adequate. In practice, the sequence of interest is often that of the partial sum process of x_j, that is $\{S_j\}_{j=1}^n$, or a scaled version of this sequence. When it is the case that time is of the essence, then the time series notation $\{S_t\}_{t=1}^T$ will be preferred. In the case of random sequences or sequences of random functions then, as noted in the introduction to this section, this raises some interesting questions about what convergence could be taken to mean when there is a possibly infinite number of outcomes. Four concepts of convergence are outlined in this section, together with related results.

4.2.1 Convergence in distribution (weak convergence): $\Rightarrow_D$

Consider the sequence of random variables $\{x_j\}_{j=1}^n$, with a corresponding sequence of distribution functions given by $\{F_j(X)\}_{j=1}^n$. Convergence in distribution, or weak convergence, is the property that $F_n(X)$ converges to F(X); that is:

$$\lim_{n\to\infty} F_n(X) = F(X) \tag{4.3}$$

or, in shorthand, $F_n(X) \Rightarrow_D F(X)$. (The symbol $\Rightarrow$ is sometimes used, but this notation is reserved here for 'implication', that is $A \Rightarrow B$, means A implies B.)

The weak convergence condition is qualified by adding that it holds for each X that is a continuity point of F(.); if there is a point, or points, of discontinuity in F(.), (4.3) is not required to hold at those points – broadly they are irrelevant (see example 14.4 of Billingsley, 1995). F(X) is referred to as the limiting distribution of the sequence. Although this form of convergence concerns the limiting distribution of x_n, it is sometimes written in terms of the random variables as $x_n \Rightarrow_D x$ (or an equivalent notation), which should be taken as having the same meaning as (4.3).

That the definition (4.3) requires comment is evident on considering the nature of a distribution function, which could, for example, involve an infinity of values of X. The condition can equivalently be stated as:

$$\lim_{n\to\infty} P(x_n \leq X) = P(x \leq X) \tag{4.4}$$

for every continuity point X. Points of discontinuity in the limit distribution function are excepted so that, for example, discrete limiting distributions are permitted, see McCabe and Tremayne (1993, chapter 3). As $P(x \leq X) \in [0, 1]$, the convergence of a distribution concerns the evaluation of 'closeness' in a sense that is familiar except, perhaps, for the idea that the evaluation is over a (possibly infinite) range of values (or points).

In the context of convergence in distribution, the probability spaces of x_n and x need not be the same, unlike the concepts of convergence in probability and convergence almost surely that are considered below, as the following example shows.

Example 4.3: Convergence to the Poisson distribution

A well-known example of this kind, referred to in Chapter 3, Section 3.5.3, is the case of n Bernoulli trials, where each trial results in a 0 ('failure') or a 1 ('success'). The probability space is the triple (Ω_n, F_n, P_n). In n trials, the sample space, Ω_n, is the space of all n-tuples of 0s and 1s, $\omega = (\omega_1, ..., \omega_n)$, where ω_j is either 0 or 1; the σ–field, F_n, is the field of all subsets of Ω_n; and the probability measure P_n assigns probability to each ω, comprising k successes and n – k failures in a sequence, as $p_n^k(1 - p_n)^{n-k}$, where $p_n = \lambda/n$. (The probability measure is as in Equations (3.25) and (3.26), with an appropriate change of notation and $\delta = 1$). Let the random variable $x_n(\omega)$, or simply x_n, be the number, k, of successes in n trials, that is the number of 1s in a sequence of length n; then the probability mass function is that of the binomial distribution:

$$P(x_n(\omega) = k) = {}_nC_k p_n^k (1 - p_n)^{n-k} \tag{4.5}$$

However, we have already seen that as $n \to \infty$, with $p_n = \lambda/n$, the probabilities in (4.5) converge to those of the Poisson distribution, namely:

$$\lim_{n\to\infty} P(x_n(\omega) = k) = e^{-(\lambda)} \frac{(\lambda)^k}{k!} \tag{4.6}$$

The probability space for this random variable is that of a Poisson random variable. Thus, the Poisson distribution is the limiting distribution of a sequence of binomial distributed random variables; see Billingsley (1995, p. 330) and McCabe and Tremayne (1993, p. 53). (Note that in making the notational translation to Chapter 3, Section 3.5.3, use n for m and k for n.) ♦

4.2.2 Continuous mapping theorem, CMT

An important result in the context of convergence in distribution is the continuous mapping theorem, which states that:

$$\text{if } x_n \Rightarrow_D x \text{ and } P(x \in D_g) = 0, \text{ then } g(x_n) \Rightarrow_D g(x) \tag{4.7}$$

where g(.) is a continuous function and D_g is the set of discontinuity points of g(.). For an elaboration, see Billingsley (1995, Theorem 25.7) and Davidson (1994 Theorem 22.11, 2000, Theorem 3.1.3). A familiar example from elementary texts is when $x \sim N(0, 1)$, and $g(x) = x^2$, then g(x) has the $\chi^2(1)$ distribution; thus, if x_n is asymptotically normal, then x_n^2 is asymptotically $\chi^2(1)$. An analogous result holds for convergence in probability, see Section 4.2.6.

4.2.3 Central limit theorem (CLT)

The CLT is a particularly important example of convergence in distribution. Let $\{x_j\}_{j=1}^n$ be a sequence of iid random variables with constant mean and constant variance, that is, $E(x_j) = \mu_j = \mu$ and $\sigma^2(x_j) = \sigma_j^2 = \sigma_x^2$. Next consider $S_n = \Sigma_{j=1}^n x_j$, which defines another sequence $\{S_j\}_{j=1}^n$; S_n will have a mean of $n\mu$ and variance of $n\sigma_x^2$ (by the iid assumption). S_n is then standardised by subtracting its mean and dividing by its standard deviation:

$$z_n = \frac{S_n - n\mu}{\sigma_x \sqrt{n}} \tag{4.8}$$

By the central limit theorem, the distribution function of z_n, say $F(Z_n)$, tends to that of the standard normal as $n \to \infty$; thus, $F(Z_n) \Rightarrow_D \Phi(Z)$, where the latter is the (cumulative) distribution function of the standard normal random variable, with zero mean and unit variance, *N*(0, 1). Sometimes this convergence is written in terms of z_n although, strictly, it applies to the cdf of z_n; nevertheless, the same meaning is to be attributed to $z_n \Rightarrow_D z$, where $z \sim N(0, 1)$.

This result in Equation (4.8) can also be stated as $\sqrt{n}(\bar{x}_n - \mu) \Rightarrow N(0, \sigma_x^2)$, where $\bar{x}_n = S_n/n$, with the interpretation that the distribution of the average, $\bar{x}_n$, converges to a random variable that is normally distributed with mean μ and variance σ_x^2/n, even though the component random variables are not normally distributed.

The assumption that $\{x_j\}_{j=1}^n$ is a sequence of iid random variables is sufficient rather than necessary for the CLT; for example, the CLT still goes through if $\{x_j\}_{j=1}^n$ is a martingale difference sequence, see Billingsley (1995, p. 475). For generalisations and references, the interested reader is referred to Merlevède, Peligrad and Utev (2006) and to Ibragimov and Linnik (1971) for the extension to strict stationarity and strong mixing.

Example 4.4: Simulation example of CLT

In these examples, the sequence of interest is $\{S_i\}_{i=0}^n$, where $S_j = \sum_{j=1}^n x_j$, and the x_j are drawn from non-normal distributions. Specifically, there are two cases for the distribution of x_j:

case 1: x_j is a random variable with outcomes +1 and –1 with equal probability;

case 2: x_j is a random variable uniformly distributed over [–1, +1].

The variance of $x_j = 1$ for case 1, so that the appropriate standardisation is $z_n = S_n / \sqrt{n}$. The variance of a uniformly distributed random variable distributed over [a, b] is $\sigma_{unif}^2 = (b - a)^2/12$, so the standardisation for case 2 is $z_n = S_n / (\sigma_{unif} \sqrt{n})$; for the simulations, b = +1 and a = –1, so that x_j is centred on 0 and $\sigma_{unif}^2 = 1/3$. The CLT applies to both of these distributions; that is notwithstanding the non-normal inputs, in the limit $z_n \Rightarrow_D z$, where $z \sim N(0, 1)$.

Convergence in distribution (that is of the cdfs) implies that the corresponding pdfs converge when they exist, as in this example. The results are illustrated for n = 20 and n = 200, with 10,000 replications used to obtain the empirical pdfs. Case 1 is shown in Figure 4.1 and case 2 in Figure 4.2; in each case, the familiar bell-shaped pdf of the standardised normal distribution is overlaid on the graph. Considering case 1 first, the convergence is evident as n increases; for n = 20, the empirical pdf is close to the normal pdf and becomes closer as the sample size is increased to n = 200. The situation is similar for case 2, although the effect of the non-normal inputs is more evident for n = 20; however, the CLT is working clearly for n = 200. ♦

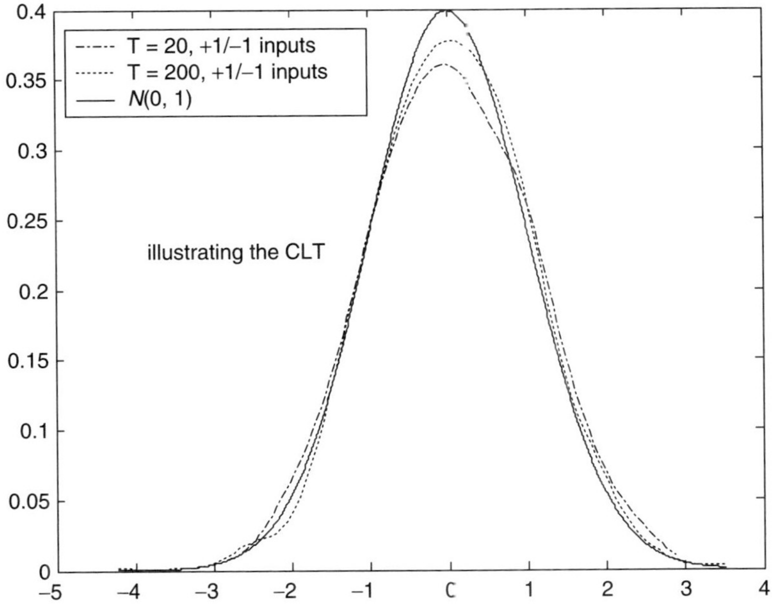

Figure 4.1 Density estimates, +1, –1 inputs

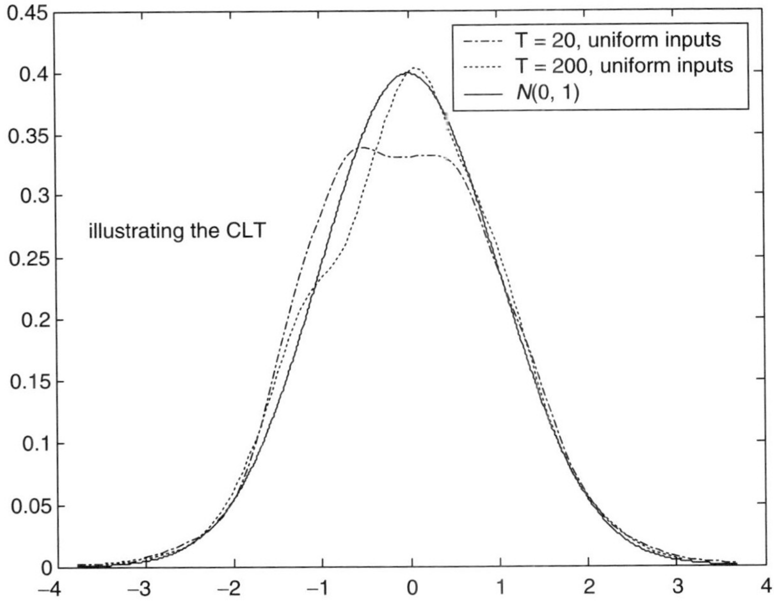

Figure 4.2 Density estimates, uniform inputs

4.2.4 Convergence in probability: $\rightarrow_p$

Consider the sequence of random variables $\{x_1\}_{j=1}^{n}$ and the single random variable x defined on the same probability space. The random variable x_n is said to converge in probability to x if, for all $\varepsilon > 0$, the following condition holds:

$$\lim_{n\rightarrow\infty} P(|x_n - x| < \varepsilon) = 1 \text{ or, equivalently,}$$
$$\lim_{n\rightarrow\infty} P(|x_n - x| \geq \varepsilon) = 0 \tag{4.9}$$

This is written $x_n \rightarrow_p x$, or some variant thereof; a common shorthand uses the 'plim' terminology, so that plim $x_n = x$. It turns out to be helpful to define the random variable w, such that $w \equiv |x_n - x|$, so that the condition (4.9) can be stated as:

$$\lim_{n\rightarrow\infty} P(w < \varepsilon) = 1 \text{ or, equivalently, } \lim_{n\rightarrow\infty} P(w \geq \varepsilon) = 0 \tag{4.10}$$

To illustrate what convergence in probability means, choose a 'small' value for ε, say $\varepsilon = 0.1$; then as $n \rightarrow \infty$, it must be the case that $P_n(w < 0.1) = 1$. To visualise what is happening, consider a continuous random variable with a probability space on the positive half-line of real numbers, $\Re^+ = [0, \infty)$ (for example, this is the probability space for the square of a normally distributed variable), then the inequality w defines a subset $w \in [0, 0.1)$. Convergence in probability requires that the probability of this subset tends to 1 as n increases. As this condition is required to hold for all positive ε then it must hold for $\varepsilon = 0.01$, $\varepsilon = 0.001$ and so on. In other words there must be an n such that the probability of even the slightest deviation of w from zero tends to zero as n increases without limit. Convergence in probability implies convergence in distribution, but the reverse implication does not hold; indeed the distributions of x_n and x need not be defined on the same probability space which, with the exception of convergence to a constant (see below) would rule out applicability of the concept.

Considering the joint distribution of two random variables, x_n and x, McCabe and Tremayne (op. cit.,) note that the case that indicates convergence in probability is when the contours of the joint density are elongated around a 45° line with a slope of –1, indicating perfect correlation. A lack of association is indicated by contours that are circular, centred at zero. Indeed, this latter case is particularly instructive for if two variables are independent then one cannot converge to the other in probability, an example in point being two uncorrelated normal

distributed random variables since then a lack of correlation implies independence.

Example 4.5: Two independent random variables

The distribution of w depends on the joint distribution of x_n and x, with a sample space that derives from the sample space of the two univariate distributions, as the following example shows. Let x and y denote independent random variables with each having the two outcomes 0 and 1, which occur with a probability ½; the random variables are, therefore, defined on the same sample space. Then the random variable $x - y$ has three possible outcomes, which are: −1 with $p(-1) = ¼$, 0 with $p(0) = ½$ and 1 with $p(+1) = ¼$; hence, the random variable $w = |x - y|$ has two possible outcomes, $w = 0$ with $p(w = 0) = ½$ and $w = 1$ with $p(w = 1) = ½$; see (Billingsley, 1995, section 25). ♦

4.2.5 Convergence in probability to a constant

A slightly modified form of convergence in probability occurs when x_n converges in probability to a constant. The constant can be viewed as a degenerate random variable, such that $x(\omega) = c$ for all $\omega \in \Omega$. In this case, the equivalent of the $\to_p$ condition is:

$$\lim_{n\to\infty} P(|x_n - c| < \varepsilon) = 1 \tag{4.11}$$

This condition is, therefore, one on the absolute value of the centred random variable $x_n - c$. Because the x_j do not have to be defined on the same probability space, Billingsley (1995, Theorem 25.3) suggests distinguishing this form of convergence from $\to_p$ convergence; however, rather than introduce a separate notation, and in common with a number of texts, only one notation, that is $\to_p$, is used here. This case is also the exception in that convergence in distribution to a constant (that is to a degenerate distribution) implies convergence in probability.

4.2.6 Slutsky's theorem

Let x_n be the n-th term in the sequence $\{x_j\}_1^n$, with $x_n \to_p c$, and let $g(x_n)$ be a continuous function, except on a set of measure zero, then $g(x_n) \to_p g(c)$. This is a very useful theorem as it is often relatively easy to determine the plim of x_n by direct means, but less easy to obtain the plim of $g(x_n)$ in the same manner. Slutsky's theorem shows how to do it quite simply.

A related theorem is the analogue of the CMT for convergence in probability. Let x_n be the n-th term in the sequence $\{x_j\}_1^n$, with $x_n \rightarrow_p x$, and let g(x) be a continuous function of x, except on a set of measure zero, then $g(x_n) \rightarrow_p g(x)$. In plim notation, plim $g(x_n) = g(x)$ and in words, 'the probability limit of the function is the function of the probability limit', Fuller (1996, p. 222 and Theorem 5.1.4). This generalises Slutsky's theorem by allowing the limit to be a random variable, rather than a constant.

4.2.7 Weak law of large numbers (WLLN)

A simple form of the weak law of large numbers is as follows. Consider again the sequence $\{S_j\}_{j=1}^n$, where $S_n = \sum_{j=1}^n x_j$ and $x_j \sim \text{iid}(\mu, \sigma_x^2)$, as in the CLT, and let $\bar{x}_n = S_n/n$. Then for every $\varepsilon > 0$, the WLLN states:

$$\lim_{n\rightarrow\infty} P(|\bar{x}_n - \mu| < \varepsilon) = 1 \qquad (4.12)$$

This can be stated as $\bar{x}_n \rightarrow_p \mu$ or plim $\bar{x}_n = \mu$. It provides a justification for using the average as an estimator of the population mean. In fact the conditions can be weakened quite substantially (as they are here sufficient for the strong law of large numbers, see below), whilst still achieving the same result; see, for example, Rao's (1973) presentations of Chebyshev's, Khinchin's and Kolgomorov's theorems.

4.2.8 Sure convergence

We start here from the concept of sure convergence, which although not generally used serves to underline the idea of almost sure convergence. Sure convergence is probably closest to an intuitive understanding of what is meant by convergence of a random variable. Recall that a random variable is a function that maps a sample space Ω into a measurable space, typically the set, or some subset, of the real numbers; for example, in tossing a coin, the outcomes heads and tails are mapped into the real numbers (0, 1) or (–1, +1). For each element ω in the sample space, that is $\omega \in \Omega$, we could ask whether the measurable quantity $x_n(\omega) - x(\omega)$ is 'large'; typically, negative and positive deviations are treated equally, so we could look at $|x_n(\omega) - x(\omega)|$ and ask whether this magnitude is less than an arbitrary 'small' number ε. It is somewhat unrealistic to expect this distance to be small for all values of the index n, but convergence would occur if $\varepsilon = 0$ in the limit as $n \rightarrow \infty$, since then $x_n(\omega) = x(\omega)$. An important feature of this kind of convergence is that it is being assessed for each $\omega \in \Omega$, so that it is sometimes referred to as element-wise (or point-wise) convergence; moreover, it does not then

make sense unless Ω is the sample space common to $x_n(\omega)$ and $x(\omega)$, for these are being compared element-by-element.

Sure convergence requires the following:

$$\lim_{n\to\infty} x_n(\omega) = x(\omega) \quad \text{for all } \omega \in \Omega \tag{4.13}$$

Clearly this is a strong notion of convergence and an interesting question is whether it can be weakened slightly, whilst still retaining the idea of element-wise convergence.

4.2.9 Almost sure convergence, $\to_{as}$

The answer is to take the probability of the limit, which leads to the concept of almost sure convergence, as follows:

$$P\{\omega \in \Omega \mid \lim_{n\to\infty} x_n(\omega) = x(\omega)\} = 1 \tag{4.14}$$

The corresponding shorthand notation is $x_n \to_{as} x$ Sometimes statements are qualified as holding almost surely or, simply, a.s. See Stout (1974) for a detailed analysis of the concept of almost sure convergence.

The 'almost' refers to the following qualification to the condition. It does not apply to $\omega \in G \subset \Omega$ where $P(G) = 0$, this is the 'almost'; that is, there may be elements ω of Ω, in the subset G, for which convergence does not hold, but this does not matter provided that the probability of the set of such elements (if any) is zero. An example will illustrate this point and the idea of the concept.

Example 4.6: Almost sure convergence

The basic idea in this example is to define two random variables that differ only in a term that tends to zero as $n \to \infty$, with the exception of some part of the sample space that has zero probability, which provides the 'almost' sure part of convergence. With that aim, suppose that $\omega \in \Omega = [0, \infty)$ and let $x_n(\omega) = \omega + (1 + \omega)^{-n}$ and $x(\omega) = \omega$ be two continuous random variables. Note that $x_n(\omega) \to x(\omega)$ as $n \to \infty$ for $\omega > 0$; but $x_n(0) = 1 \neq x(0) = 0$ for any n. Thus, convergence is not sure; however, $P(\omega = 0)$ by the continuity of the pdf and, therefore, $x_n \to_{as} x$. ♦

Note that convergence in probability makes a statement about the limiting probability, whereas almost-sure convergence makes a statement about the probability of the limit. Almost sure convergence is stronger than convergence in distribution and convergence in probability, and implies both of these forms of convergence.

4.2.10 Strong law of large numbers (SLLN)

Consider again the sequence $\{S_j\}_{j=1}^{n}$, where $S_n = \Sigma_{j=1}^{n} x_j$ and $x_j \sim$ iid (μ, σ^2), as in the CLT and the WLLN, and let $\bar{x}_n = S_n/n$. Then for every $\varepsilon > 0$, the SLLN states:

$$P(\lim_{n\to\infty} |\bar{x}_n - \mu| < \varepsilon) = 1 \tag{4.15}$$

Thus, there is almost sure convergence of $\bar{x}_n$ ('the average') to μ ('the population mean'); that is, with probability 1, $\bar{x}_n$ converges to a constant, μ, as $n \to \infty$; the assumptions on x_j can be weakened quite substantially, see, for example McCabe and Tremayne (1993) and Koralov and Sinai (2007).

4.2.11 Convergence in mean square and convergence in r-th mean: $\to_r$

Other concepts of convergence not covered in detail here include convergence in mean square, which is a special case of convergence in r-th mean. We note this case briefly. The sequence of random variables with n-th term x_n converges in mean square to the random variable x, written $x_n \to_{ms} x$ or $x_n \to_{r=2} x$, if:

$$\lim_{n\to\infty} E(\{x_n - x\}^2) = 0 \tag{4.16}$$

Thus, analogous to the elementary concept of variance, a measure of variation is the expected value of the squared difference between x_n and the (limiting) random variable x, if this tends to zero with n, x_n converges in mean square to x. This idea is extended in convergence in r-th mean, defined for x_n as follows:

$$\lim_{n\to\infty} E(|x_n - x|^r) = 0 \tag{4.17}$$

As noted, the case with $r = 2$ is convergence in mean square as $|x_n - x|^2 = (x_n - x)^2$. Otherwise the principle is the same, but the metric different, for different values of r. An intuitive case arises for $r = 1$, which might be described (loosely) as convergence in mean; consider the variable $w = |x_n - x|$, which is the absolute difference between the two random variables (as in the case of convergence in probability), and necessarily non-negative, then if the expected value of w is zero in the limit, x_n is said to converge to x in mean.

4.2.12 Summary of convergence implications

Convergence in r-th mean for $r \geq 1$ implies convergence in probability and, hence convergence in distribution. The relationship between the convergence concepts is summarised in Table 4.1.

Table 4.1 Convergence implications

Almost surely		In probability		In distribution
$x_n \to_{as} x$	$\Rightarrow$	$x_n \to_p x$	$\Rightarrow$	$x_n \Rightarrow_D x$
		$\Uparrow$		
		$x_n \to_r x$		
		In r-th mean		

The reverse implications do not hold in general; however, an important exception is: if $x_n \Rightarrow_D c$, where c is a constant, then $x_n \to_p c$.

4.3 Order of Convergence

The order or magnitude of stochastic sequences is important at several stages in the development of unit root and stationarity tests. For example, consider a test statistic that is the ratio of two stochastic sequences. The asymptotic behaviour of the ratio, for example does it converge or diverge, depends on the order of convergence of the numerator and denominator components.

We start with the order of nonstochastic sequences as this is simply extended to stochastic sequences. Following mathematical convention, it is usual to use n, rather than t (or T), as an index for the last term in a sequence. This convention is followed in this section apart from where time series are being directly addressed.

4.3.1 Nonstochastic sequences: 'big-O' notation, 'little-o' notation

By way of example, consider two sequences with the n-th terms given by $x_n = a_0 + a_1 n$ and $y_n = b_0 + b_1 n + b_2 n^2$, where a_0, a_1, b_0, b_1 and b_2 are constants. Both are unbounded as $n \to \infty$, but require different normalising factors to reduce them to a bounded sequence in the limit. In the case of x_n the required factor is n^{-1} and for y_n it is n^{-2}, so that:

$$n^{-1}x_n = a_0/n + a_1 \quad \text{with } \lim_{n\to\infty} n^{-1}x_n = a_1 \tag{4.18a}$$

$$n^{-2}y_n = b_0/n^2 + b_1/n + b_2 \quad \text{with } \lim_{n\to\infty} n^{-2}y_n = b_2 \tag{4.18b}$$

The sequences $\{x_n\}$ and $\{y_n\}$ are said to be of order n and n^2, denoted O(n) and $O(n^2)$, respectively, read as order of magnitude; this is an example of the 'big-O' notation.

Note that all that matters when the function under examination comprises elements that are polynomials in n, is the dominant power of n. For example, if $x_n = \Sigma_k^K a_k n^k$, then the dominant term is $a_K n^K$ and the sequence of which the n-th term is x_n is $O(n^K)$.

More generally, to say that a sequence $\{x_n\}$ is $O(n^\delta)$, written $\{x_n\} = O(n^\delta)$, means that:

$$\lim_{n\to\infty} \frac{|x_n|}{n^\delta} \le c \ne 0 < \infty \tag{4.19}$$

Thus, the normalised sequence $\{|x_n|/n^\delta\}$ is bounded as $n \to \infty$. Note that if division by n^δ will ensure that a sequence is bounded, then so will division by, for example, $n^{\delta+1}$, $n^{\delta+2}$ and so on; therefore, implicit in the definition is the assumption that n^δ is the minimum factor necessary to induce a bounded series; sometimes this is recognised by saying that x_n is 'at most of order' n^δ. Note that the order of magnitude necessarily refers to a sequence, although it is sometimes referred to without that qualification as applying to the n-th term, and written $x_n = O(n^\delta)$.

If x_n and y_n are to be reduced to zero rather than a non-zero constant, then the normalising factors have to be marginally greater than n^δ, say $n^{\delta+\varepsilon}$, where $\varepsilon > 0$. For example, in the case of $x_n = a_0 + a_1 n$, which is O(n), division by $n^{1+\varepsilon}$ results in:

$$\frac{x_n}{n^{(1+\varepsilon)}} = \frac{a_0}{n^{(1+\varepsilon)}} + \frac{a_1}{n^\varepsilon} \tag{4.20}$$

so that $\lim_{n\to\infty} n^{-(1+\varepsilon)} x_n = 0$ for $\varepsilon > 0$.

Generally, a sequence is said to be 'of smaller order' than $n^{\delta+\varepsilon}$, written as $\{x_n\} = o(n^{\delta+\varepsilon})$, if for some $\varepsilon > 0$, then the following holds:

$$\lim_{n\to\infty} \frac{x_n}{n^{\delta+\varepsilon}} = 0 \text{ for } \varepsilon > 0 \tag{4.21}$$

Note that the definition is such that $\{x_n\} = O(n^\delta) \Rightarrow \{x_n\} = o(n^{(\delta+\varepsilon)})$ for $\varepsilon > 0$. Conversely if a sequence is $o(n^\delta)$ then it is $O(n^{\delta-\varepsilon})$ for some $\varepsilon > 0$. In fact, if x_n is $o(n^\delta)$ then, by definition, it is also $O(n^\delta)$, the bound being zero, but it is useful to capture the idea that an $o(n^\delta)$ sequence dominates the $\{x_n\}$ sequence, whereas a $O(n^{\delta-\varepsilon})$ sequence 'matches' the $\{x_n\}$ sequence.

There are two points to note on notation for order concepts. If the normalising factor is $n^0 \equiv 1$, the convention is to write O(1) and o(1), respectively. The use of the equality symbol is not universal for these order concepts and here we follow, for example, Spanos (1986), Fuller (1976, 1996) and Davidson (1994); Hendry (1995), uses ≈, so that $\{x_n\} \approx O(n^\delta)$ means the same as $\{x_n\} = O(n^\delta)$; in mathematical use, set notation is sometime used, for example $\{x_n\} \in O(n^\delta)$.

Generalising further, it may be the case that the normalising factor is something other than a power of n; for example, g(n) = log(n) or g(n) = loglog(n), in which case, the definitions of O(g(n)) and o(g(n)) are:

$$\lim_{n\to\infty} \frac{|x_n|}{g(n)} \leq c \neq 0 < \infty \qquad \{X_n\} = O(g(n)) \tag{4.22}$$

$$\lim_{n\to\infty} \frac{x_n}{g(n)} = 0 \qquad \{X_n\} = o(g(n)) \tag{4.23}$$

In both cases, the idea is the same as in the simpler case where only powers of n were involved. Generally, in the case of O(g(n)), the sequence g(n) matches the $\{x_n\}$ sequence, whereas in the case of o((g(n)), the sequence g(n) dominates the $\{x_n\}$ sequence, both in the limit.

Lastly in this section and as an application of the 'big-O' notation, one possible explanation of a sustained movement in a time series is that there is a deterministic trend, so that a polynomial regression in time may be used as part of the analysis. For example, $y_t = \sum_{j=0}^{K} \beta_j t^j + \omega_t$, where ω_t is a stochastic input, is a simple form of a trend. In such cases, sums of the t^j appear in the subsequent analysis and their order of magnitude is of interest. The most common cases are sums of linear and quadratic trends, respectively. These are:

$$\sum_{t=1}^{T} t = \frac{1}{2}T(T+1) = O(T^2)$$

$$\sum_{t=1}^{T} t^2 = \frac{1}{6}T(T+1)(2T+1) = O(T^3)$$

Thus, in general, $\sum_{t=1}^{T} t^K$ is $O(T^{K+1})$. For a more comprehensive list and analysis, see Banerjee et al. (1993).

4.3.2 Stochastic sequences: $O_p(n^\delta)$ and $o_p(n^\delta)$

The $O(n^\delta)$ and $o(n^\delta)$ definitions are extended to the case of stochastic sequences by considering the probability of 'extreme' events, see Mann and Wald (1943).

4.3.2.i At most of order n^δ in probability: $O_p(n^\delta)$

The analogue of $O(n^\delta)$ is $O_p(n^\delta)$, read as at most of order n^δ in probability. It is defined as follows: for any $\varepsilon > 0$, there exists a finite real number $c(\varepsilon)$, such that for all $n \geq 1$,

$$P\left(\frac{|x_n|}{n^\delta} > c(\varepsilon)\right) < \varepsilon \tag{4.24}$$

This is written as $\{x_n\} = O_p(n^\delta)$, or sometimes without the braces around x_n. In words, the probability of the absolute value of the n-th term in a bounded sequence exceeding the (finite) real number $c(\varepsilon)$ is less than ε. Consider the case of $O_p(1)$, then this implies that $|x_n|$ is bounded in probability by a number $c(\varepsilon)$, such that:

$$P(|x_n| > c(\varepsilon)) < \varepsilon \tag{4.25}$$

For example, suppose that x_n is a random variable distributed as niid(0, 1) then, for all $n \geq 1$, it is trivial to find a $c(\varepsilon)$ from standard normal tables, such that this inequality is satisfied. Notice that c(.) is written as a function of ε, since as ε changes then so, generally, will the value of $c(\varepsilon)$.

4.3.2.ii Of smaller order in probability than n^δ: $o_p(n^\delta)$

Analogous to the $o(n^\delta)$ case, x_n is said to be of smaller order in probability than n^δ, written $\{x_n\} = o_p(n^\delta)$ if:

$$\lim_{n\to\infty} P\left(\frac{x_n}{n^\delta}\right) = 0 \tag{4.26}$$

The $o_p(1)$ case means that:

$$\lim_{n\to\infty} P(x_n) = 0 \tag{4.27}$$

The order notation is often used to indicate by how much, in terms of order of probability, x_n differs from x; for example, if $x_n \to_p x$ then $x_n = x + o_p(1)$, which is to say that x_n differs from x only in terms that are $o_p(1)$ and thus tends to zero in the probability limit. A related result is that if $x_n \Rightarrow_D x$, then $\{x_n\} = O_p(1)$.

Example 4.7: $x_n = O_p(\sqrt{n})$

A case of particular importance is when $x_n = O_p(\sqrt{n})$, so that:

$$P\left(\frac{|x_n|}{\sqrt{n}} > c(\varepsilon)\right) < \varepsilon \tag{4.28}$$

Thus, whilst x_n is not bounded in probability, the scaled sequence with n-th term $|x_n|/\sqrt{n}$ is bounded. To illustrate this case, consider the sequence of partial sums where $S_n = \sum_{j=1}^{n} \varepsilon_j$, with ε_j a random variable distributed as niid(0, 1). The variance of S_n is $n\sigma^2 = n$, so that the standard deviation of S_n grows linearly with $\sqrt{n}$. The normalised quantity $S_n/\sqrt{n}$ is *N*(0, 1), which is $O_p(1)$, and, therefore, $\{S_n\}$ is $O_p(\sqrt{n})$.

To illustrate what the scaling is doing consider Figures 4.3 and 4.4, each of which has four sub-plots. The top panel of Figure 4.3 shows two realisations of S_n for n = 1, ..., 5,000, whereas the corresponding lower panel shows the same realisations scaled by $\sqrt{n}$; whilst the paths of S_n are unbounded, those of $S_n/\sqrt{n}$ are bounded (in probability). Then in Figure 4.4, the upper panel shows what happens when S_n is 'overscaled' by n rather than $\sqrt{n}$; the result is that S_n/n is close to the zero axis throughout. The lower panel shows that the distributions of S_n/n for n = 2,000 approach a degenerate distribution centred on zero, whereas $S_n/\sqrt{n}$ is known to be distributed as *N*(0, 1). When n = 1,000 the probability of occurrences between ±0.05 is about 90%, and for n = 2,000 it is nearly 98%, indicating the converging degeneracy of the distributions. (The densities shown in the figure are estimated from 1,000 simulations of S_n) ♦

4.3.3 Some algebra of the order concepts

Table 4.2 provides a summary of the relations between the order concepts for two sequences of nonstochastic or stochastic variables and is based on Mittlehammer (1996, lemma 5.2, p. 232). These relationships also hold if O(.) and o(.) are replaced by $O_p(.)$ and $o_p(.)$, respectively, and if more general functions, say $\delta(n)$ and $\lambda(n)$ replace n^δ and n^λ.

Other relations of use include multiplication by a constant, λ: if $\{x_n\} = O(n^\delta)$, then $\{\lambda x_n\} = O(n^\delta)$, with similar results for $o(n^\delta)$ and the stochastic equivalent. If $\{x_n\}$ is $O(n^\delta)$ and $\{y_n\}$ is $o(n^\lambda)$, then $\{x_n/y_n\}$ is $o(n^{\delta-\lambda})$.

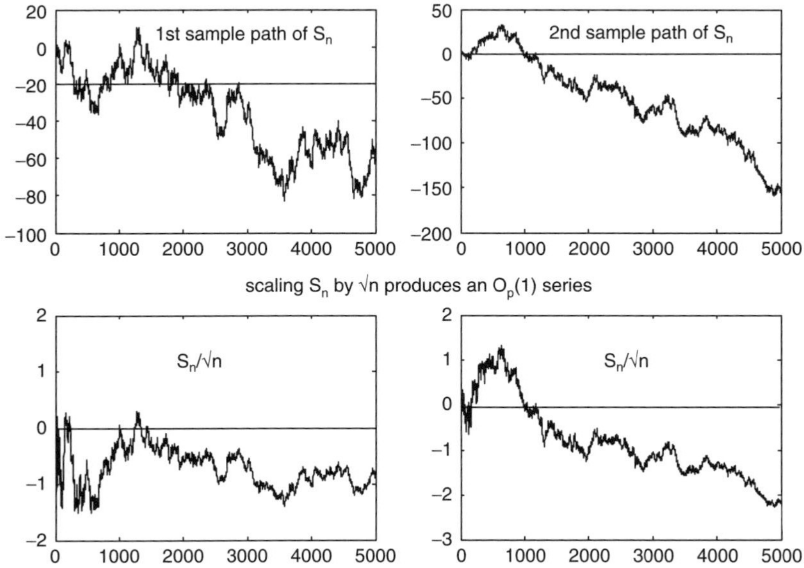

Figure 4.3 Appropriate scaling of a partial sum process

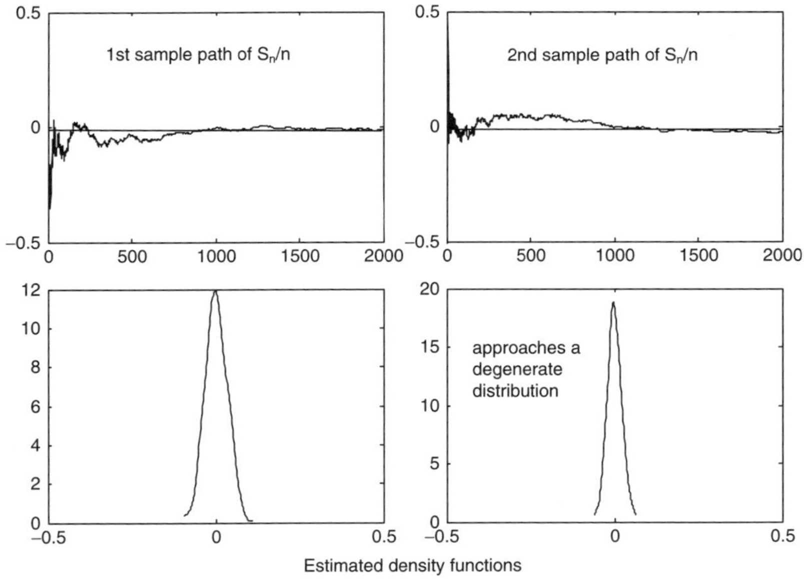

Figure 4.4 Scaling by S_n by n produces a degenerate distribution

Table 4.2 The order of some simple derived sequences

Component sequences		**Simple functions**	
$\{x_n\}$	$\{y_n\}$	$\{x_n + y_n\}$	$\{x_n y_n\}$
$O(n^{\delta})$	$O(n^{\lambda})$	$O(n^{\max\{\lambda,\delta\}})$	$O(n^{\lambda+\delta})$
$O(n^{\delta})$	$o(n^{\lambda})$	$O(n^{\max\{\lambda,\delta\}})$	$o(n^{\lambda+\delta})$
$o(n^{\delta})$	$o(n^{\lambda})$	$o(n^{\max\{\lambda,\delta\}})$	$o(n^{\lambda+\delta})$

Notes: x_n and y_n are, respectively, the n-th terms in the sequences $\{x_j\}_{j=1}^{n}$ and $\{y_j\}_{j=1}^{n}$ of real numbers.

Source: Mittlehammer (1996, lemma 5.2, p. 232); see also White (1984).

4.4 Convergence of stochastic processes

Recall from Chapters 1 and 3 that a stochastic process is a collection of random variables organised into a sequence indexed by time. The question then arises as to what is meant by the convergence of one stochastic process to another. This is a different concept from convergence of a sequence of random variables, as considered in previous sections. For example, consider the sequence of random variables $\{x_j\}_{j=1}^{n}$ with a corresponding sequence of distribution functions given by $\{F_j(X)\}_{j=1}^{n}$, and recall that convergence in distribution relates to asking whether $F_n(X)$ converges to $F(X)$ as $n \to \infty$, for some $F(X)$, written as $F_n(X) \Rightarrow_D F(X)$ or, equivalently, $x_n \Rightarrow_D x$. This is often an interesting property of the sequence when the 'generic' random variable x_j is an estimator of a quantity of interest, such as the mean or a regression parameter, and the index represents the sample size; in that case interest centres on whether there is a limiting distribution for the estimator as the sample size increases without limit.

In contrast, when the sequence of random variables is a stochastic process, so that the elements are indexed by t, representing time, the focus is now on the sample paths and the function space generated by such stochastic processes. The generation of these sample paths depends not just on the distribution of each random variable in the sequence, but also on their joint distributions. To consider these further, it is convenient to view the random variables that comprise the stochastic process as generated in continuous time, so that $Y = (y(t, \omega): t \in T \subseteq \Re, \omega \in \Omega)$, see Chapter 1, Section 1.4. Each random variable is a function of time and the sample space and, although typically the dependence on ω is suppressed, it is as ω varies that different sample paths are realised as t varies.

What can we say about the many (possibly infinite number of) sample paths that could be generated in this way? It is clear that we would need to know not only about the distribution of each of the component random variables y(t), but also how they are related. The relationships between component random variables of the stochastic process are captured by the joint distribution functions of Y:

$$P[y(t_1) \le Y_1, \dots, y(t_n) \le Y_n] \tag{4.29}$$

where $t_1 \le t_2 \le \dots \le t_n$, for all possible values of t_i and n. These are the finite-dimensional distributions, or fidis, of the stochastic process. For example, we could specify a Gaussian stochastic process comprising independent $N(0, 1)$ random variables. Such a process is generated with each component random variable having a (marginal) distribution that is $N(0, 1)$ and each possible set of joint distributions is multivariate normal, that is:

$$\text{marginal distributions: } y(t_i) \sim N(0, 1) \text{ for all } t_i \in T \tag{4.30a}$$

joint distributions (fidis):

$$P[y(t_1) \le Y_1, \dots, y(t_n) \le Y_n] = P(y(t_1) \le Y_1)P(y(t_2) \le Y_2) \dots \\ P(y(t_n) \le Y_n) = \Phi(Y_1)\Phi(Y_2) \dots \Phi(Y_n) \tag{4.30b}$$

for all t_i and n; and where Φ(.) is the cdf of the standard normal distribution and the assumption of independence is used in obtaining the joint distribution(s).

Whilst establishing the convergence of one stochastic process to another is more than just the convergence of the respective fidis, that is a good place to start. To that effect consider another stochastic process $U = U(t_1), \dots, U(t_n)$, with fidis given by:

$$P[U(t_1) \le Y_1, \dots, U(t_n) \le Y_n] \tag{4.31}$$

Then convergence of the finite-dimensional distributions occurs if for all t_j, Y_j and n, then:

$$P[y(t_1) \le Y_1, \dots, y(t_n) \le Y_n)] \Rightarrow_D P[U(t_1) \le Y_1, \dots, U(t_n) \le Y_n)] \tag{4.32}$$

The shorthand is $Y \Rightarrow_D U$, which says that the (joint) distribution of Y converges to the (joint) distribution of U. This is not sufficient by itself to enable us to say that one stochastic process converges to another; the additional condition is uniform tightness, a condition that is also required for a sequence of cdfs to have a cdf as its limit. The following statement of this condition is from Davidson (1994, section 22.5, see also sections 26.5 and 27.5). As in the concept of weak convergence let $\{F_t(X)\}$ be a sequence of distribution functions indexed by t, then uniform tightness requires that for $\varepsilon > 0$, there exists a, b with $b - a < \infty$, such that:

$$\sup_{t \in T}\{F_t(b) - F_t(a)\} > 1 - \varepsilon \tag{4.33}$$

The condition (4.33) will fail for distributions that spread the density out too thinly over the support of the distribution, for example a uniform distribution over an infinite interval (support) see Davidson (ibid). Subject to this point the convergence in (4.32) will be described as weak convergence and is the sense in which convergence of stochastic processes is used in Chapters 6–8.

4.5 Concluding remarks and further reading

Convergence is a concept with wide applications in econometrics. Indeed, it is hard to make sense of the properties of estimators without knowledge of, for example, convergence in distribution (weak convergence) and convergence in probability (plim). In essence this form of convergence relates to the limiting behaviour of the n-th term in a sequence of random variables. A prototypical case would be a sequence of estimators of the same population quantity, for example a regression parameter or a test statistic, where the terms in the sequence are indexed by the sample size. Interest then centres on the limiting behaviour of the estimator as the sample size increases without limit.

Related to convergence is the 'speed' of convergence. By itself, convergence is uninformative about whether the approach to limiting quantity (distribution, scalar, random function) is slow or fast, it just says that as $n \to \infty$, the limiting quantity is reached. However given two estimators of the same quantity, we would prefer the one that is quicker in approaching the limit. In this context it is of interest to know the order of convergence of the two estimators.

Once the groundwork of convergence of a sequence is achieved, it is possible to move onto the idea of the convergence of a stochastic process. The technical detail of this form of convergence is beyond the scope of this book, but much of the intuition derives from weak convergence and the convergence of the finite dimensional distributions.

For further reading, see Mittelhammer (1996) for an excellent treatment of the concepts of convergence and, for their application in a time series context, see Brockwell and Davis (2006). For the next level on stochastic processes, the reader could consult Mikosch (1998) and Brzeźniak and Zastawniak (1999), McCabe and Tremayne (1993) and some parts of Billingsley (1995) and Davidson (1994). Classic texts on stochastic processes include Doob (1953) and Gihman and Skorohod (1974).

Questions

Q4.1 Show that $\sqrt{n}(\bar{x}_n - \mu) \Rightarrow_D N(0,\sigma^2)$.

A4.1 Define z_n as:

$$z_n = \frac{S_n - n\mu}{\sigma\sqrt{n}}$$

Dividing the numerator and denominator by n gives:

$$\begin{aligned} z_n &= \frac{(S_n / n) - \mu}{\sigma / \sqrt{n}} \\ &= \frac{\bar{x}_n - \mu}{\sigma / \sqrt{n}} \\ &= \sqrt{n}\left(\frac{\bar{x}_n - \mu}{\sigma}\right) \Rightarrow_D N(0,1) \end{aligned}$$

Hence, $\sqrt{n}(\bar{x}_n - \mu) \Rightarrow N(0, \sigma^2)$.

Q4.2 Let x and y denote independent random variables, each with two outcomes, 0 and 1, which occur with a probability of ½. Are the following statements correct? i) $x \Rightarrow_D y$; ii) $y \Rightarrow_D x$; iii) $x \to_p y$ (see Billingsley, 1995, section 25).

A4.2 Statements i) and ii) are correct, but iii) is not because $P(|x - y| = 1) = \frac{1}{2}$, contradicting (4.9). (The sample space of $|x - y|$ was considered in example 4.5: $w = |x - y|$ has two possible outcomes, $w = 0$ and $w = 1$ each with a probability of $\frac{1}{2}$.)

Q4.3 What are the O(.) and o(.) of $\{x_n\}$, where:

$$x_n = \frac{4n^2 + 3n + 2}{6n + 1}?$$

A4.3 The only terms that matter asymptotically are $4n^2/6n = (2/3)n$, therefore $\{x_n\} = O(n)$, since $[(2/3)n]/n = 2/3$ As $\{x_n\} = O(n)$, then $\{x_n\} = o(n^{1+\varepsilon})$for $\varepsilon > 0$, as $[(2/3)n]/n^{1+\varepsilon} = (2/3)n^{\varepsilon} \to 0$.

Q4.4 Consider the Taylor series expansion of the exponential:

$$e^x = 1 + x + \frac{x^2}{2!} + \frac{x^3}{3!} + \frac{x^4}{4!} + \ldots$$

For $|x| < 1$, what is the O(.) of the error in approximating e^x by ignoring all terms in x^k, $k \geq 4$?

A4.4 Write the remainder from ignoring such higher order terms as R, so that:

$$e^x = 1 + x + \frac{x^2}{2!} + \frac{x^3}{3!} + R$$

$$R = \frac{x^4}{4!} + \ldots$$

Note that R/x^4 is:

$$\frac{R}{x^4} = \frac{1}{4!} + \frac{x}{5!} + \frac{x^2}{6!} + \ldots$$

Given that $|x| < 1$, then $x^k > x^{k+1}$ and $x^k/(4 + k)! \to 0$ as $k \to \infty$; hence R/x^4 is bounded and, therefore, $R = O(x^4)$.

5
An Introduction to Random Walks

This chapter introduces the idea of a random walk. In the first section, the emphasis is on the probability background of the random walk. It introduces the classic two-dimensional walk, primarily through the fiction of a gambler, which can be illustrated graphically. This serves two purposes, it underlies the motivation for the sample paths taken by some economic times series and it serves to introduce the partial sum (the gambler's winnings), which is a critical quantity in subsequent econometric analysis. Some economic examples are given that confirm the likely importance of the random walk as an appropriate model for some economic processes.

The random walk is a natural introduction to Brownian motion, which is the subject of the next chapter, and is an example of a stochastic difference equation, in which the steps in the walk are driven by a random input. By making the steps in the walk smaller and smaller, the random walk can be viewed in the limit as occurring in continuous time and the stochastic difference equation becomes a stochastic differential equation. Equally, one might consider the random process as occurring in continuous time and the discrete-time version, that is the random walk, is what is observed.

This chapter is organised as follows. The basic idea of a random walk is introduced in Section 5.1, with some illustrative simulations of symmetric random walks in Section 5.2 and some useful random walk probabilities in Section 5.3. Variations on the random walk theme are considered in Section 5.4. Some intuition about the nature of random walks is provided by looking at the variance of a partial sum process in Section 5.5 and the number of changes of sign on a random walk path in Section 5.6. Section 5.7 links random walks in with the presence of a unit root and Section 5.8 provides two examples.

5.1 Simple random walks

In this section, we consider a particular example of a random walk in order to motivate its use as a prototypical stochastic process for economic time series. It is an important process in its own right and has been the subject of extension and study It is an example of a process that is both a martingale and a Markov process (see Chapter 3, Sections 3.5.1 and 3.5.2).

5.1.1 'Walking'

In the first instance, consider a 'walker' who starts at the origin (0, 0) on a two-dimensional graph; looking down on this walker, who walks from left to right on the imaginary graph, he takes a step to the north on the graph, that is into the region above the zero axis, with probability p, and a step to the right (south on the graph), that is into the region below the zero axis, with probability q. He continues walking in this way, taking one step at a time, indexed by t, so t = 1, 2, ..., T. His steps at each t are independent; that is the direction of the step at t is not affected by any step taken previously. If $p = q = 1 - p$, that is $p = ½$, then the random walk is symmetric, otherwise it is nonsymmetric. (The reader may recognise this as a particularly simply Markov Chain, the theory of which offers a very effective means of analysing random walks, see for example, Ross, 2003.)

In this random walk, not all points are possible, since the walker must, at each stage, take a step to the north or to the south. This suggests that an interesting variation would be to allow the walker to continue in a straight line, perhaps with a relatively small probability, and we consider this in Section 5.4.3.i. The possible paths are shown in Figure 5.1 for T = 3. The coordinate corresponding to the vertical axis is denoted S_t (and called the 'tally' in Section 5.1.2). In this case there are $8 = 2^3$ distinct paths, but some of the paths share the last two coordinates; for example, paths [0, 1, 0, 1] and [0, –1, 0, 1] are at the same point for t = 3. To enable such a distinction in Figure 5.1, the overlapping paths are artificially separated. Note that at T = 3, the path cannot end at $S_t = 0$, or $S_t = \pm 2$; and, generally, odd outcomes are not possible if T is even and even outcomes are not possible if T is odd.

5.1.2 'Gambling'

Some of the insights into random walks can be developed with a frequent variation in which the walker is replaced with a gambler! It starts with a fictitious gambler usually called 'Peter', who plays a game that

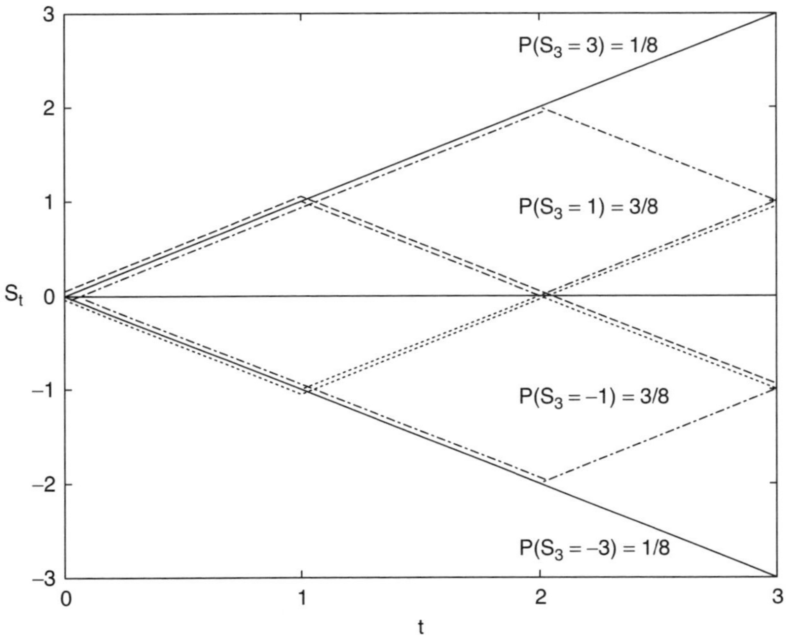

Figure 5.1 Random walk paths for T = 3, there are $8 = 2^3$ paths ending in 6 distinct outcomes

pays 1 unit in the event that the toss of a fair coin results in a head, but results in a loss of 1 unit in the event that the coin lands tails. Each toss of the coin is referred to as a 'trial', a term that originates from Bernoulli trials, resulting in the binary outcomes 'success' or 'failure', with probabilities p and q, respectively. His overall tally is kept by a banker who allows Peter credit should he find that either at the first throw, or subsequently, that Peter is losing on the overall tally. (In a variation of the game, Peter starts with a capital sum, but this development is not required here.) We assume that there are T individual games played sequentially, where the precise nature of T is yet to be determined, but serves the purpose of indicating that time is an essential element of this game. For simplicity, the games are assumed to be played at the rate of one per period t, so t increments in units of 1 from 1 to T.

In terms of the probability concepts of Chapter 1, a random variable has been constructed that is a mapping of the original sample space from the coin-tossing experiment which, in the case of one toss of the coin, is $\Omega_1 = \{H, T\}$ onto the real line $\Re$. The random variable is $y_1(\omega) = \{-1, +1\}$, with measurable sets $F_1^y = \{(\varnothing), (-1), (+1), (-1, +1)\}$ to which

are assigned the probabilities (measures) $P_1^y = (0, q, p, 1)$, respectively, see Chapter 1, Section 1.2.2. If p = q, then this set-up generates what is known as a symmetric binomial random walk; if p ≠ q then it is an asymmetric binomial random walk. The probability space associated with this experiment is $(\Omega_1^y, F_1^y, P_1^y)$. In the case of two independent tosses of the coin, the sample space is the product space $\Omega_2^y = (\Omega_1^y)^2 = \Omega_1^y \times \Omega_1^y$, that is the Cartesian product of the sample spaces Ω_1^y. The Borel field is the Cartesian product of the one-dimensional Borel fields $F_2^y = F_1^y \times F_1^y$, and P_2^y is the product measure $(P_1^y)^2 = P_1^y \times P_1^y$. A question explores this case further. This set-up generalises to t = 1, ..., T, independent tosses of the coin with probability space $(\Omega_t^y, F_t^y, P_t^y) = [(\Omega_1^y)^t, (F_1^y)^t, (P_1^y)^t]$.

To keep a running counter, the 'tally' is introduced denoted S_t, which is the partial sum process of $\{y_t\}$:

$$\begin{aligned} S_t &= y_1 + y_2 + \ldots + y_{t-1} + y_t \\ &= S_{t-1} + y_t \end{aligned} \tag{5.1}$$

A realisation of the random variable S_t is the net sum of the +1 and –1 outcomes of the t component random variables. It is clear that S_t is simply the partial sum of the y_t up to and including t, and that the progression of S_t is determined by a simple one-period recursion. For example, in order to obtain S_{t+1}, y_{t+1} is added to S_t, which is taken as given (predetermined for t + 1). In effect, a stochastic process has been defined as: $S = (S_0, ..., S_t, ..., S_T)$, where $S_0 = 0$. We can also keep the banker's tally. This is the random walk given by:

$$\begin{aligned} S_{B,t} &= -y_1 - y_2 - \ldots - y_{t-1} - y_t \\ &= S_{B,t-1} - y_t \end{aligned} \tag{5.2}$$

5.2 Simulations to illustrate the path of a random walk

The progress of a particular game can be shown graphically by plotting S_t against t. The representation is a time series plot of the partial sums, which are Peter's 'winnings'; later, the Banker's tally may also be of interest. Some examples of (symmetric) random walking are given in Figures 5.2a–5.2d; here the walk is the path of a gamble, with the partial sum S_t plotted against t, and T = 500 for these figures. Students and professional alike are often surprised by the time series patterns that can be generated by this process. A not unusual anticipation is that since the coin is fair, Peter's winnings will fluctuate more or less

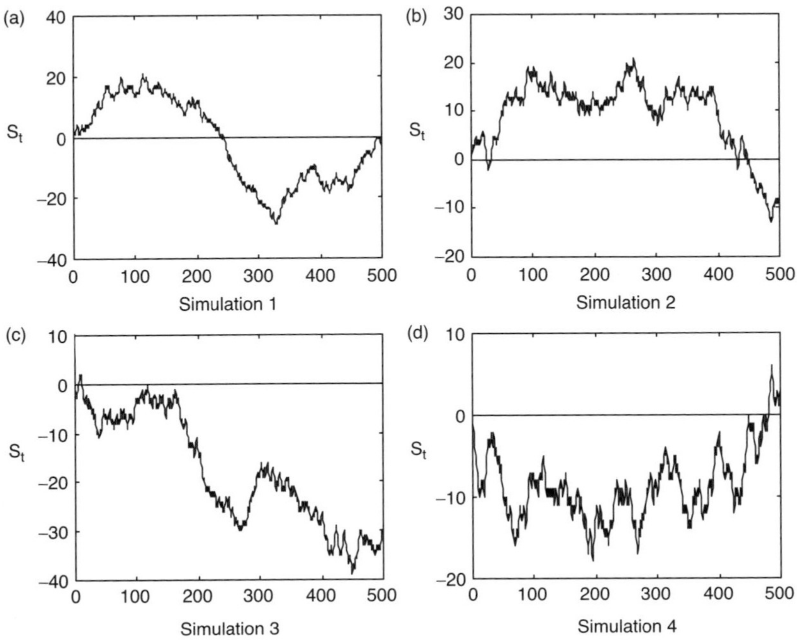

Figure 5.2 Simulated random walks

evenly about the positive and negative halves of the graph. The line of argument here is that the expected value of $S_t = 0$ for all t, so the mean should prevail (eventually?). Moreover, the variance of y_t is σ_y^2 where $\sigma_y^2 = E\{y_t - E(y_t)\}^2 = \{(-1) - 0\}^2\ ½ + \{(+1) - 0\}^2\ ½ = 1$; however, the variance of S_t increases with the number of repetitions and from Chapter 1, example 1.9, we know that $var(S_t) = t\sigma_y^2$, so that the bounds on the process are increasing over time.

To illustrate some key features of the random walk, the results from four simulations of a symmetric binomial random walk are reported in Table 5.1. The table reports a number of characteristics for four simulations with T = 5,000 and, in the final column, gives the averages of 5,000 trials. To check that the coin is indeed fair in each of the simulations, the results in Table 5.1 point up some interesting characteristics. The table reports the proportion of positive and negative outcomes for each individual trial. It also reports: the proportion of times that Peter is on the positive and negative sides of the zero axis, respectively $Prop(S_t > 0)$ and $Prop(S_t < 0)$; the proportion of time that winnings and losses are equalised $Prop(S_t = 0)$; and, the number of times that the lead changes

hands from Peter to the Banker or vice-versa, Prop(Change Sign). The final row gives the length of the maximum sequence in which Peter is not losing, as a percentage of the total time; and the final column reports the average of 5,000 trials.

It is reasonably evident from the first two rows that the coin is fair, but S_t is predominantly positive in simulation 2 and predominantly negative in simulations 3 and 4. Even in the case of simulation 1, where $Prop(S_t > 0)$ and $Prop(S_t < 0)$ are reasonably balanced, it is not the case that the lead changes hands evenly; S_t is first always positive until it switches to being negative, when it then stays negative.

Whatever the pattern, it confounds the sense that each walk generates some kind of equality between positive and negative outcomes. This is emphasised in the last two rows. First, note that there are very few changes of sign over each of the sequences; for example, even in the apparently evenly balanced simulation 1, there are only 0.6% changes of sign in the 5,000 realisations. Second, there is another interesting aspect that is apparent from the last row, which reports the maximum length of the sequence within each simulation where Peter stays on the winning side. For example, in simulation 1, most of the time (47.8%) for which $S_t > 0$, is actually spent in one continuous sequence of 47.4%; and in simulation 2, of the 86.8% of the time that $S_t > 0$, most of this was made up of one sequence of 79.4%. The last column (the averages) confirms that the walks were indeed constructed from outcomes that were equally likely – on average.

As fascinating as this process is, its importance as far as economic time series are concerned may not yet be clear. However, it turns out to contain some very important insights into economic processes, and by

Table 5.1 Positive and negative walks

Simulation	**1**	**2**	**3**	**4**	**Average**
Prop(+) (%)	49.6	49.0	46.8	50.4	50
Prop(–) (%)	50.4	51	53.2	49.6	50
$Prop(S_t > 0)$ (%)	47.8	86.8	1.0	4	49.2
$Prop(S_t = 0)$ (%)	1.4	1.6	0.6	0.8	1.1
$Prop(S_t < 0)$ (%)	50.8	11.6	98.4	95.2	49.7
Prop(Change Sign) (%)	0.6	1.0	0.4	0.2	0.5
Prop(MaxSeq) (%)	47.4	79.4	1.0	4	35.6

Note: For simulations 1 to 4, Prop(.) denotes the proportion relative to T = 5,000.

considering some of the 'unexpected' patterns that it generates we can find some motivation for considering it as prototypical stochastic process for economic data.

5.3 Some random walk probabilities

In this section we state and interpret some probabilities of interest, see especially Feller (1968, chapter III). Throughout this section, except where noted, we adopt the convention that n is defined such that 2n = T and t is, therefore, an index than runs over 1, ..., 2n (the exception is Equation (5.9) for changes of sign).

The first probability of interest is:

$$P(S_t = r) = \frac{{}_{n}C_{h}}{2^{n}} \qquad \text{where } h = (n+r)/2 \tag{5.3}$$

This is the probability that at time t the partial sum $S_t = r$, $|r| \leq n$. The binomial coefficient ${}_nC_h$ (see below for definition) is assumed to be zero unless $0 \leq h \leq n$ is an integer.

Next is the probability that Peter is always winning. This is the probability that S_t is everywhere positive:

$$P(S_1 > 0, \ldots, S_{2n} > 0) = 0.5\left(\frac{{}_{2n}C_{n}}{2^{2n}}\right) \tag{5.4}$$

The probability that Peter is never losing, which is the probability that S_t is never negative, is:

$$P(S_1 \geq 0, \ldots, S_{2n} \geq 0) = \left(\frac{{}_{2n}C_{n}}{2^{2n}}\right) \tag{5.5}$$

The paths implied by the second and third probabilities share the first coordinate (1, 1), since by assumption Peter does not lose on the first throw of the coin, but may differ as to the subsequent paths.

The binomial coefficient, as in (5.3), denoted ${}_nC_h$, is the number of ways of choosing h from n without regard to the order of choice. For example, ${}_nC_h$ and ${}_{2n}C_n$ are, respectively:

$${}_{n}C_{h} = \frac{n!}{h!(n-h)!} \tag{5.6}$$

$$
\begin{aligned}
{}_{2n}C_n &= \frac{(2n)!}{n!((2n)-n)!} \\
&= \frac{(2n)!}{(n!)^2}
\end{aligned}
\tag{5.7}
$$

where n! = n(n – 1)(n – 2) ... (1), read as 'n factorial'.

To illustrate these probabilities, let n = 2, so that 2n = T = 4, and the relevant probabilities are as follows:

$$P(S_T = r) = (2^{-4})\,{}_4C_{(4+r)/2} \text{ for } r \in A = [4, 2, 0, -2, -4] \Rightarrow$$

$$P(S_T = 0) = \left(\frac{{}_4C_2}{2^4}\right) = \frac{3}{8};\ P(S_T = 2) = \left(\frac{{}_4C_3}{2^4}\right) = \frac{1}{4};\ P(S_T = -2) = \left(\frac{{}_4C_1}{2^4}\right) = \frac{1}{4};$$

$$P(S_T = 4) = \left(\frac{{}_4C_4}{2^4}\right) = \frac{1}{16};\ P(S_T = -4) = \left(\frac{{}_4C_0}{2^4}\right) = \frac{1}{16};\ \sum\nolimits_{r \in A} P(S_T = r) = 1.$$

$$P(S_1 > 0, \ldots, S_4 > 0) = 0.5\left(\frac{{}_4C_2}{2^4}\right) = \frac{3}{16} \qquad \text{'always winning'}$$

$$P(S_1 \geq 0, \ldots, S_4 \geq 0) = \left(\frac{{}_4C_2}{2^4}\right) = \frac{3}{8} \qquad \text{'never losing'}$$

In a game consisting of 4 (sequential) tosses of a fair coin, the probability that Peter is always winning is 3/16, and the probability that he is never losing is 3/8. Continuing the illustration, in the case of n = 5, so that T = 10, the respective probabilities are 0.123 and 0.246. Already, these values might be quite surprising: the probability that Peter has not spent any time below the zero axis in ten tosses is just under ¼.

A related problem of interest, of which the last is a special case, is what fraction of the *overall* time Peter spends on the positive side of the axis. Intuition might suggest that this should be close to ½, but this is not the case. The formulation of the solution we use is due to Feller (1968, chapter III, Theorem 2 and corollary). It gives a general result that we can interpret as follows. Again let there be 2n = T sequential tosses at the rate of one per unit of time, t; define $\lambda \equiv 2k/2n = k/n$ as the fraction of time Peter spends on the positive side; then k = 0 and k = n correspond to no time and all the time, respectively, with percentages of 0 and 100%.

In the time interval from t = 0, ..., = 2n = T, the probability that Peter spends exactly λ of the time on the positive side and, therefore, exactly (1 – λ) of the time on the negative side is given by:

$$P(\lambda) = \left(\frac{{}_{2k}C_k}{2^{2k}}\right)\left(\frac{{}_{2(n-k)}C_{(n-k)}}{2^{2(n-k)}}\right) \tag{5.8a}$$

$$\approx \frac{1}{n}\frac{1}{\pi\sqrt{\lambda(1-\lambda)}} \qquad 0 < \lambda < 1 \tag{5.8b}$$

where ≈ indicates is approximately equal – see Feller (op. cit., Theorem 2) for details. Since k varies across all possible values, these probabilities must sum to unity. Further, the approximation, or direct calculation using Equation (5.8a) shows that as $n \to \infty$, the probability associated with a particular k tends to zero; hence, taking the integral to obtain the distribution function makes more sense and suggests that the cumulative probability is also of interest. The probability that the fraction of time spent on the positive side is less than or equal to λ is:

$$F(\lambda) = \sum\nolimits_{(k/n)\le\lambda} P(k/n) \tag{5.9}$$

F(λ) can be approximated by integrating the right-hand-side of (5.8b), so that:

$$F(\lambda) \approx \frac{2}{\pi}\sin^{-1}\sqrt{\lambda} \tag{5.10}$$

It may be helpful to illustrate some of these probabilities graphically. In the first case, we focus on $P(S_1 \ge 0, ..., S_{2n} \ge 0)$ and allow n to vary; this is shown in Figure 5.3. This graph shows how the probability that Peter is never on the losing side varies as the number of trials increases. (In effect this is the graph for k = n, as n increases.) Thus, the probabilities are, sequentially: $P(S_1 \ge 0, S_2 \ge 0) = 2/4 = ½$, for n = 1; $P(S_1 \ge 0, ..., S_4 \ge 0) = 6/16 = {}^3/_8$, for n = 2; and so on as n increases. Although these probabilities decline, they do so very slowly; for example, if n = 31, so that T = 62, then the probability that Peter never has a negative tally is 0.101; and even at n = 80 (T = 160), there is a 0.063 probability that Peter never has a negative tally.

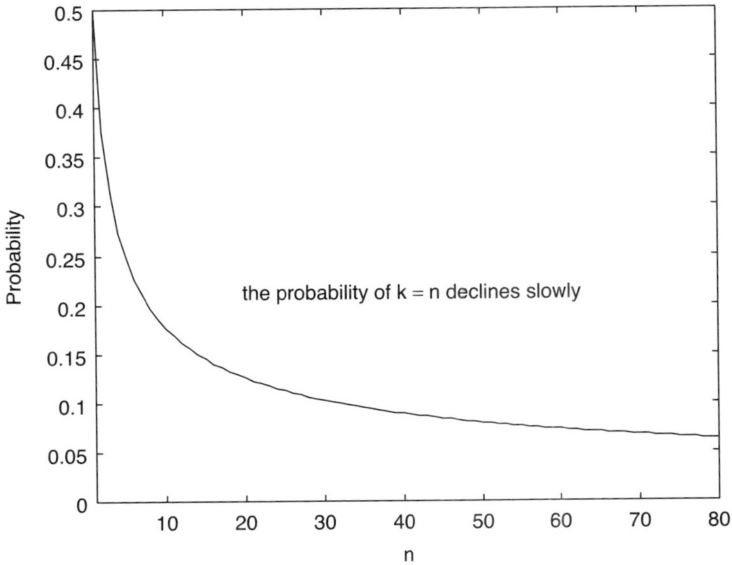

Figure 5.3 Probability of no negative tally as n varies

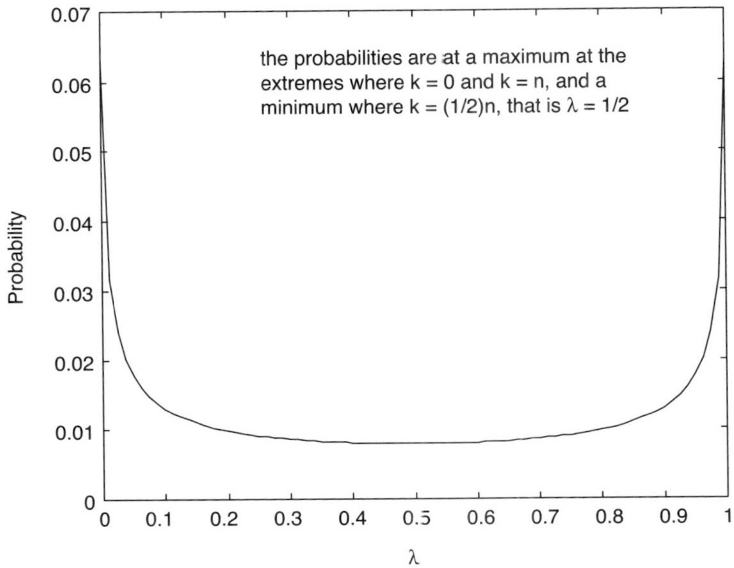

Figure 5.4 Probabilities as k/n varies for fixed n

In the case of Figure 5.4, n is fixed and k varies, therefore, $\lambda = k/n$ varies between 0 and 1; in this figure n = 80 (T = 160). Note that the probabilities are greatest at the extremes k = 0 and k = n, corresponding to $\lambda = 0$ and $\lambda = 1$, respectively; and the minimum is at $\lambda = ½$. Figure 5.4 shows

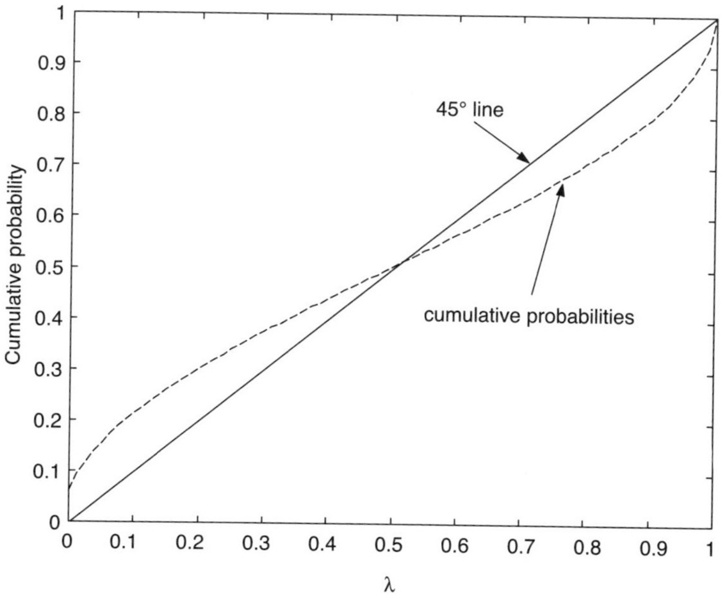

Figure 5.5 Cumulative distribution function, F(λ)

that the least likely, not the most likely, outcome is that Peter spends ½ the time on the positive side; the most likely single events are that he either spends all of his time on the positive side or all of his time on the negative side! These probabilities exhaust the sample space and, therefore, sum to unity, see Figure 5.5.

5.4 Variations: Nonsymmetric random walks, drift and other distributions

In this section, we briefly illustrate some variations on the basic random walk. The first two variations are concerned with imparting a direction to the random walk; the third to generalising the distribution and range of outcomes.

5.4.1 Nonsymmetric random walks

In the first variation, the walk is nonsymmetric so that $\text{Prob}(H) \neq \text{Prob}(T)$; for example, this follows in the gambling game when the coin is biased. This change will impart a direction to the random walk given by the larger probability. To illustrate this effect, as before four simulations were carried out, but the 'coin' was made gradually more biased, with $\text{Prob}(T) = 0.55$, 0.6, 0.65 and 0.7. These simulations are shown in Figures 5.6a–5.6b, but in this case the random walk is viewed from the

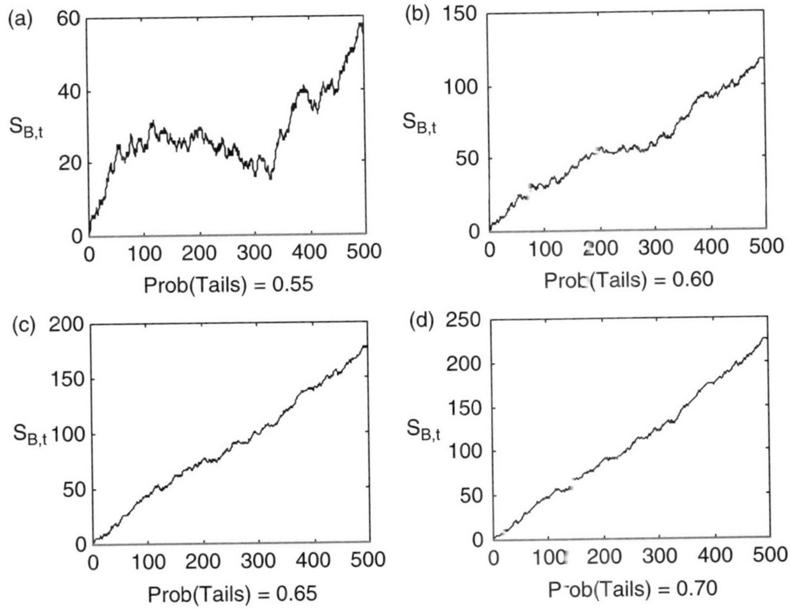

Figure 5.6 Nonsymmetric random walk (banker's view)

Banker's point of view since he, not Peter, has substituted a biased coin for an unbiased coin. Even a relatively small bias is sufficient to move the walk in the positive (Banker's) direction, see Figure 5.6a; and by the time that Prob(T) = 0.7, illustrated in Figure 5.6d, the systematic nature of the direction is very clear.

5.4.2 Drift

There is another way, frequently used in practice, that the random walk can gain direction. To continue the gambling analogy, if Peter has to 'pay-to-play' each game, say a fixed amount, μ, then the walk will tend to stay on one side of the axis. The quantity μ is usually referred to as drift. To illustrate the effect of drift, four cases are shown in Figures 5.7a–5.7d (from the Banker's view, hence drift will be positive; from Peter's point of view, the drift and walk are negative). Figure 5.7a is the base case, with $\mu = 0$, then in the other figures $\mu = 0.05$, 0.10 and 0.15, respectively; as $\sigma = 1$, the drift can also be viewed in units of the standard error. The impact of the drift becomes apparent quickly, imparting a clear direction to the random walk.

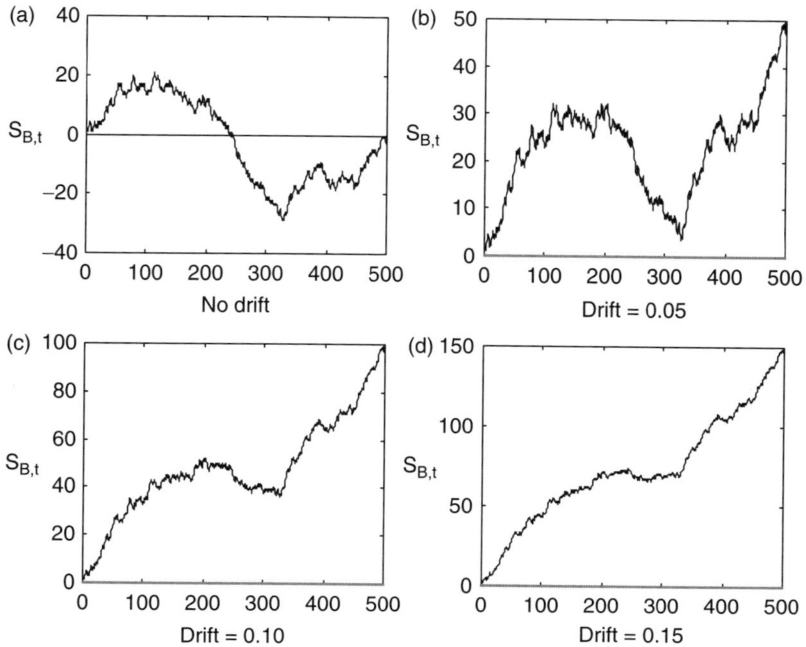

Figure 5.7 Random walk with drift (banker's view)

5.4.3 Other options and other distributions

So far the analysis has focussed on the symmetric binomial random walk. This section considers some variations on the random walk theme.

5.4.3.i A no-change option

We start with a simple idea. That is, even in a simple random walk there are actually three options: to the left, to the right and straight on; hence, probabilities can be assigned to each of these outcomes. In a gambling context, although the probability of a coin landing on an edge might be considered so unlikely as to be assigned a probability of zero, in some card games there is a 'no-hand' option, which leaves the gambler's position unchanged. Now there are three probabilities, say p_1 of a positive outcome, p_2 of no change and p_3 of a negative outcome. In order to ensure that there is no change in the variance of the process compared to the symmetric random walk, the positive and negative outcomes are symmetric, but are varied so that in each case the variance is standardised at unity.

To illustrate this variation, Figure 5.8a reproduces the symmetric random walk of Figure 5.2a, whereas Figures 5.8b–5.8d set $p_1 = p_3$ and $p_2 = 0.2$, 0.4 and 0.6, respectively and, to maintain comparability, start from the same 'seed' in the generation of the random outcomes. The simulations here are for T = 5,000, partly because the clear differences only become apparent as T increases. When the probability of no change is positive it tends to extend the sojourn times. For example, in this case, the walk first extends into the negative region, and to move out of this region requires a sequence of positive outcomes, whereas a no-change or negative outcome keeps the walk in the negative region; but the probability of the latter two now exceeds ½, hence the length of time on the negative side is extended – compare Figures 5.8a and 5.8d.

5.4.3.ii A random walk comprising Gaussian inputs

To continue the direction of the argument, we could define a continuous distribution to generate the sample space; for example, this could be continuous on a finite interval, for example a uniform distribution, or continuous over an infinite interval, for example a normal distribution. As noted in Chapter 1, this can be viewed as assigning probabilities to

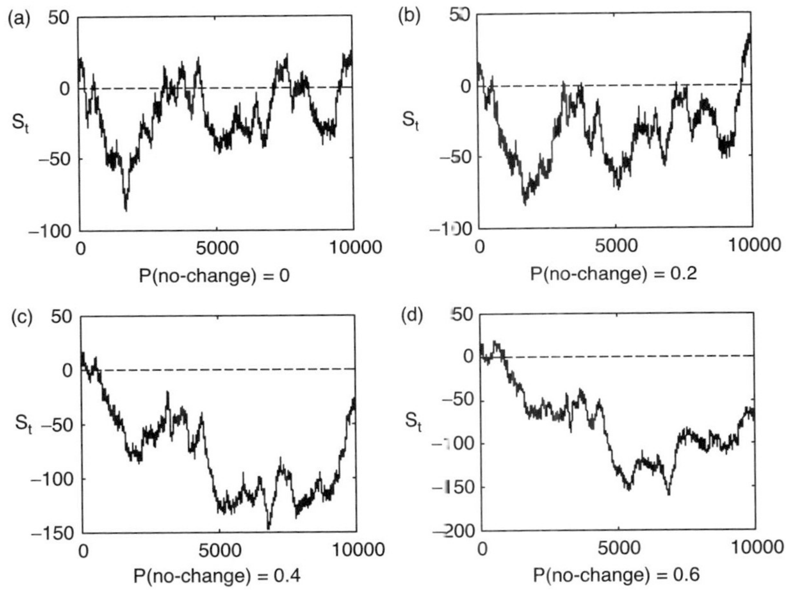

Figure 5.8 Simulated random walks as P(no-change) varies

intervals in the outcome space (which are linear Borel sets); for example, in the case of a normal distribution, the probability of an outcome in the range (+0.5, +1.0) is 0.15. As might be anticipated, when the outcomes are drawn from a normal distribution, the random walk path becomes smoother than in the discrete cases so far considered.

To consider this case further, let $y_t = \varepsilon_t$, where $\varepsilon_t \sim \text{niid}(0, \sigma^2)$, then the partial sum process is $S_t = S_{t-1} + \varepsilon_t = \sum_{j=1}^{t} \varepsilon_j$, assuming that $S_0 = 0$; that is, it is just the accumulation of normal white noise inputs. To illustrate, the simulations of Figures 5.2a–5.2d, were re-run with draws from $N(0, 1)$, and are shown in Figures 5.9a–5.9d. The smoother nature of the path is better illustrated with a fairly low value for T, and here T = 100. However, although smoother than in the case of (–1, +1) outcomes, the sample paths are still quite sharp at the micro level and hint that they do not have the property of differentiability.

We may also note at this point a feature of the way that the graphs have been drawn. Following convention, the discrete coordinates have been joined by straight lines, in effect interpolating adjacent points, to produce a continuous, albeit on occasion quite 'jerky', line, whereas a case could be made for using a step function since, in discrete time, the position S_t is held until just before the next gamble at t + 1, whereupon

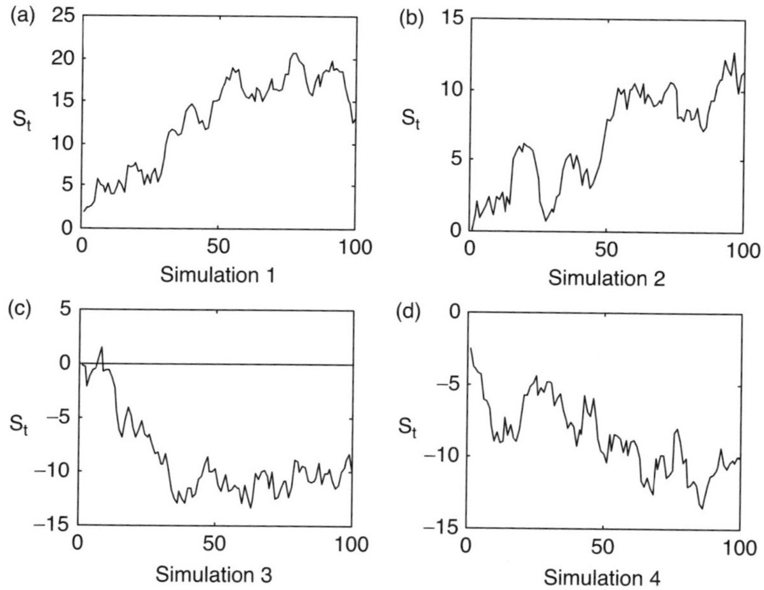

Figure 5.9 Simulated random walks, with draws from $N(0, 1)$

the position S_{t+1} is known; we continue with the convention, but return to this point in Chapter 6 where CADLAG functions are introduced.

5.5 The variance

Returning to the partial sum, it is evident that if $y_t \sim \text{iid}(0, \sigma_y^2)$, $y_t \sim \text{WN}(0, \sigma_y^2)$ or an MDS, then the variance of S_t evolves as $t\sigma_y^2$. In general:

$$\text{var}(S_t) = \sum\nolimits_{j=1}^{t} \text{var}(y_j) + 2\sum\nolimits_{i=1}^{t}\sum\nolimits_{j>i}^{t} \text{cov}(y_i, y_j) \tag{5.11}$$

So that if $\text{var}(y_j) = \sigma_y^2$ and $\text{cov}(y_i, y_j) = 0$ for $i \neq j$, then $\text{var}(S_t) = t\sigma_y^2$. If the y_t are heteroscedastic with $\text{cov}(y_i, y_j) = 0$, then the variance of S_t is:

$$\text{var}(S_t) = \sum\nolimits_{j=1}^{t} \text{var}(y_j) \tag{5.12}$$

Again, this will increase with t.

The covariances of the partial sums will also be of interest. We can infer the general pattern from some simple examples. Recall from example 1.9 that:

$$\text{cov}(S_2, S_3) = 2\sigma_y^2 + 2\,\text{cov}(y_1, y_2) + \text{cov}(y_1, y_3) + \text{cov}(y_2, y_3)$$

If the covariances are zero, then:

$$\text{cov}(S_2, S_3) = 2\sigma_y^2$$

In general, there are min(s, t) variances in common and the expectation of all terms involving subscripts that are not equal will be zero by the iid, MDS or white noise assumption; hence, in general:

$$\text{cov}(S_s, S_t) = \min(s, t)\sigma_y^2 \tag{5.13}$$

Later we will also be interested in the variance of the differences in the partial sums, $\text{var}(S_t - S_s)$. For convenience, assume that $t > s$, then the difference between these partial sums is just $\sum\nolimits_{j=1}^{t} y_j - \sum\nolimits_{j=1}^{s} y_j = \sum\nolimits_{j=s+1}^{t} y_j$, and, hence, $\text{var}(S_t - S_s) = (t - s)\sigma_y^2$.

Figure 5.10 illustrates how the variance of the partial sums increases with t, with values of $\text{var}(S_t)$ from R = 1,000 replications of a walk of length T = 500, plotted against t. The random walk in this case is a

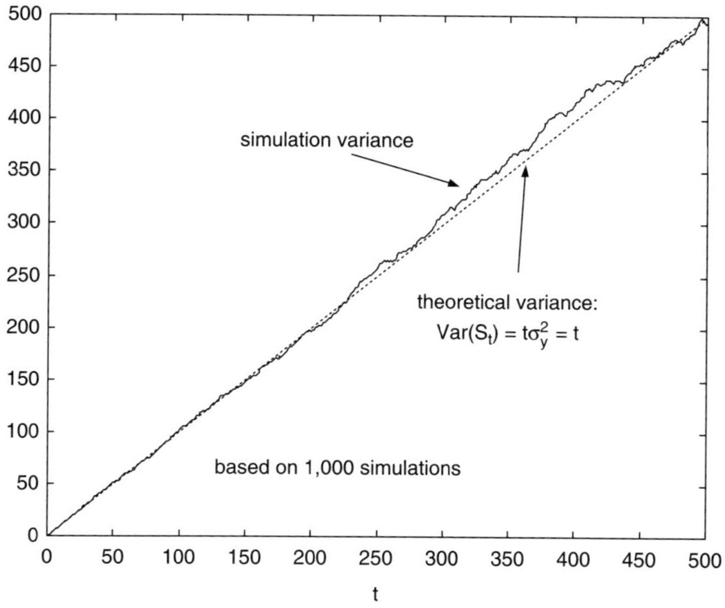

Figure 5.10 Simulation variance: var(S_t) as t varies

symmetric binomial random walk, with $\sigma_y^2 = 1$, but the pattern would be almost indistinguishable with draws from niid(0, 1).

To understand what these variances are, and what they are not, imagine the data arranged into a T × R matrix; then there is a variance for each column and a variance for each row. The R column variances are the 'sample' variances, for which there is no theoretical counterpart; however, the T row variances have a well-defined theoretical counterpart in var(S_t) = $t\sigma_y^2$ = t, when, as here, $\sigma_y^2 = 1$. We can make the correspondence of the simulated var(S_t) to $t\sigma_y^2$ as good as we like by increasing R. In this case R = 1,000 and the simulated var(S_t) are clearly very close to t (an exact correspondence would be a 45° line). Although the increase in the variance of the partial sum of a random walk is a clear identifying feature, in practice it is only a single column 'sample' variance that is available and that is not the appropriate concept; however, tests of the random walk hypothesis can be based on a variance ratio, see for example Lo and MacKinlay (2001).

5.6 Changes of sign on a random walk path

In a sense to be made precise, there are few changes of sign in a random walk path, and this a one of its key distinguishing features. For

example, in the four illustrative simulations reported in Table 5.1 (and Figures 5.2a–5.2d), the maximum changes of sign was 1% in simulation 2. The average number of changes of sign in 5,000 trials was just 27 in a sample of T = 5,000 (0.54%).

A change of sign means that the path crosses the zero axis, which here marks the expected value of S_t; it is for this reason that a sign change is referred to as mean reversion. Thus, a frequent descriptive feature by which to broadly judge whether a path has been generated by a random walk, is to look for mean reversion or, equivalently, sign changes taking $E(S_t)$ as the reference point. This heuristic also provides the basis of a test statistic for a unit root, see Burridge and Guerre (1996) and Garciá and Sansó (2006), which is developed in Chapter 8.

5.6.1 Binomial inputs

To make these ideas more precise we refer to Feller (1968, chapter III.5, Theorem 1) for the symmetric binomial random walk. A change of sign is dated at t if S_{t-1} and S_{t+1} are of opposite sign, in which case $S_t = 0$. (The identification of sign changes is slightly different if the underlying random variable is continuous.) The probability of k changes of sign in T realisations is given by:

$$2P(S_T = 2k + 1) = 2\left(\frac{{}_T C_h}{2^T}\right) \tag{5.14}$$

where T = 2n + 1 and h = (2n + 2k +2) / 2 = (n − k + 1). As Feller (ibid) notes, this probability declines with k: thus, the largest probability is actually for *no* change of sign, which is illustrated for three choices of T = 99, 59 and 19 in Figure 5.11. The expected values of the number of sign changes are 3.48, 2.58 and 1.26, respectively.

Thus, it is incorrect to assume that the lead will change hands quite evenly. If this was the case then the graph of Peter's winnings would show frequent crossings of the zero axis, but this event has negligible probability in a sense that can be made more precise as follows. Let $\upsilon_T = k / \sqrt{T}$ be the normalised number of changes of sign in a symmetric binomial random walk starting at the origin, where k is the number of changes of sign and T the number of trials. Let $F(\upsilon_T)$ be the distribution function of υ_T for T trials. Then Feller (1968, chapter III.5, Theorem 2) derives the following limiting result as $T \to \infty$:

$$F(\upsilon_T) \Rightarrow_D 2\Phi(2\upsilon_T) - 1 \tag{5.15}$$

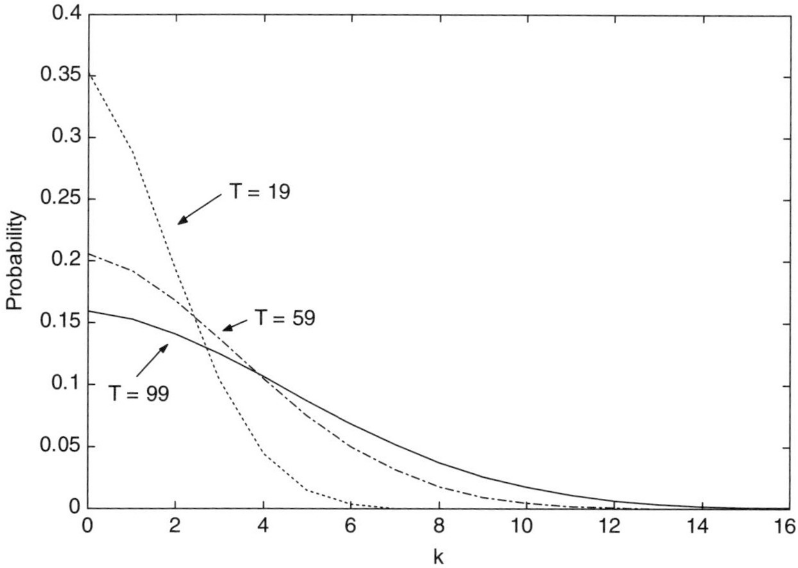

Figure 5.11 Probability of k sign changes

where Φ(.) is the cdf of the standard normal distribution (see Chapter 1, example 1.2). An equivalent statement in terms of the random variables, rather than the distribution functions, is $\upsilon_T \Rightarrow_D \nu$ where ν has the distribution given on the right of Equation (5.15). The limiting distribution of $F(\upsilon_T)$ is plotted in Figure 5.12 (solid line); it is, of course, defined only for $\upsilon \geq 0$. The median is approximately 0.337, so that the median number of changes of sign for T trials is about $0.337\sqrt{T}$; for example if T = 100, then the median is about 3 (it has to be an integer). The limiting distribution is a remarkably good approximation for finite values of T. For example, the implied probabilities from the limit distribution and the exact probabilities from (5.14) for T = 19 are plotted in Figure 5.13 in the form of a bar chart; note that the bar heights are virtually indistinguishable.

In the case of a symmetric binomial random walk, just counting the sign changes will exclude the number of reflections; that is where the random walk reaches the zero axis, but it is reflected back in the same direction on the next step. In our sense this is also mean reversion as it is a 'return to the origin', although it is not a sign change. Since a change of sign implies a return to the origin, a count of mean reversions will include the sign changes; Burridge and Guerre (1996) note

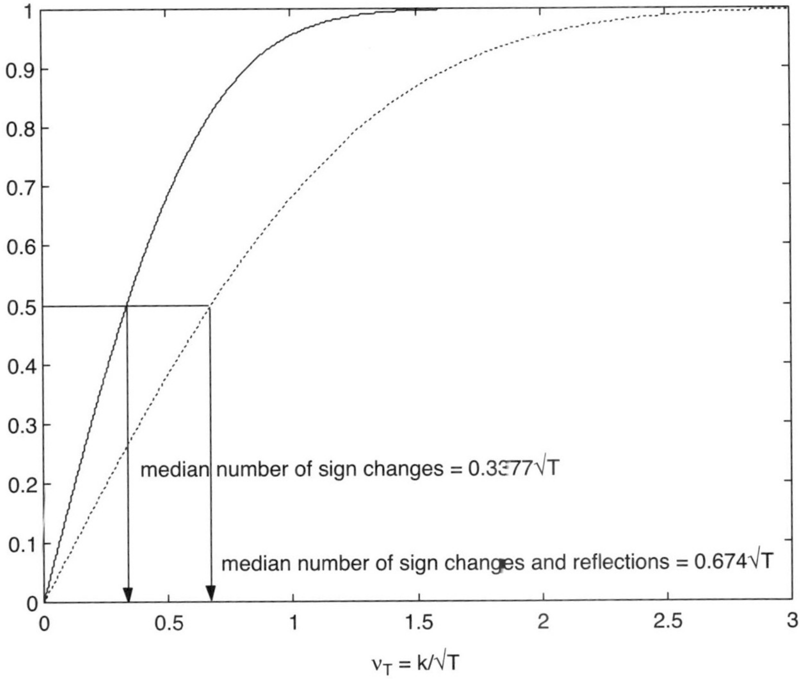

Figure 5.12 Distribution functions of changes of sign and reflections

that reflections are as numerous as sign changes and capture this in their Theorem 2. The notation adopted is in preparation for Chapter 8. Let $\zeta \equiv K_{B,T}(0) = S_T / \sqrt{T}$ be the normalised number of visits to the origin (including reflections) of a symmetric binomial random walk of length T and let $F(K_{B,T})$ be the distribution function of $K_{B,T}(0)$, then:

$$F(K_{B,T}) \Rightarrow_D F(\zeta) = 2\Phi(\zeta) - 1 \tag{5.16}$$

The limiting distribution function in (5.16) is also shown in Figure 5.12 (dotted line). The median of this distribution is 0.674, so that the median number of mean reversions for T trials is about $0.674\sqrt{T}$; for example if T = 100, then median is about 7. The distribution function $F(\zeta) = 2\Phi(\zeta) - 1$ is the half normal, that is the distribution function for the absolute value of a normally distributed random variable with mean $\mu = 0$ and variance σ^2; for $\sigma^2 = 1, E(\zeta) = \sqrt{1/2\pi} = 0.7979$, so that

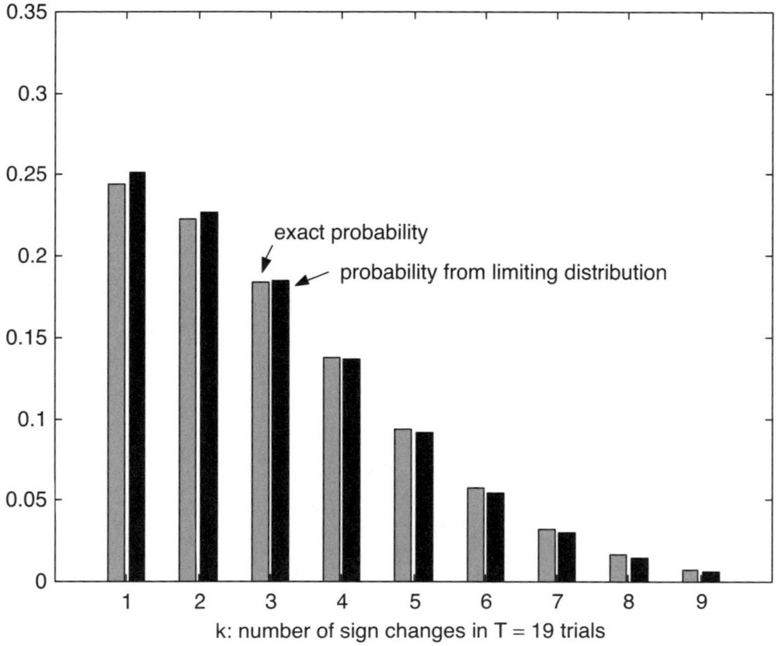

Figure 5.13 Exact and approximate probability of k sign changes

the mean number of reversions is $0.7979\sqrt{T}$. The distribution in (5.16) reappears in Chapter 8 in connection with the Burridge and Guerre (1996) nonparametric test for a unit root based on the number of mean reversions.

5.6.2 Gaussian inputs

If the random inputs are Gaussian, then the random walk is $S_t = S_{t-1} + \varepsilon_t$, where $\varepsilon_t \sim \text{niid}(0, \sigma^2)$. This implies that the level $S_t = 0$ is crossed if:

$$S_{t-1} < 0 \text{ and } S_t > 0 \text{ or } S_{t-1} > 0 \text{ and } S_t < 0$$

That is a crossing of zero occurs if S_{t-1} moves from negative to positive or from positive to negative; in either case there is a sign change. Table 5.2 gives the expected number of crossings for some values of T.

There are fewer crossings of the zero axis in the case of a symmetric binomial random walk, because the limitation of the inputs to draws from the pair (+1, –1), implies that some mean reversions, in the sense of returns to the origin, are not counted (as noted in the previous section).

Table 5.2 Number of crossings of the zero axis for two random walk processes

T =	100	500	1,000	3,000
Binomial inputs without reflections	3.5	8.4	12.1	21.4
Binomial inputs with reflections	6.4	17.3	24.7	43.2
Gaussian inputs	6.4	14.2	20.1	34.9

Source: Gaussian inputs, Burridge and Guerre (1996, table 1); binomial inputs, exact probabilities for T = 100 using (5.4); otherwise (5.15) and (5.16) were used.

For example, the sequence $S_{t-1} < 0$, $S_t = 0$, $S_{t+1} < 0$, is not counted as a sign change, but it is an example of mean reversion. If the reflections are counted then there are slightly more mean reversions for the symmetric binomial random walk. Burridge and Guerre (op. cit.,) find that the expected number of sign changes (mean reversions) in the case of Gaussian inputs is $0.6363\sqrt{T}$, whereas for the analogous case of mean reversion for a symmetric binomial random walk, this is $0.7979\sqrt{T}$ (see Section 5.6.1). (The reason for this difference is explained in Chapter 8, Section 8.5.1.)

5.7 A unit root

Notice that a partial sum process such as (5.1), is constructed as $S_t = S_{t-1} + y_t$, hence the 'slope' relating S_t to S_{t-1} is +1; another way of looking at this is to write the partial sum process using the lag operator, in which case $(1 - L)S_t = y_t$, from which it is evident that the process generating S_t has a unit root. A useful graphic to inform at least in this simple case, whether there is a unit root, is a scatter graph of S_t on S_{t-1}. To illustrate, Figure 5.14a shows one sample path for T = 200, together with the associated scatter graph in Figure 5.14b, on which a line with a slope of +1, that

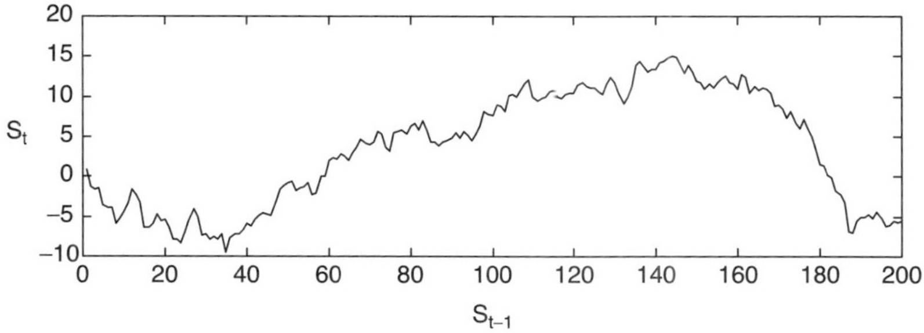

Figure 5.14a A random walk sample path

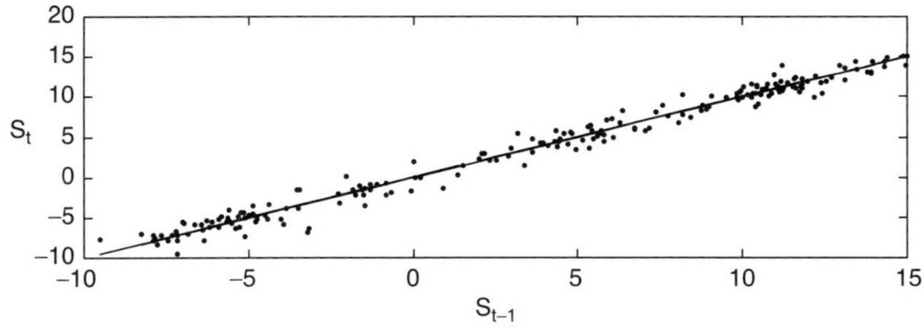

Figure 5.14b Scatter graph of S_t on S_{t-1}

is a 45° line, has been superimposed. The following economic examples illustrate this and other points connected with random walks.

5.8 Economic examples

In this section we examine some economic time series to see if they exhibit the characteristics of a random walk.

5.8.1 A bilateral exchange rate, UK:US

The first series to be considered comprises 7,936 observations on the (nominal) UK:US exchange rate (expressed as the number of units of one £ it takes to buy one US$). The data are daily, excluding weekends and Public Holidays, over the period June 1975 to May 2006. The data are graphed in Figure 5.15 (upper panel). The first point to note is that despite the widespread analysis of nominal exchange rates for random walk behaviour, the limitation of non-negativity rules out a simple random walk, although it allows an exponential random walk. One could view the lower limit as a 'reflecting' barrier in the random walk. The strategy we adopt is to reintroduce 'Peter' who gambles on whether the exchange rate will move up, with respective 'outcomes' of +1 (up) and –1 (down), and 0 for no change. (In effect, the original sample space has been mapped into a much simpler sample space.) The random variable at each stage in the sequence therefore has outcomes corresponding to a multinomial trial. The sequence so defined is (S_t, t = 1, ..., T), whereas the original sequence is denoted ($S_{E,t}$, t = 1, ..., T).

The sequence corresponding to the 'gamble' is shown in Figure 5.15 (lower panel). The potential sequences from this formulation do not have the non-negativity limitation of the original series and have a theoretical mean of zero. They can, then, be considered as being generated

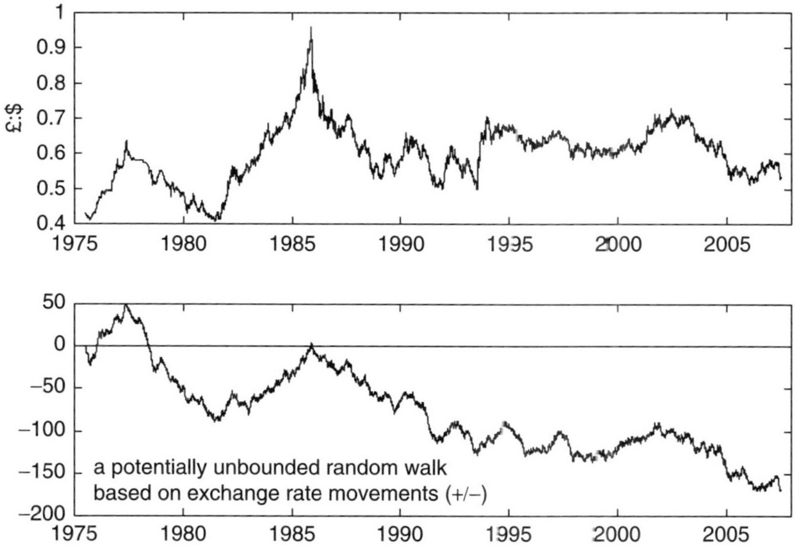

Figure 5.15 US:UK exchange rate (daily)

by a simple symmetric random walk. Some of the characteristics of this process are summarised in Tables 5.3a and 5.3b.

In the case of the overall sample, almost exactly 50% of the outcomes are negative, and just under 48% are positive, see Table 5.3a. Informally this is close enough to the prototypical situation in which these outcomes have equal probability. However, as in an idealised random walk, despite these almost equal overall figures, most of the observations are on one side of the axis, in this case the negative side, with just over 67% of the outcomes forming one continuous sequence on the negative side. Further, there are just 8 changes of sign in over 7,900 observations. Taken together, these features are strongly suggestive that the outcomes are being generated by a random walk process.

Another aspect of interest is to examine 'windows' of observations, where, in this case, the windows each comprise 1,000 observations. At the beginning of each sub-sample, the start is re-centred to zero. The proportions of positive and negative changes within each sub-sample are broadly between 45% and 53%, but there are relatively few changes of sign for the partial sum, S_t, and some very long sequences on one side or the other; for example, between (re-centred) observations 1,001 and 2,000, 97.8% of the S_t are negative, whereas between (re-centred) observations 2,001 and 3,000, 94.4 of the S_t are positive.

Table 5.3a Characteristics of a sequence of gambles on the UK:US exchange rate

	+ ve outcomes	**No-change**	**– ve outcomes**	**sign changes**	**Longest + sequence**	**Longest – sequence**
Number	3,797	172	3,966	8	585	5,347
Proportion (%)	47.8	2.2	50.0	0.1	7.4	67.3

Table 5.3b Sub-samples of the sequence of gambles on the UK:US exchange rate

	1,001–2,000	**2,001–3,000**	**3,001–4,000**	**4,001–5,000**	**5,001–6,000**	**6,001–7,000**
Prop(+)	48.3	51.2	44.7	48.7	49.1	49.4
Prop(=)	1.6	1.1	1.9	1.5	1.0	1.7
Prop(–)	50.1	47.7	53.4	49.8	49.9	48.9
Prop($S_t > 0$)	0.1	97.1	0.8	65.5	27.7	98.1
Prop($S_t = 0$)	0.3	0.4	1.1	4.9	2.6	0.3
Prop($S_t < 0$)	99.6	2.5	98.1	29.6	69.7	1.6
Prop(Change Sign)	0.2	0.2	0.9	2.3	1.2	0.3
Prop(MaxSeq+)	0.1	94.4	0.5	25.3	21.9	97.8
Prop(MaxSeq–)	97.8	2.5	97.0	17.5	46.8	1.5

Note: overall data period, June 1975 to May 2006, comprising 7,936 observations.

To illustrate, Figure 5.16 shows the scatter graph of $S_{E,t}$ on $S_{E,t-1}$ for the last 1,000 observations, with a 45° line superimposed on the scatter. (The scatter is so dense around the line that the number of observations is limited; also using S_t rather than $S_{E,t}$ results in a similar plot.) The tightness of the scatter plot around the 45° line is evident, which suggests quite strongly that the exchange rate has the properties associated with a random walk.

5.8.2 The gold-silver price ratio

The second series to be considered is the ratio of gold to silver price, obtained from the daily London Fix prices for the period 2 January 1985 to 31 March 2006; weekends and Bank holidays are excluded, giving an overall total of $T = 5{,}372$ observations. Whilst either of these prices might be considered singly, they are nominal prices and it makes more economic sense to apply a numeraire, with the cost of gold in terms of silver well established in this respect.

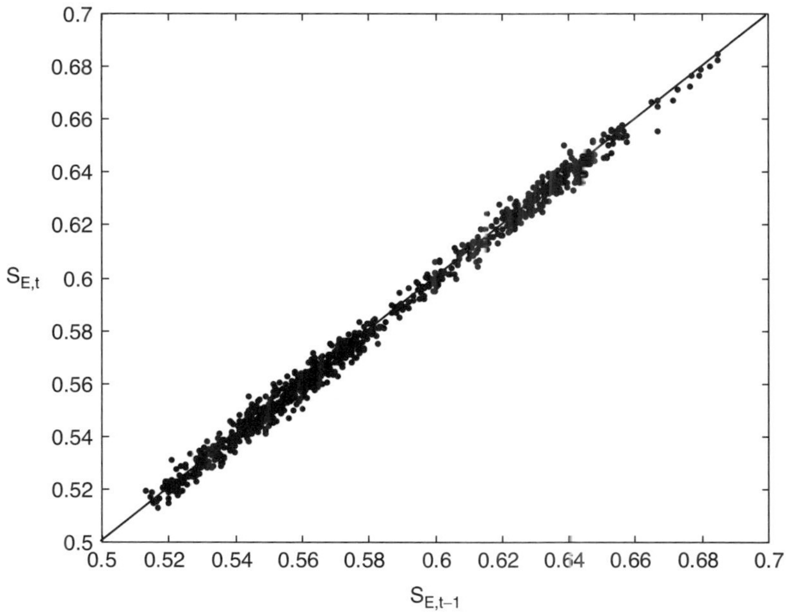

Figure 5.16 Scatter graph of daily exchange rate

In this case, the variable considered is the log of the gold-silver price ratio, thus negative values are possible; the ratio is normalised at unity at the start of the sample, so the log of the ratio is zero at the start point. The data are presented in ratio form in the upper panel of Figure 5.17 and in log ratio form in the lower panel. In the latter, the opportunity is taken to introduce a time indexing transformation that is of use in the next chapter; specifically, the variable $0 \leq r \leq 1$ is introduced, which refers to the fraction of the overall sample T. For example, given T = 5,372, then if r = ½, rT = 2,686, so that the complete sample can be indexed by moving r through its range.

Table 5.4 presents a number of summary characteristics of the log (ratio) data, which is S_t in this context. Note that the proportion of positive (+) and negative (–) changes in the sequence, at very close to 50% each, almost exactly fits a symmetric random walk. There are relatively few, just 32, changes of sign of the series, S_t, itself, with 98.2% of the S_t on the positive side of the axis, and one positive sequence of nearly 98% of the observations. These characteristics are strongly suggestive of a generating process for the sequence that is a random walk.

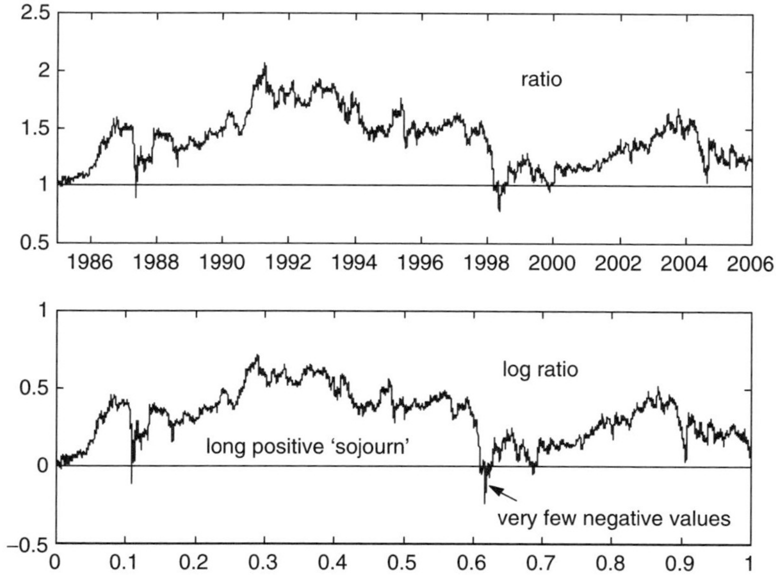

Figure 5.17 Gold-silver price ratio (daily data)

Table 5.4 Gold-silver price ratio (log): Characteristics in the sample

	+	=	–	$S_t > 0$	$S_t = 0$	$S_t < 0$	Change Sign	Max Seq+	Max Seq–
Number	2,702	4	2,665	5,277	0	94	32	5,261	78
Per cent	50.3	0.07	49.6	98.2	0.0	1.8	0.6	97.9	1.5

The scatter graph of S_t on S_{t-1} for the last 1,000 observations is shown in Figure 5.18 for the last 1,000 observations, with a 45° line superimposed on the scatter. Although there are some departures from the 45° line, there is a clear indication that the points cluster around the line, suggesting a stochastic process with random walk properties.

5.9 Concluding remarks and references

Random walks have been an enduring subject of intrigue and study. Hald (2003) takes the story back to before 1750 and to the relationship of the random walk to the problem of gambler's ruin. Telcs (2006) continues the

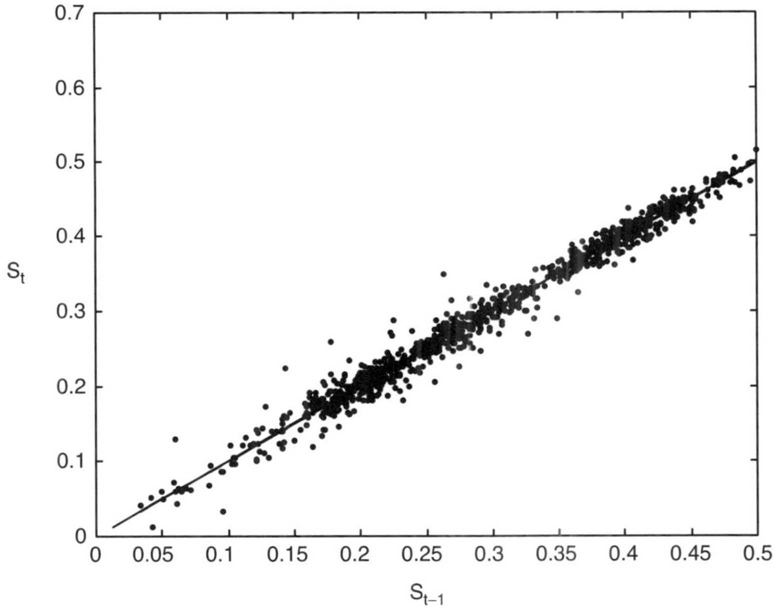

Figure 5.18 Scatter graph of gold-silver price ratio (log)

historical picture of random walks and also includes many recent developments. Hughes (1995, 1996) is a comprehensive two volume work on random walks and, whilst it is based on examples from physics, physical chemistry, and engineering, it contains much of more general interest, as does Révész (2005).

Several modern texts on probability have a chapter on random walks, see for example Fristedt and Gray (1997) and Tuckwell (1995); it is also usual to include coverage of the random walk as part of the development of Brownian motion, see for example Koralov and Sinai (2007). Feller's two volumes (1966, 1968) are classics, which should also be consulted. In an economic context, there has been a considerable interest in random walks as a baseline model for pricing financial assets, see, for example, Shreve (2004) especially chapter 3; and Lo and MacKinlay (2001) summarise many of the arguments and link and distinguish the random walk hypothesis from the theory of efficient markets. The econometric literature on random walks is too vast to summarise here, but some early key references include Nelson and Plosser (1982), Phillips (1987) and Phillips and Perron (1988).

Questions

Q5.1 Peter visits the gambling casino for the second time having won handsomely the night before. He is betting on whether the ball on a roulette wheel lands red or black, winning or losing an equal amount. After 20 games his cumulative winnings have not been negative and, therefore, he argues that his winning streak is continuing and that he should continue to bet because luck must be on his side! Is he right?

On the other hand Peter argues that if he had only spent half the time in a winning position, he would not have felt so lucky and would have stopped betting. Is he right?

A5.1 First, consider the probability that his tally would never be negative after 20 games. His tally S_t is a symmetric binomial random walk, with the probability that S_t is always positive given by (5.5) with $t = 2n$. For $t = 20$, this is:

$$P(S_t \geq 0 : t = 1, \ldots, 20) = \left(\frac{{}_{20}C_{10}}{2^{20}} \right) = 0.1762$$

A probability of 0.1762 that Peter's tally did not go negative in 20 plays, that is about a one-in-six chance, so although Peter might consider himself lucky, the probability is perhaps larger than he thought. As to whether he has a lucky streak, the random walk has independent increments, so the probability of winning on the next gamble is unaffected by his previous good fortune: it is still ½.

The next question is what is the probability of Peter spending half of his time in a winning position in 20 games? To answer this, we use (5.8a), to obtain the probability of spending exactly $\lambda = ½$ of his time on the positive side. Set $2k = 10$, $2n = 20$, then:

$$P(½) = 2\left(\frac{{}_{10}C_5}{2^{10}} \right) = 0.0606$$

Note that the approximation in (5.8b) gives the probability as 0.0637. Thus, the probability of $\lambda = ½$ is just over 6%, which reflects the general pattern shown in Figure 5.4 that $P(\lambda)$ is at a minimum where $\lambda = ½$, and is symmetric about this point, increasing towards the two extremes $\lambda = 0$ and $\lambda = 1$. So as to Peter's judgement, the least likely outcome was

that he would spend exactly half his time on the positive side, but if he did, again it would not affect the probability of winning on the next gamble.

Q5.2 Let $S_t = \sum_{j=1}^{t} y_j, y_j \sim (0, \sigma_y^2)$, show the following and establish the general pattern for $\text{cov}(S_t, S_{t+1})$:

$$\text{cov}(S_1, S_2) = 2\sigma_y^2 + \text{cov}(y_1, y_2)$$
$$\text{cov}(S_2, S_3) = 2\sigma_y^2 + 2\,\text{cov}(y_1, y_2) + \text{cov}(y_1, y_3) + \text{cov}(y_2, y_3)$$

Also show that $\text{cov}(S_t, S_{t+1}) = \text{var}(S_t) + \sum_{i=1}^{t} \text{cov}(y_i y_{t+1})$.

A5.2 Working through the examples remembering that $E(y_j) = 0$ and expectation is a linear operator, then the following sequence is established:

$$\begin{aligned}
\text{cov}(S_1, S_2) &= \text{cov}(y_1, y_1 + y_2) \\
&= E[y_1(y_1 + y_2)] \\
&= \sigma_y^2 + \text{cov}(y_1 y_2) \\
\text{cov}(S_2, S_3) &= \text{cov}(y_1 + y_2, y_1 + y_2 + y_3) \\
&= E(y_1^2) + E(y_2^2) + 2E(y_1 y_2) + E(y_1 y_3) + E(y_2 y_3) \\
&= 2\sigma_y^2 + 2\,\text{cov}(y_1 y_2) + \text{cov}(y_1 y_3) + \text{cov}(y_2 y_3) \\
\text{cov}(S_3, S_4) &= \text{cov}(y_1 + y_2 + y_3, y_1 + y_2 + y_3 + y_4) \\
&= 3\sigma_y^2 + 2E(y_1 y_2) + 2E(y_1 y_3) + 2E(y_2 y_3) + E(y_1 y_4) + E(y_2 y_4) \\
&\quad + E(y_3 y_4) \\
&= 3\sigma_y^2 + 2\sum_{i=1}^{2}\sum_{j=i+1}^{3} \text{cov}(y_i y_j) + \sum_{i=1}^{3} \text{cov}(y_i y_4) \\
\text{cov}(S_4, S_5) &= 4\sigma_y^2 + 2\sum_{i=1}^{3}\sum_{j=i+1}^{4} \text{cov}(y_i y_j) + \sum_{i=1}^{4} \text{cov}(y_i y_5)
\end{aligned}$$

In general:

$$\begin{aligned}
\text{cov}(S_t, S_{t+1}) &= t\sigma_y^2 + 2\sum_{i=1}^{t-1}\sum_{j=i+1}^{t} \text{cov}(y_i y_j) + \sum_{i=1}^{t} \text{cov}(y_i y_{t+1}) \\
&= \text{var}(S_t) + \sum_{i=1}^{t} \text{cov}(y_i y_{t+1})
\end{aligned}$$

The last result follows either on noting the relationship directly or

$$\begin{aligned}
\text{cov}(S_t, S_{t+1}) &= \text{cov}(S_t, S_t + y_{t+1}) \\
&= \text{var}(S_t) + \text{cov}(S_t, y_{t+1}) \\
&= \text{var}(S_t) + \text{cov}(y_1 + \ldots + y_t, y_{t+1}) \\
&= \text{var}(S_t) + \sum_{i=1}^{t} \text{cov}(y_i y_{t+1})
\end{aligned}$$

Q5.3 The time series of the ratio of the gold to silver price shows 32 changes of sign in 5,372 observations. Is this prima facie evidence of a random walk? Suppose that the variable of interest is the log of the ratio of the gold to silver price: how many changes of sign will there be in the log ratio series?

A5.3 In the case of Gaussian inputs, the expected number of sign changes is $0.6363\sqrt{T}$, which is 46.4 for T = 5,372; whereas for binomial inputs, it is $0.7979\sqrt{T} = 58.5$. In both cases, the actual number of changes is below the expected number, but it is on the right side to suggest that the data could be generated by a random walk process. A more formal test can be designed and this is the subject of Chapter 8, Section 8.5. As to the second part of the question, the number of times that a particular level is crossed is invariant to a continuous monotonic transformation. Intuitively, if the original series is subject to a monotonic transformation then so is the level, so that the number of crossings in the transformed series is just the same as in the original series. This is useful if a random walk is suspected, but there is there is uncertainty as to whether it is in the original series or some (monotonic) transformation of the series.

6
Brownian Motion: Basic Concepts

Introduction

Brownian motion is a key concept in economics in two respects. It underlies an important part of stochastic finance, which includes the pricing of risky assets, such as stock prices, bonds and exchange rates. For example a central model for the price of a risky asset is that of geometric Brownian motion (see Chapter 7). It also plays a key role in econometrics, especially in the distribution theory underlying test statistics for a unit root. For example, the limiting distribution of the familiar Dickey-Fuller pseudo-t test for a unit root is a functional of Brownian motion.

In both cases, but in different contexts, it is possible to relate the importance of Brownian motion to the limit of a random walk process in which the steps of the random walk become smaller and smaller. The process can be viewed in the limit as occurring in continuous time; the stochastic difference equation becomes a stochastic differential equation and the random walk generates a sample path of Brownian motion. Solving the stochastic differential equation requires use of the Itô calculus. This chapter outlines the key concept of Brownian motion, whereas the next chapter is a non-technical introduction to Itô calculus. Together these chapters provide some familiarity with the language that is used in more advanced texts and especially in the asymptotic distribution theory for unit root tests. A number of references to more advanced works are provided at the end of the chapter for the interested reader.

This chapter is organised as follows. Section 6.1 introduces the definition of Brownian motion and Section 6.2, picking up on Chapter 5, links this to the limit of a random walk; Section 6.3 outlines the function space

on which BM is defined and Section 6.4 summarises some key properties of Brownian motion. Brownian bridges occur quite frequently in the distribution theory of unit root tests and these are introduced in Section 6.5. The central limit theorem and the continuous mapping theorem, as they apply to functional spaces, are two essential tools for the analysis of unit root test statistics and these are outlined in Section 6.6. The use of these theorems is illustrated in Chapter 8, to obtain the limiting distributions of two widely used test statistics for a unit root due to Dickey and Fuller (see Fuller, 1976).

6.1 Definition of Brownian motion

The concept of Brownian motion is critical to the development of many scientific disciplines, including biology, engineering, physics, meteorology and chemistry, as well as economics. The stochastic process W(t) defined in continuous time is said to be a Brownian motion (BM) process if the following three conditions are met:

BM1: $W(0) = 0$.
BM2: the increments are independent and stationary over time.
BM3: $W(t) \sim N(0, t\sigma^2)$; that is W(t) is normally distributed with mean zero and variance $t\sigma^2$.

This process is also referred to as a Weiner process (Weiner, 1923). It is a standard Brownian motion process if $\sigma^2 = 1$, when it will be denoted B(t). If $\sigma^2 \neq 1$ and $W(0) = 0$, then $B(t) = W(t)/\sigma$ converts the process to have a unit variance and become standard BM. If $W(0) = \mu \neq 0$, and $\sigma^2 \neq 1$, then $B(t) = [W(t) - \mu]/\sigma$ is standard BM $\Rightarrow W(t) = \mu + \sigma B(t)$. A trended BM is obtained if $W(t) = \beta t + \sigma B(t)$, so that $B(t) = [W(t) - \beta t]/\sigma$ is standard BM.

A word on notation is appropriate at this stage: a reasonably standard notation in this area is to denote time in general by letters of the alphabet, for example s and t and, thus, to refer to, say, W(s) and W(t) as Brownian motion at times s and t. If the context does not require reference to more than two or three distinct times, then this notation will suffice. Otherwise, if a time sequence of general length is defined, the convention is to use a subscript notation on t, otherwise too many letters are required; thus, $t_1, t_2, \ldots t_N$ is an increasing sequence of the time index, for example corresponding to the Brownian motions $W(t_1)$, $W(t_2)$ and $W(t_N)$. As time is here a continuous index, there is no requirement that any of these indices are integers.

What are the characteristics of Brownian motion that make it attractive as a model of physical and human behaviour? BM provides a mathematical model of the diffusion, or motion over time, of erratic particles; consider two examples, the first being Robert Brown's original observation in 1827 that pollen grains suspended in water exhibited a ceaseless erratic motion; being bombarded by water molecules, the pollen seemed to be the subject of a myriad of chance movements. A similar phenomenon can be observed with smoke particles colliding with air molecules. In both examples, the trajectory of the particle over any small period is spiky and seemingly chaotic, but observed over a longer period the particle traces out a smoother path that has local trends.

In an economic context, it is evident that the behaviour of stock prices over time, particularly very short periods of time, can be quite erratic – or noisy; however, over a longer period, a direction is imparted to the level of the series. The point then is how to model this process: what is required is a model in which at any one point, or small interval, movement, as captured by the 'increments', is erratic and seemingly without structure, whereas over a longer period, the individual erratic movements are slight relative to the whole path. Hence, a key element of BM is the way that the erratic increments are built up into the level of the series. Whilst BM specifies normal increments, it can be generalised to increments from other distributions as might be appropriate for some financial asset prices, whose distributions exhibit much greater kurtosis than would be found in a normal distribution.

6.2 Brownian motion as the limit of a random walk

It is helpful to revisit the random walk of Chapter 5, and view Brownian motion as the limiting version of this process, where the limit is taken as the time interval between steps in the random walk is made smaller and smaller. Thus, in the limit the random walk becomes a continuous process.

6.2.1 Generating sample paths of BM

As an artificial, but helpful, device consider the length of the walk, T, as fixed and view this length as being divided into 'small' steps, where there are N of these relative time divisions, so that $\Delta t = T/N$. By allowing N to increase, these time divisions become smaller, approaching 0 and, thus, in the limit, with T fixed, as $N \to \infty$, the random walk process becomes continuous. In such a case,

there is no loss in fixing the length of walk as the unit interval, so that T = 1, and, therefore, $\Delta t = 1/N$. The time index is not a set of integers, so we adopt the notation (referred to above), that the time index is $t_1 < t_2 < \ldots < t_N$; in general, $\Delta t_j \equiv t_j - t_{j-1}$, but we may, for convenience, set Δt equal to a constant so that $t_j = t_{j-1} + \Delta t$. Having established the limit of the random walk, which turns out to be Brownian motion, the method can also be used to establish the limit of some important partial sum processes, which are scaled random walks, arising in econometric theory.

The other parameter in the random walk is the size of each step, or win/loss amount in a gamble, which is taken to be $\Delta S_t = (\sqrt{\Delta t})\varepsilon_t$ where ε_t is distributed as iid(0, σ^2). We could alternatively base the random walk on the inputs $y_t = (-1, +1)$ and $p = q = ½$, which defines a symmetric binomial random walk, with the same limiting results see Equations (6.2) and (6.3) below, and see also Shreve (2004, section 3.2.5) and Iacus (2008, section 1.6.1). A question, see **Q6.1** below, further explores this variant.

The variance of ΔS_t is $(\Delta t)\sigma^2$ and if we return to the case where $\Delta t = 1$, that is time increments by one (whole) unit, then $\text{Var}(\Delta S_t) = \sigma^2$, which is as before. The random walk is now:

$$S_{t_j} = S_{t_{j-1}} + (\sqrt{\Delta t})\varepsilon_{t_j} \tag{6.1}$$

The variance of S_{t_j}, $\text{var}(S_{t_j})$, will be needed, but we know this to be $\text{var}(S_{t_j}) = t_j\sigma^2$; if $\sigma^2 = 1$, then $t_j\sigma^2 = t_j$.

The limit of interest is obtained as $N \to \infty$, with T fixed, such that:

$$\frac{S_{t_j}}{\sigma\sqrt{N}} \Rightarrow_D N(0, t_j) \tag{6.2}$$

This result follows by application of the standard central limit theorem, see Chapter 4, Section 4.2.3. Thus, scaled by $\sigma\sqrt{N}$, the asymptotic (with N) partial sum process, or random walk, has a normal distribution with variance $\text{var}(S_{t_j}) = t_j$; therefore, dividing the scaled partial sum by $\sqrt{t_j}$ results in a random variable, defined as Z_{t_j}, which is distributed as $N(0, 1)$. In summary:

$$Z_{t_j} \equiv \frac{S_{t_j}}{\sigma\sqrt{t_j}\sqrt{N}} \Rightarrow_D N(0, 1) \tag{6.3}$$

This result could have been obtained directly by appeal to the CLT.

Some insight into the idea of BM can be gained by considering a simple program to generate some sample paths as N varies, with T fixed, from 50 to 200. The program here is written in MATLAB, but the principles are transparent and easily translated across to other programming environments. (For example, Iacus, 2008, provides an R code algorithm to simulate a BM sample path.) The program is written to take draws from $N(0, 1)$, but a routine could be inserted to convert this to a +1, –1 step by mapping a positive draw to +1 and a negative draw to –1 (see **Q6.1**). An index, H, is introduced to govern the size of the time partition, $\Delta t_j = \Delta t$.

The program ends by plotting the generated data in Figure 6.1. (As an exercise, the reader could vectorise the generation of the data, rather than use a 'for' loop, for example, using a cumsum function.) As $N \to \infty$ (achieved in the program by increasing H), the sample path is that of a BM. As usual the plotting function joins up adjacent points on the graph by straight lines; this seemingly innocent device is related to a more profound issue, which is considered further below.

```
Program to generate an approximation to BM
% a variation in which the number of time divisions increases so that
% their size decreases
% this variation generates random inputs as N(0, 1)
% a variation could map this into +1 or –1 inputs

H = 4;                        % the number of times the divisions change
T = 1;                        % set T = 1, divide T into lengths = dt
for k = 1:H;                  % start the outer loop
N = 50*k;                     % the number of divisions (varies with k)
randn('state',100)            % set the state of random (sets the seed)
dt = T/N;                     % the time divisions, 1/50, 1/100 and so on
dS = zeros(1,N);              % allocate arrays
S = zeros(1,N);               % required for unscaled RW
Z = zeros(1,N);               % required for scaled RW
dS(1) = sqrt(dt)*randn;       % first approximation outside the loop
S(1) = dS(1);                 % since S(0) = 0 is assumed
for j = 2:N;                  % start inner loop to generate the data
   dS(j) = sqrt(dt)*randn;    % general increment
   S(j) = S(j–1) + dS(j);     % the psp (or use a cumsum type function)
end;                          % end inner loop
Z = S./(sqrt(dt)*sqrt(N));    % scale so that distributed as N(0, 1)
plot([0:dt:T],[0,Z],'k-');    % plot Z against t, with increments dt
```

```
hold on;                    % plots all H figures on one graph
pause
  ylabel('Z(t)','FontSize',14)
  title('Figure 6.1 Random walk approximation to BM','FontSize',14)
end;                        % end outer loop
                            % end of program
```

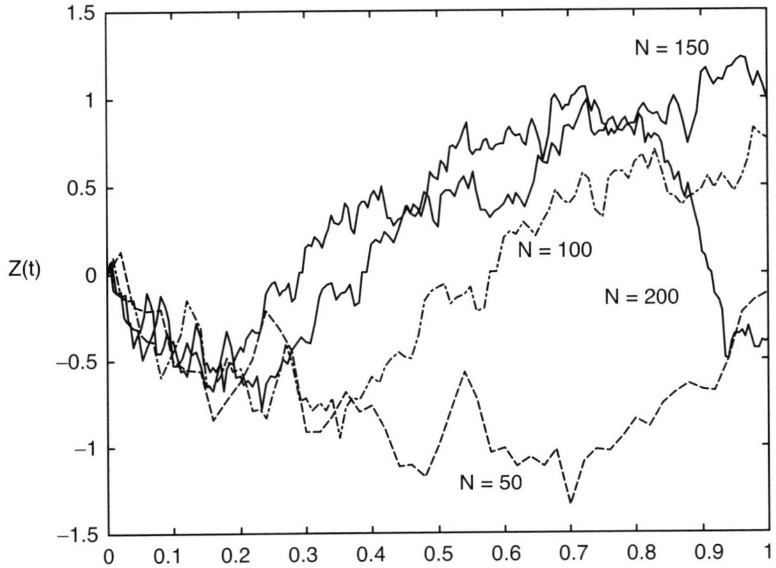

Figure 6.1 Random walk approximation to BM

6.3 The function spaces: C[0, 1] and D[0, 1]

In the previous section the random walk was viewed as taking place over the domain [0, 1] and the divisions in [0, 1], over which the random walk was evaluated, were then made smaller and smaller so that in the limit, the discretely realised random walk became continuous. The notation of continuous time was adopted with time index $t_1 < t_2 < \ldots < t_N$.

A similar strategy, but with a different notational convention, is widely adopted in analysing unit root tests. It acknowledges the feature of economic time series data that they tend to be equally spaced. In this case T is variable and the domain is converted to [0, 1] by the creation of equally spaced divisions of length 1/T resulting in the series [0, 1/T, 2/T,…, t/T,…, 1]. The movement across the domain is indexed by r,

where [rT] is the integer part of rT and $r \in [0, 1]$. On this basis the partial sum process is given by:

$$S_T(r) = \sum_{t=1}^{[rT]} \varepsilon_t \qquad r \in [0, 1] \tag{6.4}$$

where $\varepsilon_t \sim iid(0, \sigma^2)$. In detail, $S_T(r)$ is:

$$\begin{array}{ll} S_T(r) = \varepsilon_0 = 0 & 0 \le r < 1/T \\ S_T(r) = \varepsilon_1 & 1/T \le r < 2/T \\ S_T(r) = \varepsilon_1 + \varepsilon_2 & 2/T \le r < 3/T \\ \vdots \qquad \vdots & \qquad \vdots \\ S_T(r) = \sum_{t=1}^{T-1} \varepsilon_t & (T-1)/T \le r < 1 \\ S_T(r) = \sum_{t=1}^{T} \varepsilon_t & r = 1 \end{array}$$

where $\varepsilon_0 = 0$ has been assumed, implying $S_T(0) = 0$.

Note that the function so defined is a mapping from $r \in [0, 1]$ to $\Re$. Also of interest is the scaled version of this partial sum process defined by:

$$Z_T(r) \equiv \frac{S_T(r)}{\sigma\sqrt{T}} \qquad 0 \le r \le 1 \tag{6.5}$$

This differs from $S_T(r)$ in dividing each element by $\sigma\sqrt{T}$. A graph of $S_T(r)$ against r will be a step function because $S_T(r)$ remains at the same value for each value of r in the range $(j - 1)/T \le r < j/T$.

The function could be viewed as continuous (but not smooth) by interpolating between adjacent points (which is what a graph plotting routine does). This suggests the variation given by:

$$\begin{aligned} Y_T(r) &\equiv \frac{\sum_{t=1}^{[rT]} \varepsilon_t + (rT - [rT])\varepsilon_{[rT]+1}}{\sigma\sqrt{T}} \\ &= \frac{S_T(r) + (rT - [rT])\varepsilon_{[rT]+1}}{\sigma\sqrt{T}} \end{aligned} \tag{6.6}$$

In this case, the additional term linearly interpolates $\varepsilon_{[rT]+1}$ across two adjacent points; graphically a straight line joins $Y_T(r)$ at $r = (j - 1/T)$ and $r = j/T$. As defined $Y_T(r)$ is a continuous random function on the space

usually referred to as C[0,1]; it is a continuous function, but it is not differentiable because of its piecewise nature; and it is a random function because the inputs, $\{\varepsilon_i\}_{i=1}^{t}$, t = 1, ..., T, are random. Thus, different drawings from the random inputs result in a different set of realisations in the mapping from C[0, 1] $\mapsto \Re$. For a given T there is a distribution of such functions and an interesting question is what is the limiting distribution of these functions? (Here T is variable, so the limit is as T $\to \infty$.) This question is answered below by the functional central limit theorem, see Section 6.6.1.

Some realisations of such a process for given T, but with N varying, were graphed in Figure 6.1. In Figure 6.2, some sample paths of $Y_T(r)$ are illustrated for three increasing values of T, namely T = 100, 800 and 2,700; even though T differs, the domain is still [0, 1] in each case. Note that as T increases the graph of $Y_T(r)$ does not become smooth, but increasingly 'prickly' emphasising its non-differentiability.

The 'interpolation' terms in (6.6) become negligible as T increases (or for T given as the sub-divisions are made finer and finer), and it is possible to work directly with $Z_T(r)$ rather than $Y_T(r)$, noting that $Z_T(r)$ is defined on a slightly different space known as D[0, 1] $\mapsto \Re$; this space allows jump discontinuities. The function(s) so defined are known as cadlag functions (continue à droite, limites à gauche), which have a left

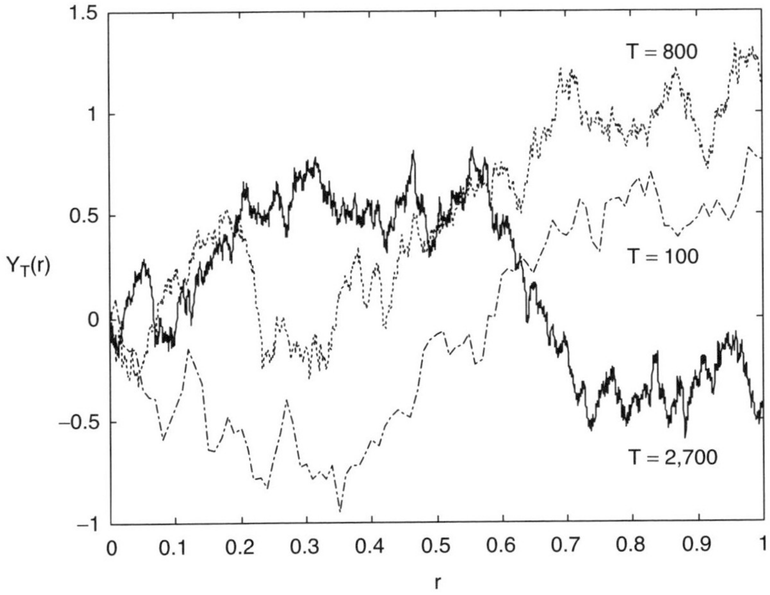

Figure 6.2 Realisations of $Y_T(r)$ as T varies

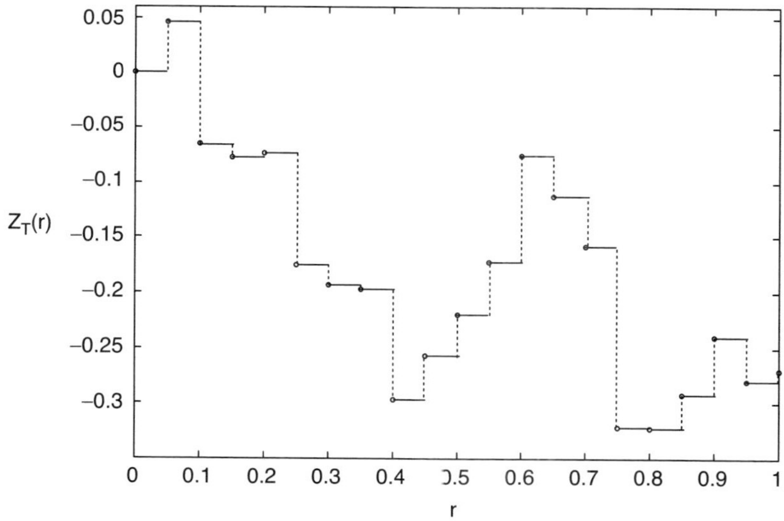

Figure 6.3 The partial sum process as a cadlag function: a graph of $Z_T(r)$ as a step function

limit, that is $Z_T(r)$, where r is such that rT is an integer, and are continuous on the right, that is the horizontal 'piece' of the step function. This is illustrated in Figure 6.3, where the left limit (that is the point at which rT is an integer) is indicated by a circle, to the right of this is a continuous line and then a discontinuity, that is the jump to the next value of r such that rT + 1 is an integer.

6.4 Some properties of BM

Some properties of a BM process that are useful to note are summarised below.

BM1. The covariance and correlation of W(s) and W(t).
The covariance is:

$$\begin{aligned} \text{cov}[W(s)W(t)] &= E\{W(s)W(t)\} \\ &= s\sigma^2 \end{aligned} \tag{6.7a}$$

where s < t has been assumed. Otherwise, this is written as min (s, t)σ^2 or, equivalently, $(s \wedge t)\sigma^2$, where $\wedge$ is the minimum operator.

The correlation of W(s) and W(t) is the covariance standardised by the variance. For, for s < t this is:

$$\text{cor}[W(s)W(t)] = \sqrt{\frac{s}{t}} \tag{6.7b}$$

BM2. Multivariate normality of the increments and the levels.

Let $0 = t_0 < t_1 < t_2 < \ldots < t_N = t$, then the BM for t_j is denoted $W(t_j)$ and the increments over these intervals are given by $\Delta W(t_j) \equiv W(t_j) - W(t_{j-1})$. Let W and ΔW be defined by the vector collections of these quantities:

$$W \equiv (W(t_1), W(t_2), \ldots, W(t_N))'$$
$$\Delta W \equiv (W(t_1) - 0, W(t_2) - W(t_1), \ldots, W(t_N) - W(t_{N-1}))'$$

Then W has a multivariate normal distribution with covariance matrix E[WW′], where the i-th diagonal element is $t_i\sigma^2$ and ij-th off-diagonal element is min $(t_i, t_j)\sigma^2$; the covariance matrix of E[ΔWΔW′] has i-th diagonal element equal to $(t_i - t_{i-1})\sigma^2$ and all off-diagonal elements are zero; the latter follows as the increments of a BM process are independent.

BM3. A BM process is a martingale.

$E[W(t_j)|F_0^{t_i})] = W(t_i)$ for all $i \leq j$, where the filtration $F_0^{t_i} = \sigma(W(t_i), W(t_{t-1}) \ldots W(t_0))$; and $\{W(t_j) - W(t_{j-1})\}_{j=1}^N$ forms a martingale difference sequence (MDS), see **Q6.2** and Chapter 3, Section 3.5.1 for the definition of a martingale and an MDS.

BM4. A BM process has the Markov property (see Chapter 3, Section 3.5.2).

That is: $E[f(W(t_j)) \mid F_0^{t_i})] = g(W(t_i))$, where f(.) and g(.) are Borel-measurable functions; (for an elaboration of both the martingale and Markov properties of BM, see, for example, Shreve, 2004; for the concept of Borel-measurable functions see Chapter 1).

BM5. Unbounded variation.

Brownian motion has unbounded variation along a sample path for $p \leq 2$ and bounded variation for $p > 2$, where p is the order of variation. Consider $p = 1$ and $p = 2$, being first and second order (or quadratic), respectively, then BM5.i and BM5.ii elaborate on these properties.

BM5.i The limiting first order path-wise variation is infinite for BM.

Define the p-th order variation, $p > 0$, of the general function f(t) over the interval $[t_0, t_N]$ as:

$$V_N^p(t) \equiv \sum_{j=0}^{N-1} |f(t_{j+1}) - f(t_j)|^p \tag{6.8}$$

Next, take the limit so that the partition, denoted δ, of $[t_0, t_N]$, becomes finer with the maximum subinterval → 0 as N → ∞, and define $V^p(t)$ as:

$$V^p(t) \equiv \lim_{N\to\infty} V^p_N(t) \tag{6.9}$$

Then the p-th order variation is bounded if:

$$\sup_\delta V^p(t) < \infty$$

First-order variation (p = 1) is a measure of the 'up-and-down' movement of a function ignoring the sign of the movement. If f(t) = W(t), that is f(.) is Brownian motion, then the path-wise variation is infinite; see, for example, Brzeźniak and Zastawniak (1999, Theorem 6.5).

BM5.ii Quadratic path-wise variation increases without limit for BM.

The quadratic variation along a Brownian motion path (referred to as 'pathwise') is given by:

$$V^2_N(t) = \sum_{j=0}^{N-1} [W(t_{j+1}) - W(t_j)]^2 \tag{6.10}$$

$V^2_N(t)$ is path-dependent as it refers to a particular sample path of the realisations of a Brownian motion process. Taking the limit N → ∞, then $V^2(t) = t$, so that the quadratic variation converges in mean square to t (see Shreve, 2004, Theorem 3.4.3, and Section 4.2.11), which implies that $E[V^2_N(t)] = t$ and $var[V^2_N(t)] = 0$. As t increases, the quadratic variation increases uniformly with t. This stands in contrast to continuous functions with continuous derivatives, which have quadratic variation of zero. The next property should, therefore, not be a surprise.

BM6. Neither Brownian motion nor its increments are differentiable.

Intuitively, this is due to the 'spiky' or erratic nature of the increments. Consider taking the limit of $\Delta W(t_j)$ as $\Delta t_j \to 0$, which is the derivative if the limit exists. We know from the properties of BM that $\Delta W(t_j) \sim N(0, \Delta t_j \sigma^2)$, hence:

$$\frac{\Delta W(t_j)}{\Delta t_j} \sim N\left(0, \frac{\Delta t_j \sigma^2}{(\Delta t_j)^2}\right) = N\left(0, \frac{\sigma^2}{\Delta t_j}\right) \tag{6.11}$$

Thus, if $\Delta t_j \rightarrow 0$, then $1/\Delta t_j \rightarrow \infty$, so that the variance increases without limit, see for example, McCabe and Tremayne (1993) and Davidson (2000).

6.5 Brownian bridges

Brownian bridges are important in econometric theory as they can be related to mean or trend adjusted series. A Brownian bridge is Brownian motion that is 'tied' down at the end of the interval. For these purposes let t = rT, where r is confined to the interval [0 1], and write $V_1(r)$ for a first order Brownian bridge stochastic process:

$$V_1(r) = W(r) - rW(1) \qquad r \in [0, 1] \tag{6.12}$$

where W(r) is a BM on $r \in [0, 1]$. A Brownian bridge can be tied down to any finite value, but typically, as in (6.12), the case of interest is where it both starts and ends at zero. It follows that $V_1(0) = V_1(1) = 0$. The need to tie the Brownian bridge down at the end means that its increments are dependent.

The expectation of the Brownian bridge is $E\{V_1(r)\} = E\{W(r)\} - rE\{W(1)\} = 0$. The covariance of the Brownian bridge is given by:

$$\begin{aligned} \text{cov}\{V_1(s), V_1(t)\} &= [(s \wedge t) - st)]\sigma^2 \\ &= s(1 - t)\sigma^2 \end{aligned}$$

where the second line follows for $s < t$ and $\wedge$ is the minimum operator.

For a general discussion of Brownian motion and the Brownian bridge, see, for example, Ross (2003). Two illustrative sample paths for a Brownian motion process and their associated Brownian bridges are shown in Figures 6.4a and 6.4b. (Demeaning, detrending and Brownian bridges are considered in Chapter 7, Section 7.6).

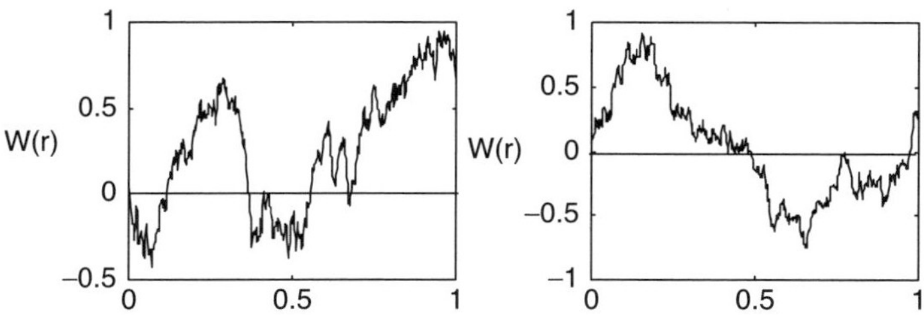

Figure 6.4a Sample paths of BM

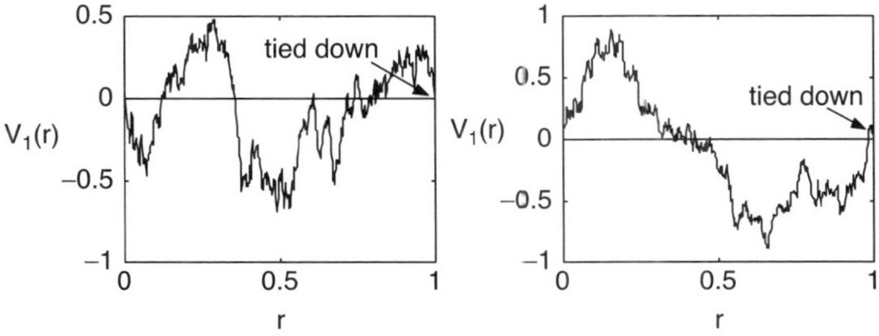

Figure 6.4b Associated sample paths of Brownian bridge

6.6 Functional: function of a function

Without explicit acknowledgement, a functional was introduced in Chapter 1, and this concept is of considerable importance in the econometrics of unit root testing. A functional is a function that has a function as its argument; it returns a number to a function argument. To understand what this means, recall that a function, y = f(x) takes the argument x and returns the value y. The domain of x denoted D is such that $x \in D$. For example, $y = f(x) = x^2$ for $x \in D = \Re$. If we then take this function as the argument of another function, we have a functional, say F[f(.)]; for example, the functional F[.] given by the definite integral $F[.] = \int_a^b f(x)dx$, so that with a = –1, b = +1 and $y = x^2$, then $F[x^2] = \int_{-1}^{+1} x^2 dx = 2/3$ and the functional assigns the number $2/3$ as the functional outcome.

6.6.1 Functional central limit theorem, FCLT (invariance principle)

The FCLT is an important part of the 'toolkit' for the development of unit root test statistics. It deals with the extension of the standard CLT to functionals. We start with a particularly simple version, in which the stochastic inputs are $\varepsilon_t \sim iid(0, \sigma^2)$, with $\sigma^2 < \infty$.

Consider the partial sum process and scaled partial sum process given, respectively, by:

$$S_T(r) \equiv \sum_{t=1}^{[rT]} \varepsilon_t \tag{6.18}$$

$$Z_T(r) \equiv \frac{S_T(r)}{\sigma\sqrt{T}} \tag{6.19}$$

Then the FCLT states that:

$$Z_T(r) \Rightarrow_D B(r) \tag{6.20}$$

This is sometimes stated in slightly abbreviated form as $Z_T \Rightarrow_D B$ (or with a variant of the $\Rightarrow_D$ notation). The FCLT (and CLT) is sometimes referred to as an invariance principle, IP, meaning that the convergence result is invariant to the distribution of the stochastic inputs that drive $S_T(r)$. Of course, some assumptions have to be made about these inputs, but these assumptions, discussed below, are relatively weak, and the FCLT is simply extended to cover such cases.

The notation $\Rightarrow_D$ is used as in the case of conventional asymptotics where it indicates convergence in distribution; here it refers to the weak convergence of the probability measures, which is more encompassing than simply convergence in distribution, where the latter compares the distribution of one random variable with another. The nature of Brownian motion B(r) means that it is normally distributed for all r in the domain, its increments are normally distributed and it is jointly normally distributed for different values of r. The CLT is in this sense a by-product of the FCLT.

6.6.2 Continuous mapping theorem (applied to functional spaces), CMT

This is the extension of the CMT, which was introduced earlier, see section 4.2.2 Chapter 4, and it is often used in conjunction with the FCLT. This statement of the theorem is based on Davidson (1994, Theorem 26.13; 2000, Theorem 14.2.3) and is, in essence, the CMT applied to functionals rather than to functions.

Let g be a functional that maps D to the real line, expressed as g: $D \mapsto \Re$, which is continuous apart from a set of measure zero, expressed as $D_g \in D$, $P(B \in D_g) = 0$. Next, let the FCLT apply to Z_T, such that $Z_T(r) \Rightarrow_D B(r)$, then $g(Z_T(r)) \Rightarrow_D g(B(r))$. Important continuous functions for which this theorem is essential in unit root asymptotics are sums of $Z_T(r)$ and sums of squared $Z_T(r)$. (See Table 7.1 in Chapter 7, which summarises some frequently occurring functions in unit root econometrics.)

6.6.3 Discussion of conditions for the FCLT to hold and extensions

As in the case of the (standard) CLT and CMT, the FCLT and extended CMT are remarkable theorems that greatly simplify the derivation of

the limiting distributions of test statistics with integrated processes that involve the ratio and products of Brownian motion. The simplest context of interest is when the data is generated by the AR(1) process:

$$y_t = \rho y_{t-1} + u_t \qquad t = 1, \dots, T$$

so that

$$u_t = y_t - \rho y_{t-1} \qquad t = 1, \dots, T$$

and the partial sum process is defined in terms of u_t.

As in the (standard) CLT, the convergence is invariant to the precise nature of the distribution of u_t, provided some generally quite minimal conditions are met. It applies most evidently when $u_t \sim \text{niid}(0, \sigma_u^2)$ or $u_t = \varepsilon_t \sim \text{iid}(0, \sigma^2)$; however, it also applies under much broader conditions that allow weak dependence and some forms of heterogeneity. The conditions stated here, which are sufficient rather than minimal, are due to Phillips (1987), Phillips and Perron (1988), Herndorf (1984) and see also McLeish (1975).

First, to enable the generalisation, let u_t denote the stochastic input into the psp, such that $S_{T,u}(r) = \sum_{t=1}^{[rT]} u_t$, thus reserving the notation ε_t for a white noise random variable, with variance denoted σ^2; then in the simplest case $u_t = \varepsilon_t$ and $S_{T,u}(r) = \sum_{t=1}^{[rT]} \varepsilon_t$. Specifying $u_t \neq \varepsilon_t$ enables stochastic processes with properties other than those of ε_t, to drive the partial sum process. More generally, a standard set of assumptions, stated in a form due to Phillips (1987), is:

i) $E(u_t) = 0$ for all t
ii) $\sup_t E|u_t|^{\beta+\delta} < \infty$ for some $\beta > 2$ and $\delta > 0$
iii) $\lim_{T\to\infty} E(S_{T,u}^2 / T) \equiv \sigma_{lr,u}^2 > 0$
iv) $\{u_t\}$ is strong mixing, with mixing coefficients α_m, such that $\sum_{m=1}^{\infty} \alpha_m^{1-2/\beta} < \infty$.

Assumption i) is straightforward. Assumption ii) controls the heterogeneity that is permitted in the $\{u_t\}$ sequence jointly with a condition that controls the dependence (condition iv). Notice that heterogeneity is allowed, with no requirement that the variance is constant. The parameter β controls the 'fatness' of the tails of the distribution of u_t, with the probability of outliers increasing as β tends to 2. As to assumption iii), given that $E(S_{T,u}) = 0$, this is a condition that the average variance, $T^{-1}E(S_{T,u}^2)$, converges to a finite constant, denoted $\sigma_{lr,u}^2$, which is usually referred to as the long-run variance, a description that motivates the

use of the subscript, and is considered further below; see also Chapter 2, Section 2.3.2 for an outline of the long-run variance.

Finally, assumption iv) relates to the allowable asymptotic weak dependence in the $\{u_t\}$ sequence. (The idea of strong mixing was outlined in Chapter 3, Section 3.1.2.) Note that the parameter β in the strong mixing condition is related to the permitted heterogeneity of condition ii), so that as the probability of outliers increases, the memory (dependence) of the process must decline so that they are forgotten more quickly, see Phillips (1987).

These assumptions do not limit the $\{u_t\}$ sequence to be iid, for example, in general allowing finite order ARMA models and martingale difference sequences. For a convenient statement of the CLT and FCLT where $\{u_t\}$ is a MDS sequence, see Fuller (1996, Theorems 5.3.4 and 5.3.5, respectively). However, there are some exceptions indicated by the qualification 'in general'. Andrews (1983, especially Theorem 3), and see also Davidson (1994, Theorem 14.7), provides an exception to the presumption that AR(1) processes are necessarily strong mixing. His counter-example is the class of AR(1) processes where $\rho \in (0, \frac{1}{2}]$, with stochastic inputs that are generated by a Bernoulli process (0, 1, with probabilities p and 1 – p, respectively), which are not strong mixing even though the random inputs are iid; and the result is conjectured to apply for $\rho > \frac{1}{2}$. To ensure strong mixing, Andrews (op. cit.) introduces a smoothness condition on the density of the stochastic inputs, which is satisfied by such common distributions as the normal, exponential, uniform and Cauchy amongst others. For an informative discussion of the problem and solutions, see Davidson (1994).

Condition iii) refers to the long-run variance, which was introduced in Chapter 2, Sections 2.3.2 and 2.6.1. The simplest case is when there is homoscedasticity and no serial correlation, so that $E(u_t^2) = \sigma_u^2$ and $E(u_t u_{t+s}) = 0$ for $t \neq s$. In this case:

$$\begin{aligned} T^{-1}E(S_{T,u}^2) &= T^{-1}(T\sigma_u^2) \\ &= \sigma_u^2 \end{aligned} \tag{6.21}$$

so that $\sigma_{lr,u}^2 \equiv \lim_{T\to\infty} E(S_{T,u}^2 / T) = \sigma_u^2$. Those familiar with spectral analysis may note that if $\{u_t\}$ is a covariance stationary sequence, then $\sigma_{lr,u}^2 = 2\pi f_u(0)$, where $f_u(0)$ is the spectral density of $\{u_t\}$ at the zero frequency. In the event that u_t is white noise $u_t = \varepsilon_t$, then $f_u(0) = f_\varepsilon(0) = (2\pi)^{-1}\sigma^2$ and so $\sigma_{lr,u}^2 = 2\pi(\sigma^2 / 2\pi) = \sigma^2$.

In the case that $\sigma^2_{lr,u} \neq \sigma^2$, with $0 < \sigma^2_{lr,u} < \infty$, then the partial sum process is normalised using $\sigma^2_{lr,u}$ rather than σ. The invariance principle is restated as follows. Let $S_{T,u}(r)$ and $Z_T(r)$ be defined by:

$$S_{T,u}(r) \equiv \sum_{t=1}^{[rT]} u_t \tag{6.22}$$

$$Z_T(r) \equiv \frac{S_{T,u}(r)}{\sigma_{lr,u}\sqrt{T}} \tag{6.23}$$

where u_t satisfies the conditions i) to iv) above, then, as before, but with these redefinitions:

$$Z_T(r) \Rightarrow_D B(r) \tag{6.24}$$

The conditions i) – iv) are not the only way to approach the characterisation of permissible heterogeneity and dependence in the $\{u_t\}$ sequence. The generality of the FCLT to processes that generate weakly dependent and heterogeneous errors has been studied by a number of authors; for different approaches see, for example, Wooldridge and White (1988), Phillips and Solo (1992), Andrews and Pollard (1994), Davidson (1994), de Jong (1997) and de Jong and Davidson (2000a, b).

Another way of approaching the invariance principle is to seek the normalising sequence $\{a_T\}$ for $S_T(r)$ such that:

$$Z_T(r) = \frac{S_T(r)}{a_T} \Rightarrow_D B(r) \tag{6.25}$$

Then the cases so far correspond to $a_T = \sigma\sqrt{T}$ and $a_T = \sigma_{lr,u}\sqrt{T}$, respectively. In these cases $\{u_t\}$ is said to lie in the domain of normal attraction (DNA) of the normal law. That is despite heterogeneity, non-normality and weak dependence, $Z_T(r)$ acts, in the limit, as if it was normal. A case where this does not occur is when the variances of the elements of $\{u_t\}$ are infinite, as when the $\{u_t\}$ are drawn from the Cauchy distribution; even so $S_T(r)$ can be normalised so that it does converge, but to a Levy motion rather than a Brownian motion. These results have been generalised to other distributions. Let u_t belong to the domain of attraction (DA) of a stable law with index $\alpha \in (0, 2)$, then the norming sequence is $a_T = T^{1/\alpha}L(T)$, where $L(T)$ is a slowly varying function. If u_t belongs to the domain of normal attraction, then the norming sequence simplifies to $a_T = \sigma_{lr,u}\sqrt{T}$, see Chan and Tran (1989) and Kourogenis and Pittis (2008).

6.7 Concluding remarks and references

Whilst it is possible to understand the general principles of unit root testing without reference to Brownian motion, for example the familiar DF pseudo-t test is just a t test, but with a non-standard distribution, some knowledge is essential for the asymptotic distribution theory. An understanding of Brownian motion also serves to emphasise the link with random walks and extensions, such as when the stochastic inputs are no longer Gaussian.

As noted in the previous chapter, most modern texts on probability theory include a section on Brownian motion and the references cited there will also be useful for BM; Fristedt and Gray (1997) is particularly good reference in this respect. Mikosch (1998) and Iacus (2008) are useful introductory references on Brownian motion, geometric Brownian motion and Brownian bridges, with the latter including program code in R. The monograph by Hida (1980) is devoted to Brownian motion. Shreve (2004) places the development of Brownian motion in the context of modelling the prices of financial assets. For an econometric perspective, at a more advanced level, see Davidson (1994) and Hamilton (1994).

Questions

Q6.1 Rewrite the program in Section 6.2 to generate an approximation to BM from a symmetric binomial random walk.

AQ6.1 This variation requires that the partial sum process is defined as:

$$S_{t_j} = S_{t_{j-1}} + (\sqrt{\Delta t})y_t$$

where $y_t = (-1, +1)$ with $p = q = ½$, hence $\sigma_y^2 = 1$. A program to generate the resulting approximation to BM follows for N = 100, …, 800. The resulting output is shown in Figure **Q6.1**; note that the path is 'spikier' than when the inputs are *N*(0, 1), but that as the time divisions become smaller, the sample paths look very similar.

Program to generate an approximation to BM, via a symmetric binomial random walk

```
% the number of time divisions increases so that their size decreases
% this variation generates random inputs as +1 or –1
```

```
H = 8;                        % the number of times the divisions change
T = 1;                        % set T = 1, divide T into lengths = dt
for k = 1:H;                  % start the outer loop
N = 100*k;                    % the number of divisions (varies with k)
randn('state',100)            % set the state of random (sets the seed)
dt = T/N;                     % the time divisions, 1/50, 1/100 and so on
dS = zeros(1,N);              % allocate arrays
S = zeros(1,N);               % required for unscaled RW
Z = zeros(1,N);               % required for scaled RW
dS(1) = randn;                % take draw from N(0, 1)
if dS(1)> 0;
  dS(1)= +1;                  % set to +1 if draw > 0
else;
  dS(1)= –1;                  % set to –1 if draw ≤ 0
end;
dS(1) = sqrt(dt)*dS(1);       % scale the increment
S(1) = dS(1);                 % the first input
for j = 2:N;                  % start inner loop to generate the data
  dS(j) = randn;
if dS(j)> 0;
  dS(j)= +1;                  % set input to +1
else;
  dS(j)= –1;                  % set input to –1
end;
  dS(j)=sqrt(dt)*dS(j); % increment based on –1/+1 inputs
  S(j) = S(j–1)+dS(j); % the psp
end;                          % end inner loop
Z = S./(sqrt(dt)*sqrt(N));    % scale so that distributed as N(0, 1)
plot([0:dt:T],[0,Z],'k-');    % plot Z against t, with increments dt
hold on;                      % plots all H figures on one graph
pause
ylabel('Z(r)','FontSize',14)
xlabel('r','FontSize',14)
title('Figure Q6.1 Symmetric binomial random walk approximation
to ... BM','FontSize',14);
end;                          % end outer loop
% end of program
```

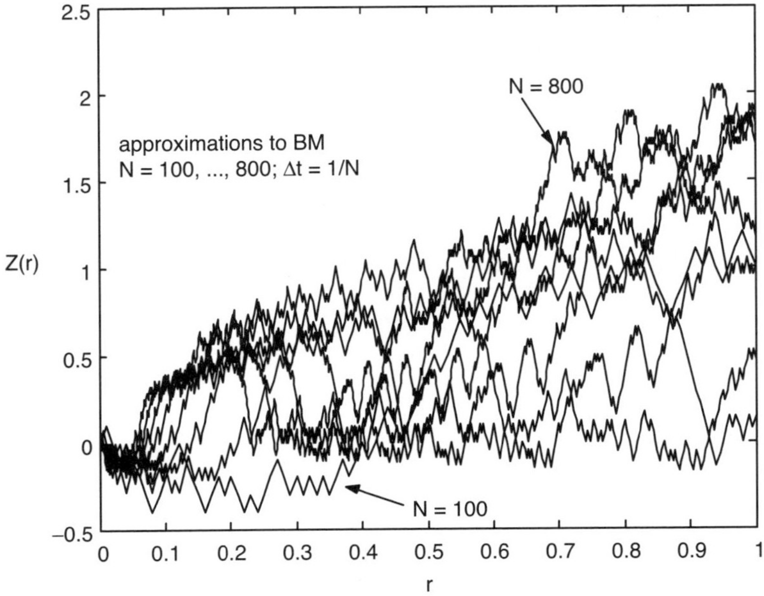

Figure Q6.1 Symmetric binomial random walk approximation to BM

The binomial inputs could also be generated via the uniform distribution, see Iacus (2008, Section 1.6.1).

Q6.2 Show that the covariance between W(s) and W(r) for $s < r$ is $s\sigma^2$.

A6.2 First add and subtract W(s) to W(r) in the second term of the covariance:

$$\begin{aligned}\text{cov}[W(s), W(r)] &= \text{cov}[W(s), (W(s) + W(r) - W(s)]\\ &= \text{cov}[W(s)W(s) + W(s)(W(r) - W(s))]\\ &= \text{cov}[W(s)W(s)]\\ &= \text{var}[W(s)]\\ &= s\sigma^2\end{aligned}$$

The result uses (2nd to 3rd line) the increment W(r) – W(s) is independent of W(s) and (4th to 5th line) the variance of W(s) is $s\sigma^2$ or s if $W(s) \equiv B(s)$.

Q6.3 Prove that a BM process is a martingale and that $\{W(t_j)\} - W(t_{j-1})\}_{j=1}^{n}$ forms a martingale difference sequence.

A6.3 If BM is a martingale it must satisfy $E[W(t)|F_0^s] = W(s)$ for $s < t$, where $F_0^s = \sigma\{W(u)\text{: } u \leq s\}$. To show this, first add and subtract

W(s) within the expectation:

$$\begin{aligned} E[W(t) \mid F_0^s] &= E[\{W(t) - W(s)\} + W(s) \mid F_0^s] \\ &= E[\{W(t) - W(s)\} \mid F_0^s] + E[W(t) \mid F_0^s] \\ &= E[W(s) \mid F_0^s] \\ &= W(s) \end{aligned}$$

where $E[W(t) - W(s) \mid F_0^s]$ because the increment $W(t) - W(s)$ is independent of F_0^s; $E[W(s) \mid F_0^s] = W(s)$ because F_0^s includes W(s), so it is known at s. It then follows that the sequence of differences, $\{W(t) - W(s)\}$, each being a difference of a martingale, is a martingale difference sequence.

7

Brownian Motion: Differentiation and Integration

Introduction

It was noted in Chapter 6 that Brownian motion is not differentiable along its path, that is with respect to t, see property **BM6**. However, even just a passing familiarity with the literature on random walks and unit root tests will have alerted the reader to the use of notation that corresponds to derivatives and integrals. In particular, the limiting distributions of various unit root test statistics invariably involve integrals of Brownian motion. Given that these are not conventional integrals, what meaning is to be attributed to them? This chapter is a brief introduction to this topic, starting by a contrast with the nonstochastic case. As usual, further references are given at the end of the chapter.

This chapter is organised as follows. Section 7.1 comprises a brief review of integration in the nonstochastic case; the concept of integration is extended to the stochastic case in Section 7.2, with the Itô formula and corrections outlined in Section 7.3. Some particular examples of stochastic differential equations, namely the Ornstein-Uhlenbeck process and geometric Brownian motion, are introduced in Sections 7.4 and 7.5, respectively. Section 7.6 is concerned with the frequently occurring and important case where some form of detrending is first applied to a time series. Section 7.7 provides a tabular summary of some results involving functional of Brownian motion and a simulation example.

7.1 Nonstochastic processes

To start, consider a nonstochastic process that is a continuous function of time; for example, suppose the process evolves as $dU(t) = \alpha U(t)dt$, which is a first order differential equation. The path of U(t) can be obtained

by integrating dU(t) to obtain the solution $U(t) = U(0)e^{\alpha t}$, where U(0) is the initial condition. We can check that this does indeed satisfy the differential equation by differentiating U(t) with respect to t: thus, $dU(t)/dt = \alpha U(0)e^{\alpha t} = \alpha U(t)$, as required.

Analogously, as Brownian motion is a continuous-time process, it might be tempting to write its derivative with respect to time as dW(t)/dt, the idea being to measure the change with respect to time along a Brownian motion path; however, as noted, this 'derivative' does not exist, although, of course, changes in the form of increments and decrements do exist. Neither does the 'anti-derivative' or integral, in the conventional sense, exist, so that the solution, W(t), cannot be obtained by conventional integration.

To make the point in another way, suppose the first order differential equation for U(t) is amended by adding a function of the increments of Brownian motion, say f(t)dW(t), where dW(t) is an increment on the Brownian motion path, so that $dU(t) = \alpha U(t)dt + f(t)dW(t)$; it might be tempting to divide through by dt and let $dt \to 0$; however, such an operation is not valid given the non-differentiability of W(t). The first part of the solution is still valid, but in obtaining a complete solution a special meaning has to be attached to $\Delta S_t = (\sqrt{\Delta t})\varepsilon_t$ other than that of the conventional Reimann integral. As the path of a Brownian motion process is continuous and can be reconstructed from its increments/decrements and an initial condition, it must be possible to do something. The solution to this problem is to use the Itô calculus, in which conventional (Reimann) integrals are replaced with Itô integrals. Reimann integrals are briefly reviewed in the next section as a precursor to the solution when deterministic functions are replaced by stochastic functions.

7.1.1 Reimann integral

It is helpful to first take a step back and consider an integral for a function whose derivatives exist. In this case the conventional integral is a Reimann integral. Consider the function f(t) where (at least) df(t)/dt exists.

The integral is written $\int_{s=0}^{t} f(s)ds$, where s is the variable of integration, which can be viewed as the limit of the following discretisation:

$$I_R^N(t) = \sum\nolimits_{j=0}^{N-1} f(t_{[j]})(t_{j+1} - t_j) \tag{7.1}$$

where $0 = t_0 < t_1 < t_2 < \ldots < t_N = t$ and $f(t_{[j]})$ is the function f(t) evaluated in the interval t_j to t_{j+1}; for convenience assume that $\Delta t_{j+1} \equiv (t_{j+1} - t_j) = \Delta t$, so

that the time increments are equal. Provided that the limit converges, the Reimann integral, $I_R(t)$, is obtained as $N \rightarrow \infty$, so that the overall interval (0, t) is split into smaller and smaller parts such that $\Delta t \rightarrow 0$. Each small interval is multiplied by the value of the function f(t) for a value of t in the interval Δt_{j+1}; the resulting areas are then summed over all the disjoint partitions of the overall interval. In summary:

$$I_R(t) \equiv \lim_{N\rightarrow\infty} I_R^N(t) \tag{7.2}$$

We will often be interested in the integral over $0 = t_0 < \ldots < t_N = 1$, in which case the Reimann integral is $\int_{s=0}^{1} f(s)ds$.

Example 7.1: Revision of some simple Reimann indefinite and definite integrals

By way of revision, consider the simple polynomial function $y = f(t) = at^b$, $b \neq -1$, with derivative $f_t \equiv \partial y/\partial t = abt^{b-1}$; then the indefinite integral is $\int f_t dt = \int (ab)t^{b-1}dt$. Often we are interested in the reverse procedure, that is given the indefinite integral what is $y = f(t)$? In this case, the solution is easy to obtain if we write $\int \alpha x^\beta dx$, and note that $\beta = b - 1$ and $\alpha = ab$ imply $b = \beta + 1$ and $a = \alpha/b$; for example, $\int 4t^3 dt$ implies $b = 3 + 1 = 4$ and $a = 4/4 = 1$, so that $y = t^4$ and, to check, $f_t = 4t^3$, as required. However, there is an element of non-uniqueness in this solution, because $y = t^4 + C$, for $C \neq 0$, results in the same derivative as for $C = 0$; hence, we should write $\int f_t dt = f(t) + C$, where C is referred to as the constant of integration. The definite integral corresponds to setting an upper and a lower limit to the range of integration, $\int_g^h f_t dt = t^4]_g^h$, where $h \geq g$; for example, $\int_0^1 4t^3 dt = t^4]_0^1 = (1)^4 - (0) = 1$. ♦

7.1.2 Reimann-Stieltjes integral

An extension of the integration problem can be formulated by introducing a continuous function of t, say, g(t), as the function of integration, rather than t itself. The problem is to integrate the function f(t), the integrand, with respect to the function g(t), the integrator. This leads to the Reimann-Stieltjes integral, where $I_R^N(t)$ is replaced by:

$$I_{RS}^N(t) = \sum_{j=0}^{N-1} f(t_{[j]})[g(t_{j+1}) - g(t_j)] \tag{7.3}$$

This corresponds to the Reimann integral when $g(t) = t$, so that $\Delta g(t_{j+1}) = \Delta t_{j+1}$, but in the case of the Reimann-Stieltjes (RS) integral, each $f(t_{[j]})$ is weighted by $\Delta g(t_{j+1})$. In summary:

$$I_{RS}(t) \equiv \lim_{N\to\infty} I_{RS}^{N}(t) \tag{7.4}$$

The typical notation for the RS integral is $\int_{s=0}^{t} f(s)dg(s)$. As the functions are deterministic, if the limit exists then it is an element of the real line and the definite integral is a number, not a function.

The function g(t) may have jump discontinuities, but if it has bounded variation, then the RS integral will exist. If g(t) is everywhere differentiable and the derivative $g_t \equiv \partial g(t)/\partial t$ is continuous, then the RS integral $\int_{s=0}^{t} f(s)dg(s)$ coincides with the simple Reimann construction $\int_{s=0}^{t} f(s)g_t ds$; but continuity of g(t) is not sufficient to ensure this, rather absolute continuity is required (see end of book glossary).

The bounded variation of g(t) is a sufficient condition for existence of the RS integral; however, Mikosch (1998) gives a more general sufficient condition that is close to necessity. We cite one of his results here, see (Mikosch, op. cit., pp. 94–5), which uses the following sufficient conditions.

1. The functions f(t) and g(t) do not have discontinuities at the same point of $t \in [0, 1]$;
2. f(t) and g(t) have bounded p-variation and q-variation, respectively, where $p^{-1} + q^{-1} > 1$ for $p > 0$ and $q > 0$. (For the definition of p-th order variation see **BM5**.)

The RS integral does exist for some combinations of f(t) and g(t) when g(t) is replaced by Brownian motion, W(t). Let the function f(t) be a deterministic function of t or the sample path of a stochastic process on $t \in [0, 1]$, $0 = t_0 < \ldots < t_N = 1$; assume f(t) is differentiable with a bounded derivative on [0, 1], for example $f(t) = \sin(t)$ or $f(t) = t^p$; and W(s) is a Brownian motion on the same space. If conditions 1 and 2 are satisfied, then the following RS integral exists for every BM sample path:

$$I_{RS}(t) \equiv \int_{s=0}^{1} f(s)dW(s) \tag{7.5}$$

See Mikosch (op. cit., p. 95). For example, $I_{RS}(t) = \int_{s=0}^{1} sdW(s)$ exists in the RS sense. However, this does not mean that the RS integral exists for general integrands; for example, the integral $\int_{s=0}^{1} W(s)dW(s)$, which is of particular interest in an econometric context, does not exist in the

RS sense; in this case, f(t) = g(t) = W(t) and variation is bounded only for $p > 2$, so the test for condition 2 is now on $p^{-1} + p^{-1} = 2p^{-1}$, but this is < 1 for $p > 2$. Further arguments show that the failure of this sufficient condition also implies failure of the integral to be defined in the RS sense (see Mikosch, op. cit.).

In what sense, therefore, does an integral exist and do the rules of classical calculus still apply? The answer to the first question is yes, an integral exists, but it differs from the Reimann-Stieltjes integral; the answer to the second question is no, not in general. These matters are considered in the next section.

7.2 Integration for stochastic processes

When dealing with stochastic processes, the starting point for defining an integral looks similar to that for the RS integral, but it leads to a different development. Consider the particular example where we would like to obtain the integral $\int_{s=0}^{t} W(s)dW(s)$ and, as usual, W(t) is Brownian motion and s is the variable of integration. Then we could start by analogy with the Reimann-Stieltjes sum, so that:

$$\sum_{j=0}^{N-1} W(t_{[j]})(W(t_{j+1}) - W(t_j)) \tag{7.6}$$

where $W(t_{j+1}) - W(t_j)$ is just an increment to Brownian motion, so it is unambiguously defined; the problem is with $W(t_{[j]})$, the critical point being that, in contrast to when W(t) was a differentiable function of t, it now matters where $t_{[j]}$ is chosen in the subinterval t_j to t_{j+1}. Consider three possibilities:

$$t_{[j]} = t_j; \qquad t_{[j]} = \tfrac{1}{2}(t_j + t_{j+1}); \qquad t_{[j]} = t_{j+1}.$$

That is the beginning of the interval, the mid-point of the interval and the end of the interval. Taking the former results in the Itô integral and taking the second results in the Stratonovich integral, whereas the latter choice does not appear to be in general use.

The Itô integral is in widespread use, not least because of its importance in finance, where $t_{[j]} = t_j$ relates to an 'opening' position rather than the 'closing' position that relates to choosing $t_{[j]} = t_{j+1}$, see, for example, Shreve (2004, especially chapter 4). It also corresponds to the space of cadlag functions on C[0, 1] as illustrated in Figure 6.3, with the

step function starting at the 'opening' position. Making this choice, the sum of interest is:

$$I_I^N(t) = \sum_{j=0}^{N-1} W(t_j)(W(t_{j+1}) - W(t_j)) \quad (7.7)$$

Also letting $N \to \infty$, so that the divisions become finer and finer, then:

$$I_1(t) \equiv \lim_{N\to\infty} I_I^N(t) \quad (7.8)$$

which is the limit of $I_I^N(t)$ as $N \to \infty$. To obtain the limiting expression, which will be the Itô integral, first consider $I_I^N(t)$. Write a typical component of the sum as $a(b - a)$, noting that this is identically equal to $½[(b^2 - a^2) - (b - a)^2]$. Using this identity, the sum can be expressed as:

$$\begin{aligned}\sum_{j=0}^{N-1} W(t_j)(W(t_{j+1}) - W(t_j)) \\ = \frac{1}{2}\left(\sum_{j=0}^{N-1}\left[W(t_{j+1})^2 - W(t_j)^2\right] - \sum_{j=0}^{N-1}\left[W(t_{j+1}) - W(t_j)\right]^2\right)\end{aligned} \quad (7.9)$$

Next, note that the first sum is equal to $W(t_N)^2 - W(t_0)^2$ and the second is the quadratic variation in $W(t)$, so that:

$$I_I^N(t) = \frac{1}{2}\left(W(t_N)^2 - W(t_0)^2 - V_N^2(t)\right) \quad (7.10)$$

Finally, noting that $W(t_0) = W(0) = 0$, by the definition of Brownian motion, and that the limit of $V_N^2(t)$ is $V^2(t) = t$, see **BM5.ii**, then the Itô integral of $\int_{s=0}^{t} W(s)dW(s)$ is:

$$\begin{aligned}I_I(t) &= \lim_{N\to\infty} I_I^N(t) \\ &= \frac{1}{2}\left(W(t)^2 - t\right)\end{aligned} \quad (7.11)$$

Note that this differs from the Reimann integral by a term $\frac{1}{2}t$, that depends on the quadratic variation of Brownian motion, which is zero for nonstochastic functions.

To show that the integral is sensitive to the point at which the function is evaluated, note that if $t_{[j]} = t_{j+1}$ then the resulting integral gives $½(W(t)^2 + t)$, whereas if $t_{[j]} = ½(t_j + t_{j+1})$ then the Stratonovich integral results in $½W(t)^2$. Only in this last case does the integral coincide with the classical result that if $w(t)$ is a continuous

deterministic function (reserving W(t) in upper case for BM) then $\int_{s=0}^{T} w(s)dw(s) = \int_{s=0}^{T} w(s)(\partial w/\partial s)ds = \frac{1}{2} w(t)^2\Big]_0^T = \frac{1}{2} w(T)$, where $]_0^T$ indicates the limits of the definite integral and, by analogy with BM, we assume that w(0) = 0.

A particular application of the Itô integral result occurs when the variable of integration is limited to the interval $0 \le r \le 1$, and the integral is taken over the whole range, then $I_I(1) = \frac{1}{2}(W(1)^2 - 1)$. Such an integral is sometimes written in conventional notation; in this case it would be $\int_{s=0}^{1} W(s)dW(s)$, but this only makes sense on the understanding that the integral referred to is the Itô integral (or another form of stochastic integral).

Returning to the stochastic differential equation $dU(t) = \alpha U(t)dt + f(t) dW(t)$, the meaning of this can now be framed in terms of well-defined integrals as:

$$U(t) - U(0) = \int_{s=0}^{t} \alpha U(s)ds + \int_{s=0}^{t} f(s)dW(s) \qquad (7.12)$$

where the first integral is a conventional integral and the second is an Itô integral (or an Reimann integral depending on the properties of f(t)), both of which now have well-defined meanings.

7.3 Itô formula and corrections

7.3.1 Simple case

The result that $I_I(t) = \int_{s=0}^{t} W(s)dW(s) = \frac{1}{2}(W(t)^2 - t)$, where W(t) is Brownian motion, is one example of an Itô integral. It contains the additional term, $\frac{1}{2}t$, relative to the nonstochastic case. This term is related to the Itô correction of the standard integral and, in general, the additional term can be obtained by means of the Itô formula, which is given in simple and then more complex forms below.

If f(t) = f{W(t)}, so that there is no dependence on t apart from through W(t), with derivatives $f_W \equiv \partial f(.)/dW(.)$ and $f_{WW} \equiv \partial^2 f(.)/\partial W(.)^2$, then the Itô formula (which is a simplified version of the more general case given below) is:

$$f(T) - f(0) = \frac{1}{2}\int_0^T f_{WW}dt + \int_0^T f_W dW(t) \qquad (7.13)$$

The second term on the right-hand-side is present in a conventional integral but the first term, which is the Itô correction, is not. Note that

the correction term $\frac{1}{2}\int_0^T f_{WW}dt$ is a conventional Reimann integral. In the case that f(0) = 0, a simple rearrangement of (7.13) gives the following form that is often convenient:

$$\int_0^T f_W dW(t) = f(T) - \frac{1}{2}\int_0^T f_{WW}dt \tag{7.14}$$

The differential form of this simple version of the Itô formula is written as:

$$df(t) = \frac{1}{2}f_{WW}dt + f_W dW(t) \tag{7.15}$$

However, this is a convenient notation that takes meaning from the underlying rigorous statement in (7.13).

To consider the nature of the correction, we take a simple example and contrast it with the deterministic case. In the case of a continuous differentiable deterministic function of the form $f(t) = w(t)^k$, with $w(0) = 0$, then it holds that $w(T)^k = k\int_0^T w(t)^{k-1}dt$. However, in the case of Brownian motion, an additional term is required. Consider $f(t) = W(t)^k$ where, as usual, W(t) is Brownian motion, then the following derivatives are required: $f_W = kW(t)^{k-1}$and $f_{WW} = k(k-1)W(t)^{k-2}$.

Application of the Itô formula results in:

$$W(T)^k = \frac{1}{2}k(k-1)\int_0^T W(t)^{k-2}dt + k\int_0^T W(t)^{k-1}dW(t) \tag{7.16}$$

where $k - 2 \geq 0$, $W(t)^0 \equiv 1$ and $W(0)^k = 0$. The differential form of the Itô formula in this case is:

$$d\{W(T)^k\} = \frac{1}{2}[k(k-1)W(t)^{k-2}]dt + [kW(t)^{k-1}]dW(t) \tag{7.17}$$

Example 7.2: Polynomial functions of BM (quadratic and cubic)

If $f(t) = W(t)^2$ then by direct application of the Itô formula of (7.13), we obtain:

$$\begin{aligned} W(T)^2 &= \int_{t=0}^T dt + 2\int_{t=0}^T W(t)dW(t) \\ &= T + 2\int_{t=0}^T W(t)dW(t) \end{aligned}$$

The correction term is $\int_{t=0}^{T} dt = T$, which arises from the accumulation of quadratic variation along the sample path of BM, see property **BM5.i**. (This could also have been obtained by rearranging $\int_{s=0}^{t} W(s)dW(s)$, see the development below (7.11)). Next consider $f(t) = W(T)^3$, then with $k = 3$, the Itô formula results in:

$$W(T)^3 = 3\int_0^T W(t)dt + 3\int_0^T W(t)^2 dW(t)$$

$$\int_0^T W(t)^2 dW(t) = \frac{1}{3}W(T)^3 - \int_0^T W(t)dt \qquad \blacklozenge$$

The following results are often of use:

$$\int_{s=0}^{t} s dW(s) = tW(t) - \int_{s=0}^{t} W(s)ds \tag{7.18}$$

$$\int_{r=0}^{1} r dW(r) = W(1) - \int_{r=0}^{1} W(r)dr \tag{7.19}$$

$$\int_{s=0}^{t} W(s)^2 dW(s) = \frac{1}{3}W(t)^3 - \int_{s=0}^{t} W(s)ds \tag{7.20}$$

$$\int_{r=0}^{1} W(r)^2 dW(r) = \frac{1}{3}W(1)^3 - \int_{r=0}^{1} W(r)dr \tag{7.21}$$

7.3.2 Extension of the simple Itô formula

An extension of the results of the previous section occurs if the function being considered has two arguments. First, consider the deterministic case f[t, w(t)], which is a real-valued function of t and w(t), with continuous partial derivatives and where w(t) is a non-random function of t. This is a classical case to which standard procedures can be applied. Denote the partial derivatives as:

$$f_t \equiv \partial f(.)/\partial t,\ f_w \equiv \partial f(.)/\partial w,\ f_{ww} \equiv \partial^2 f(.)/\partial w^2 \tag{7.22}$$

The differential and integral forms of this relationship are:

$$df[(t, w(t)] = f_t dt + f_w dw(t) \tag{7.23}$$

$$f[T, w(T)] = f[0, w(0)] + \int_0^T f_t dt + \int_0^T f_w dw(t) \tag{7.24}$$

This is the classical case because w(t) is a deterministic function t; however, the case of interest here is when W(t) is a stochastic function, in

particular a Brownian motion process. In that case, the Itô formula, in integral and differential forms, is:

$$f[T, W(T)] = f[0, W(0)] + \int_0^T \{f_t + \tfrac{1}{2} f_{WW}\} dt + \int_0^T f_W dW(t) \tag{7.25}$$

$$df[(t, W(t)] = \{f_t + \tfrac{1}{2} f_{WW}\} dt + f_W dW(t) \tag{7.26}$$

where the first integral in (7.25) is a Reimann integral (it is a function of t) and the second integral is an Itô integral (it is a function of W(t)). As in the simpler case of (7.13), comparing the two forms, there is an additional term involving the second derivative, f_{ww}, of f[t, W(t)], which is the Itô correction; as noted, this arises because of the path-wise quadratic variation of Brownian motion.

Example 7.3: Application of the Itô formula

Consider the function f[t, W(t)] = $tW(t)^2$, then $f_t = W(t)^2$, $f_w = 2tW(t)$ and $f_{ww} = 2t$. Hence, in integral and differential forms, the Itô formula results in:

$$f[T, W(T)] = \int_0^T \{W(t)^2 + t\} dt + 2\int_0^T tW(t) dW(t)$$
$$d\{tW(t)\} = (W(t)^2 + t) dt + 2tW(t) dW(t) \quad \blacklozenge$$

Example 7.4: Application of the Itô formula to the exponential martingale

Let Y(t, W(t)) = $e^{w(t)}e^{-(1/2)t}$, which is a process known as an exponential martingale (see Brzeźniak and Zastawniak, 1999): obtain the integral and differential forms, as in (7.25) and (7.26). First note that the required derivatives are:

$$\begin{aligned} f_t &= -\tfrac{1}{2} e^{W(t)} e^{-(1/2)t} = -\tfrac{1}{2} Y(t, W(t)) \\ f_W &= e^{W(t)} e^{-(1/2)t} = Y(t, W(t)) \\ f_{WW} &= e^{W(t)} e^{-(1/2)t} = Y(t, W(t)) \end{aligned}$$

Substituting these derivatives into (7.25) and (7.26), respectively, results in:

$$\begin{aligned} Y(t, W(t)) &= e^{W(0)} + \int_0^T \left\{ f_t + \frac{1}{2} f_{WW} \right\} dt + \int_0^T f_W dW(t) \\ &= \int_0^T \left(-\frac{1}{2} e^{W(t)} e^{-(1/2)t} + \frac{1}{2} e^{W(t)} e^{-(1/2)t} \right) dt + \int_0^T e^{W(t)} e^{-(1/2)t} dW(t) \\ &= \int_0^T e^{W(t)} e^{-(1/2)t} dW(t) \\ &= \int_0^T e^{W(t)} e^{-(1/2)t} dW(t) \end{aligned}$$

$$\begin{aligned} dY(t, W(t)) &= e^{W(t)} e^{-(1/2)t} dW(t) \\ &= Y(t, W(t)) dW(t) \end{aligned}$$

In a simplified notation, this is $dY(t) = Y(t)dW(t)$, so that the proportionate rate of growth is a Brownian motion increment. ♦

7.3.3 The Itô formula for a general Itô process

Note that examples 7.4 and 7.5 are examples of an Itô process, given by:

$$X(T) = X(0) + \int_0^T a(t)\, dt + \int_0^T b(t) dW(t) \tag{7.27}$$

with differential form given by:

$$dX(t) = a(t)dt + b(t)W(t) \tag{7.28}$$

In the case of (7.13), $a(t) = \frac{1}{2} f_{WW}$ and $b(t) = f_W$, and for (7.25), $a(t) = f_t + f_{WW}$ and $b(t) = f_W$. However, these are special cases. The more general case is where $Y(t) = f[t, X(t)]$, with $X(t)$ an Itô process. In this case, the Itô formulae, in integral form, is:

$$\begin{aligned} Y(T) = Y(0) + \int_0^T \left\{ f_t[t, X(t)] + f_X[t, X(t)]a(t) + \frac{1}{2} f_{XX}[(t, X(t)]b(t)^2 \right\} dt \\ + \int_0^T f_X[t, X(t)]b(t)dW(t) \end{aligned} \tag{7.29}$$

7.4 Ornstein-Uhlenbeck process (additive noise)

The following stochastic differential equation is a continuous-time analogue of an AR(1) process:

$$dX(t) = \alpha X(t)dt + \sigma dB(t) \tag{7.30}$$

Apart from the stochastic input, the motion of the process is provided by a first order differential equation with coefficient α; B(t) is a standard BM, which is multiplied by σ, interpreted as a scalar calibrating the volatility of the process (note that $W(t) = \sigma B(t)$). The equation (7.30) can be viewed as one way of randomising the first order differential equation by introducing additive noise. The discrete-time form of (7.30) is the familiar AR(1) model:

$$\Delta X_t = \gamma X_{t-1} + u_t \tag{7.31}$$

with $\gamma = \alpha$, and $u_t = \sigma(B_t - B_{t-1})$ is the stochastic input, which is distributed as $N(0, \sigma^2)$.

However, the differential form is not the rigorous form of this continuous-time process, as the terms in (7.30) only take meaning from the integral form which, in this case, is:

$$X(t) = X(0) + \alpha\int_0^t X(s)ds + \sigma\int_{s=0}^t dB(s) \tag{7.32}$$

This equation is referred to in the physics literature as the Langevin equation, see for example, Mikosch (1998). The expression (7.32) is of interest in econometrics as the continuous-time limiting form of (7.31), and is referred to as an Ornstein-Uhlenbeck process (sometimes with the condition that X(0) is non-random), which is of particular interest in the near-unit root case when α is close to zero; see Uhlenbeck and Ornstein (1930).

The solution of the non-random first order differential equation $dX(t) = \alpha X(t)dt$ is $X(t) = e^{\alpha t}X(0)$, whereas the solution to the randomised version (7.32) involves a second term due to the BM random input:

$$X(t) = e^{\alpha t}X(0) + \sigma e^{\alpha t}\int_0^t e^{-\alpha s}dB(s) \tag{7.33}$$

The Itô formula can be used to establish the relationship between (7.32) and (7.33). The solution can be obtained by first transforming X(t), such that $Y(t) = f[t, X(t)] = e^{-\alpha t}X(t)$, noting that $Y(0) = X(0)$, with the following derivatives: $f_t = -\alpha Y(t)$, $f_x = e^{-\alpha t}$ and $f_{xx} = 0$.

By reference to the form of an Itô process (7.27), note that $a(t) = \alpha X(t)$ and $b(t) = \sigma$. Next, substituting these particular values and the derivatives

into the Itô formula of (7.29), then the solution for Y(t) is:

$$\begin{aligned} Y(t) &= Y(0) + \int_0^t \{-\alpha Y(s) + e^{-\alpha t}\alpha X(s)\} ds + \sigma\int_0^s e^{-\alpha s} dB(s) \\ &= Y(0) + \int_0^t \{-\alpha Y(s) + \alpha Y(s)\} ds + \sigma\int_0^s e^{-\alpha s} dB(s) \\ &= Y(0) + \sigma\int_0^s e^{-\alpha s} dB(s) \end{aligned} \tag{7.34}$$

Finally, bearing in mind the original transformation, the solution for $X(t) = e^{\alpha t}Y(t)$, where $X(0) = e^0Y(t) = Y(0)$, is:

$$X(t) = e^{\alpha t}X(0) + e^{\alpha t}\sigma\int_0^t e^{-\alpha s} dB(s) \tag{7.35}$$

The solution comprises the deterministic solution plus weighted increments of Brownian motion, with weights that decline as s increases. (Note that some authors write (7.30) with $-\alpha$ rather than α as the coefficient on dt, which changes the sign on the exponential coefficients in (7.35).)

7.5 Geometric Brownian motion (multiplicative noise)

A development of the additive noise model is the proportional growth or multiplicative noise model of the kind that has been applied to economic time series where the realisations are necessarily non-negative, such as the price of a financial asset or GDP. In this case, the stochastic input is proportional to X(t) and the differential version of the equation is:

$$dX(t) = \alpha X(t)dt + \sigma X(t)dB(t) \tag{7.36}$$

where B(t) is standard Brownian motion. The interpretation of this expression is that growth, for example of an asset price, is a constant α plus a random shock, which is a scaled increment of Brownian motion; noting that $dW(t) = \sigma dB(t)$, then as in the Ornstein-Uhlenbeck process, σ is a volatility parameter. The integral form of the equation is:

$$X(t) = X(0) + \alpha\int_0^t X(s)ds + \sigma\int_{s=0}^t X(s)dB(s) \tag{7.37}$$

As $X(t) \geq 0$, then a natural transformation is $Y(t) = \ln X(t)$, with derivatives: $f_t = 0$, $f_x = X(t)^{-1}$ and $f_{xx} = -X(t)^{-2}$. Noting that (7.36) is an Itô process

with a(t) = αX(t) and b(t) = σX(t), then applying the Itô formula of (7.29) results in:

$$Y(t) = Y(0) + \int_0^t \left\{ \alpha X(t)X(t)^{-1} - \frac{1}{2}X(t)^2 X(t)^{-2}\sigma^2 \right\} dt + \sigma\int_0^T X(t)X(t)^{-1} dB(s)$$

$$= Y(0) + \int_0^t \left\{ \alpha - \frac{1}{2}\sigma^2 \right\} ds + \sigma\int_0^s dB(s) \tag{7.38}$$

In differential form this is:

$$dY(t) = \left\{ \alpha - \frac{1}{2}\sigma^2 \right\} dt + \sigma dB(t) \tag{7.39}$$

Transforming back to X(t), using X(t) = exp{Y(t)}, gives:

$$X(t) = X(0)\exp\left\{ \int_0^t (\alpha - \frac{1}{2}\sigma^2) ds + \sigma\int_0^t dB(s) \right\}$$

$$= X(0)\exp\left\{ (\alpha - \frac{1}{2}\sigma^2)\int_0^t ds + \sigma\int_0^t dB(s) \right\} \tag{7.40}$$

This expression can be simplified on noting that $(\alpha - \frac{1}{2}\sigma^2)\int_0^t ds = (\alpha - \frac{1}{2}\sigma^2)t$ and $\sigma\int_0^t dB(s) = \sigma B(t)$. Hence, (7.40) is written more simply as:

$$X(t) = X(0)\exp\left\{ (\alpha - \frac{1}{2}\sigma^2)t + \sigma B(t) \right\} \tag{7.41}$$

In this form X(t) is usually referred to as geometric Brownian motion, which is an important model in economics and finance.

7.6 Demeaning and detrending

It is frequently necessary to adjust observations by removing the mean or trend. This section summarises some important results on the limiting distributions that result from this procedure.

7.6.1 Demeaning and the Brownian bridge

A strategy often used in dealing with polynomial trends in constructing unit root tests is to remove the trend, so that the detrended data is used in the testing procedure. In the simplest case, the trend is simply a non-zero constant and the procedure just amounts to demean-

ing the data. The other case in frequent use is where a linear trend is first fitted to the data, and the residuals from this regression, interpreted as the detrended observations, are used. The partial sum process is then constructed from the detrended data. For example, in the first case let $y_t \sim \text{iid}(0, \sigma_y^2)$, where σ_y^2 is a finite constant, and $\bar{y} = T^{-1}\sum_{t=1}^{T} y_t$. The demeaned data is $\tilde{y}_t = y_t - \bar{y}$, with partial sum $S_{T,\tilde{y}}(r) = \sum_{t=1}^{[rT]} \tilde{y}_t$. A hint that this, suitably scaled, will converge to a Brownian bridge is given by $S_{T,\tilde{y}}(1) = \sum_{t=1}^{T}(y_t - \bar{y}) = \sum_{t=1}^{T} y_t - T\left(\sum_{t=1}^{T} y_t / T\right) = 0$, so that $S_{T,\tilde{y}}(1)$ is 'tied down' for r = 1.

As in the standard case, see Equation (6.19), the quantity of interest is:

$$\tilde{Z}_T(r) \equiv T^{-1/2} \frac{S_{T,\tilde{y}}(r)}{\sigma_y} \tag{7.42}$$

The limiting result is then:

$$\tilde{Z}_T(r) \Rightarrow_D V_1(r) \tag{7.43a}$$

$$V_1(r) \equiv B(r) - rB(1) \tag{7.43b}$$

where $V_1(r)$ is a first level Brownian Bridge. A question considers the proof of this statement, see **Q7.4**.

The previous result should be distinguished from what is known as demeaned Brownian motion, which is also important in the distribution theory for unit root tests, see Chapter 8. The difference is that it is $\{S_{T,y}(r)\}$ not the basic input sequence $\{y_t\}$ that is demeaned. Thus, in the usual way, define a normalised quantity as:

$$R_T(r) \equiv T^{-1/2} \frac{[S_{T,y}(r) - \bar{S}_{T,y}(r)]}{\sigma_y} \tag{7.44}$$

where $\bar{S}_{T,y}(r) = T^{-1}\sum_{t=1}^{T} S_{t,y}(r)$. The limiting result of interest is then as follows:

$$R_T(r) \Rightarrow_D B(r) - \int_0^1 B(s)ds \tag{7.45a}$$

$$\equiv B(r)_\mu \tag{7.45b}$$

where B(r) and B(s) are standard Brownian motion.

7.6.2 Linear detrending and the second level Brownian bridge

The second frequently used case is where the original data is detrended by fitting a linear trend. As before let $S_{T,\tilde{y}}(r) = \sum_{t=1}^{[rT]} \tilde{y}_t$, but now $\tilde{y}_t$ is the residual $\tilde{y}_t = y_t - (\hat{\beta}_0 + \hat{\beta}_1 t)$, where ^ over indicates a consistent estimator, usually the LS estimator. Let $\tilde{X}_T(r)$ be defined as follows:

$$\tilde{X}_T(r) \equiv T^{-1/2} \frac{S_{T,\tilde{y}}(r)}{\sigma_y} \tag{7.46}$$

Then the limiting result is:

$$\tilde{X}_T(r) \Rightarrow_D V_2(r) \tag{7.47a}$$

$$V_2(r) \equiv B(r) + (2r - 3r^2)B(1) + 6(r^2 - r)\int_0^1 B(s)ds \tag{7.47b}$$

$$= V_{(1)}(r) + 6r(1-r)\left(\frac{1}{2}B(1) - \int_0^1 B(s)ds\right)$$

where $V_2(r)$ is a second level Brownian bridge; see, for example, MacNeill (1978, especially Equation (8)), who provides a general expression for the p-th level Brownian bridge.

As in the case of demeaned Brownian motion, detrended Brownian motion relates to the case where $\{S_{T,y}(r)\}$ rather than $\{y_t\}$ is detrended. Thus, let

$$Q_T(r) \equiv T^{-1/2} \frac{[S_{T,y}(r) - \tilde{S}_{T,y}(r)]}{\sigma_y} \tag{7.48}$$

where $\tilde{S}_{T,y}(r)$ is the value of $S_{T,y}(r)$ estimated by a constant and a trend. Then the limiting result for detrended Brownian motion is:

$$Q_T(r) \Rightarrow_D B(r) + (6r - 4)\int_0^1 B(s)ds - (12r - 6)\int_0^1 sB(s)ds \tag{7.49a}$$

$$\equiv B(r)_\beta \tag{7.49b}$$

Throughout these expressions, if $\sigma_y \neq \sigma_{lr,y}$ then $\sigma_{lr,y}$ should be used in place of σ_y.

Note that the shorthand adopted for the functionals (7.45a) and (7.49a) is $B(r)_\mu$ and $B(r)_\beta$, respectively, this notation being indicative of the underlying demeaning or detrending that has taken place.

7.7 Summary and simulation example

7.7.1 Tabular summary

Some results that involve a correspondence between sample quantities, their limiting distributions and functionals of Brownian motion are summarised in Table 7.1.

Table 7.1 Summary: functionals of Brownian motion and sample moments

Limiting form	Closed form, if available	Example sample quantity
$\int_0^1 W(r)dr = \sigma\int_0^1 B(r)dr$	$N(0, \frac{1}{3}\sigma^2)$	$T^{-1/2}\bar{y} = T^{-3/2}\sum_{t=1}^{T} y_t$, $T^{-3/2}\sum_{t=1}^{T} y_{t-1}$
$\int_0^1 W(r)^2 dr = \sigma^2\int_0^1 B(r)^2 dr$		$T^{-2}\sum_{t=1}^{T} y_t^2$, $T^{-2}\sum_{t=1}^{T} y_{t-1}^2$
$\int_0^1 r dW(r) = \sigma\int_0^1 r dB(r)$	$N(0, \frac{1}{3}\sigma^2)$	$T^{-3/2}\sum_{t=1}^{T} t\varepsilon_t$
$\int_0^1 rW(r)dr = \sigma\int_0^1 rdB(r)dr$		$T^{-5/2}\sum_{t=1}^{T} ty_{t-1}$
$W(1) = \sigma B(1)$	$N(0, \sigma^2)$	$T^{-1/2}y_T$
$W(1)^2 = \sigma^2 B(1)(2)$	$\sigma^2\chi^2(1)$	$T^{-1}y_T^2$
$\int_0^1 W(r)dW(r) = \frac{1}{2}\{W(1)^2 - \sigma^2\}$ $= \frac{1}{2}\sigma^2\{B(1)^2 - 1\}$	$\frac{1}{2}\sigma^2\{\chi^2(1) - 1\}$	$T^{-1}\sum_{t=1}^{T} y_{t-1}\varepsilon_t$

Notes: the DGP for the quantities in the third column is $y_t = y_{t-1} + \varepsilon_t$, $y_0 = 0$, and $\varepsilon_t \sim \text{iid}(0, \sigma^2)$.
Sources: Banerjee et al. (1993, table 3.3); see also Davidson (2000), Phillips (1987) and Fuller (1996, Corollary 5.3.6).

7.7.2 Numerical simulation example

Where no closed form exists for the functional in the left-hand column of Table 7.1, or, for example, a product or ratio involving these elements, the distribution function can be obtained by numerical simulation using the form given in the right-hand column and the CMT.

Example 7.5: Simulating a functional of Brownian motion

To illustrate, consider obtaining by such means a limiting distribution where this distribution is known; this will act as a simple check on the procedure. An example is $\int_0^1 W(r)dr$, where for simplicity $\sigma^2 = 1$ is assumed, so that the simulation is just a functional of standard BM, $\int_0^1 B(r)dr$, which is normally distributed with a variance of $^1/_3$. The

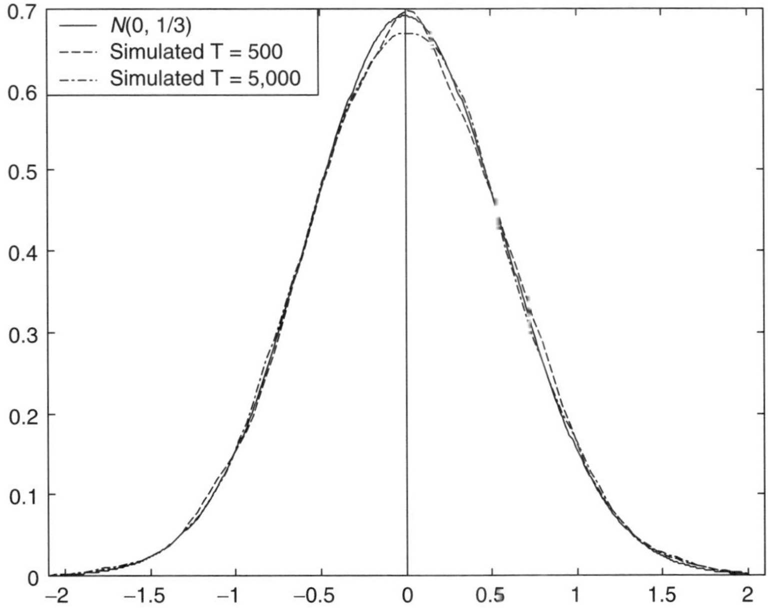

Figure 7.1 Estimated densities of ∫B(r)dr

simulated quantity is $T^{-1/2}\bar{y} = T^{-3/2}\sum_{t=1}^{T} y_t$, with $y_t = y_{t-1} + \varepsilon_t$, $y_0 = 0$, and $\varepsilon_t \sim$ niid(0, 1). In the illustrative set-up, T = 500 and T = 5,000 and there are 5,000 replications. The estimated density is overlaid with the pdf from N(0, $^1/_3$). The resulting densities, simulated and theoretical, are graphed in Figure 7.1 and show very slight differences at the peak, but are virtually indistinguishable elsewhere, even for the smaller sample size.

7.8 Concluding remarks

Brownian motion underpins the distribution theory of unit root tests. It is, therefore, necessary to have some understanding of this process, its properties and, especially, functionals of Brownian motion, for even the simplest of unit root test statistics. Whilst Brownian motion generates continuous sample paths, these paths are nowhere differentiable, with the result that classical calculus, with concepts such as derivatives and integrals, cannot be applied; what is required is a different form of calculus with different rules. This calculus due to Itô is not the only one designed for random functions, but it is appropriate for present purposes because it ties in with the space of cadlag functions on [0, 1].

In conventional integration, the ordinary Reimann integral of a function f(t) can be viewed as the limiting value of a weighted sum, which is obtained as follows. First create a partition of the evaluation interval, for example $t \in [0, 1]$, into n smaller intervals Δt_i and then compute the weighted sum of the Δt_i, where the weights are the function evaluations at points s_i, where $s_i \in \Delta t_i$, say $f(s_i)$. Taking s_i as the left-end point, t_{i-1}, the right-end point, t_i, the middle point or some other point in the interval, will not affect the limiting value of the weighted sum (where the limit refers to making the partition finer and finer). This is not the case if the function to be evaluated involves a Brownian motion input. The Itô calculus results from taking the left-end point for the evaluation of the weighted sum, which can be viewed as a non-anticipative choice; in terms of stochastic finance this relates to the opening position, and in terms of the distribution theory for partial sums it relates to the sum to the integer part of rT, where T is the sample size and $r \in [0, 1]$. The end result is that a correction, the Itô correction, is required to obtain the stochastic integral compared to the classical case where the function components are entirely non-random.

A particular interest in econometrics is the distribution of quantities such as sample moments and test statistics that arise in least squares and maximum likelihood estimation of AR and ARMA models, a simple example being the DF test statistic $T(\hat{\rho} - 1)$, when the null generating model is $y_t = y_{t-1} + \varepsilon_t$, $y_0 = 0$ and $\varepsilon_t \sim \text{niid}(0, \sigma^2)$. This can be expressed as the ratio of two functionals of Brownian motion, specifically the ratio of $\int_0^1 W(r)dW(r)$ to $\int_0^1 W(r)^2 dr$; recall that a functional takes a function as its argument and maps this into a scalar, integrals being a classic example. The power driving various results in asymptotic distribution theory for unit root test statistics is then a combination of the central limit theorem (CLT) and the continuous mapping theorem (CMT), extended to functionals, see Chapter 6, Sections 6.6.1 and 6.6.2, respectively. Together these provide many of the results that have become standard in unit root testing.

There are number of books to which the reader may turn for an elaboration of the concepts introduced in this chapter. A selective and partial list follows. An excellent place to start for a review of classical calculus, and its extension to stochastic functions, is the introductory book by Mikosch (1998); this could usefully be followed by one of Brzeźniak and Zastawniak (1999), Henderson and Plaschko (2006) and Kuo (2006); these books include important material on martingales and also include examples from economics, finance and

engineering. Continuing the finance theme, the reader could consult Shreve (2004) and Glasserman (2004). Books with a more explicit econometric orientation include Banerjee et al. (1993), McCabe and Tremayne (1993), Hamilton (1994) and Davidson (1994, 2000); the most extensive in terms of the probability background being Davidson (1994).

Questions

Q7.1 Generalise the Ornstein-Uhlenbeck process so that the implied long-run equilibrium can be non-zero.

A7.1 The basic Ornstein-Uhlenbeck process is, see Equation (7.30):

$$dX(t) = \alpha X(t)dt + \sigma dB(t)$$

with integral solution, see Equation (7.35), as follows:

$$X(t) = e^{\alpha t}X(0) + e^{\alpha t}\sigma\int_0^t e^{-\alpha s}dB(s)$$

In this specification, X(t) evolves as a function of its level and a stochastic input, which is scaled Brownian motion, with σ interpreted as a constant volatility parameter. The analogous discrete-time process is an AR(1) model without drift. The change that is necessary is to relate the nonstochastic part of the driving force to the deviation of X(t) from its steady state, $\mu - X(t)$; in the simple version, which is Equation (7.30), $\mu = 0$, so that the implied steady state is zero. The revised specification is:

$$dX(t) = \theta\{\mu - X(t)\}dt + \sigma dB(t)$$

The first term is now the deviation of X(t) from μ and θ characterises the speed of adjustment. If $X(t) = \mu$, then X(t) only changes if the stochastic input is non-zero and if that is zero then $X(t) = \mu$, justifying the description of μ as the equilibrium or steady state of X(t). Note that if $\mu = 0$, then $\theta = -\alpha$.

All that changes in obtaining the solution is that $a(t) = \theta\{\mu - X(t)\}$, rather than $\alpha X(t)$. To obtain the integral solution take $Y(t) = f[t, X(t)] = e^{\theta t}X(t)$, with derivatives: $f_t = \theta Y(t)$, $f_X = e^{\theta t}$ and $f_{XX} = 0$. Then make the

appropriate substitutions into (7.29), as follows:

$$Y(T) = Y(0) + \int_0^T \{\theta Y(t) + e^{\theta t}\theta[\mu - X(t)]\} dt + \sigma \int_0^s e^{\theta s} dB(s)$$

$$Y(T) = Y(0) + \int_0^T \theta\mu e^{\theta t} dt + \sigma \int_0^s e^{\theta s} dB(s)$$

$$Y(T) = Y(0) + \mu e^{\theta t}]_0^T + \sigma \int_0^s e^{\theta s} dB(s)$$

$$Y(T) = Y(0) + \mu(e^{\theta T} - 1) + \sigma \int_0^s e^{\theta s} dB(s)$$

Finally, reverse the original substitution $X(t) = e^{-\theta t}Y(t)$, to obtain:

$$X(T) = e^{-\theta t}Y(0) + \mu e^{-\theta T}(e^{\theta T} - 1) + \sigma e^{-\theta T} \int_0^s e^{\alpha s} dB(s)$$

$$= e^{-\theta t}X(0) + \mu - \mu e^{-\theta T} + \sigma e^{-\theta T} \int_0^s e^{\theta s} dB(s)$$

$$= \mu + [X(0) - \mu]e^{-\theta T} + \sigma e^{-\theta T} \int_0^s e^{\theta s} dB(s)$$

Notice that the solution for the simpler case with $\mu = 0$, as in (7.35), obtains by making the substitution $\theta = -\alpha$.

Q7.2 Confirm the following results from Table 7.1:

i. $T^{-2}\sum_{t=1}^{T} y_{t-1}^2 \Rightarrow_D \int_0^1 W(r)^2 dr$

ii. $T^{-1}\sum_{t=1}^{T} y_{t-1}\varepsilon_t \Rightarrow_D \int_0^1 W(r)dW(r)$

A7.2 First define the partial sum process of ε_t and its scaled equivalent given, respectively, by:

$$S_T(r) \equiv \sum_{t=1}^{[rT]} \varepsilon_t$$

$$Z_T(r) \equiv \frac{S_T(r)}{\sigma\sqrt{T}}$$

Then from the FCLT:

$$Z_T(r) \Rightarrow_D B(r) \qquad 0 \le r \le 1$$

i. Turning to the question and considering $T^{-2}\sum_{t=1}^{T} y_{t-1}^2$, it is also convenient to define $Y_T(r)$ and note the associated convergence result:

$$Y_T(r) \equiv \frac{S_T(r)}{\sqrt{T}} \Rightarrow_D W(r) = \sigma B(r)$$

The quantity of direct interest is $Y_T(r)^2 = T^{-1}S_T^2(r)$. The terms of which are given by:

$$\begin{aligned}
&Y_T(r)^2 = y_0^2/T = 0 && 0 \le r < 1/T\\
&Y_T(r)^2 = (\varepsilon_1 + \varepsilon_2)^2/T = y_1^2/T && 1/T \le r < 2/T\\
&\vdots \qquad\qquad \vdots \qquad\qquad \vdots && \vdots\\
&Y_T(r)^2 = \left(\sum\nolimits_{j=1}^{T-1} \varepsilon_j{}^2\right)/T = y_{T-1}^2/T && (T-1)/T \le r < 1\\
&Y_T(r)^2 = \left(\sum\nolimits_{j=1}^{T} \varepsilon_j{}^2\right)/T = y_T^2/T && r = 1
\end{aligned}$$

Note that r changes by 1/T each time a further step is taken. Taking the sum of these terms each weighted by 1/T is the first step in obtaining the integral:

$$\left(\sum\nolimits_{t=1}^{T} y_t^2/T\right)\frac{1}{T} = T^{-2}\sum\nolimits_{t=1}^{T} y_t^2$$

The integral of $Y_T(r)^2$ with respect to $r \in [0, 1]$, $\int_0^1 Y_T(r)^2 dr$, is the limit of the last expression. Then from the FCLT applied to $Y_T(r)$ and the CMT applied to $Y_T(r)^2$ it follows that:

$$\int_0^1 Y_T(r)^2 dr \Rightarrow_D \int_0^1 W(r)^2 dr = \sigma^2 \int_0^1 B(r)^2 dr$$

$T^{-2}\sum\nolimits_{t=1}^{T} y_t^2$ differs from $T^{-2}\sum\nolimits_{t=1}^{T} y_{t-1}^2 = T^{-2}\sum\nolimits_{t=1}^{T-1} y_t^2$ by one term, that is y^2_T/T^2, which is asymptotically negligible, so both $T^{-2}\sum\nolimits_{t=1}^{T} y_t^2$ and $T^{-2}\sum\nolimits_{t=1}^{T} y_{t-1}^2 \Rightarrow_D \int_0^1 W(r)^2 dr = \sigma^2 \int_0^1 B(r)^2 dr$.

ii. Turning to the second part of the question consider $T^{-1}\sum\nolimits_{t=1}^{T} y_{t-1}\varepsilon_t$. Note that $y_t^2 = (y_{t-1} + \varepsilon_t)^2 = (y_{t-1}^2 + 2y_{t-1}\varepsilon_t + \varepsilon_t^2)$, therefore, $y_{t-1}\varepsilon_t = \frac{1}{2}(y_t^2 - y_{t-1}^2 + \varepsilon_t^2)$. Hence, making the substitution:

$$\begin{aligned}
&T^{-1}\sum\nolimits_{t=1}^{T} y_{t-1}\varepsilon_t\\
&\quad = \tfrac{1}{2}T^{-1}\sum\nolimits_{t=1}^{T}(y_t^2 - y_{t-1}^2 + \varepsilon_t^2)\\
&\quad = \tfrac{1}{2}T^{-1}\left(\sum\nolimits_{t=1}^{T} y_t^2 - \sum\nolimits_{t=1}^{T} y_{t-1}^2 + \sum\nolimits_{t=1}^{T} \varepsilon_t^2\right)\\
&\quad = \tfrac{1}{2}T^{-1}\left(y_T^2 - \sum\nolimits_{t=1}^{T} \varepsilon_t^2\right)
\end{aligned}$$

Noting from Table 7.1 that $T^{-1}y_T^2 \Rightarrow_D W(1)^2 = \sigma^2 B(1)^2 = \sigma^2\chi^2(1)$ as $B(1) \sim N(0, 1)$; also $\text{plim}\left(T^{-1}\sum_{t=1}^{T}\varepsilon_t^2\right) = \sigma^2$, it then follows that:

$$T^{-1}\sum y_{t-1}\varepsilon_t \Rightarrow_D \frac{1}{2}\sigma^2(B(1)-1) \sim \frac{1}{2}\sigma^2\left(\chi^2(1)-1\right)$$

Q7.3 Prove that if W(r) is Brownian motion, then $V(r) = W(r) - rW(1)$ is a Brownian bridge.

A7.3 First note that V(r) has zero expectation:

$$\begin{aligned} E[V(r)] &= E[W(r)] - rE[W(1)] \\ &= 0 \end{aligned}$$

The first term and second terms are zero by the property of Brownian motion:

$$\begin{aligned} \text{cov}[V(s), V(r)] &= E[W(s) - sW(1)][W(r) - rW(1)] \\ &= E[W(s)W(r)] - rE[W(s)W(1)] - sE[W(r)W(1)] + rsE[W(1)^2] \\ &= (s - rs - sr + rs)\sigma^2 \\ &= s(1-r)\sigma^2 \end{aligned}$$

where $s < r$ has been assumed. The result follows on noting that $E[W(s), W(r)] = \text{cov}[W(s), W(r)] = s\sigma^2$ for $s < r$. Hence, the first and second moments are the same as for a Brownian bridge and as V(r) is Gaussian, V(r) is a Brownian bridge; see Ross (2003, chapter 10).

Q7.4 Prove the following:

$$\frac{S_{T,\bar{y}}(r)}{\sigma_y\sqrt{T}} \Rightarrow_D B(r) - rB(1) \equiv V_1(r)$$

where $S_{T,\bar{y}}(r) = \sum_{t=1}^{[rT]}(y_t - \bar{y})$ and $y_t \sim \text{iid}(\mu, \sigma_y^2)$.

A7.4 Starting from the definition of $S_{T,\bar{y}}(r)$:

$$\begin{aligned} S_{T,\bar{y}}(r) &= \sum_{t=1}^{[rT]}(y_t - \bar{y}) \\ &= \sum_{t=1}^{[rT]}y_t - [rT]\sum_{t=1}^{T}y_t/T \\ &= \sum_{t=1}^{[rT]}y_t - r\sum_{t=1}^{T}y_t + o_p(T) \end{aligned}$$

Hence, noting that:

$$(\sigma_y\sqrt{T})^{-1}\sum_{t=1}^{[rT]} y_t \Rightarrow_D B(r) \text{ and } (\sigma\sqrt{T})^{-1}\sum_{t=1}^{T} y_t \Rightarrow_D B(1)$$

then the required result follows:

$$\frac{S_{T,\tilde{y}}(r)}{\sigma_y\sqrt{T}} \Rightarrow_D B(r) - rB(1) \qquad r \in [0, 1]$$

which is a standard first level Brownian bridge.

8

Some Examples of Unit Root Tests

Introduction

It is not the intention in this chapter to provide a comprehensive review of unit root tests; that would be a task far more substantial than space allows. Rather, the idea is to introduce some tests that link in with developments in earlier chapters. Examples are given of two types of test: parametric and nonparametric. In the former case, probably the most frequently applied test is a version of the standard t test from the family of Dickey-Fuller (DF) tests, usually referred to as a $\hat{\tau}$ test. This is a pseudo-t test in the sense that whilst it is constructed on the same general principle as a t test, it does not have a t distribution under the null hypothesis of a unit root. A closely related test is the coefficient or normalised bias test, referred to here as a $\hat{\delta}$ test, which is just T times the numerator of the pseudo-t statistic. Whilst the $\hat{\delta}$ test is generally more powerful than the $\hat{\tau}$ test, it is not so stable when the error process in the underlying model has a serially correlated structure, and is not so widely used as the $\hat{\tau}$ test.

One of the problems of testing a hypothesis that a parameter takes a particular value under the null hypothesis is that power, the probability of rejecting the null hypothesis when the alternative hypothesis is correct, is likely to be low for alternatives very close to the null value. This is a problem generic to testing hypotheses that a parameter takes a particular value. In context, it means that processes with a near-unit root are going to be very difficult to discover. Tests for a unit root are very vulnerable to this criticism and the DF tests are known to have low power for near-unit root alternatives. Thus, one fruitful line of development has been to obtain tests that are more powerful. The second set of parametric tests described here, due to Elliott, Rothenberg and Stock

(1996) and Elliott (1999), gain power by demeaning or detrending the time series for an alternative close to the unit root.

There are also several nonparametric tests for a unit root. The one outlined here is due to Burridge and Guerre (1996), extended by García and Sansó (2006). The principle underlying this test is based on the intuition provided by Chapter 5 that random walks have infrequent mean reversion. We saw in Chapter 5, Section 5.6 that it was possible to obtain the distribution of the number of sign changes for a random walk; hence, in principle, a test for a unit root can be based on the number of sign changes observed in a time series. Nonparametric tests are unlikely to be more powerful than parametric tests when the assumptions underlying the latter are correct, however they often have an appealing intuitive rationale and may have features that make them useful in combination with parametric tests.

This chapter is organised as follows. The basic testing framework is outlined in Section 8.1 and is extended in Section 8.2 to consider how to deal with deterministic terms that are particularly likely to be present under the alternative hypothesis. In a practical application of a unit root test, it is usually necessary to consider the possibility of dynamics in the error term and Section 8.3 considers this complication. An alternative family of unit root tests, based on 'efficient' detrending, is considered in Section 8.4. A nonparametric test, based on the observed number of crossings of a particular level, is considered in Section 8.5.

8.1 The testing framework

We consider the simplest case first to lay out a framework that is easily modified for more complex cases.

8.1.1 The DGP and the maintained regression

The simplest DGP of interest is that of the pure random walk:

$$y_t = y_{t-1} + u_t \tag{8.1}$$

$$u_t = \varepsilon_t \tag{8.2}$$

The specification in (8.2) just sets u_t to the special case of white noise, with finite variance, but allows for the more general case when $u_t \neq \varepsilon_t$ to be developed in later sections. Equation (8.1) is the special case of the following AR(1) model, with $\rho = 1$:

$$y_t = \rho y_{t-1} + \varepsilon_t \tag{8.3}$$

Hence, $\rho = 1$ corresponds to the unit root. We could proceed by estimating (8.3) and setting up the null hypothesis $H_0 : \rho = 1$ to be tested against the alternative hypothesis $H_A : |\rho| < 1$. In this specification, the case $\rho = -1$ is excluded from the parameter space under H_A, since it also corresponds to a negative unit root, with unit modulus; however, notwithstanding this point, the alternative hypothesis is usually just specified as $H_A : \rho < 1$ on the understanding that the relevant part of the parameter space under H_A is likely to be that which is close to the positive unit root.

The regression that is estimated in order to form a test statistic is referred to as the maintained regression; thus, in the present context, (8.3) is the maintained regression in order to test $H_0 : \rho = 1$ against $H_A : \rho < 1$. As it is generally easier to test a null hypothesis that a coefficient is equal to zero, y_{t-1} is subtracted from both sides of (8.3), to obtain:

$$\begin{aligned}\Delta y_t &= (\rho - 1)y_{t-1} + \varepsilon_t \\ &= \gamma y_{t-1} + \varepsilon_t\end{aligned} \tag{8.4}$$

where $\gamma = (\rho - 1)$. The corresponding null and alternative hypotheses are now: $H_0 : \gamma = 0$ against $H_A : \gamma < 0$. H_A is sometimes written more explicitly to indicate that the negative unit root is excluded, so that $-2 < \gamma < 0$.

Whilst a good place to start to establish some general principles, specifying the maintained regression as in (8.3) is unlikely in practice. The reason for this is that the specification under H_A summarises our view of how the data has been generated if the generating process is stationary. Thus, for (8.3) to be relevant for $\rho < 1$, there must be reversion to a mean of zero rather than to a non-zero mean; whilst there might (rarely) be good reasons to impose such a feature of the DGP under H_A, if its imposition is invalid, so that the maintained regression should include an intercept, then the power of standard unit root tests, such as the pseudo-t, will tend to zero as the absolute value of the intercept increases. In intuitive terms, the presence of an intercept under H_A, which is not included in the maintained regression, leads the test statistic to interpret the data as being generated by a nonstationary process.

8.1.2 DF unit root test statistics

The reason for starting with the simple case represented by Equations (8.1) – (8.3) is that they provide an introduction to obtaining the distribution of two well-known unit root test statistics and the use of the FCLT and CMT. The two test statistics are the normalised bias and the

t-type test statistic, denoted $\hat{\delta}$ and $\hat{\tau}$, respectively. These are:

$$\hat{\delta} = T(\hat{\rho} - 1) \tag{8.5}$$

$$\hat{\tau} = \frac{(\hat{\rho} - 1)}{\hat{\sigma}(\hat{\rho})} \tag{8.6}$$

where $\hat{\delta}$ is the LS estimator of $\hat{\rho}$ and $\hat{\sigma}(\hat{\rho})$ is the estimated standard error of $\hat{\rho}$.

We will consider $\hat{\delta}$ first. The LS estimator $\hat{\rho}$, $\hat{\rho} - 1$ and $\hat{\delta}$ are, respectively, given by:

$$\hat{\rho} = \frac{\sum_{t=1}^{T} y_t y_{t-1}}{\sum_{t=1}^{T} y_{t-1}^2} \tag{8.7}$$

$$\hat{\rho} - 1 = \frac{\sum_{t=1}^{T} y_{t-1}(y_t - y_{t-1})}{\sum_{t=1}^{T} y_{t-1}^2} \tag{8.8}$$

$$= \frac{\sum_{t=1}^{T} y_{t-1}\varepsilon_t}{\sum_{t=1}^{T} y_{t-1}^2} \qquad \text{using } y_t - y_{t-1} = \varepsilon_t$$

$$\hat{\delta} \equiv T(\hat{\rho} - 1)$$

$$= T\frac{\sum_{t=1}^{T} y_{t-1}\varepsilon_t}{\sum_{t=1}^{T} y_{t-1}^2}$$

$$= \frac{\sum_{t=1}^{T} y_{t-1}\varepsilon_t / T}{\sum_{t=1}^{T} y_{t-1}^2 / T^2} \tag{8.9}$$

The numerator and denominator on the right-hand-side of this inequality are familiar from Chapter 7.

There are several variants of a set of sufficient assumptions that lead to the same limiting null distributions of $\hat{\delta}$ and $\hat{\tau}$, and the extensions of these statistics to include deterministic regressors. For example, from Fuller (1996, Theorem 10.1.1) we may specify that $\{\varepsilon_s\}_1^t$ is a martingale difference sequence, MDS, see Chapter 3, Section 3.5.1, as follows:

$$E(\varepsilon_t \mid F_1^{t-1}) = 0$$

$$E(\varepsilon_t^2 \mid F_1^{t-1}) = \sigma^2 < \infty$$

$$E(|\varepsilon_t|^{2+\eta} = F_1^{t-1}) = K$$

where $\eta > 0$, K is a finite constant and F_1^t is the σ–field generated by $\{\varepsilon_s\}_1^t$ (see Chapter 1, Section 1.2.3 for the definition of a σ–field). Alternatively, it may be assumed that $\varepsilon_t \sim \text{iid}(0, \sigma^2)$. Additionally y_0 is assumed to be a finite constant, which is satisfied for cases such as $y_0 = 0$, or y_0 is a bounded random variable. The set of assumptions, which relate to the invariance of the functional central limit theorem, outlined in Chapter 6, Section 6.6.1, can also be adopted.

Considering (8.9), the limiting distributions of interest can be read off from Table 7.1 of Chapter 7:

$$T^{-1}\sum\nolimits_{t=1}^{T} y_{t-1}\varepsilon_t \Rightarrow_D \int_0^1 W(r)dW(r) = \sigma^2 \int_0^1 B(r)dB(r) \tag{8.10}$$

$$T^{-2}\sum\nolimits_{t=1}^{T} y_{t-1}^2 \Rightarrow_D \int_0^1 W(r)^2 dr = \sigma^2 \int_0^1 B(r)^2 dr \tag{8.11}$$

These are the limiting distributions of the numerator and denominator quantities of $\hat{\delta}$ and the next question is whether the limiting distribution of the ratio is the ratio of the limiting distributions. This follows from the CMT extended to function spaces, see Chapter 6, Section 6.2.2 and, for example, Davidson (2000, Theorem 14.2.3) and Billingsley (1995, Theorem 25.7), so that:

$$\begin{aligned} \hat{\delta} &\Rightarrow_D \frac{\int_0^1 B(r)dB(r)}{\int_0^1 B(r)^2 dr} \equiv F(\hat{\delta}) \\ &= \tfrac{1}{2}\frac{\{B(1)^2 - 1\}}{\int_0^1 B(r)^2 dr} \end{aligned} \tag{8.12}$$

Notice that the second line uses the result that $\int_0^1 B(r)dB(r) = \frac{1}{2}[B(1)^2 - 1]$, see Chapter 7, Equation (7.11) for t = 1.

Whilst the limiting distribution of the numerator of (8.12) exists in closed form, see Chapter 7, Table 7.1, this is not the case for the denominator so that, in practice, the percentiles are obtained by simulating the distribution function, as in Fuller (1976, 1996). This is considered in more detail in the next section and in an appendix.

Perhaps the most frequently used test statistic for the unit root null hypothesis is $\hat{\tau}$, the t-statistic based on $\hat{\rho}$, sometimes referred to as a pseudo-t statistic in view of the fact that its distribution is not the 't' distribution. The numerator of $\hat{\tau}$ is $(\hat{\rho}-1)$ and the denominator is $\hat{\sigma}(\hat{\rho})$,

the estimated standard error of $\hat{\rho}$, where:

$$\hat{\sigma}(\hat{\rho}) = \tilde{\sigma}\left(\sum_{t=1}^{T} y_{t-1}^2\right)^{-1/2} \tag{8.13}$$

$$\tilde{\sigma} = T^{-1}\sum_{t=1}^{T} \hat{\varepsilon}_t^2 \tag{8.14a}$$

$$\hat{\varepsilon}_t = y_t - \hat{\rho} y_{t-1} \tag{8.14b}$$

The estimator $\tilde{\sigma}$ could be replaced by the LS estimator that makes an adjustment for degrees of freedom, but this does not affect the asymptotic results. Making the substitution for $\hat{\sigma}(\hat{\rho})$, $\hat{\tau}$ is given by:

$$\begin{aligned}\hat{\tau} &= \frac{\sum_{t=1}^{T} y_{t-1}\varepsilon_t}{\tilde{\sigma}\left(\sum_{t=1}^{T} y_{t-1}^2\right)^{-1/2}\left(\sum_{t=1}^{T} y_{t-1}^2\right)} \\ &= \frac{\sum_{t=1}^{T} y_{t-1}\varepsilon_t}{\tilde{\sigma}\left(\sum_{t=1}^{T} y_{t-1}^2\right)^{1/2}} \\ &= \frac{T^{-1}\sum_{t=1}^{T} y_{t-1}\varepsilon_t / \tilde{\sigma}}{\left(T^{-2}\sum_{t=1}^{T} y_{t-1}^2\right)^{1/2}}\end{aligned} \tag{8.15}$$

The limiting distribution of $\hat{\tau}$ is now obtained by taking the limiting distributions of the numerator and denominator, and noting that $\tilde{\sigma} \to_p \sigma$. This results in:

$$\begin{aligned}\hat{\tau} &\Rightarrow_D \frac{\int_0^1 B(r)dB(r)}{\left(\int_0^1 B(r)^2 dr\right)^{1/2}} \equiv F(\hat{\tau}) \\ &= \tfrac{1}{2}\frac{[B(1)^2 - 1]}{\left(\int_0^1 B(r)^2 dr\right)^{1/2}}\end{aligned} \tag{8.16}$$

As in the case of $T(\hat{\rho} - 1)$, the limiting distribution can be obtained by simulation as illustrated in the next section.

8.1.3 Simulation of limiting distributions of $\hat{\delta}$ and $\hat{\tau}$

In this section, the limiting distributions of $\hat{\delta}$ and $\hat{\tau}$ are obtained by simulation, where the DGP is $y_t = y_{t-1} + \varepsilon_t$, with $\varepsilon_t \sim niid(0, 1)$, and the

maintained regression is $y_t = \rho y_{t-1} + \varepsilon_t$; note that the test statistics are invariant to σ^2 so that, for convenience, it may be set equal to unity. The test statistics $\hat{\delta}$ and $\hat{\tau}$ were obtained for T = 1,000 and 5,000 replications. Figure 8.1 shows the simulated cdf of $\hat{\delta}$, from which a skew to the left, inherited from the distribution of $(\hat{\rho} - 1)$, is evident. The corresponding pdf is shown in Figure 8.2; although the mode is zero, the distribution is not symmetric. The estimated 1%, 5% and 10% percentiles for $\hat{\delta}$ are: –13.2(–13.7), –8.1(–8.1), –5.8(–5.7), respectively; these are very close to the percentiles from Fuller (1996, table 10A.1), shown in parentheses and obtained from a larger number of replications. Figure 8.3 shows the simulated cdf of $\hat{\tau}$, together with the cdf of the standard normal distribution; and Figure 8.4 shows the corresponding pdfs. The distribution of $\hat{\tau}$ is shifted to the left compared to the normal distribution, with the result that the critical values typically used for testing are more negative than those from the standard normal distribution. The estimated 1%, 5% and 10% percentiles for $\hat{\tau}$ are: –2.58, –1.95 and –1.62, which are identical to the percentiles from Fuller (1996, table 10A.1).

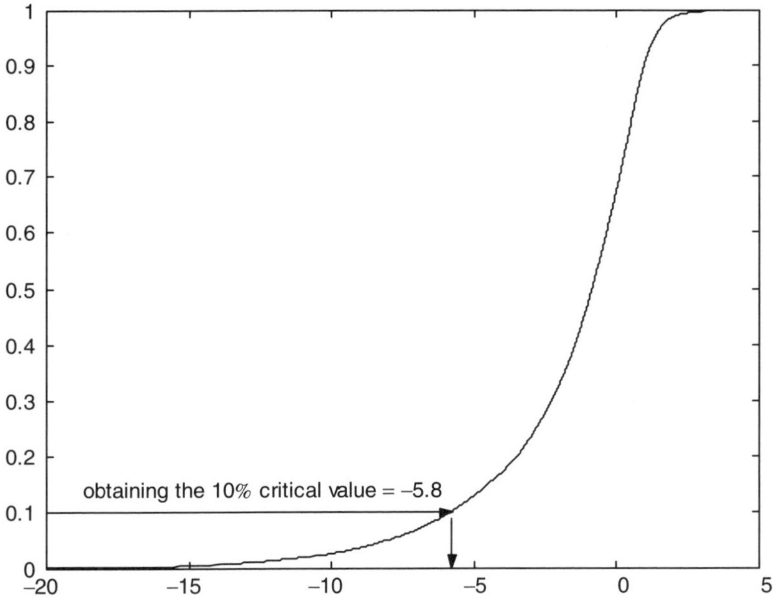

Figure 8.1 Simulated distribution function of $\hat{\delta}$

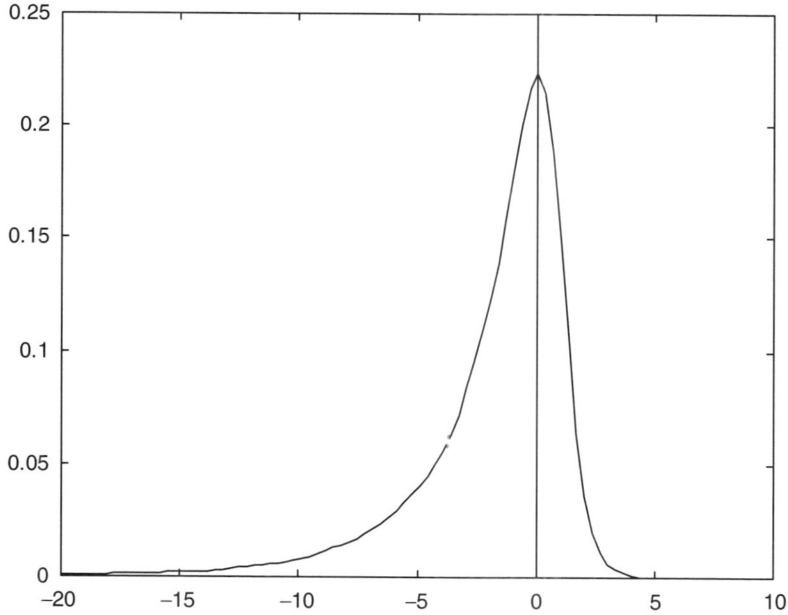

Figure 8.2 Simulated density function of $\hat{\delta}$

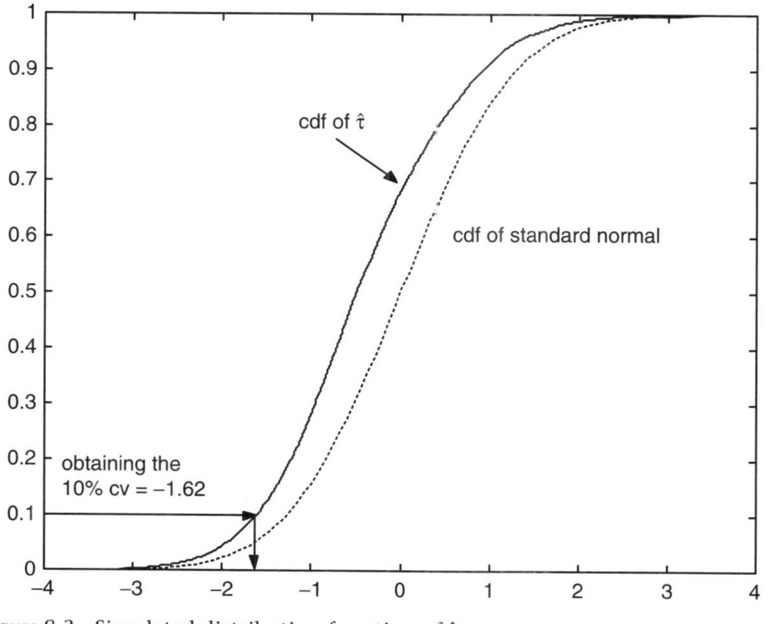

Figure 8.3 Simulated distribution function of $\hat{\tau}$

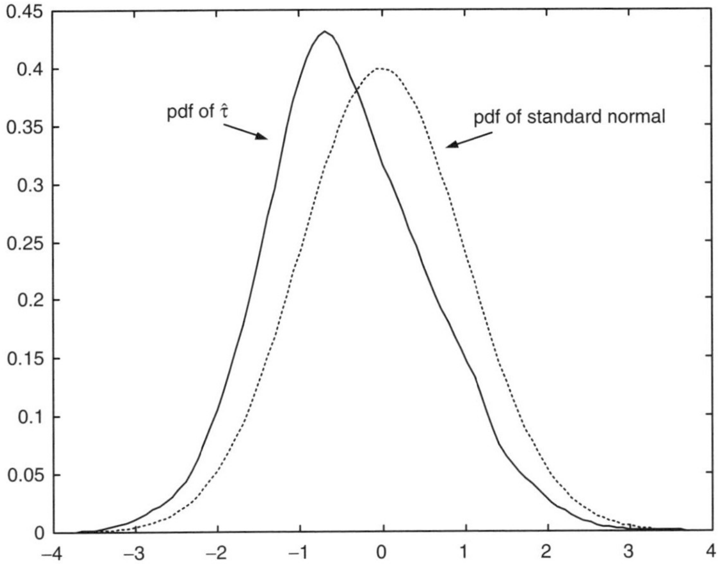

Figure 8.4 Simulated density function of $\hat{\tau}$

8.2 The presence of deterministic components under H_A

It is rarely the case that under the alternative hypothesis, the time series of interest reverts to a zero mean in the long run. Two more likely cases are that of long-run reversion to a constant and, alternatively, reversion to a trend. Economic examples in the former case include unemployment and real inflation rates, and in the latter case many macroeconomic series formed by aggregating individual components, such as consumption expenditure and GDP.

8.2.1 Reversion to a constant or linear trend under the alternative hypothesis

As noted in Section 8.1.1, the case where the maintained regression does not contain any deterministic terms is likely to be the exception rather than the rule. The two most familiar cases are $\mu_t = \mu$ and $\mu_t = \beta_0 + \beta_1 t$, corresponding to AR(1) models of the following form:

$$y_t - \mu = \rho(y_{t-1} - \mu) + \varepsilon_t \tag{8.17}$$

$$y_t - \mu_t = \rho(y_{t-1} - \mu_{t-1}) + \varepsilon_t \tag{8.18a}$$

$$\mu_t = \beta_0 + \beta_1 t \tag{8.18b}$$

First, consider the specification in (8.17): then according to H_0, $\rho = 1$, which reduces (8.17) to (8.3), the data is generated by a pure random walk; however, according to H_A, the data has the characteristics of a stationary process, but with a non-zero, long-run mean, μ, to which the stationary series reverts. Second, in the case of (8.18) under H_A, the stationary series reverts to a linear trend.

Figures 8.5 and 8.6 show two simulated series for T = 500, each generated by a stationary but near-unit root process with $\rho = 0.975$, that revert to a constant mean or to a trend, respectively. In the first case, the DGP is as in (8.17) with $\mu = 10$ and in the second as in (8.18) with $\beta_0 = 10$ and $\beta_1 = 0.1$, where $\varepsilon_t \sim \text{niid}(0, 1)$ in both cases. Note from Figure 8.5, that the near-unit root leads to long sojourns away from the long-run mean and from Figure 8.6 that whilst the trend is the attractor, there are long periods when observations are away from the trend.

What is evident from these figures is that the maintained regression must include a mechanism that is capable of capturing the behaviour of y_t according to H_A as well as according to H_0. As a result,

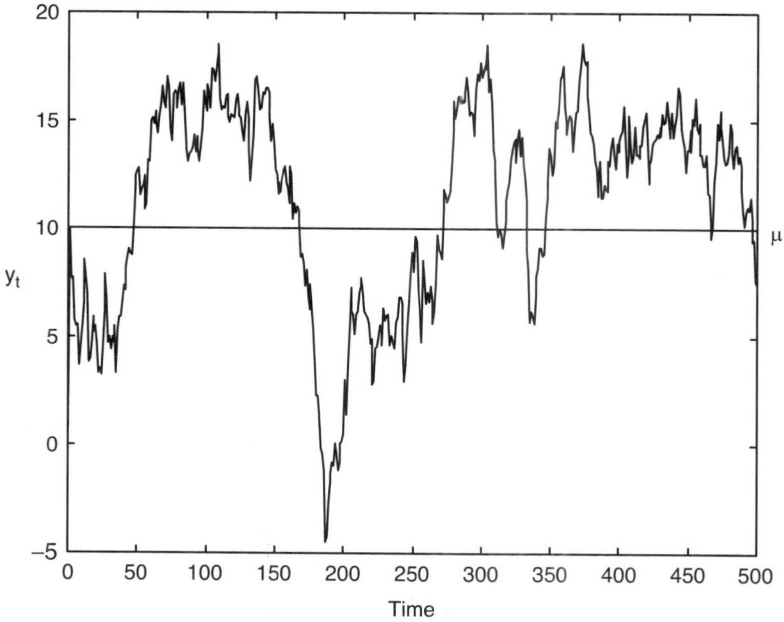

Figure 8.5 Data generated by a stationary mean-reverting process
Note: Near-unit root leads to long periods away from the long-run mean, $\mu = 10$

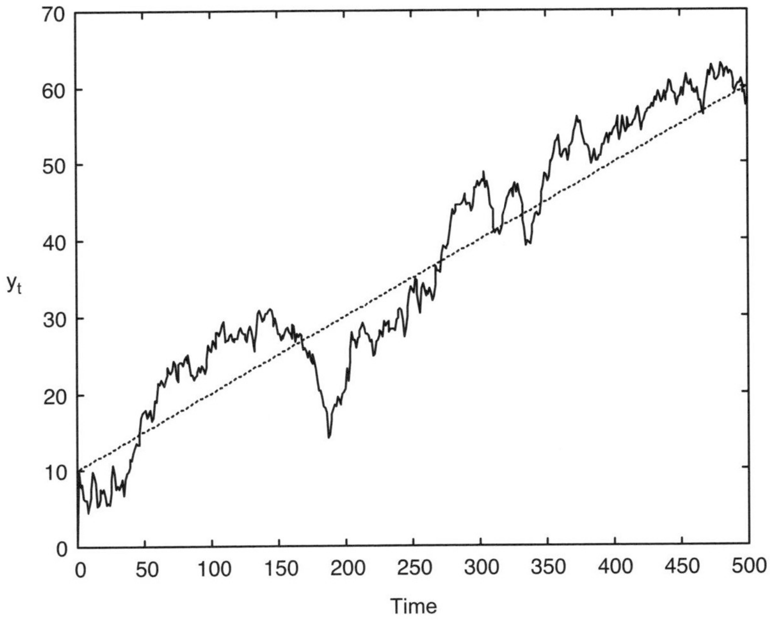

Figure 8.6 Data generated by trend stationary process
Note: Near-unit root leads to long periods away from long-run trend

the specification $\mu \neq 0$ will generally represent the minimum inclusion of deterministic terms and, hence, the maintained regression will be of the form of (8.17). To obtain the test statistic, first, estimate μ by, say, $\hat{\mu}$, the usual estimator being the sample mean $\bar{y} = T^{-1}\sum_{t=1}^{T} y_t$, then use the demeaned observations $\hat{\tilde{y}}_t = y_t - \bar{y}$, so that the maintained regression is:

$$\hat{\tilde{y}}_t = \rho\hat{\tilde{y}}_{t-1} + \xi_t \tag{8.19}$$

where $\xi_t = \varepsilon_t + (1 - \rho)(\mu - \bar{y})$. Let $\hat{\rho}$ be the LS estimator from (8.19), then form $\hat{\delta}_\mu = T(\hat{\rho} - 1)$ and $\hat{\tau}_\mu = (\hat{\rho} - 1)/\hat{\sigma}(\hat{\rho})$, where the subscript μ serves to indicate the use of demeaned observations.

An analogous procedure can be followed if $\mu_t = \beta_0 + \beta_1 t$. The first step is to detrend the data by regressing y_t on a constant and a linear trend, then forming $\hat{\mu}_t = \hat{\beta}_0 + \hat{\beta}_1 t$, where ^ over indicates a LS estimator; the second step, analogous to (8.19), is to specify the AR(1) model in terms of the detrended data:

$$y_t - \hat{\mu}_t = \rho(y_{t-1} - \hat{\mu}_{t-1}) + \xi_t \tag{8.20}$$

The test statistics are formed as in the case of (8.19), but are distinguished by the subscript β as $\hat{\delta}_\beta$ and $\hat{\tau}_\beta$, to indicate that a linear trend has been removed from the observations.

The limiting distributions of the test statistics, which assume that the DGP according to the null is $\Delta y_t = \varepsilon_t$, are as follows:

$$\hat{\delta}_i \Rightarrow_D \frac{\int_0^1 B(r)_i dB(r)_i}{\int_0^1 B(r)_i^2 \, dr} \equiv F(\hat{\delta}_i) \tag{8.21}$$

$$\hat{\tau}_i \Rightarrow_D \frac{\int_0^1 B(r)_i dB(r)_i}{\left(\int_0^1 B(r)_i^2 \, dr\right)^{1/2}} \equiv F(\hat{\tau}_i) \tag{8.23}$$

where i = μ, β and the functionals of Brownian motion are as follows:

$$B(r)_\mu = B(r) - \int_0^1 B(s)ds$$

$$B(r)_\beta = B(r) + (6r - 4)\int_0^1 B(s)ds - (12r - 6)\int_0^1 sB(s)ds$$

Notice that $B(r)_\mu$ and $B(r)_\beta$ are demeaned and detrended Brownian motion, as defined in Chapter 7, Equations (7.45) and (7.49), respectively; thus, the limiting distributions are of the same form as in (8.12) and (8.16) except for the substitution of the appropriate form of Brownian motion. The critical values of these distributions have been obtained by simulation see, for example, Fuller (1996, Appendix A); a response function approach to obtaining the critical values (quantiles) is described in the appendix to this chapter.

The simulated pdfs of $\hat{\tau}$, $\hat{\tau}_\mu$ and $\hat{\tau}_\beta$ are shown in Figure 8.7 for T = 100. Note the leftward shift in the density functions as the number of deterministic terms is increased. For example, the 5% quantiles are: –1.95, –2.90 and –3.45 for $\hat{\tau}$, $\hat{\tau}_\mu$ and $\hat{\tau}_\beta$, respectively. Simulated power for T = 100 for the DF tests is shown in Figure 8.8. (The initial observation is drawn from the unconditional distribution of u_t; for more discussion of this point, see Section 8.4.) Notice that power declines substantially as more deterministic terms are included, with power($\hat{\tau}$) ≤ power($\hat{\tau}_\mu$) ≤ power(τ_β); for example, estimated power at ρ = 0.9 is 83% for $\hat{\tau}$, 35% for $\hat{\tau}_\mu$ and 20% for $\hat{\tau}_\beta$. Much of the research on different unit root test statistics has been directed to obtaining test statistics that improve on the power of the DF tests, and we outline one such approach in Section 8.4.

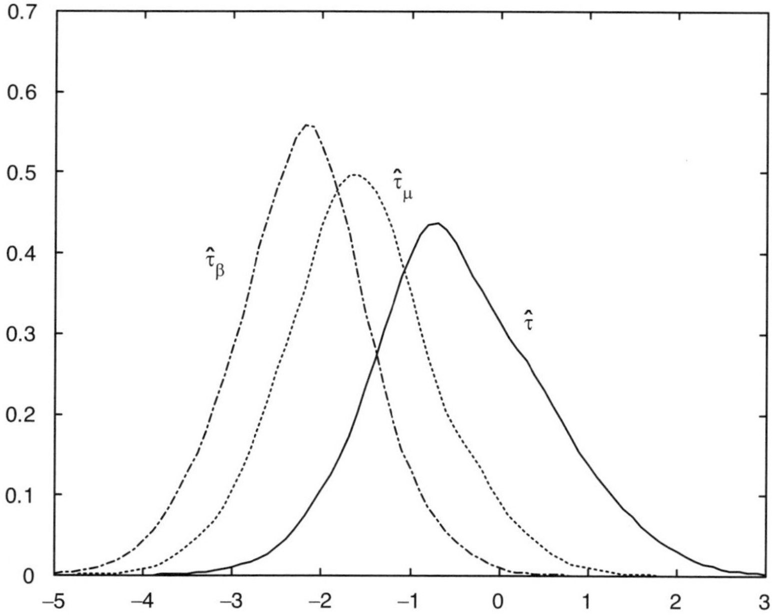

Figure 8.7 Estimated pdfs of $\hat{\tau}$, $\hat{\tau}_\mu$ and $\hat{\tau}_\beta$, T = 100

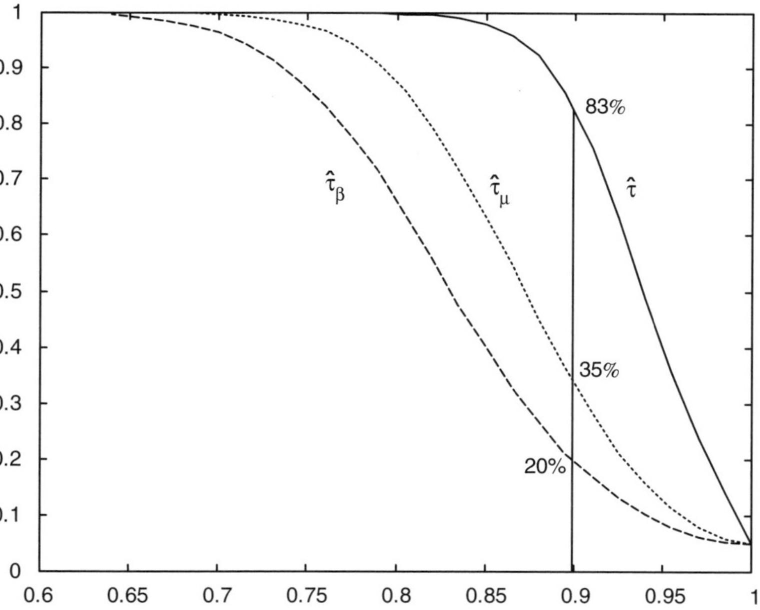

Figure 8.8 Power of DF tests: $\hat{\tau}$, $\hat{\tau}_\mu$ and $\hat{\tau}_\beta$, T = 100

8.2.2 Drift and invariance: The choice of test statistic and maintained regression

There are two typical cases in which unit root tests are used. In the first, the issue is to decide whether an observed time series is best described as being generated by a process with a unit root, but no drift, or a stationary process that generates observations that would, in equilibrium, revert to a constant, non-zero mean, see, for example, the pattern graphed in Figure 8.5 for a stylised view of the data. In this case, a test statistic based on Equations (8.19) or (8.20) would be appropriate, perhaps subject to an extension for possible serial correlation, which is described in Section 8.3 below.

In the second case, the observed data has a trend, which must be capable of explanation in terms of a nonstationary process and, alternatively, in terms of a stationary process. As to the former, there are two possibilities, the first is that the underlying random walk does not inherently have a direction, but the direction it has taken is just as likely as any other and so provides an ex post explanation of the observed data. This explanation is not entirely satisfactory, as it suggests that if another 'run' of history was possible we might observe a trend in the opposite direction. Evidently, this would be a difficulty for series such as GDP and consumption!

Alternatively, the direction has been driven by drift in the random walk process, for example positive drift for GDP. According to the explanation under H_A, the direction is accounted for by a linear trend (or other polynomial trend) and once the data is adjusted for this trend, a stationary series results. Thus, the competing explanations are matched in terms accounting for a central feature of the observed data. The practical implication of the explanation under H_0 is that an appropriate DGP would be $\Delta y_t = \mu + \varepsilon_t$, rather than $\Delta y_t = \varepsilon_t$, and a desirable characteristic of any unit test statistic in this context is that its limiting null distribution should be invariant to μ, otherwise, with μ unknown, there would be a problem in determining the appropriate critical values. To achieve this invariance, the maintained regression including a linear trend must be used, which would reduce to $\Delta y_t = \mu + \varepsilon_t$, $\mu = \beta_1$, according to the null hypothesis. The resulting DF test statistics are $\hat{\delta}_\beta$ and $\hat{\tau}_\beta$. The test statistics $\hat{\delta}_\mu$ and $\hat{\tau}_\mu$ are not invariant to μ, whereas the limiting null distributions of $\hat{\delta}_\beta$ and $\hat{\tau}_\beta$ are invariant to μ; as a corollary, this invariance means that μ may be set equal to zero in obtaining the percentiles required for hypothesis testing. This method is part of a general procedure in that including in the maintained regression a

polynomial of one higher order than specified under the null ensures invariance of the test statistic.

The approach described in Section 8.2.1 is an example of the common factor or error dynamics approach, see Bhargava (1986). That is, an equivalent way of writing (8.18a) is as follows:

$$y_t = \mu_t + u_t \tag{8.25a}$$

$$u_t = \rho u_{t-1} + v_t \tag{8.25b}$$

$$v_t = \varepsilon_t \tag{8.25c}$$

Note that (8.25c) plays no effective part at this stage, just setting v_t to a white noise random variable. These equations can be regarded as the structural equations, with the reduced form equation obtained on substituting $u_t = y_t - \mu_t$ into (8.25b), and using (8.25c), resulting in:

$$(y_t - \mu_t) = \rho(y_{t-1} - \mu_{t-1}) + \varepsilon_t \tag{8.26a}$$

With some slight rearrangement, this can be expressed as:

$$y_t = \mu_t^* + \rho y_{t-1} + \varepsilon_t \tag{8.27a}$$

$$\mu_t^* = (1 - \rho L)\mu_t \tag{8.27b}$$

If $\mu_t = \mu$ and $\hat{\mu} = \bar{y}$, then the maintained regression is as in (8.19).

There is a subtle but important difference in this approach compared to the original DF specification; (see also Dickey (1984) and Dickey, Bell and Miller (1986) for a specification in the spirit of the common factor approach). To see this, take the case where a constant is included in the maintained regression, then:

$$y_t = \mu^* + \rho y_{t-1} + \varepsilon_t \tag{8.28}$$

Estimation of (8.19) and (8.28) will produce asymptotically equivalent results, only differing due to some finite sample effects, see **Q8.1.** However, a difference in interpretation arises if μ^* is considered a parameter that is unrelated to ρ, rather than related as in (8.27b); in effect, (8.28) is considered a 'stand-alone' regression. Then consider the situation with $\rho = 1$. The specification of (8.28) reduces to:

$$\Delta y_t = \mu^* + \varepsilon_t \tag{8.29}$$

whilst that of (8.27a,b) reduces to:

$$\Delta y_t = \varepsilon_t \tag{8.30}$$

Note that (8.29) includes a drift term μ^*, implying a deterministic trend in y_t as well as the stochastic trend from the cumulated values of current and lagged ε_t, whereas (8.30) just implies the latter. If (8.29) is what is regarded as the most likely specification under the null, perhaps informed by a prior graphical analysis, then the maintained regression should include a linear trend, as follows:

$$y_t = \mu^* + \rho y_{t-1} + \beta^* t + \varepsilon_t \tag{8.31}$$

The specification in (8.29) can then be tested by an F-type test that jointly tests $\rho = 1$ and $\beta^* = 0$. Dickey and Fuller (1981) suggested such a test and a number of other joint tests, and provided some critical values; see also Patterson (2000) for critical values.

Also, unless $\mu^* = (1 - \rho)\mu$ is imposed there will be a difference under H_A in the two formulations. Consider the difference in a simulation set-up in order to assess power. In the common factor approach, the long-run mean, μ, is kept constant, whereas in the DF specification, the long-run mean varies because μ^* is kept constant. Further, in order to ensure stationarity under the alternative, the initial value, y_0, should be a draw from $N(\mu, \sigma_y^2)$, where $\sigma_y^2 = (1 - \rho^2)^{-1}\sigma^2$ is the unconditional variance.

Schmidt and Phillips (1992) show that the power curves, for a given value of $\rho < 1$ under H_A, from the two approaches cross. For consistency of treatment of the deterministic components under H_0 and H_A, the common factor approach is preferred. For a more detailed discussion of the issues, especially power comparisons see Marsh (2007).

8.3 Serial correlation

The specification of the maintained regression has so far assumed that ε_t is not serially correlated, implying $\sigma_{lr,v}^2 = \sigma^2$. In practice, this may not be the case and so the testing procedure must be flexible enough to allow $\sigma_{lr,v}^2 \neq \sigma^2$. The approach we take here is to model v_t as generated by the ARMA process, although it applies to more general linear processes, see Chang and Park (2002). The reduced form equation of the underlying system of structural equations that becomes the basis of the testing model is known as an augmented Dickey-Fuller, ADF, regression.

In the case of serial correlation in v_t, it transpires that the ratio $\sigma/\sigma_{lr,v}$ is a nuisance parameter that affects the null distribution of the $\hat{\delta}$-type statistic, both finite sample and limiting, but not that of the $\hat{\tau}$-type statistic. In the former case, the limiting distribution of the DF $\hat{\delta}$-type test is a simple scalar multiple of the corresponding DF distribution and multiplying $\hat{\delta}$ by $(\sigma/\sigma_{lr,v})^{-1} = \sigma_{lr,v}/\sigma$ gives a test statistic with a DF distribution; thus, to obtain a feasible test statistic, a consistent estimator of $\sigma/\sigma_{lr,v}$ is required.

8.3.1 The ADF representation

A leading specification for v_t is that it is generated by a stationary and invertible ARMA process. The structural equations are now:

$$y_t = \mu_t + u_t \tag{8.32a}$$

$$u_t = \rho u_{t-1} + v_t \tag{8.32b}$$

$$\varphi(L)v_t = \theta(L)\varepsilon_t \tag{8.32c}$$

where $\varphi(L) = 1 - \sum_{i=1}^{p-1} \varphi_i L^i$, $\theta(L) = 1 + \sum_{j=1}^{q} \theta_j L^j$ and $\varphi(L)$ and $\theta(L)$ are assumed to be invertible. From (8.32c) we can obtain that $\sigma^2_{lr,v} = [\theta(1)/\varphi(1)]^2\sigma^2$; (see Chapter 2, Section 2.6.2 and note that here we are obtaining the long-run variance of v_t).

To obtain the reduced form of (8.32a)–(8.32c), first, as usual, define $\tilde{y}_t \equiv y_t - \mu_t = u_t$ and then substitute y_t from (8.32a) into (8.32b) and use (8.32c), to obtain:

$$\varphi(L)(1 - \rho L)\tilde{y}_t = \theta(L)\varepsilon_t \tag{8.33}$$

$$\Rightarrow$$

$$\phi(L)\tilde{y}_t = \varepsilon_t \tag{8.34}$$

where $\phi(L) = \theta(L)^{-1}\varphi(L)(1 - \rho L)$. The order of $\phi(L)$ will be infinite if $\theta(L)$ is of order $q \geq 1$ or if $\varphi(L)$ is of infinite order. The AR form of (8.34), and the general nature of $\phi(L)$, should be familiar from Chapter 2.

It is convenient to write $\phi(L)$ as $\phi(L) = 1 - \Phi(L)$, where $\Phi(L) = \sum_{i=1}^{\infty} \phi_i L^i$. Next, a useful representation of $\Phi(L)$ is through the DF decomposition:

$$\Phi(L) = \Phi(1)L + c(L)(1 - L) \tag{8.35}$$

where $c(L) = \sum_{j=1}^{\infty} c_j L^j$. Using this decomposition, the original form, (8.34), can be separated into two parts, one comprising the lag of $\tilde{y}_t$ and the other comprising lags of $\Delta\tilde{y}_t$. Then, substituting (8.35) in (8.34), we obtain:

$$\tilde{y}_t = \Phi(1)\tilde{y}_{t-1} + c(L)\Delta\tilde{y}_t + \varepsilon_t \tag{8.36}$$

$$\Rightarrow$$

$$\Delta\tilde{y}_t = \gamma\tilde{y}_{t-1} + c(L)\Delta\tilde{y}_t + \varepsilon_t \tag{8.37}$$

where $\gamma = \Phi(1) - 1$. Note that if there is a unit root, then $\Phi(1) = 1$ (see Chapter 2, Section 2.1.3), implying that $\gamma = 0$, which forms the basis of using the pseudo-t test on $\hat{\gamma}$ as a unit root test, where $\hat{\gamma}$ is the LS estimator from a feasible version of (8.37).

The form of the model in (8.37) is known as an augmented Dickey-Fuller (ADF) regression. If the original AR order in (8.34) is AR(p), $p < \infty$, then the corresponding ADF model, (8.37), is ADF(p – 1), where (p – 1) is the order of the c(L) polynomial.

To proceed to a feasible model, first assume that c(L) is of infinite order, so that (8.37) is:

$$\Delta\tilde{y}_t = \gamma\tilde{y}_{t-1} + \sum_{j=1}^{\infty} c_j\Delta\tilde{y}_{t-j} + \varepsilon_t \tag{8.38}$$

This cannot be estimated because of the infinite number of lags on Δy_t, so a truncation rule is required to ensure a finite order for c(L), resulting in, say, an ADF(p – 1) model, as follows:

$$\Delta\tilde{y}_t = \gamma\tilde{y}_{t-1} + \sum_{j=1}^{p-1} c_j\Delta\tilde{y}_{t-j} + \varepsilon_{t,p} \tag{8.39}$$

$$\varepsilon_{t,p} = \sum_{j=p}^{\infty} c_j\Delta\tilde{y}_{t-j} + \varepsilon_t \tag{8.40}$$

A condition is required on the expansion rate for $p^* = p - 1$, so that p^* increases with the sample size. A sufficient condition in this case has already been considered in Chapter 2, Section 2.6.2 (see below Equation (2.51)); it requires that $p^*/T^{1/3} \to 0$ as $T \to \infty$, and there exist constants, ζ and s, such that $\zeta p^* > T^{1/s}$, see Said and Dickey (1984), Xiao and Phillips (1998, Assumption A4). This expansion rate governs the case where T is variable, so it does not directly provide guidance in a single sample, where T is fixed. As noted in Chapter 2, a rule of the form

$p^* = [K(T/100)^{1/3}]$ is often used, with K = 4, 12, but the sensitivity of the results to increasing p* should be assessed.

8.3.2 Limiting null distributions of the test statistics

Let $\hat{\gamma}$ denote the LS estimator from (8.39) and let the pseudo-t be $\hat{\tau}^{adf} = \hat{\gamma}/\hat{\sigma}(\hat{\gamma})$, where $\hat{\sigma}(\hat{\gamma})$ is the estimated standard error of $\hat{\gamma}$, and assume that p* expands at the required rate. Then, it is still the case that the limiting null distribution of $\hat{\tau}^{adf}$ is the DF distribution, see Fuller (1996, Theorem 10.1.4), that is:

$$\hat{\tau}^{adf} \Rightarrow_D F(\hat{\tau}) \qquad (8.41)$$

$$\hat{\tau}_{\mu}^{adf} \Rightarrow_D F(\hat{\tau}_{\mu}) \qquad (8.42)$$

$$\hat{\tau}_{\beta}^{adf} \Rightarrow_D F(\hat{\tau}_{\beta}) \qquad (8.43)$$

These results mean that the limiting percentiles are still those of the corresponding DF distribution; there are, however, differences in the finite sample distributions, which are sensitive to the lag length in the ADF regression, see Cheung and Lai (1995a, b) and Patterson and Heravi (2003), who provide critical values from a response surface approach.

It is not, however, the case that $\tilde{\delta} = T\hat{\gamma}$ has a DF limiting null distribution. To achieve this result it is necessary to make an adjustment. Xiao and Phillips (1998, Theorem 1) show that the limiting null distribution of $\tilde{\delta}$ is a scalar multiple of the DF distribution, that is:

$$\begin{aligned}\hat{\delta} &\Rightarrow_D \frac{\sigma}{\sigma_{lr,v}}\left(\frac{\int_0^1 B(r)dB(r)}{\int_0^1 B(r)^2 dr}\right) \\ &= \frac{\sigma}{\sigma_{lr,v}} F(\hat{\delta})\end{aligned} \qquad (8.44)$$

Notice that the 'sigma' ratio $\sigma/\sigma_{lr,v}$ is a nuisance parameter that scales the DF distribution, $F(\hat{\delta})$; thus, multiplying by the inverse of the sigma ratio removes the nuisance parameter from the asymptotic distribution. That is:

$$\begin{aligned}\hat{\delta}^{adf} &\equiv \frac{\sigma_{lr,v}}{\sigma}\tilde{\delta} \Rightarrow_D \left(\frac{\int_0^1 B(r)dB(r)}{\int_0^1 B(r)^2 dr}\right) \\ &= F(\hat{\delta})\end{aligned} \qquad (8.45)$$

As in the case of the pseudo-t tests, this result extends to the case where the data are demeaned or detrended, so that:

$$\hat{\delta}_{\mu}^{adf} \equiv \frac{\sigma_{lr,v}}{\sigma}\tilde{\delta}_{\mu} \Rightarrow_D F(\hat{\delta}_{\mu}) \tag{8.46}$$

$$\hat{\delta}_{\beta}^{adf} \equiv \frac{\sigma_{lr,v}}{\sigma}\tilde{\delta}_{\beta} \Rightarrow_D F(\hat{\delta}_{\beta}) \tag{8.47}$$

where $\tilde{\delta}_{\mu}$ and $\tilde{\delta}_{\beta}$ are as $\tilde{\delta}$, but in the demeaned and detrended cases, respectively.

A feasible test statistic results from replacing $\sigma_{lr,v}$ and σ by consistent estimators, denoted $\hat{\sigma}_{lr,v}$ and $\hat{\sigma}$, respectively. Estimation of the long run variance was considered in Chapter 2, Section 2.6. The parametric estimator of $\hat{\sigma}_{lr,v}$ is a natural one to consider in this context. In the case of the ADF(p*) model of (8.39), $\hat{\sigma}^2_{lr,v}$ is obtained as follows:

$$\hat{\sigma}^2_{lr,v} = \left(\frac{1}{(1-\hat{c}(1))}\right)^2 \hat{\sigma}^2_p \tag{8.48}$$

$$\hat{\sigma}^2_p = T^{-1}\sum\nolimits_{t=p}^{T} \hat{\varepsilon}^2_{t,p} \tag{8.49}$$

where $\hat{c}(1) = \sum\nolimits_{j=1}^{p^*} \hat{c}_j$, $\hat{c}_j$ is the LS estimator of c_j and $\hat{\varepsilon}_{t,p}$ is the t-th residual from estimation of (8.39). Hence, a consistent estimator of the inverse sigma ratio is given by:

$$\begin{aligned}\frac{\hat{\sigma}_{lr,v}}{\hat{\sigma}} &= \frac{1}{\hat{\sigma}_p}\left(\frac{1}{(1-\hat{c}(1))}\right)\hat{\sigma}_p \\ &= \left(\frac{1}{(1-\hat{c}(1))}\right)\end{aligned} \tag{8.50}$$

This provides the required scalar multiple for (8.45), (8.46) or (8.47), so that:

$$\begin{aligned}\hat{\delta}^{adf} &\equiv \frac{\hat{\sigma}_{lr,v}}{\hat{\sigma}}\tilde{\delta} \\ &= \frac{T\hat{\gamma}}{(1-\hat{c}(1))}\end{aligned} \tag{8.51}$$

$$\Rightarrow_D \left(\frac{\int_0^1 B(r)dB(r)}{\int_0^1 B(r)^2 dr} \right) \tag{8.52}$$

Example 8.1: Deriving an ADF(1) regression model from the basic components

The set-up for this example is the basic model augmented by an additional AR(1) process in the error dynamic component. The three parts of the model are:

$$y_t = \mu_t + u_t \tag{8.53a}$$

$$u_t = \rho u_{t-1} + v_t \tag{8.53b}$$

$$(1 - \varphi_1 L)v_t = \varepsilon_t \tag{8.53c}$$

The first and second equations are familiar from (8.25a) and (8.25b); the third equation specifies v_t to be generated from an AR(1) process, rather than being white noise. In the sequence of steps that follows, the three component equations are brought into one equation and then written as an ADF(1) model. As usual, $\tilde{y}_t \equiv y_t - \mu_t$.

$(1-\varphi_1 L)(1-\rho L)\tilde{y}_t = \varepsilon_t$	substitute (8.53a) and (8.53b) into (8.53c)
$(1-(\varphi_1+\rho)L + \varphi_1\rho L^2)\tilde{y}_t = \varepsilon_t$	expand the left-hand-side polynomial
$(1-\phi_1 L - \phi_2 L^2)\tilde{y}_t = \varepsilon_t$	write the lag polynomial in the form $\phi(L)$
$\tilde{y}_t = \phi_1\tilde{y}_{t-1} + \phi_2\tilde{y}_{t-2} + \varepsilon_t$	rearrange as an AR(2) model
$\tilde{y}_t = (\phi_1 + \phi_2)\tilde{y}_{t-1} + c_1\Delta\tilde{y}_{t-1} + \varepsilon_t$	rearrange: collect ϕ_j coefficients on $\tilde{y}_{t-1}$
$\Delta\tilde{y}_t = \gamma\tilde{y}_{t-1} + c_1\Delta\tilde{y}_{t-1} + \varepsilon_t$	write as an ADF(1) model (8.54)

where $\phi_1 = \varphi_1 + \rho,\ \phi_2 = -\varphi_1\rho,\ c_1 = -\phi_2$

$\gamma = \phi_1 + \phi_2 - 1 = \varphi_1 + \rho - \varphi_1\rho - 1 = (1 - \varphi_1)(\rho - 1)$

Note that $\rho = 1$ implies $\gamma = 0$, which provides an intuitive basis for the invariance of limiting null distribution of $\hat{\tau}$ when obtained from an ADF or a simple DF regression.

From $\gamma = (1 - \varphi_1)(\rho - 1)$, it is evident that:

$$(\rho - 1) = \frac{\gamma}{(1 - \varphi_1)}$$

Hence, if φ_1 is known, $(\rho - 1)$ and, therefore, ρ can be obtained. Under the null hypothesis $c_1 = \varphi_1\rho = \varphi_1$, so that:

$$(\rho - 1) = \frac{\gamma}{(1 - c_1)} \quad \text{conditional on } \rho = 1$$

For example, suppose that $\mu_t = \beta_0 + \beta_1 t$, then from estimation of (8.54), the $\hat{\delta}$ type test statistic can be obtained as:

$$\hat{\delta}_{\beta}^{adf} = \frac{T\hat{\gamma}}{(1 - \hat{c}_1)}$$

where $\hat{\delta}_{\beta}^{adf}$ has the limiting null distribution given in (8.47). Note that this procedure fails under the alternative hypothesis; an alternative in that case is to estimate φ_1 and ρ from (8.54) imposing the nonlinear constraints. ♦

Example 8.2: Deriving an ADF(∞) regression model from the basic components

In this example v_t is modelled as generated from an invertible MA(1) process. This results in an ADF of infinite order and illustrates some principles that are applicable to higher order MA and infinite AR processes. As before, there are three component equations:

$$y_t = \mu_t + u_t \tag{8.55a}$$

$$u_t = \rho u_{t-1} + v_t \tag{8.55b}$$

$$v_t = (1 + \theta_1 L)\varepsilon_t \tag{8.55c}$$

The reduced form can be obtained as follows:

$$(1 - \rho L)\tilde{y}_t = (1 + \theta_1 L)\varepsilon_t$$ substitute (8.55a) into (8.55b) and use (8.55c)

$$(1 + \theta_1 L)^{-1}(1 - \rho L)\tilde{y}_t = \varepsilon_t$$ the MA lag polynomial is invertible

$(1-\phi_1 L - \phi_2 L^2 - \ldots)\tilde{y}_t = \varepsilon_t$	multiply out the two lag polynomials
$\tilde{y}_t = \Phi(L)\tilde{y}_t + \varepsilon_t$	$\Phi(L) = \sum_{i=1}^{\infty} \phi_i L^i$: an infinite AR model
$\tilde{y}_t = \Phi(1)\tilde{y}_{t-1} + c(L)\Delta\tilde{y}_t + \varepsilon_t$	rearrange: collect ϕ_j coefficients on $\tilde{y}_{t-1}$
$\Delta\tilde{y}_t = \gamma\tilde{y}_{t-1} + c(L)\Delta\tilde{y}_t + \varepsilon_t$	ADF(∞): subtract $\tilde{y}_{t-1}$ from both sides

(8.56)

$$\phi_j = (-1)^{j-1}\theta_1^{j-1}(\theta_1 + \rho), \Phi(1) = \sum_{j=1}^{\infty} \phi_j, \gamma = \phi(1) - 1$$

$$c(L) = \sum_{j=1}^{\infty} c_j L^j, c_j = -\sum_{i=j+1}^{\infty} \phi_i$$

Note that the ADF model of Equation (8.56) can be viewed as the reduced form of the structural Equations (8.55a)–(8.55c); it is of infinite order due to the presence of the invertible MA component in (8.55c). As far as estimation is concerned, it is necessary to adopt a truncation rule to fix the lag order of the polynomial c(L) at a finite value. The pseudo-t test is then just the usual t test on $\hat{\gamma}$; however, the $\hat{\delta}$-type test is based on $T(\hat{\rho} - 1)$, where $\hat{\rho}$ is a derived estimator of ρ from (8.56).

To obtain ρ, and hence $\hat{\rho}$, we have to show that:

$$(\rho - 1) = \frac{\gamma}{(1 - c(1))} \quad \text{conditional on } \rho = 1$$

Notice that ϕ_j are the coefficients on L^j in the lag polynomial $\Phi(L)$, where:

$$\Phi(L) = 1 - \frac{(1 - \rho L)}{(1 + \theta_1 L)}$$
$$= \frac{(\theta_1 + \rho)L}{(1 + \theta_1 L)} \tag{8.57}$$

$$\Phi(1) = \frac{(\theta_1 + \rho)}{(1 + \theta_1)} \tag{8.58}$$

$$\gamma = \frac{(\rho - 1)}{(1 + \theta_1)} \tag{8.59}$$

Hence, if $\rho = 1$ (and $\theta_1 \neq -1$), then $\gamma = 0$ and, as in the previous example, this motivates the continued use of the pseudo t-statistic on $\hat{\gamma}$ as a

unit root test, even in an ADF model. However, from (8.59), note that $\gamma \neq (\rho - 1)$; specifically, from (8.59)

$$(\rho - 1) = \gamma(1 + \theta_1) \tag{8.60}$$

To obtain c(L) and hence c(1) note that the ADF decomposition of $\Phi(L)$ is, with c(L) to be determined:

$$\begin{aligned}
\frac{(\theta_1 + \rho)L}{(1 + \theta_1 L)} &= \left(\frac{\theta_1 + \rho}{1 + \theta_1}\right)L + c(L)(1 - L) \Rightarrow \\
c(L)(1 - L) &= \frac{(\theta_1 + \rho)L}{(1 + \theta_1 L)} - \left(\frac{\theta_1 + \rho}{1 + \theta_1}\right)L \\
&= (\theta_1 + \rho)L\left[\frac{1}{(1 + \theta_1 L)} - \frac{1}{(1 + \epsilon_1)}\right] \\
&= (\theta_1 + \rho)L\left[\frac{\theta_1}{(1 + \theta_1 L)(1 + \theta_1)}\right](1 - L) \Rightarrow \\
c(L) &= \left(\frac{\theta_1(\theta_1 + \rho)L}{(1 + \theta_1 L)(1 + \theta_1)}\right) \\
c(1) &= \left(\frac{\theta_1(\theta_1 + \rho)}{(1 + \theta_1)^2}\right)
\end{aligned}$$

Conditional on $\rho = 1$, c(1) reduces to:

$$\begin{aligned}
c(1) &= \left(\frac{\theta_1}{(1 + \theta_1)}\right) \Rightarrow 1 - c(1) = 1 - \frac{\theta_1}{(1 + \theta_1)} = \frac{1}{(1 + \theta_1)} \\
\frac{\gamma}{(1 - c(1))} &= \frac{(\rho - 1)}{(1 + \theta_1)}(1 + \theta_1) \\
&= (\rho - 1) \text{ as required.}
\end{aligned}$$

Hence, the $\hat{\delta}$-type test statistic is obtained as:

$$\hat{\delta} = \frac{T\hat{\gamma}}{(1 - \hat{c}(1))} \tag{8.61}$$

Note that, as in the AR(1) case of the previous example, $\hat{\delta}T^{-1}$ is not a consistent estimator of $(\rho - 1)$ under the alternative hypothesis that $\rho < 1$. ♦

8.3.3 Limiting distributions: Extensions and comments

The distribution results summarised in the previous section extend to linear processes, other than ARMA processes, of the form $v_t = \pi(L)\varepsilon_t$ where $\pi(L) = \sum_{j=0}^{\infty} \pi_j L^j$, with $\pi(z) \neq 0$ for all $|z| < 1$ and $\sum_{j=0}^{\infty} |j|^k \pi_j < \infty$ for some $k \geq 1$, see Chang and Park (2002). The latter authors emphasise that conditional heterogeneous error processes, such as covariance stationary ARCH and GARCH models, are permitted, and some forms of unconditional heterogeneity (see also Chapter 6, Section 6.6.3) as in the case of the modified test statistics suggested by Phillips and Perron (1988). Notably, in the present context, Chang and Park (op. cit.) derive that in the case of $\hat{\tau}^{adf}$ (but not $\hat{\delta}^{adf}$) the rate of expansion of the lag length in the ADF regression may be $p^* = o(T)^{1/2}$, compared to the Said and Dickey rate of $p^* = o(T)^{1/3}$. However, $p^* = o(T)^{1/2}$ is not sufficient for consistency of the LS estimators $\{\hat{c}_j\}_{j=1}^{p^*}$, so that lag selection techniques that rely on this consistency require a slower rate of expansion. The required rate differs depending on the heterogeneity in the MDS, with $p^* = o(\{T/\ln(T)\}^{1/2})$ for a homogenous MDS and $p^* = o(T)^{1/3}$ for a possibly heterogeneous MDS.

8.4 Efficient detrending in constructing unit root test statistics

A well-known problem with DF tests is that they lack power when the dominant root is close to unity. A uniformly powerful test across the whole range of values for ρ does not exist, but power can be improved for a particular value of ρ. This section describes one of a family of tests due to Elliott, Rothenberg and Stock (1996), hereafter ERS, and Elliott (1999). The idea is that when there is no UMP test, one possibility is maximise power for a given alternative very local to $\rho = 1$ (see also Cox and Hinkley (1974)).

The method consists of two steps. In the first step, referred to as efficient detrending, the data is detrended by a GLS-type procedure for a fixed value ρ_c of ρ, chosen such that ρ_c is 'local-to-unity' in a well-defined sense; in the second step, a unit root test is then carried out on the detrended data. There are a number of tests based on this idea and the one described here is the extension of the DF $\hat{\tau}$ family of tests.

The idea of a near-integrated process, and the testing framework associated with it, is one in which under H_A, ρ takes a value that is 'local-to-unity'. To capture this idea, consider the alternative hypothesis

specified as

$$H_A : \rho = \rho_c = 1 + c/T < 1 \tag{8.62}$$

where $c < 0$ and $c \in C$, so that C is the set of possible values of c. For example, with T = 100, values of c = –5 and –10 imply $\rho_c = 0.95$ and $\rho_c = 0.9$, and as T increases ρ_c gets closer to unity. It is this part of the parameter space where the power of standard unit root tests, such as $\hat{\delta}$ and $\hat{\tau}$, have low power, see Figure 8.8.

In the local-to-unity framework, in principle, power can be maximised for each value of c, which gives the power envelope, $\pi(c)$, that is the outer bound of power for $c \in C$. This seems to imply an infeasible procedure since c is a continuous variable and there is, therefore, an infinity of tests indexed by $c \in C$. Consider one of these, so that c is fixed at, say, c* and a test statistic is constructed conditional on this value, then its power function, $\pi(c, c^*)$ will be tangential to the power envelope at $c = c^*$, but elsewhere will, generally, lie below it. It is then possible to choose a value for power, say 0.5, and solve (by simulation) for the value of c, say $\bar{c}$, that generates that value. ERS (op. cit.) suggest choosing $c = \bar{c}$ corresponding to 50% power on the power envelope, so that $\pi(c, \bar{c}) = 0.5$ and, therefore, the test designed for $c = \bar{c}$ will have a tangent to the power envelope at power = 50%. The form of such a test is outlined in the next two sections.

8.4.1 Efficient detrending

The framework is best interpreted in the form of (8.25), which can be viewed as estimating a trend function subject to a serially correlated error, for which it is natural to turn to generalised least squares (GLS) and feasible GLS for a solution. To start, consider the common factor representation of the DGP, where μ_t is the trend function and u_t is a serially correlated error:

$$y_t = \mu_t + u_t \qquad t = 1, \ldots, T \tag{8.63a}$$

$$(1 - \rho L)u_t = v_t \qquad t = 2, \ldots, T \tag{8.63b}$$

$$v_t = \varepsilon_t \tag{8.63c}$$

Substituting for u_t from (8.63a) into (8.63b) gives observations y_1, y_2 and so on, that evolve as:

$$y_1 = \mu_1 + u_1 \tag{8.64a}$$

$$(1 - \rho L)y_t = (1 - \rho L)\mu_t + \varepsilon_t \qquad t = 2,\ldots,T \tag{8.64b}$$

The initial specification of $v_t = \varepsilon_t$, where ε_t is white noise, is a starting point that is relaxed below. The dependent variable in (8.64b) is the 'quasi-difference' of y_t, that is $y_t - \rho y_{t-1}$, and the regressors comprise the quasi-differenced (QD) trend, that is $\mu_t - \rho\mu_{t-1}$. Of course ρ is unknown, but (8.64b) can be evaluated for a given value of ρ as in the case of $H_A : \rho = \rho_c < 1$ in (8.62), leading to $y_t - \rho_c y_{t-1}$ and $\mu_t - \rho_c\mu_{t-1}$, respectively.

The treatment of the first observation, (8.64a), depends on what is assumed about $u_1 = y_1 - \mu_1$ under the alternative hypothesis. There are two leading cases due to ERS (1996) and Elliott (1999), respectively, corresponding to whether u_1 is a draw from the conditional distribution or the unconditional distribution of u_t. In the first case, $u_1 \sim (0, \sigma^2)$ under the alternative hypothesis; whereas in the second case $u_1 \sim (0, \sigma^2_u)$ when $|\rho| < 1$, as under H_A, so that u_1 is drawn from its unconditional distribution. Under the null hypothesis, both approaches assume $u_0 = 0$ (or a bounded second moment for u_0), which implies, from (8.63a), that $u_1 = v_1$; in turn, this implies $y_1 = \mu_1 + v_1$, so that y_1 is a random variable with a finite variance. Given $|\rho| < 1$, the variance of the unconditional distribution of u_t is $\sigma^2_u = \sigma^2/(1 - \rho^2)$. This is usually the preferred assumption, see Pantula et al. (1994) and Harvey and Leybourne (2005, 2006), as it implies that according to H_A, the initial observation is part of the same (stationary) process that generates the remainder of the observations and, in particular, it has the same unconditional variance.

The difference these assumptions make is on how the first observation is transformed. The following approach assumes the unconditional distribution assumption, $u_1 \sim (0, \sigma^2_u)$. To see what the quasi-differencing looks like consider the linear trend case:

$$\begin{aligned}\mu_t &= \beta_0 + \beta_1 t \\ &= (1 \quad t)\beta\end{aligned} \tag{8.65}$$

where $\beta = (\beta_0\ \beta_1)'$. The data for the QD detrending regression model are, assuming $\rho = \rho_c < 1$:

$$y_c = ((1 - \rho_c^2)^{1/2}\ y_1,\ y_2 - \rho_c y_1,\ y_3 - \rho_c y_2,\ \ldots,\ y_T - \rho_c y_{T-1})' \tag{8.66}$$

$$X_{1,c} = ((1 - \rho_c^2)^{1/2},\ 1 - \rho_c,\ 1 - \rho_c,\ \ldots,\ 1 - \rho_c)' \tag{8.67a}$$

$$X_{2,c} = ((1 - \rho_c^2)^{1/2},\ 2 - \rho_c,\ldots,\ t - \rho_c(t - 1),\ \ldots,\ T - \rho_c(T - 1))' \tag{8.67b}$$

$$X_c = (X_{1,c} \quad X_{2,c}) \tag{8.67c}$$

Apart from the first observation, the data are quasi-differenced: the typical observation on the dependent variable is $y_t - \rho_c y_{t-1}$; the typical observation on the first explanatory variable is just the constant $1 - \rho_c$; and the typical observation on the second explanatory variable is $t - \rho_c(t - 1)$.

If the conditional distribution assumption is used, then the first observation in y_c is just y_1 and the first elements of $X_{1,c}$ and $X_{2,c}$ are each 1, all other elements are unchanged, so that (8.66a)–(8.68a) are replaced by the following.

$$y_c = (y_1, y_2 - \rho_c y_1, y_3 - \rho_c y_2, \dots, y_T - \rho_c y_{T-1})' \tag{8.68}$$

$$X_{1,c} = (1, 1 - \rho_c, 1 - \rho_c, \dots, 1 - \rho_c)' \tag{8.69a}$$

$$X_{2,c} = (1, 2 - \rho_c, \dots, t - \rho_c(t - 1), \dots, T - \rho_c(T - 1))' \tag{8.69b}$$

The next step is to estimate the following detrending regression model (for a given value of $c \in C$):

$$y_c = X_c \beta_c + v_c \tag{8.70}$$

$$v_c = (v_{c,1}, v_{c,2}, \dots, v_{c,T})' \tag{8.71}$$

Note that the coefficient vector is denoted β_c to indicate its dependence on the selected value of c implied in ρ_c. This regression is estimated by LS as it incorporates the QD adjustment motivated by GLS (generalised least squares). Let $\hat{\beta}_c = (\hat{\beta}_{0,c}\ \hat{\beta}_{1,c})'$ denote the LS estimator of β_c from (8.70), then the detrended series is obtained as:

$$\tilde{y}_c = y - X\hat{\beta}_c \tag{8.72}$$

So that $\tilde{y}_{c,t}$ is given by:

$$\tilde{y}_{c,t} = y_t - (\hat{\beta}_{0,c} + \hat{\beta}_{1,c} t) \qquad t = 1, \dots, T \tag{8.73}$$

The QD detrended data, $\tilde{y}_{c,t}$, conditional on $\rho = \rho_c$, are used in place of the LS detrended data $\tilde{y}_t$ in the usual DF/ADF regression model and associated test statistics. Note that setting $\rho_c = 0$ results in the LS detrended data without any GLS adjustment.

In the case that a trend is not present under the alternative, all that is required is 'efficient' demeaning, in which case the second column of X_c is omitted and the regression of (8.70) becomes just a regression of y_c on $X_{1,c}$. As in the case of detrending, there are two options depending on how the first observation is treated, that is either as in (8.66) and (8.67a) or as in (8.68) and (8.69a).

The detrended data is then used as in the standard DF case for example in a DF or ADF regression as in (8.4) and (8.39), respectively:

$$\Delta\tilde{y}_{c,t} = \gamma\tilde{y}_{c,t-1} + \varepsilon_t \tag{8.74}$$

$$\Delta\tilde{y}_{c,t} = \gamma\tilde{y}_{c,t-1} + \sum\nolimits_{j=1}^{p-1} c_j \Delta\tilde{y}_{c,t-j} + \varepsilon_{t,p} \tag{8.75}$$

The maintained regression does not include a constant or a trend as these have been accounted for in the first step. The DF-type test statistics are denoted $\hat{\delta}^{gls}$ and $\hat{\tau}^{gls}$, subsequently these will be further distinguished depending on the assumption about the starting value of y_t.

8.4.2 Limiting distributions of test statistics

Xiao and Phillips (1998), extending the approach of ERS (1996), have obtained the asymptotic null distributions for the ADF $\hat{\delta}$-type tests applied to QD data, where v_t is generated by a stationary and invertible ARMA process; their results apply by extension to the $\hat{\tau}$-type test. Given the results in Chang and Park (2002), it seems safe to conjecture that the Xiao and Phillips' results will also hold for more general linear processes. Just as in the case of standard ADF tests, the use of ADF tests, but with QD data, is appropriate for the case that v_t exhibits serial correlation so that $\sigma^2_{lr,v} \neq \sigma^2$.

Elliott (1999) has also suggested a DF $\hat{\tau}$-type test applied to QD data, but in the framework where u_1 is a draw from the unconditional distribution of u_t. The notation adopted here is that $\hat{\delta}_i^{glsc}$ and $\hat{\tau}_i^{glsc}$ refer to tests based on the conditional distribution assumption, whereas $\hat{\delta}_i^{glsu}$ and $\hat{\tau}_i^{glsu}$ refer to tests based on the unconditional distribution assumption.

In the case of test statistics $\hat{\delta}_i^{glsc}$ and $\hat{\tau}_i^{glsc}$, the QD data as summarised in Equations (8.68) and (8.69a,b) are used in obtaining the detrended series y_c, see Equation (8.72). Thus, apart from the use of QD data in the detrending (or demeaning) regression, the general principle is as in the standard LS case; in that case, the detrending is sometimes referred to as projecting y on X, where X comprises a constant (a column of 1s) and a trend, whereas in the QD case, $\tilde{y}_c$ is projected on $X_{1,c}$ and $X_{2,c}$.

Xiao and Phillips (op. cit.) show that:

$$\hat{\delta}_i \equiv T\tilde{\gamma} \Rightarrow_D \frac{\tilde{\sigma}}{\tilde{\sigma}_{lr}} \left(\frac{\int_0^1 \bar{B}_c(r)dB(r)}{\int_0^1 \bar{B}_c(r)^2 dr} \right) \qquad i = \mu, \beta \tag{8.76}$$

where $\tilde{\gamma}$ is obtained from LS estimation of (8.75). $\bar{B}_c(r)$ is given by:

$$\bar{B}_c(r) = \left(B(r) - X(r)' \frac{\int_0^1 X_c(r)dB(r) - \bar{c}\int_0^1 X_c(r)B(r)dr}{\int_0^1 X_c(r)X_c'(r)dr} \right) \tag{8.77}$$

Where $X(r) = (1, r)'$, $X_c(r) = (-\bar{c}, 1 - \bar{c}r)'$ and $\bar{c} \neq 0$ if the trend function includes a constant, see Xiao and Phillips (op. cit., section 3). (Note that Xiao and Phillips use the notation W(r) not B(r) for standard BM.)

The quantities $\tilde{\sigma}_{lr,v}$ and $\tilde{\sigma}$ in (8.76) are consistent estimators of $\sigma_{lr,v}$ and σ, respectively, which can be obtained from (8.48) and (8.49), that is using data that is not quasi-differenced or, analogously, using data that is quasi-differenced from LS estimation of (8.75).

Multiplying (8.76) through by the inverse sigma ratio results in:

$$\hat{\delta}_i^{glsc} \equiv T\tilde{\gamma}\frac{\tilde{\sigma}_{lr}}{\tilde{\sigma}} \Rightarrow_D \left(\frac{\int_0^1 \bar{B}_c(r)dB(r)}{\int_0^1 \bar{B}_c(r)^2 dr} \right) \neq F(\hat{\delta}_{DF}) \tag{8.78}$$

It can be inferred from these results that the $\hat{\tau}$-type test based on (8.75) has the following limiting distribution:

$$\hat{\tau}_i^{glsc} = \frac{\tilde{\gamma}}{\tilde{\sigma}(\tilde{\gamma})} \Rightarrow_D \left(\frac{\int_0^1 \bar{B}_c(r)dB(r)}{\left(\int_0^1 \bar{B}_c(r)^2 dr\right)^{1/2}} \right) \neq F(\hat{\tau}_{DF}) \tag{8.79}$$

The versions of these tests based on the unconditional distribution assumption are $\hat{\delta}_i^{glsu}$ and $\hat{\tau}_i^{glsu}$. These have limiting distributions of the same form as (8.78) and (8.79), differing only in the underlying projections, since the detrended or demeaned data on which they are based is defined differently for the first observation, see (8.66) and (8.67a,b). For more on the limiting distributions of these and related test statistics see Elliott (1999, p. 773) and Müller and Elliott (2003, especially table I).

8.4.3 Choice of c and critical values

There is a test statistic for each value of $c = \bar{c}$, so that there is a family of tests indexed by $\bar{c}$. As noted in the opening to this section, in order to use a single test statistic rather than a multiplicity of such tests, a single value of $c = \bar{c}$ is chosen. ERS (op. cit.) suggest choosing $\bar{c}$ where the power function $\pi(c, \bar{c}) = 0.5$, that is at 50% power. In the case of the conditional tests, the suggested values are $\bar{c} = 7.0$ for the demeaned case, and $\bar{c} = -13.5$ for the detrended case, see also Xiao and Phillips (1998). For example, if T = 100, these values of $\bar{c}$ correspond to $\rho_{\bar{c}} = 0.93$ and 0.865, respectively, whereas if T = 500, then $\rho_{\bar{c}} = 0.986$ and 0.973, respectively. For the unconditional tests, Elliott (1999) found $\bar{c} = -10$ to work well in both cases. Some critical values for the conditional and unconditional versions of the tests are provided in Tables 8.1 and 8.2.

Table 8.1 Critical values (conditional distribution)

	1%	5%	10%
$\hat{\tau}_{\mu}^{glsc}(-7)$			
100	–2.77	–2.14	–1.86
200	–2.69	–2.08	–1.76
∞	–2.55	–1.95	–1.63
$\hat{\tau}_{\beta}^{glsc}(-13.5)$			
100	–3.58	–3.03	–2.74
200	–3.46	–2.93	–2.64
∞	–3.48	–2.89	–2.57

Table 8.2 Critical values (unconditional distribution)

	1%	5%	10%
$\hat{\tau}_{\mu}^{glsu}(-10)$			
100	–3.59	–2.78	–2.47
200	–3.44	–2.79	–2.47
∞	–3.26	–2.73	–2.46
$\hat{\tau}_{\beta}^{glsu}(-10)$			
100	–3.77	–3.23	–2.97
200	–3.78	–3.20	–2.94
∞	–3.69	–3.17	–2.91

Sources: ERS (op. cit., table I), Elliott (op. cit., table 1) and own calculations based on 50,000 replications.

8.4.4 Power of ERS-type tests

To illustrate the potential gains in power, Figures 8.9–8.12 summarise the results from 5,000 simulations with T = 100. In each case the DGP is $y_t = \rho y_{t-1} + \varepsilon_t$, where $\varepsilon_t \sim N(0, 1)$; $\rho = 1$ corresponds to the null hypothesis and $\rho < 1$ to the alternative hypothesis. The simulated power function records the proportion of correct decisions to reject the null hypothesis when carrying out a unit root test at the 5% significance level.

The comparisons are illustrated as follows: $\hat{\tau}_\mu$ and $\hat{\tau}_\mu^{glsc}$ in Figure 8.9; $\hat{\tau}_\beta$ and $\hat{\tau}_\beta^{glsc}$ in Figure 8.10; $\hat{\tau}_\mu$ and $\hat{\tau}_\mu^{glsu}$ in Figure 8.11; and $\hat{\tau}_\beta$ and $\hat{\tau}_\beta^{glsu}$ in Figure 8.12. The power functions using efficiently detrended data lie above those for the standard DF tests for both variants. For example, in the case of the conditional distribution assumption, power at $\rho = 0.85$ is 62% for $\hat{\tau}_\mu$ and 93% for $\hat{\tau}_\mu^{glsc}$, and 41% for $\hat{\tau}_\beta$ and 58% for $\hat{\tau}_\beta^{glsc}$; when the initial draw is from the unconditional distribution, the powers are 62% for $\hat{\tau}_\mu$ and 72% for $\hat{\tau}_\mu^{glsu}$, and 40% for $\hat{\tau}_\beta$ and 49% for $\hat{\tau}_\beta^{glsu}$. Notice that on a pairwise basis for $\hat{\tau}_\mu^{glsc}$ and $\hat{\tau}_\mu^{glsu}$, and $\hat{\tau}_\beta^{glsc}$ and $\hat{\tau}_\beta^{glsu}$, power is greater for the conditional distribution assumption

These simulations suggest that the initial condition may be influential in determining the power of a unit root test and, indeed, this is the case;

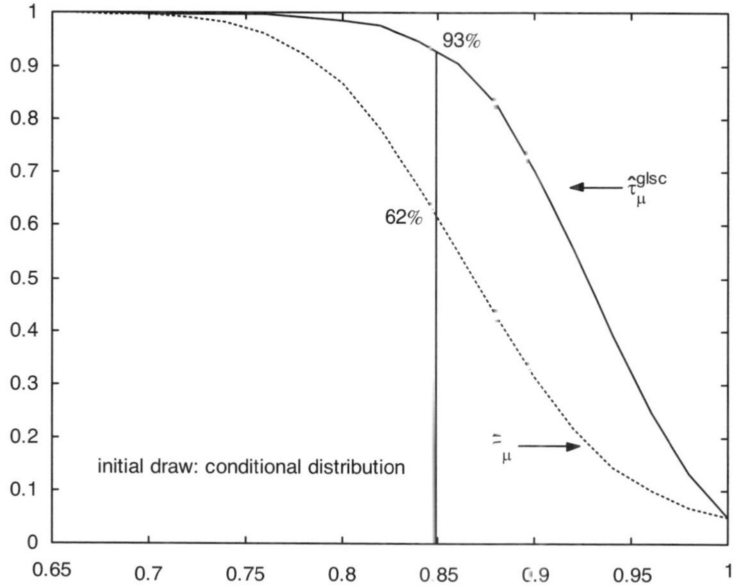

Figure 8.9 Comparison of power, $\hat{\tau}_\mu^{glsc}$, (demeaned) T = 100

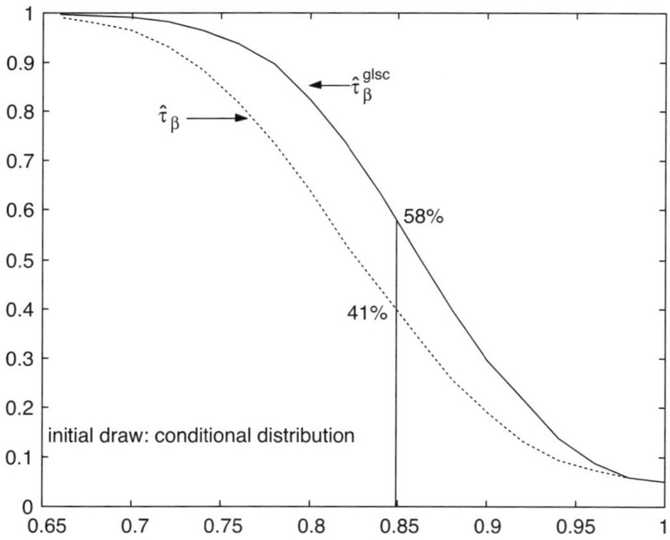

Figure 8.10 Comparison of power, $\hat{\tau}^{glsc}_{\beta}$, (detrended) T = 100

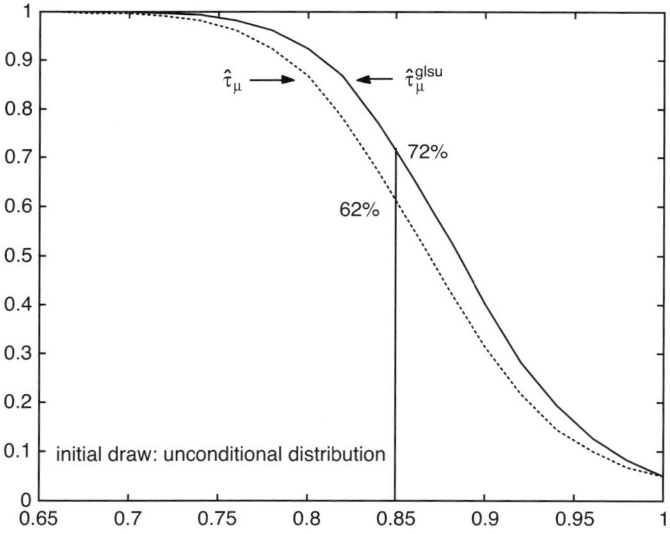

Figure 8.11 Comparison of power, $\hat{\tau}^{glsu}_{\mu}$, (demeaned) T = 100

see for example, and Müller and Elliott (2006), Elliott and Müller (2006), Harvey and Leybourne (2005, 2006) and Harvey, Leybourne and Taylor (2009) and Müller (2009). For example, typically the sample period, and so the starting date for a unit root regression, is chosen subject to the

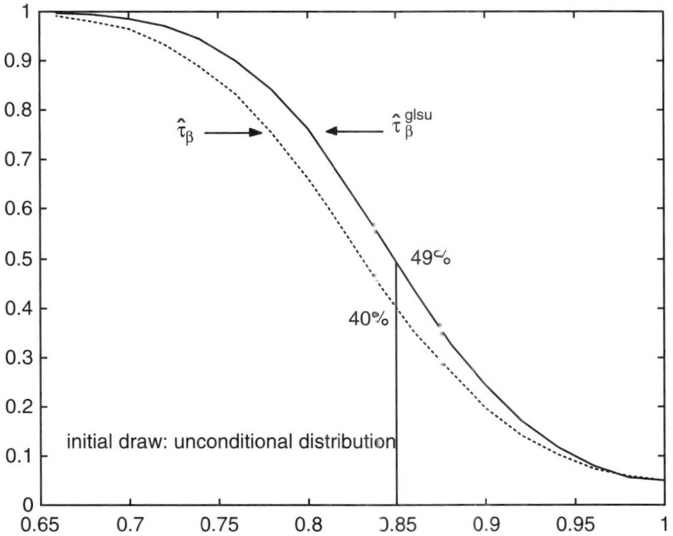

Figure 8.12 Comparison of power, $\hat{\tau}_\beta^{glsu}$, (detrended) T = 100

constraints of data availability; yet quite different results can be obtained by varying the start date and the key to understanding this problem is the role of the initial condition on the outcome of the test. Starting the regression when the initial observation is far from the trend line can have a marked effect on the outcome of the test. It transpires that the standard DF tests can regain their relative power when the initial observation is far from the trend. The interested reader is referred to *Econometric Theory* (2009), Volume 25, No 3, for a number of articles on this topic.

8.4.5 Empirical example: US industrial production

The example in this section illustrates some of the practical issues arising in the implementation of the DF tests and their extensions for efficient detrending. The data series is for the logarithm of US industrial production (monthly, seasonally adjusted) for the period 1919m1 to 2006m10, comprising 1,054 observations. The data is graphed in Figure 8.13, from which a trend is evident, so that prior detrending is appropriate.

The model is as specified in Equations (8.63a)–(8.63c). In summary, these are:

$$y_t = \mu_t + u_t$$
$$(1 - \rho L)u_t = v_t$$
$$v_t = \pi(L)\varepsilon_t$$
$$\mu_t = \beta_0 + \beta_1 t$$

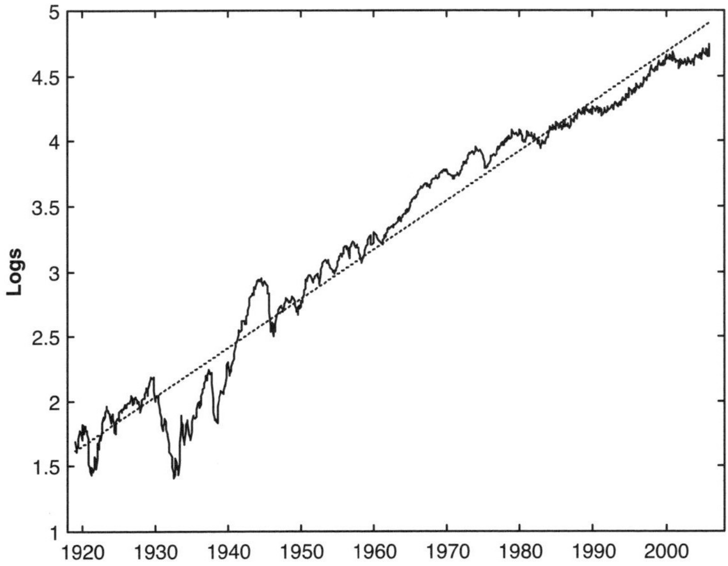

Figure 8.13 US industrial production (logs, p.a, s.a)

Together these imply an ADF model of the following general form (see Equation (8.75)):

$$\Delta\hat{\hat{y}}_t = \gamma\hat{\hat{y}}_{t-1} + \sum\nolimits_{j=1}^{p-1} c_j \Delta\hat{\hat{y}}_{t-j} + \varepsilon_{t,p}$$

where $\hat{\hat{y}}_t = y_t - \hat{\mu}_t = y_t - (\hat{\beta}_0 + \hat{\beta}_1 t)$. In the case of 'efficient' detrending, $\hat{\hat{y}}_t$ is replaced by $\hat{\hat{y}}_{c,t}$ where detrending is based on either the conditional or unconditional assumption for the initial draw, referred to as GLSC and GLSU, respectively.

The detrending results are summarised in Table 8.3 and the ADF test results are reported in Table 8.4. The order, p*, of the ADF regression was chosen by a general-to-specific search using the marginal t criterion, that is the longest lag was omitted if its estimated coefficient was not significant at the $\alpha\%$ two-sided significance level. The maximum lag was set at 20 and $\alpha\%$ was set equal to 1% to avoid unwanted accumulation of type I error. This resulted in a lag length of 14 for the ADF model, where the marginal t statistic had a p-value of less than 0.5%.

The values of the test statistics differ only marginally. None of the $\hat{\tau}_\beta$–type tests lead to rejection of the null hypothesis of a unit root at the 5% significance level but, because the limiting null distributions differ,

the implied p-values of each test value do differ, with p-values decreasing in order for $\hat{\tau}_\beta$, $\hat{\tau}_\beta^{glsu}$ then $\hat{\tau}_\beta^{glsc}$. For example, using a 10% significance level leads to rejection with $\hat{\tau}_\beta^{glsc}$, but not with $\hat{\tau}_\beta$ or $\hat{\tau}_\beta^{glsu}$. The $\hat{\delta}_\beta$ tests are also reported in Table 8.4. Using $\hat{\delta}_\beta$ and $\hat{\delta}_\beta^{glsu}$ leads to the same conclusion as using their pseudo-t counterparts. Whilst using $\hat{\delta}_\beta^{glsc}$ leads to rejection of the null hypothesis at the 5% significance level, it is probably the case that of the two GLS-type tests, this is the less preferred.

It is known that these test statistics can be sensitive to the initial observation and, as is evident from Figure 8.13, there are some substantial deviations from trend. For example, the observations around 1932/33 are a long way from trend, as could be expected from the onset of the Great Crash, and the test statistics start to differ quite noticeably from 1929 onward. For example, if the starting date of the test regression is taken to be 1933m1, then the test statistics do give quite different results. These are summarised in Table 8.5, where it is now the case that whilst the DF versions of the test statistics are almost unchanged, the test value of $\hat{\tau}_\beta^{glsc}$ becomes less negative as does $\hat{\tau}_\beta^{glsu}$, but less so, which, ceteris paribus, would be taken as evidence not to reject the null hypothesis. There are a number of ways around this sensitivity, for example by forming a weighted test statistic, see Harvey and Leybourne

Table 8.3 Estimation of trend coefficients: LS and 'efficient' detrending

	LS	GLSC, $\bar{c} = -13.5$	GLSU, $\bar{c} = -10.0$
$\hat{\beta}_0$	1.614	1.682	1.666
$\hat{\beta}_1$	0.00315	0.00303	0.00302

Table 8.4 Unit root test statistics from ADF(14) maintained regression

	DF	GLSC	GLSU
$\hat{\gamma}$	−0.0108	−0.0103	−0.0104
$\hat{\tau}$-type test	$\hat{\tau}_\beta = -2.737$	$\hat{\tau}_\beta^{glsc} = -2.687$	$\hat{\tau}_\beta^{glsu} = -2.703$
$\hat{\delta} = \frac{T\hat{\gamma}}{(1-\hat{c}(1))}$	$\hat{\delta}_\beta = \frac{-11.26}{(1-0.424)} = -19.54$	$\hat{\delta}_\beta^{glsc} = \frac{-10.73}{(1-0.419)} = -18.47$	$\hat{\delta}_\beta^{glsu} = \frac{-10.80}{(1-0.419)} = -18.61$

Notes: 5% (10%) critical values, $\hat{\tau}_\beta$: −3.41 (−3.13); $\hat{\tau}_\beta^{glsc}$: −2.89 (−2.57); $\hat{\tau}_\beta^{glsu}$: −3.17 (−2.91); $\hat{\delta}_\beta$: −21.7 (−18.3); $\hat{\delta}_\beta^{glsc}$: −16.53 (−13.49); $\hat{\delta}_\beta^{glsu}$: −19.79 (−16.17).

Table 8.5 Unit root test statistics if 1933m1 is taken as the start date

	DF	GLSC	GLSU
$\hat{\tau}_\beta$	–2.802	–0.730	–2.065
$\hat{\delta}_\beta$	–20.36	–1.76	–11.05

(2005, 2006), or constructing a new statistic that is not (as) sensitive to the initial observation, see Elliott and Müller (2006).

8.5 A unit root test based on mean reversion

This section introduces a simple test for a unit root based on the number of times that a series crosses a particular level; for example, in the case of a pure random walk starting at zero, the level of particular interest is zero. However, to be of practical use, a unit root test of this form must also be able to accommodate random walks with drift and serially dependent random inputs. This section deals with each of these in turn. The test statistics in this section are based on Burridge and Guerre (1996) as extended by Garciá and Sansó (2006). Although not the most powerful of unit root tests, the development links in with the basic characteristics of a random walk process, as outlined particularly in Chapter 5, Sections 5.6.1 and 5.6.2, and may be useful when combined with a parametric unit root test.

A notational convention that is close to universally adopted in the literature on random walks created as the partial sum process of random inputs, is to refer to the resulting stochastic process as $S = (S_t, 0 \leq t \leq T)$, with S_t as the typical component random variable. This convention was followed in Chapter 5, for example in considering whether the exchange rate had the characteristics of a random walk. In contrast, the convention in time series analysis is to refer to the stochastic process that is the object of study, as $Y = (y_t, 0 \leq t \leq T)$, so that y_t is the typical component random variable. As the context of the derivation of the test considered here is that of a partial sum, we use the notation S_t to enable reference back to Chapter 5.

Note that a test based on the number of times that a particular level is crossed is invariant to continuous monotonic transformations. Let S_t be the time series under consideration, $t = 1, \ldots, T$, and let $K(s)$ be the number of times that the level s is crossed; consider the monotonic transformation $f(S_t)$, so that $f(s)$ is the crossing level corresponding to

the transformed variable, then the number of times that $f(S_t)$ crosses f(s) is also K(s). This feature has a constructive and a nonconstructive aspect. For example, suppose that we are unsure whether to test for mean reversion in the log or the level of a series. If a standard DF test is used, different results will be produced if $\ln S_t$ and S_t are used. This will not be the case for a test based on K(s), so non-rejection is non-rejection for all monotonic transformations; but this does not tell us for which transformation (including no transformation) the unit root exists. To determine that question, other tests are needed.

8.5.1 No drift in the random walk

In this case, the random walk is of the form given by the partial sum process $S_t = S_{t-1} + \varepsilon_t$, $t \geq 1$, where $\{\varepsilon_t\}_{t=1}^{T}$ is a sequence of continuous random variables distributed as iid(0, σ^2). S_0 and ε_1 are assumed to be random variables with bounded pdfs and finite variance; thus, the often assumed starting assumption $S_0 = 0$ is permitted, interpreting S_0 as a degenerate random variable. (Also the boundedness condition can be relaxed, see Burridge and Guerre, op. cit. Remark 1.)

The first problem is to determine the distribution of a test statistic based on the number of level crossings under the null that the data generating process was a simple random walk. The number of crossings of the level s, normalised by $\sqrt{T}$, is:

$$K_T(s) = T^{-1/2}\left(\sum\nolimits_{t=1}^{T}[I(S_{t-1} \leq s, S_t > s) + I(S_{t-1} > s, S_t \leq s)]\right) \tag{8.82}$$

where I(.) is the indicator function, equal to 1 if the condition is true and 0 otherwise. The first part of the condition (8.82) captures the case when the level s is crossed from below and the second part of the condition captures the case when the level s is crossed from above. Burridge and Guerre (1996, Theorem 1), show for any s, then $K_T(s)$:

$$K_T(s) \Rightarrow_D \frac{E|\varepsilon_1|}{\sigma}|z| = \kappa|z| \tag{8.83}$$

where $\kappa = E|\varepsilon_1|/\sigma$ and z is a random variable distributed as standard normal, $z \sim N(0, 1)$. It follows that:

$$K_T^*(s) \equiv \kappa^{-1}K_T(s) \Rightarrow_D |z| \tag{8.84}$$

In distributional terms this is stated as:

$$F[K^*_T(s)] \Rightarrow_D \Phi(|z|) \tag{8.85}$$

where $F[K^*_T(s)]$ is the distribution function of $K^*_T(s)$ and $\Phi(|z|)$ is the half-normal distribution function, which is a special case of the folded normal distribution. It is the distribution of the absolute value of a normally distributed random variable with mean zero and variance $\sigma^2 = 1$. It 'folds' over the left-side of the normal pdf onto the right hand side. Typically we are interested in tail probabilities, for example in determining $1 - \Phi(|z|) = \alpha$ for a given value of z or finding z for a given value of α. This procedure is familiar from $\Phi(z)$; for example, $1 - \Phi(1.96) = 0.025$. In the case of $\Phi(|1.96|)$, the right tail probability is $1 - \Phi(|1.96|) = 2(1 - \Phi(1.96)) = 0.05$, and the tail probability is doubled for a given value of α. The generalisation of this result is $1 - \Phi(|z|) = 2(1 - \Phi(z)) \Rightarrow \Phi(|z|) = 2\Phi(z) - 1$.

Replacing the unknown quantities σ and $E|\varepsilon_1|$ by consistent estimators will not alter the limiting distribution. The suggested estimators are:

$$\hat{\sigma} = T^{-1/2}\left(\sum_{t=1}^{T} \Delta S_t^2\right)^{1/2} \qquad \rightarrow_p \sigma \tag{8.86}$$

$$\hat{E}|\varepsilon_1| = T^{-1}\sum_{t=1}^{T} |\Delta S_t| \qquad \rightarrow_p E|\varepsilon_1| \tag{8.87}$$

These are obtained noting that under the null hypothesis $\varepsilon_t = \Delta S_t$, and by the iid assumption $E|\varepsilon_1| = E|\varepsilon_t|$, $t = 2, \ldots, T$; hence, the estimator of $E|\varepsilon_1|$ is based on all T observations on ΔS_t. The estimator $\hat{E}|\varepsilon_1|$ is the (sample) mean absolute deviation (MAD) and the resulting test statistic, denoted $\eta^{(0)}$ for simplicity, is:

$$\eta^{(0)} \equiv \frac{\hat{\sigma}}{\hat{E}|\varepsilon_1|} K_T(s) \Rightarrow_D |z| \tag{8.88}$$

In practice, a value for the level s is chosen, the test statistic is calculated and compared to the upper quantiles of $\Phi(|z|)$. In the case of a pure random walk starting at zero, the level $s = 0$ is chosen, so that the test statistic is interpreted as a test of mean reversion. Under the alternative hypothesis of stationarity, the test statistic diverges because the number of changes of sign increases; therefore, large values of $\eta^{(0)}$ relative to the $(1 - \alpha)\%$ quantile of $\Phi(|z|)$ lead to rejection of the null

hypothesis of a unit root at the α significance level. Some finite sample critical values are provided by Burridge and Guerre (op. cit., table 1) and García and Sansó (op. cit., table 1); and see Table 8.6 below.

This distribution $\Phi(|z|) = 2\Phi(z) - 1$, has been encountered before in Chapter 5, as the distribution of the normalised number of mean reversions for a symmetric binomial random walk (see Chapter 5, Equation 5.15 in Section 5.6.1). Thus, although it has been assumed here that the ε_t are continuous random variables, the distributional result in (8.85) also holds for $\varepsilon_t = (-1, +1)$ with probability ½ for each outcome; then $\sigma = 1$ and $E|\varepsilon_1| = 1$, hence $F[K_{B,T}(0)] \Rightarrow_D \Phi(|z|)$, which is the result in Equation (5.15); (recall that the B subscript indicates binomial inputs). This also accounts for the difference in the number of mean reversions when the symmetric random walk is alternately specified with Gaussian inputs and (–1, +1) inputs – a difference that was noted in Chapter 5, Table 5.2 (see Section 5.6.2). First note that the Cauchy-Schwarz inequality implies that $\kappa^{-1} = \sigma/E|\varepsilon_1| \geq 1$, see Burridge and Guerre (op. cit., Remark 2, in the form that $0 \leq \kappa \leq 1$); then $\kappa^{-1}E[K_T(s)] = \sqrt{1/2\pi}$ implies that $E[K_T(s)] \leq E[K_{B,T}(s)]$; the mean number of reversions with continuous iid random variables is no greater than with binomial inputs. (Note that κ is a constant and the mean of a random variable distributed as half (standard) normal is $\sqrt{2/\pi}$, see Section 5.6.2.)

8.5.2 Drifted random walk

In the case of a drifted random walk, $S_t = \mu + S_{t-1} + \varepsilon_t = \mu t + S_0 + \tilde{S}_t$, where $\tilde{S}_t = \sum_{j=1}^{t} \varepsilon_j$. The deterministic trend in this series is μt, which will tend to impart a direction, or drift, to the random walk generated by the stochastic trend $\tilde{S}_t$ (for examples of drift, see Chapter 5, Section 5.4.2, Figure 5.7). This is why if a random walk is an appropriate model for aggregate macroeconomic time series, such as GDP and consumption expenditure, then it should contain a drift parameter. However, the presence of a direction to the time series will confuse the previous test for level crossings (mean reversion). For example, a series that is stationary around a positive trend, will not generate systematic crossings of any particular level, so the test statistic, $K_T^*(s)$, which was designed for the random walk without a drift, will not be able to discriminate in favour of the alternative.

What we need to consider is $\tilde{S}_t$, interpreted as a detrended random walk, rather than S_t. In order to achieve this note that:

$$\begin{aligned}\tilde{S}_t &= \sum_{j=1}^{t} \varepsilon_j \\ &= S_t - (\mu t + S_0) \end{aligned} \quad (8.89)$$

So that what is required is an estimator of μ, say $\hat{\mu}$, so that the trend component can be removed from S_t, that is:

$$\hat{\hat{S}}_t = S_t - (\hat{\mu}t + S_0) \tag{8.90}$$

Note that $\mu = \Delta S_t + \varepsilon_t$, so that a consistent estimator of μ is provided by:

$$\begin{aligned}\hat{\mu} &= T^{-1}\sum_{t=1}^{T}\Delta S_t \\ &= T^{-1}(S_T - S_0)\end{aligned} \tag{8.91}$$

$\hat{\hat{S}}_t$ is an estimator of the I(1) component $\sum_{j=1}^{t}\varepsilon_j$, just as in the case without drift. The test statistic is derived in the same way replacing S_t by $\hat{\hat{S}}_t$, so that the first step is to obtain the normalised number of sign changes:

$$\tilde{K}_T(s) = T^{-1/2}\left(\sum_{t=1}^{T}[I(\hat{\hat{S}}_{t-1} \leq s,\ \hat{\hat{S}}_t > s) + (\hat{\hat{S}}_{t-1} > s,\ \hat{\hat{S}}_t \leq s)]\right) \tag{8.92}$$

The test statistic is:

$$\eta^{(1)} = \frac{\tilde{\sigma}}{\tilde{E}\,|\,\varepsilon_1\,|}\tilde{K}_T(s) \Rightarrow_D R \tag{8.93}$$

where

$$\tilde{\sigma} = T^{-1/2}\left(\sum_{t=1}^{T}\Delta\hat{\hat{S}}_t^2\right)^{1/2}$$

$$\tilde{E}\,|\,\varepsilon_1\,| = T^{-1}\sum_{t=1}^{T}|\,\Delta\hat{\hat{S}}_t\,|$$

R is a random variable with the standard Rayleigh distribution; the density function is $f_R(x) = I(x > 0)x\exp(-\frac{1}{2}x^2)$, where I(.) is the indicator function taking the value 1 when $x > 0$ and 0 otherwise. Some critical values for $\eta^{(0)}$ and $\eta^{(1)}$ are given in Table 8.6, with more extensive tabulations in Burridge and Guerre (op. cit., table 1) and García and Sansó (op. cit., table 1).

8.5.3 Serial dependence

So far it has been assumed that stochastic input to the partial sum process denoted ε_t, was not serially dependent; however, as this is not often the case, the method must be able to deal with serially dependent inputs (referred to as 'errors'). To accommodate this possibility consider the random walk model, but with serially dependent errors, denoted by

Table 8.6 Critical values for the levels crossing test statistics, $\eta^{(0)}$ and $\eta^{(1)}$

	$\eta^{(0)}$		$\eta^{(1)}$	
	90%	**95%**	**90%**	**95%**
100	1.52	1.82	2.07	2.36
200	1.56	1.85	2.08	2.38
500	1.60	1.91	2.11	2.40
1,000	1.61	1.91	2.12	2.41
∞	1.645	1.96	2.14	2.44

Note: Source, García and Sansó (op. cit., table 1).

u_t (to distinguish them from ε_t):

$$S_t = S_{t-1} + u_t \tag{8.94}$$

$$\begin{aligned} u_t &= \sum\nolimits_{j=0}^{\infty} \pi_j \varepsilon_{t-j} \\ &= \pi(L)\varepsilon_t \end{aligned} \tag{8.95}$$

where $\varepsilon_t \sim \text{iid}(0, \sigma^2)$ and $E|\varepsilon_t|^r$ for some $r > 2$; also, $\pi_0 = 1$, $\pi(1) \neq 0$ and $\sum_{j=0}^{\infty} j|\pi_j| < \infty$, see García and Sansó (op. cit.). The moving average specification of u_t is familiar from Chapter 2, see Section 2.6, from which we note that the long-run variance of $u_t = \Delta S_t$ is $\sigma_{lr,\Delta S} = \pi(1)^2\sigma^2$. For example, if $u_t = \varphi u_{t-1} + \varepsilon_t$, then $\sigma_{lr,\Delta S} = (1 - \varphi^2)^{-1}\sigma^2$; see also Section 8.3.2. If the random walk has a drift component, as in Section 3.5.2, then S_t is detrended to obtain $\tilde{S}_t$ and the required long-run variance is denoted $\sigma_{lr,\Delta\tilde{S}}$.

The solution to the problem of serial dependence in the errors is now simple (and may now be recognised as following a general principle) and just involves replacing σ in $\eta^{(0)}$ or $\eta^{(1)}$, as the case may be, by the respective long-run standard error; that is $\sigma_{lr,\Delta S}$, for ΔS_t, and $\sigma_{lr,\Delta\tilde{S}}$ for $\Delta\hat{\tilde{S}}_t$. The sample value of the test statistic then uses a consistent estimator obtained, for example, by a semi-parametric method or an autoregressive estimator as illustrated in Chapter 2, see Sections 2.5 and 2.6. The revised test statistics are:

$$\eta_{lr}^{(0)} = \frac{\hat{\sigma}_{lr,\Delta S}}{\hat{E}|u_1|} K_T(s) \Rightarrow_D \Phi(|z|) \tag{8.96}$$

$$\eta_{lr}^{(1)} = \frac{\tilde{\sigma}_{lr,\Delta\tilde{S}}}{\tilde{\hat{E}}|u_1|}\tilde{K}_T(s) \Rightarrow_D R \tag{8.97}$$

where $\hat{E}|u_1| = T^{-1}\sum_{t=1}^{T}|\Delta S_t|$ for $\eta_{lr}^{(0)}$ and $T^{-1}\sum_{t=1}^{T}|\Delta\hat{\tilde{S}}_t|$ for $\eta_{lr}^{(1)}$; otherwise, compared to $\eta^{(0)}$ and $\eta^{(1)}$, $\hat{\sigma}$ and $\tilde{\sigma}$ have been replaced by $\hat{\sigma}_{lr}$ and $\tilde{\sigma}_{lr}$, respectively. Note that the asymptotic distributions are unchanged.

In some illustrative simulation results, with an MA(1) generating process $u_t = (1 + \theta_1 L)\varepsilon_t$, Garcia and Sanso (op. cit.) find that whilst $\eta_{lr}^{(1)}$ is not as powerful as $\hat{\tau}_{\beta}^{glsc}$, it maintains its size better especially in the problematic case when $\theta_1 \to -1$.

8.5.4 Example: Gold-silver prices

This example continues that in Chapter 5, Section 5.8.2, which used a sample of 5,372 observations on the log ratio of gold to silver prices, which is the variable S_t in this case. The price ratio was normalised to unity at the beginning of the sample implying that the log ratio was normalised at zero. The graph of the data does not reveal any evidence of drift in the ratio (see Figure 5.17), so the test statistic $\eta^{(0)}$ (or $\eta_{lr}^{(0)}$) is preferred. As previously noted, the number of sign changes in the sample of 5,372 observations was only 32, so there is strong presumption of a random walk. The expected number of sign changes for a random walk with $N(0, \sigma^2)$ inputs is 46.6. The likelihood of random walk is strongly suggested by the sample value of the test statistic calculated as follows:

$$\begin{aligned}\eta^{(0)} &= \frac{\hat{\sigma}}{(T-1)^{-1}\sum_{t=2}^{T}|\Delta S_t|}K_T(s) \\ &= \frac{0.0138}{0.0094} \times \frac{32}{\sqrt{5,372}} \\ &= 0.64\end{aligned}$$

This value is well below the 95% quantile of 1.96; indeed, the p-value of 0.64 is 0.52.

To take into account the possibility of serial dependence, the long-run variance of $u_t = \Delta S_t$ was estimated by the two methods outlined in Chapter 2, Sections 2.6.1 and 2.6.2. The first of these is semi-parametric, with two estimators depending upon whether a kernel estimator is used. To illustrate the difference it makes to the estimates, the unweighted and Newey-West estimates of $\sigma_{lr,\Delta S}^2 \times 10^3$ are graphed in

Figure 8.14. This figure makes it evident that in each case there is some variation due to the selection of m, the truncation parameter controlling the number of autocovariances included in the estimation. As noted in Chapter 2, in some cases the 'rule' $m = 12(T/100)^{1/4} = 32$ is used; another possibility is to only include those lags for which the autocorrelations are significant. The correlogram for lags 1 to 100 is shown in Figure 8.15, together with the errors bands for a 1% two-sided test. The significance level is set deliberately low in order to control the overall size (cumulative type 1 error) of the test. There is no consistent pattern of significant autocorrelations: the first lag is clearly significant and must be included; otherwise lags 5, 17 and 45 are significant, but only marginally so. The unweighted estimate and the Newey-West estimate lie between a band of approximately 0.00013 to 0.00015 for m = 1, ..., 25; to illustrate the calculation of the test statistic $\eta^{(0)}_{lr}$, we take m = 24, where $\hat{\sigma}_{lr,\Delta S}(24) = \sqrt{0.000137} = 0.0117 \approx \hat{\sigma}_{lr,\Delta S}(24, \varphi) = \sqrt{0.000139} = 0.0118$.

The second method uses an ARMA(p, q) model-based estimate of $\sigma^2_{lr,\Delta S}$, where the dependent variable is demeaned ΔS_t. An upper limit of 2 was set for each of p and q. Use of BIC suggested ARMA(1, 0), whereas using AIC suggested ARMA(2, 1), although ARMA(1, 0) was a close second. In fact there was very little difference between the estimates

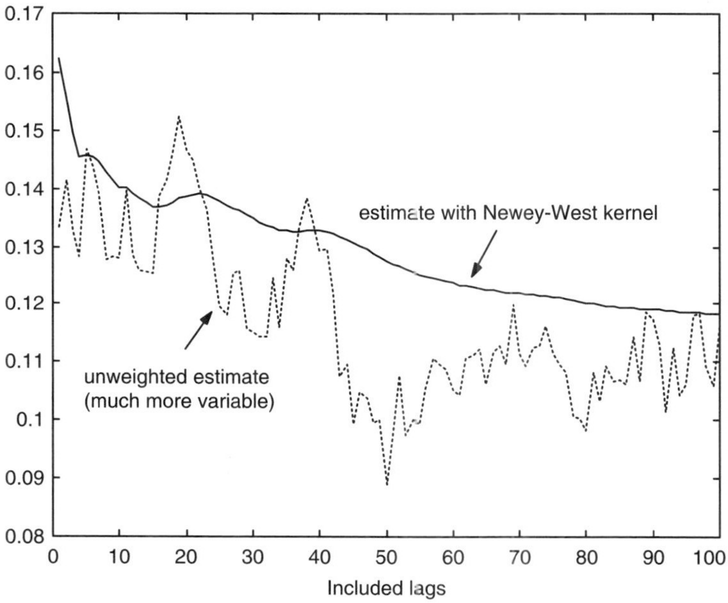

Figure 8.14 Alternative semi-parametric estimates of $\sigma^2_{lr,\Delta S}$

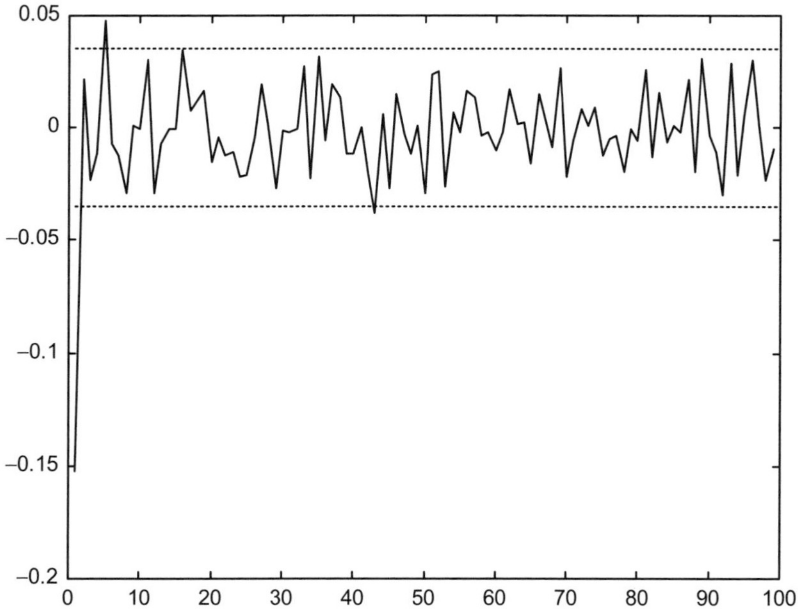

Figure 8.15 Correlogram for (log) gold-silver price

of $\sigma^2_{lr,\Delta S}$ from these two models; further, **Q2.3** (of Chapter 2) used these estimation results to show that there was a common factor in the ARMA (2, 1) model, which could, therefore be reduced to ARMA(1, 0) without loss. The results for ARMA(1, 0) are reported in Table 8.7.

The model-based estimate of $\hat{\sigma}_{lr,\Delta S}$ is close to that from the semi-parametric method and suggests that we may take $\hat{\sigma}_{lr,\Delta S} = 0.0118$ as a 'consensus' estimate. Note that as $\hat{\sigma}_{lr,\Delta S} < \hat{\sigma}$, the test statistic $\eta^{(0)}$ cannot increase in its long-run variance version $\eta^{(0)}_{lr}$, and so an insignificant value for the test statistic cannot become significant. The revised test statistic is:

$$\begin{aligned}\eta^{(0)}_{lr} &= \frac{\hat{\sigma}_{lr,\Delta S}}{(T-1)^{-1}\sum_{t=2}^{T}|\Delta S_t|}K_T(s)\\ &= \frac{0.0118}{0.0094}\times\frac{32}{\sqrt{5,372}}\\ &= 0.55\end{aligned}$$

As anticipated, this value confirms the decision not to reject the null hypothesis.

Table 8.7 ARMA model-based estimates

	$\hat{\phi}_1$	$\hat{\sigma}$	$\hat{\sigma}^2_{lr,\Delta S}$ and $\hat{\sigma}_{lr,\Delta S}$
ARMA(1, 0)	−0.152 (−11.28)	0.0137	$\hat{\sigma}^2_{lr,\Delta S} = w(1)^2\hat{\sigma}^2 = \frac{1}{(1-(-0.152))^2}\hat{\sigma}^2$ $= 0.000141$ $\hat{\sigma}_{lr,\Delta S} = \sqrt{0.000141} = 0.0119$

Notes: t statistic in parentheses; dependent variable, $\Delta S_t - \hat{\mu}_{\Delta S}$ where $\hat{\mu}_{\Delta S} = (T-1)^{-1}\sum_{t=2}^{T}\Delta S_t$

8.6 Concluding remarks

Tests for a unit root are in widespread use primarily for two reasons. First, the question of whether a time series has been generated by a process that has this form of nonstationarity is of interest in its own right with, for example, implications for the persistence of shocks and the existence or otherwise of an equilibrium to which a series will revert in the long run. Second, the concept of cointegration, which involves jointly modelling several series, is concerned with whether integrated series are related, as suggested in particular cases by economic theory.

This chapter has been but a 'dip' into some of the existing tests. Some interesting problems that arise in the theoretical and applied literature of unit root testing include the following.

1. The treatment of the initial observation under the alternative is critical, as is the specification of the deterministic components; see, for example, Harvey, Leybourne and Taylor (2009), and the references and series of comments on that article in *Econometric Theory* (2009).
2. MA errors can lead to near cancellation of unit roots, which can cause severe size distortions (oversizing) in unit root tests; hence, in the limit is it possible to discriminate between stationary and nonstationary processes? See Schwert (1987) and Müller (2008).
3. Breaks in time series, which are in a stationary in pieces ('piecewise stationarity') that is between the breaks, can look like series generated by a unit root nonstationary process. The seminal article on this topic is Perron (1989), which has led to a considerable literature on break detection see, for example, Perron (2006) for a critical overview.

4. Autoregressive processes that are 'triggered' by a variable that exceeds a threshold value and which may have a unit root, referred to as threshold autoregressive (TAR) models, have also been of theoretical and empirical interest see, for example, Caner and Hansen (2001), Van Dijk, Teräsvirta and Franses (2002), Strikholm and Teräsvirta (2004), Lundbergh, Teräsvirta, and Dijk. (2003) and for an overview of nonlinear TAR models see Teräsvirta (2006).
5. A time series 'contaminated' by outliers can also be confused with one generated by a unit root nonstationary process see, for example, Franses and Haldrup (1994), Harvey and Leybourne (2001) and Popp (2008).
6. There is empirical evidence that a time series may become stationary after applying the fractional differencing operator $(1 - L)^d$, where d is not an integer, thus restricting d to be an integer is a form of misspecification; for an overview of this concept and tests, see Gil-Alana and Hualde (2009).
7. Bounded variables: many economic time series are bounded, for example the nominal interest rate, unemployment and variables constructed as shares, such as the components of wealth relative to total wealth; however, random walks are necessarily unbounded. Can processes be constructed that generate random walks that are bounded? See, for example, Cavaliere (2002).
8. Will differencing a nonstationary series necessarily reduce it to stationarity? Clearly this will not always be the case. Such cases are of empirical interest and have been modelled as stochastic unit roots. See, for example, Leybourne, McCabe and Tremayne (1996), Granger and Swanson (1997), Leybourne, McCabe and Mills (1996) and Taylor and Van Dijk (2002).
9. Detecting more than one unit root may be a critical issue for some time series, such as those, like prices and wages, in nominal terms. What happens if the possibility of a second root is left undetected? Is the best test for two unit roots, the same as the one unit root test applied to the first difference of the series? See for example Haldrup and Lildholdt (2002), Haldrup and Jansson (2006) and Rodrigues and Taylor (2004).
10. Many time series have a seasonal pattern and the question then is whether the seasonally adjusted or the unadjusted series should be used in order to test for a unit root. For a consideration of the issues and references see Fok, Franses and Paap (2006) and for some test statistics applied to seasonally unadjusted series see, for example, Osborn and Rodrigues (2002) and Rodrigues and Taylor (2004a,b).

Questions

Q8.1 Consider the demeaned AR(1) model given by (8.17), as follows:

$$y_t - \mu = \rho(y_{t-1} - \mu) + \varepsilon_t \qquad \text{(A8.1 = 8.17)}$$

Suggest a method of demeaning the data such that the estimate of ρ and its t statistic are identical to those obtained from estimation with an explicit constant:

$$y_t = \mu^* + \rho y_{t-1} + \varepsilon_t \qquad \text{(A8.2 = 8.28)}$$

A8.1 Demean y_t and y_{t-1} separately, that is estimate:

$$y_t - \bar{y}_0 = \rho(y_{t-1} - \bar{y}_{-1}) + \xi_t \qquad \text{(A8.3)}$$

where $\bar{y}_0 = \sum_{t=2}^{T} y_t/(T-1)$ and $\bar{y}_{-1} = \sum_{t=1}^{T-1} y_t/(T-1)$; this ensures that the regressand and the regressor are identical under both methods and, hence, the estimators of ρ will be the same. Next, to ensure that the estimated standard errors of ρ are also identical, either compute the estimated standard error from (A8.3) as the square root of the residual sum of squares divided by (T – 2), hence making an adjustment for implicit estimation of the mean, as in the LS estimator from (A8.2); or divide each residual sum of squares by (T – 1). Either way, the resulting standard errors will be the same and so will the t statistics calculated using these standard errors.

Q8.2 Given the results of Q7.2 that $T^{-2}\sum_{t=1}^{T} y_{t-1}^2 \Rightarrow_D \int_0^1 W(r)^2 dr$ and $T^{-1}\sum y_{t-1}\varepsilon_t \Rightarrow_D \int_0^1 W(r)dW(r)$, confirm the following:

$$\hat{\delta} \equiv T(\hat{\rho} - 1) \Rightarrow_D \frac{1}{2}\frac{\lambda \sim (\chi^2(1) - 1)}{\int_0^1 B(r)^2 dr}$$

A8.2 From Table 7.1, we have the following:

$$T^{-2}\sum_{t=1}^{T} y_{t-1}^2 \Rightarrow_D \int_0^1 W(r)^2 dr = \sigma^2 \int_0^1 B(r)^2 dr$$

$$T^{-1}\sum y_{t-1}\varepsilon_t \Rightarrow_D \frac{1}{2}\sigma^2(B(1) - 1) \sim \frac{1}{2}\sigma^2(\chi^2(1) - 1)$$

The test statistic is:

$$\hat{\delta} = \frac{\sum_{t=1}^{T} y_{t-1}\varepsilon_t / T}{\sum_{t=1}^{T} y_{t-1}^2 / T^2}$$

The convergence results for the numerator and denominator together with the extended CMT imply that:

$$T(\hat{\rho} - 1) \Rightarrow_D \frac{\frac{1}{2}\sigma^2\lambda}{\sigma^2 \int_0^1 B(r)^2 dr} = \frac{1}{2} \frac{\lambda}{\int_0^1 B(r)^2 dr}$$

See Davidson (1994) for some expansion of this and related results.

Q8.3 Interpret the following model under the null hypothesis $H_0: \rho = 1$ and compare it with the interpretation under the alternative hypothesis $H_A: \rho < 1$.

$$y_t = \mu_t + u_t$$
$$(1 - \rho L)u_t = v_t$$
$$v_t = \varepsilon_t$$
$$\mu_t = \beta_0 + \beta_1 t$$

A8.3 First obtain the reduced form by substituting u_t and then μ_t into the second equation:

$$(y_t - \mu_t) = \rho(y_{t-1} - \mu_{t-1}) + \varepsilon_t$$
$$y_t = \beta_0(1 - \rho) + \rho\beta_1 + \beta_1(1 - \rho)t + \rho y_{t-1} + \varepsilon_t$$
$$= \beta_0^* + \beta_1^* t + \rho y_{t-1} + \varepsilon_t$$

where $\beta_0^* = \beta_0 (1 - \rho) + \rho\beta_1$ and $\beta_1^* = \beta_1(1 - \rho)$. Provided that these restrictions are used then $\rho = 1$ implies that $\Delta y_t = \beta_1 + \varepsilon_t$, so that β_1 is the drift under H_0 and the invariance of the test regression to the unknown value of β_1 is ensured by prior detrending (or directly including a trend in the maintained regression). Under $\rho < 1$, there are stationary deviations from the linear trend $\mu_t = \beta_0 + \beta_1 t$, to which observations will revert if there are no shocks. With no further dynamics in the structural equations, shocks die out geometrically.

Appendix: Response functions for DF tests $\hat{\tau}$ and $\hat{\delta}$

The form of the response functions follows MacKinnon (1991), as extended by Cheung and Lai (1995a, b) and Patterson and Heravi (2003). The general notation is C(ts, α, T, p*), which is the estimate of the α percentile of the distribution of test statistic ts, for T and p* = k – 1; 'observations' are indexed by n = 1, ..., N; and $\breve{T} \equiv T - p$ adjusts for the actual sample size. The general form of C_n(ts, α, $\breve{T}$, p*) is:

$$C_n(ts, \alpha, \breve{T}, p^*) = \kappa_\infty + \sum_{i=1}^{I} \kappa_i / \breve{T}^i + \sum_{j=1}^{J} \omega_j (p^* / \breve{T})^j + \xi_n \qquad \text{(A8.1)}$$

A factorial experimental design was used over all different pairings of T and p*, with p* = 0, 1, ..., 12. The sample size T and the increments (in parentheses) were then as follows: T = 20(1), 51(3), 78(5), 148(10), 258(50), 308(100), 508(200), 908. In all there were 66 × 13 = 858 sample points from which to determine the response functions for the 1st, 5th and 10th percentiles. The coefficient κ_∞ gives an approximate guide as to the critical value for large T.

The tables are arranged in three parts distinguished by the specification of the trend function, with $\mu_t = 0$, $\mu_t = \mu$ and $\mu_t = \beta_0 + \beta_1 t$. As an example of their use consider estimating a maintained regression with $\mu_t = \mu$, $\breve{T} = 100$ and p* = 4, then the 5% critical value for $\hat{\tau}_\mu$ is obtained as:

$$\begin{aligned} &C(\hat{\tau}_\mu, 0.05, \breve{T}, 4) \\ &\quad = -2.863 - (3.080/100) - (5.977/100^2) + \\ &\qquad 0.902(4/100) - 1.470(4/100)^2 + 1.527(4/100)^3 \\ &\quad = -2.861 \end{aligned}$$

In fact, the asymptotic 5% critical value provides quite a good 'eyeball' figure for T > 50, but the differences are more noticeable with the $\hat{\delta}$ versions of the tests.

Table A8.1 1%, 5% and 10% critical values for $\mu_t = 0$

No constant and no trend								
Coefficients for 1% critical values								
Tests	κ_∞	$\hat{\kappa}_1$	$\hat{\kappa}_2$	$\hat{\kappa}_3$	$\hat{\omega}_1$	$\hat{\omega}_2$	$\hat{\omega}_3$	R^2
$\hat{\tau}$	−2.5599	−3.03928	−33.3711	106.5659	1.20448	−2.39415	2.499499	0.914757
$\hat{\delta}$	−13.5309	117.8137	−790.263	2808.642	−18.1035	9.312984	−57.3207	0.984012
Coefficients for 5% critical values								
Tests	κ_∞	$\hat{\kappa}_1$	$\hat{\kappa}_2$	$\hat{\kappa}_3$	$\hat{\omega}_1$	$\hat{\omega}_2$	$\hat{\omega}_3$	R^2
$\hat{\tau}$	−1.93893	−0.49021	−30.6711	145.4072	0.839898	−1.21031	0.722283	0.896397
$\hat{\delta}$	−7.94693	68.47636	−494.355	1619.858	−6.20634	0.126817	−21.0683	0.980275
Coefficients for 10% critical values								
Tests	κ_∞	$\hat{\kappa}_1$	$\hat{\kappa}_2$	$\hat{\kappa}_3$	$\hat{\omega}_1$	$\hat{\omega}_2$	$\hat{\omega}_3$	R^2
$\hat{\tau}$	−1.61581	0.026171	−22.5668	108.9953	0.696141	−0.94715	0.479764	0.921401
$\hat{\delta}$	−5.65876	50.4526	−391.624	1287.258	−3.18757	−1.0887	−12.5416	0.982363

Table A8.2 1%, 5% and 10% critical values for $\mu_t = \mu$

Constant, no trend

Coefficients for 1% critical values

Tests	κ_∞	$\hat{\kappa}_1$	$\hat{\kappa}_2$	$\hat{\kappa}_3$	$\hat{\omega}_1$	$\hat{\omega}_2$	$\hat{\omega}_3$	R^2
$\hat{\tau}_\mu$	–3.42982	–7.2198	–4.111	–143.64	1.146321	–2.39972	3.064037	0.971963
$\hat{\delta}_\mu$	–20.4576	56.06736	1045.566	–9727.2	–53.7195	13.44147	–174.19	0.998422

Coefficients for 5% critical values

Tests	κ_∞	$\hat{\kappa}_1$	$\hat{\kappa}_2$	$\hat{\kappa}_3$	$\hat{\omega}_1$	$\hat{\omega}_2$	$\hat{\omega}_3$	R^2
$\hat{\tau}_\mu$	–2.86327	–3.07992	–5.97687	0	0.901746	–1.46986	1.527349	0.909708
$\hat{\delta}_\mu$	–14.0208	30.69298	278.2316	–3220.58	–27.0831	11.63782	–105.829	0.998918

Coefficients for 10% critical values

Tests	κ_∞	$\hat{\kappa}_1$	$\hat{\kappa}_2$	$\hat{\kappa}_3$	$\hat{\omega}_1$	$\hat{\omega}_2$	$\hat{\omega}_3$	R^2
$\hat{\tau}_\mu$	–2.56895	–1.76401	–2.05581	0	0.797342	–1.23508	1.320015	0.901355
$\hat{\delta}_\mu$	–11.2154	19.99818	119.392	–1732.33	–17.5616	4.636452	–71.537	0.998984

Table A8.3 1%, 5% and 10% critical values for $\mu_t = \beta_0 + \beta_1 t$

Constant and trend

Coefficients for 1% critical values

Tests	κ_∞	$\hat{\kappa}_1$	$\hat{\kappa}_2$	$\hat{\kappa}_3$	$\hat{\omega}_1$	$\hat{\omega}_2$	$\hat{\omega}_3$	R^2
$\hat{\tau}_\beta$	−3.95744	−11.1096	28.5592	−595.064	1.771437	−4.5696	6.323746	0.981384
$\hat{\delta}_\beta$	−28.718	36.30394	4921.59	−38069.8	−127.443	79.11798	−689.384	0.998701

Coefficients for 5% critical values

Tests	κ_∞	$\hat{\kappa}_1$	$\hat{\kappa}_2$	$\hat{\kappa}_3$	$\hat{\omega}_1$	$\hat{\omega}_2$	$\hat{\omega}_3$	R^2
$\hat{\tau}_\beta$	−3.41143	−5.23793	5.05483	−130.831	1.341085	−2.50943	2.930775	0.930308
$\hat{\delta}_\beta$	−21.391	37.01571	2032.085	−15884.4	−77.1933	56.6283	−433.71	0.999269

Coefficients for 10% critical values

Tests	κ_∞	$\hat{\kappa}_1$	$\hat{\kappa}_2$	$\hat{\kappa}_3$	$\hat{\omega}_1$	$\hat{\omega}_2$	$\hat{\omega}_3$	R^2
$\hat{\tau}_\beta$	−3.12798	−2.97506	−4.86709	0	1.113759	−1.44179	1.507824	0.904309
$\hat{\delta}_\beta$	−18.0093	25.05023	1439.654	−11572.5	−57.4767	39.05892	−323.521	0.999391

Glossary

Absolute continuity

Consider a function defined on the closed interval [a, b] and let there be n disjoint open intervals in this interval, say $(a_i, b_i) \subset [a, b]$, i = 1, ..., n, then for any $\varepsilon > 0$, there exists a $\delta > 0$ such that:

$$\sum_{i=1}^{n}(b_i - a_i) < \delta \Rightarrow \sum_{i=1}^{n}|f(b_i) - f(a_i)| < \varepsilon$$

When used without qualification, absolute continuity refers to absolute continuity for all closed intervals in the domain. Absolute continuity is stronger than continuity. Two implications being that there is bounded p-variation, $p > 0$, and the derivative exists almost everywhere (that is, if it does not, then the set has measure zero).

Cartesian product

A Cartesian product of two sets A and B is denoted $A \times B$ and is the direct product of the elements of the set A with those in the set B, it has a dimension which is the product of the dimensions of the component sets. For example let $C = A \times B$, where A = (1, 2, 3) and B = (1, 2), then C has dimension 3 by 2, with ordered elements (1, 1), (1, 2), (2, 1), (2, 2), (3, 1), (3, 2). The two-dimensional Cartesian product can be represented graphically as the points on a two-dimensional plane or as a matrix of rows for A and columns for B. The component sets may be discrete or continuous. An example of the latter is when, say, $A = \Re$. If $B = \Re$, then $\Re \times \Re = \Re^2$, that is all points in the two-dimensional plane; similarly $\Re \times \Re \times \Re \times \Re = \Re^4$ and so on.

Continuity

Continuity of the function f(x) at the point $x = a$, requires two conditions to be satisfied:

$f(a)$ is defined, that is given a value a in the domain of the function then the function value exists at that point;

in the limit, approaching a from the left or the right results in the same value of f(a).

When used without qualification, continuity refers to continuity for all points in the domain.

Domain

Let $x \in X \subseteq \Re$ be the domain of the function f(x); that is X is the set of values for which the function y = f(x) can be evaluated. Write f: $x \mapsto y$ to indicate that x is mapped into y via the function f; for example $y = x^2$, $x \in \Re$ and the output must be on the positive half of $\Re$, indicated as $y \in \Re^+$. The function mapping notation, f: $x \mapsto y$, may also indicate the mapping of the space of x into the space of y; for example in the case of $y = x^2$ for $x \in \Re$, then f: $\Re \mapsto \Re^+$.

Domain of attraction

Consider a sequence of identically distributed random variables x_1, $x_2, \ldots, x_n$, with common distribution function F(x). The distribution F(x) is said to belong to the domain of attraction of V if there exist constants $a_n > 0$ and b_n such that:

$$z_n \equiv \frac{\left(\sum_{i=1}^{n} x_i - b_n\right)}{a_n} \Rightarrow_D V(x) \tag{G1}$$

Where a_n and b_n are normalising constants and V(x) is a stable, nondegenerate distribution, see Feller (1966, VI.1 definition 2, IX.8).

Domain of attraction of the normal distribution

If V(x) in (G1) is the normal distribution, then F(x) belongs to the domain of attraction of the normal distribution.

Image

Let $x_1 \in X$ be in the domain of the function f(x), then f(x_1) is the image of x_1 under f(x); that is the value of f(x) applied to x_1. For example, if $y = x^2$, then the image of $x_1 = 2$ is $2^2 = 4$.

Recall from basic algebra that given the mapping $X: \Omega \mapsto \Re$ with element $\omega \in \Omega$, then $X(\omega) \in \Re$ is the image of ω under X. The image can be extended from an element to a subset in Ω, say $A \subseteq \Omega$. Then the image of A according to X is:

$$X[A] = \{r \in \Re : r = X(\omega) \text{ for some } \omega \in A\}$$

This just formalises the idea that what happens in the original space is mapped into the derived space. Conversely, the pre-image works in the reverse mapping of $X(\omega)$ back to the $\omega \in \Omega$ that resulted in $X(\omega)$. For $B \subseteq \Re$, then the pre-image of B is:

$$X^{-1}[B] = \{\omega \in \Omega: X(\omega) \in B\}$$

For example, the pre-image of the set A = (1, 4) according to the mapping $X(\omega) = \omega^2$ is the set B = (–1, 1, –2, 2).

Interval(s)

Let a and b be numbers on the real line $\Re$, then $c \in [a, b]$ indicates that c lies in the closed interval, so that $a \leq c \leq b$. If the interval is open, the relevant square bracket is replaced by the round parenthetical bracket; for example, $c \in (a, b]$, indicates $a < c \leq b$. The intervals are disjoint if they contain no elements in common.

Lebesgue measure

Lebesgue measure may be denoted either by Leb(.) or *L*.; it is the extension of the intuitive notion of the length of an interval on $\Re$ to more complex sets. The Lebesgue measure of the interval I_1 = [a, b] on $\Re$ is its length, b–a: $L(I_1)$ = b–a. The length is unchanged by replacing the closed interval by a half-open or open interval (the difference has measure zero). Now consider two intervals I_1 = [a, b] and I_2 = [d, e], the Lebesgue measure of the product $I_1 \times I_2$ is (b – a)(d – e), which accords with the intuition that this is the area of the rectangle formed by the product.

Pre-image

The pre-image is the reverse mapping from y to x, sometimes written as $f^{-1}(x)$; for example, if $y = x^2$, then the pre-image of y = 4 is x = ±2.

Range

Consider the mapping f: $x \mapsto y$ from the domain of $x \in X \subseteq \Re$ into the *range* of y; for example, if $y = x^2$, $x \in \Re$, then the range of y is $\Re^+$.

The real line $\Re$

The real line is the single-dimensional continuum of real numbers; the adjective real is to distinguish such numbers from complex numbers, which require two dimensions, one axis for the real part and a second axis for the imaginary part of the number. Often it is of interest to consider the non-negative (or positive) half line, $\Re^+$, which is the continuum starting from zero on the left.

Slowly varying function

$\psi(x)$ is a slowly varying function (of x) if for each $x > 0$, then:

$$\lim_{\lambda \to \infty} \frac{\psi(\lambda x)}{\psi(\lambda)} = 1$$

See Feller (1966, VIII.8 and IX.8); Drasin and Seneta (1986) generalise this concept and, in an econometric context, Phillips (2001) considers slowly varying regressors.

References

Akaike, H. (1974) Information theory and an extension of the maximum likelihood principle, *2nd International Symposium on Information Theory*, in B. N. Petrov and F. Csaki (eds), Budapest: Akademiai Kiado, 267–281.

Anderson, T. W. (1971) *The Statistical Analysis of Time Series*, New York: John Wiley & Sons.

Anderson, T. W., and A. M. Walker. (1964) On the asymptotic distribution of the autocorrelations of a sample from a linear stochastic process, *Annals of Mathematical Statistics* 35, 1296–1303.

Andrews, D. W. K. (1983) First order autoregressive processes and strong mixing, *Cowles Foundation Discussion Papers* 664. Cowles Foundation, Yale University.

Andrews, D. W. K., and D. Pollard. (1994) An introduction to functional central limit theorems for dependent stochastic processes, *International Statistical Review* 62, 119–132.

Banerjee, A., Dolado, J., Galbraith, J. W., and D. F. Hendry. (1993) *Co-integration, Error Correction, and the Econometric Analysis of Non-Stationary Data*, Oxford: University Press.

Bean, M. A. (2009) *Probability: The Science of Uncertainty with Applications to Investments, Insurance, and Engineering*, New York: American Mathematical Society.

Berk, K. N. (1974) Consistent autoregressive spectral estimates, *Annals of Statistics* 2, 489–502.

Bhargava, A. (1986) On the theory of testing for unit roots in observed time series, *Review of Economic Studies* LIII, 360–384.

Billingsley, P. (1995) *Probability and Measure*, 3rd edition, New York: John Wiley & Sons.

Box, G. E. P. and D. A. Pierce. (1970) Distribution of the autocorrelations in autoregressive moving average time series models, *Journal of American Statistical Association* 65, 1509–1526.

Box, G. E. P., and G. M. Jenkins. (1970) *Time Series Analysis: Forecasting and Control*, San Francisco: Holden-Day.

Bradley, R. C. (2005) Basic properties of strong mixing conditions. A survey and some open questions, *Probability Surveys* 2, 107–144.

Brockwell, P. J., and R. A. Davis. (2002) *Introduction to Time Series and Forecasting*, New York: Springer.

Brockwell, P. J., and R. A. Davis. (2006) *Time Series: Theory and Methods*, 2nd edition, New York: Springer.

Brzeźniak, Z., and T. Zastawniak. (1999) *Basic Stochastic Processes*, New York: Springer.

Burridge, P., and E. Guerre. (1996) The limit distribution of level crossings of a random walk, *Econometric Theory* 12, 705–723.

Caner, M., and B. E. Hansen. (2001) Threshold autoregression with a unit root, *Econometrica* 69, 1555–1596.

Canjels, E., and M. W. Watson. (1997) Estimating deterministic trends in the presence of serially correlated errors, *The Review of Economics and Statistics* 79, 184–200.

Cavaliere, G. (2002) Bounded integrated processes and unit root tests, *Statistical Methods and Applications* 11, 41–69.

Chan, N. H. and L. T. Tran. (1989) On the first-order autoregressive process with infinite variance, *Econometric Theory* 5, 354–362.

Chang, Y., and J. Y. Park. (2002) On the asymptotics of ADF tests for unit roots, *Econometric Reviews* 21, 431–447.

Chatfield, C. (2004) *The Analysis of Time Series*, 6th edition, London: Chapman & Hall.

Cheung, L.-W., and K. S. Lai. (1995a) Lag order and critical values of the augmented Dickey–Fuller test, *Journal of Economic and Business Statistics* 13, 277–280.

Cheung, L.-W., and K. S. Lai. (1995b) Lag order and critical values of a modified Dickey–Fuller test, *Oxford Bulletin of Economics and Statistics* 57, 411–419.

Cox, D. R., and D. Miller. (1965) *The Theory of Stochastic Processes*, London: Methuen Press.

Cox, D. R., and D. V. Hinkley. (1974) *Theoretical Statistics*, London: Chapman & Hall.

Davidson, J. (1994) *Stochastic Limit Theory*, Oxford: Blackwell Publishers.

Davidson, J. (2000) *Econometric Theory*, Oxford: Blackwell Publishers.

De Jong, R. M. (1997) Central limit theorems for dependent heterogenous random variables, *Econometric Theory* 13, 353–367.

De Jong, R. M., and J. Davidson. (2000a) The functional central limit theorem and convergence to stochastic integrals I: weakly dependent processes, *Econometric Theory*, 621–642.

De Jong, R. M., and J. Davidson. (2000b) The functional central limit theorem and convergence to stochastic integrals II: weakly dependent processes, *Econometric Theory*, 643–666.

Dhrymes, P. (1981) *Distributed Lags, Problems of Estimation and Formulation*, 2nd edition, Amsterdam: North-Holland.

Dickey, D. A. (1984) Power of unit root tests, *Proceedings of Business and Economic Statistics Section, American Statistical Association*, 489–493.

Dickey, D. A., and W. A. Fuller. (1981) Likelihood ratio statistics for autoregressive time series with a unit root, *Econometrica* 49, 1057–1022.

Dickey, D. A., Bell, W. R., and R. B. Miller. (1986) Unit roots in time series models: tests and implications, *The American Statistician* 40, 12–26.

Doob, J. L. (1953). *Stochastic Processes*, New York: John Wiley & Sons.

Dougherty, C. (2007) *Introduction to Econometrics*, 3rd edition, Oxford: Oxford University Press.

Drasin, D., and E. Seneta. (1986) A generalization of slowly varying functions, *Proceedings of the American Mathematical Society* 96, 470–472.

Elliott, G. (1999) Efficient tests for a unit root when the initial observation is drawn from its unconditional distribution, *International Economic Review* 40, 767–783.

Elliott, G., and U. K. Müller. (2006) Minimizing the impact of the initial condition on testing for unit roots, *Journal of Econometrics* 135, 285–310.

Elliott, G., Rothenberg, T. J., and J. H. Stock. (1996) Efficient tests for an autoregressive root, *Econometrica* 64, 813–836.

Escanciano, J. C., and I. N. Loboto. (2009) Testing the martingale hypothesis, Chapter 20 in T. C. Mills and K. D. Patterson (eds), *The Handbook of Econometrics, Vol 2, Applied Econometrics*, Basingstoke: Palgrave Macmillan.

Feller, W. (1966) *An Introduction to Probability Theory and Its Applications*, Volume II, New York: John Wiley & Sons.

Feller, W. (1968) *An Introduction to Probability Theory and Its Applications*, 3rd edition, Volume I, New York: John Wiley & Sons.

Fok, D., Franses, P. H., and R. Paap. (2006) Performance of seasonal adjustment procedures: simulation and empirical results, Chapter 29 in T. C. Mills and K. D. Patterson (eds), *The Handbook of Econometrics, Vol 2, Applied Econometrics*, Basingstoke: Palgrave Macmillan.

Franses, P. H., and N. Haldrup. (1994) The effect of additive outliers on test for unit root and cointegration, *Journal of business Economics and Statistics* 12, 471–478.

Fristedt, B., and L. Gray. (1997) *A Modern Approach to Probability Theory*, Boston: Birkhäuser.

Fuller, W. (1976) *An Introduction to Statistical Time Series*, 1st edition, New York: John Wiley & Sons.

Fuller, W. (1996) *An Introduction to Statistical Time Series*, 2nd edition, New York: John Wiley & Sons.

Garciá, A., and A. Sansó. (2006) A generalisation of the Burridge-Guerre nonparametric unit root test, *Econometric Theory* 22, 756–761.

Gihman, I., and A. V. Skorohod. (1974) *The Theory of Stochastic Processes*, New York: Springer-Verlag.

Gil-Alana, L. A., and J. Hualde. (2009) Fractional integration and cointegration: An Overview and an empirical application, Chapter 10 in T. C. Mills and K. D. Patterson (eds), *The Handbook of Econometrics, Vol 2, Applied Econometrics*, Basingstoke: Palgrave Macmillan.

Glasserman, P. (2004) *Monte Carlo Methods in Financial Engineering*, New York: Springer-Verlag.

Granger, C. W. J., and N. R. Swanson. (1997) An introduction to stochastic unit-root processes, *Journal of Econometrics* 80, 35–62.

Gujarati, D. (2006) *Essentials of Econometrics*, 3rd edition, New York: McGraw-Hill.

Hahn, B. D., and D. T. Valentine. (2007) *Essential MATLAB for Engineers and Scientists*, Amsterdam: Elsevier.

Hald, A. (2003) *A History of Probability and Statistics and Their Applications Before 1750*, New York: John Wiley & Sons.

Haldrup, N., and M. Jansson. (2006) Improving Power and Size in Unit Root Testing, Chapter 7 in T. C. Mills and K. D. Patterson (eds), *The Handbook of Econometrics, Vol 2, Applied Econometrics*, Basingstoke: Palgrave Macmillan.

Haldrup, N., and P. M. Lildholdt. (2002) On the robustness of unit root tests in the presence of double unit roots, *Journal of Time Series Analysis* 23, 155–171.

Hall, P., and C. C. Heyde. (1980) *Martingale Limit Theory and its Application*, New York: Academic Press.

Hamilton, J. (1994) *Time Series Analysis*, Princeton: Princeton University Press.

Hanselman, D., and B. Littlefield. (2004) *Mastering MATLAB 7*, Englewood Cliffs, NJ: Prentice Hall.

Harvey, A. C. (1993) *Time Series Models*, 2nd edition, Hemel Hempstead: Harvester Wheatsheaf.

Harvey, D. I., and S. J. Leybourne. (2005) On Testing for Unit Roots and the initial observation, *Econometrics Journal* 8, 97–111.

Harvey, D. I., and S. J. Leybourne. (2006) Power of a unit-root test and the initial condition, *Journal of Time Series Analysis* 27, 739–752.

Harvey, D. I., Leybourne, S. J., and A. M. R. Taylor. (2009) Unit root testing in practice: dealing with uncertainty over the trend and initial condition, *Econometric Theory* 25, 587–636.

Harvey, D. I., and S. Leybourne. (2001) Innovational outlier unit root tests with an endogenously determined break in level, *Oxford Bulletin of Economics and Statistics* 63, 559–575.

Hayashi, F. (2000) *Econometrics*, Princeton: Princeton University Press.

Henderson, D., and P. Plaschko. (2006) *Stochastic Differential Equations in Science and Engineering*, New Jersey: World Scientific.

Hendry, D. F. (1995) *Dynamic Econometrics*, Oxford: Oxford University Press.

Herndorf, N. (1984) A functional central limit theorem for weakly dependent sequences of random variables, *Annals of Probability* 12, 141–153.

Hida, T. (1980) *Brownian Motion*, Berlin: Springer-Verlag.

Hodges, J. L., and E. L. Lehmann. (2004) *Basic Concepts of Probability and Statistics*, 2nd edition, Philadelphia: Society for Industrial and Applied Mathematics.

Hughes, B. D. (1995) *Random Walks and Random Environments, Vol. 1: Random Walks*, Oxford: Oxford University Press.

Hughes, B. D. (1996) *Random Walks and Random Environments, Vol. 2: Random Environments*, Oxford: Oxford University Press.

Iacus, S. M. (2008) *Simulation and Inference for Stochastic Differential Equations with R Examples*, New York: Springer.

Ibragimov, I. A., and Yu. V. Linnik. (1971) *Independent and Stationary Sequences of Random Variables*, Groningen: Wolters-Noordhoff.

Jacod, J., and P. Protter. (2004) *Probability Essentials*, 2nd edition, New York: Springer.

Jeffrey, R. C. (2004) *Subjective Probability: The Real Thing*, Cambridge: Cambridge University Press.

Jones, R. H. (1975) Fitting autoregressions, *Journal of the American Statistical Association* 70, 590–592.

Karlin, S., and H. M. Taylor. (1975a) *A First Course in Stochastic Processes*, 2nd edition. New York: Academic Press.

Karlin, S., and H. M. Taylor. (1975b) *A Second Course in Stochastic Processes*, New York: Academic Press.

Kay, S. (2004) *Intuitive Probability and Random Processes using MATLAB*, New York: Springer.

Kifowit, S. J., and T. A. Stamps. (2006) The harmonic series diverges again and again, *The AMATYC Review* 27, 31–43.

Koralov, L . B., and G. Y. Sinai. (2007) *Theory of Probability and Random Processes*, 2nd edition, Berlin: Springer-Verlag.

Koreisha, S. G., and T. Pukkila. (1995) A comparison between different order-determination criteria for identification of ARIMA models, *Journal of Business and Economic Statistics* 13, 127–131.

Kourogenis, N., and N. Pittis. (2008) Testing for a unit root under errors with just barely infinite variance, *Journal of Time Series Analysis* 6, 1066–1087.

Kuo, H. H. (2006) *Introduction to Stochastic Integration*, New York: Springer-Verlag.

Larson, H. J. (1974) *Introduction to Probability Theory and Statistical Inference*, 2nd edition, New York: John Wiley & Sons.

Leybourne, S. J., McCabe, B. P. M., and A. R. Tremayne. (1996) Can economic time series be differenced to stationarity? *Journal of Business and Economic Statistics* 14, 435–446.

Leybourne, S. J., McCabe, B. P. M., and T. C. Mills. (1996) Randomized unit root processes for modelling and forecasting financial time series: Theory and applications, *Journal of Forecasting* 15, 253–270.

Ljung, G. M. and G. E. P. Box. (1978) On a measure of a lack of fit in time series models, *Biometrika* 65, 297–303.

Lo, A. W., and C. A. MacKinlay. (2001) *A Non-Random Walk Down Wall Street*, Princeton: Princeton University Press.

Lundbergh, S., Teräsvirta, T., and D. J. C. Van Dijk. (2003) Time-Varying Smooth Transition Autoregressive Models, *Journal of Business Economics and Statistics* 21, 104–121.

Lütkepohl, H. (1993) *Introduction to Multiple Time Series Analysis*, 2nd edition, Berlin: Springer-Verlag.

MacKinnon, J. (1991) Critical values for cointegration tests, in R. F. Engle and C. W. J. Granger (eds), *Long Run Economic Relationships*, Oxford: Oxford University Press, 267–276.

MacNeill, I. B. (1978) Properties of sequences of partial sums of polynomial regression residuals with applications to tests for change of regression at unknown time, *The Annals of Statistics* 2, 422–433.

Mann, H. B., and A. Wald. (1943) On stochastic limit and order relationships, *Annals of Mathematical Statistics* 14, 390–402.

Marsh, P. (2007) Constructing Optimal Tests on a Lagged Dependent Variable, *Journal of Time Series Analysis* 28, 723–743.

Martinez, W. L., and A. R. Martinez. (2002) *Computational Statistic Handbook with MATLAB*, London: Chapman & Hall.

McCabe, B., and A. Tremayne. (1993) *Elements of Modern Asymptotic Theory with Statistical Applications*, Manchester: Manchester University Press.

McLeish, D. L. (1975) A maximal inequality and dependent strong laws, *The Annals of Probability* 5, 829–839.

Merlevède, F., Peligrad., M., and S. Utev. (2006) Recent advances in invariance principles for stationary sequences, *Probability Surveys* 3, 1–36.

Mikosch, T. (1998) *Elementary Stochastic Calculus with Finance in View*, New Jersey: World Scientific.

Mittelhammer, R. C. (1996) *Mathematical Statistics for Economics and Business*, New York: Springer.

Moler, C. B. (2004) *Numerical Computing with MATLAB*, Cambridge: Cambridge University Press.

Müller, U. K. (2007) A theory of robust long-run variance estimation, *Journal of Econometrics* 141, 1331–1352.

Müller, U. K. (2008) The impossibility of consistent discrimination between I(0) and I(1) processes, *Econometric Theory* 24, 616–630.

Müller, U. K. (2009) Comment on 'Unit root testing in practice: dealing with uncertainty over the trend and initial condition' by D. I. Harvey, S. J. Leybourne and A. M. R. Taylor, *Econometric Theory* 25, 643–648.

Müller, U. K., and G. Elliott. (2003) Tests for unit roots and the initial condition, *Econometrica* 71, 1269–86.

Nelson, C. R., and C. I. Plosser. (1982) Trends and random walks in macroeconomic time series, *Journal of Monetary Economics* 10, 139–162.

Ng, S., and P. Perron. (2001) Lag length selection and the construction of unit root tests with good size and power, *Econometrica* 69, 1519–1554.

Osborn, D. R., and P. M. M. Rodrigues. (2002) Asymptotic distributions of seasonal unit root tests: a unifying approach, *Econometric Reviews* 21, 221–241.

Pantula, S. G., Gonzalez-Farias, G., and W. A. Fuller. (1994) A comparison of unit root test criteria, *Journal of Business and Economic Statistics* 12, 449–459.

Patterson, K. D. (2000) *An Introduction to Applied Econometrics*, Basingstoke: Palgrave Macmillan.

Patterson, K. D., and S. Heravi. (2003) Weighted symmetric tests for a unit root: Response functions, power, test dependence and test conflict, *Applied Economics* 35, 779–790.

Perron, P. (1989) The great crash, the oil price shock, and the unit root hypothesis, *Econometrica* 57, 1361–1401.

Perron, P. (2006) Dealing with structural breaks, Chapter 8 in Chapter 20 in T. C. Mills and K. D. Patterson (eds), *The Handbook of Econometrics, Vol 1, Theoretical Econometrics*, Basingstoke: Palgrave Macmillan.

Perron, P., and S. Ng. (1996) Useful modifications to some unit root tests with dependent errors and their local asymptotic properties, *Review of Economic Studies* 63, 435–463.

Phillips, P. C. B. (1987) Time series regression with a unit root, *Econometrica* 55, 277–301.

Phillips, P. C. B. (2001) Regression with slowly varying regressor, *Cowles Foundation Discussion Papers* 1310, Cowles Foundation, Yale University.

Phillips, P. C. B., and P. Perron. (1988) Testing for a unit root in time series regression, *Biometrika* 75, 335–346.

Phillips, P. C. B. and S. Ouliaris. (1990) Asymptotic properties of residual based tests for cointegration, *Econometrica* 58, 165–193.

Phillips, P. C. B., and V. Solo. (1992) Asymptotics for linear processes, *The Annals of Statistics* 20, 971–1001.

Popp, S. (2008) New innovational outlier unit root test with a break at an unknown time, *Journal of Statistical Computation and Simulation* 78, 1143–1159.

Porter, T. M. (1988) *The Rise Of Statistical Thinking, 1820–1900*, Princeton: Princeton University Press.

Priestley, M. B. (1981) *Spectral Analysis and Time Series*, London: Academic Press.

Pryce, J. D. (1973) *Basic Methods of Functional Analysis*, London: Hutchison University Library.

Ramanathan, R. (2002) *Introductory Econometrics with Applications*, 5th edition, Boston: South-Western College Publishers.

Rao, P. (1973) *Linear Statistical Inference and Its Applications*, New York: John Wiley & Sons.

Révész, P. (2005) *Random Walk in Random and Non-Random Environments*, 2nd edition, Singapore: World Scientific.

Rodrigues, P. M. M., and A. M. R. Taylor. (2004) On tests for double differencing: methods of demeaning an detrending and the role of initial values, *Econometric Theory* 20, 95–115.

Rodrigues, P. M. M., and A. M. R. Taylor. (2004a) Alternative estimators and unit root tests for seasonal autoregressive processes, *Journal of Econometrics* 120, 35–73.

Rodrigues, P. M. M., and A. M. R. Taylor. (2004b) Asymptotic distributions for regression-based seasonal unit root test statistics in near-integrated models, *Econometric Theory* 20, 645–670.

Rosenblatt, M. (1956) A central limit theorem and a strong mixing condition, *Proceedings of The National Academy of Sciences* 42, 43–47.

Ross, S. (2003) *Probability Models*, 8th edition, London: Academic Press.

Said, S. E., and D. A. Dickey. (1984) Testing for unit roots in autoregressive-moving average models of unknown order, *Biometrika* 71, 599–607.

Schmidt, P., and P. Phillips. (1992) LM tests for a unit root in the presence of deterministic trends, *Oxford Bulletin of Economics and Statistics* 54, 257–287.

Schwarz, G. (1978) Estimating the dimension of a model, *The Annals of Statistics* 5, 461–464.

Schwert, G. W. (1987) Test for unit roots: a Monte-Carlo investigation, *Journal of Business and Economic Statistics* 7, 147–160.

Shibata, R. (1976) Selection of the order of an autoregressive model by Akaike's information criterion, *Biometrika* 62, 117–126.

Shreve, S. E. (2004) *Stochastic Calculus for Finance II: Continuous Time Models*, New York: Springer.

Spanos, A. (1986) *Statistical Foundations of Econometric Modelling*, Cambridge: Cambridge University Press.

Stirzaker, D. (2005) *Stochastic Processes and Models*, Oxford: Oxford University Press.

Stock, J., and M. W. Watson. (2007) *Introduction to Econometrics*, 2nd edition, New York: Prentice Hall.

Stout, W. F. (1974) *Almost Sure Convergence*, New York: Academic Press.

Strikholm, B., and T. Teräsvirta. (2004) A sequential procedure for determining the number of regimes in a threshold autoregressive model, *Econometrics Journal* 9, 472–491.

Suhov, Y., and M. Kelbert. (2005) *Probability and Statistics by Example: Volume 1, Basic Probability and Statistics*, Cambridge: Cambridge University Press.

Sul, D. P., Phillips, P. C. B., and C. Y. Choi. (2005) Prewhitening bias in HAC estimation, *Oxford Bulletin of Economics and Statistics* 67, 517–546.

Taylor, A. M. R., and D. J. C. Van Dijk. (2002) Can tests for stochastic unit roots provide useful portmanteau tests for persistence?, *Oxford Bulletin of Economics and Statistics* 64, 381–397.

Telcs, A. (2006) *The Art of Random Walks*, Berlin: Springer-Verlag.

Teräsvirta, T. (2006) Univariate nonlinear time series models, Chapter 10 in T. C. Mills and K. D. Patterson (eds), *The Handbook of Econometrics, Vol 2, Applied Econometrics*, Basingstoke: Palgrave Macmillan.

Tuckwell, H. C. (1995) *Elementary Applications of Probability Theory, 2nd edition*, London: Chapman & Hall.

Uhlenbeck, G. E., and L. S. Ornstein. (1930) On the theory of Brownian motion, *Physics Review* 36, 823–841.

Van Dijk, D. J. C., Teräsvirta, T., and P. H. Franses. (2002) Smooth transition autoregressive models – A survey of recent developments, *Econometric Reviews* 21, 1–47.

Vogelsang, T. J. (1998) Trend function hypothesis testing in the presence of serial correlation, *Econometrica* 66, 123–148.

Weiner, N. (1923) Differential space, *Journal of Mathematical Physics* 2, 131–174.

White, H. (1984) *Asymptotic Theory for Econometricians*, New York: Academic Press.

Withers, F. (1981) Conditions for linear processes to be strong mixing, *Zeitschrift fur Wahrscheinlichkeitstheorie und Verwandte Gebiete* 57, 477–480.

Wooldridge, J. M., and H. White. (1988) Some invariance principles and central limit theorems for dependent heterogeneous processes, *Econometric Theory* 4, 210–230.

Wright, G., and P. Ayton. (1994) *Subjective Probability*, New York: John Wiley & Sons.

Xiao, Z., and P. C. B. Phillips. (1998) An ADF coefficient test for a unit root in ARMA models of unknown order with empirical applications to the US economy, *Econometrics Journal* 1, 27–43.

Author Index

Subject Index